PRAISE FOR
AFRICAN GODDESS INITIATION

"There is no greater hand to hold through your guided journey into the land of self-love and spiritual connection than Abiola's, who will no doubt handle it with care. She has consistently shown up for women for more than a decade and brought out their very best, and this guided journey into our most sacred rituals is no exception."

— **Charli Penn**, editorial lifestyle director, *ESSENCE* magazine

"Abiola Abrams, a true African Goddess, has put her heart and soul into this inspiring book that helps guide you to self-awareness, self-healing, and self-love. This book is a must for every woman's household!"

— **Yvette Hayward**, founder, African American Literary Awards

"We are at a crossroads spiritually and in search of answers. In African Goddess Initiation, Abiola introduces our ancient mothers back to us. It is a welcome reunion for those of us seeking a deeper connection with African spirituality and the ancient wisdom of our ancestors."

— **Yolanda Sangweni**, founder, African Women Create and senior director of programming, NPR

"Abiola Abrams is a powerful storyteller and historian. For anyone looking to explore Global African spiritual traditions laced with love, this is the text. Many of us have been forced to forget where we come from. African Goddess Initiation isn't just history; it contains rituals and ceremonies that tap into our collective DNA. Abiola's words are a soothing balm in turbulent times. This book is an offering, a gift from our ancestors, and they are felt on every page. A deep bow for Abrams as a channel, guide, and compassionate cheerleader. If African Goddess Initiation is in your hands, there is a reason. This book will permanently live on my nightstand when I need reminders, encouragement, or guidance. She's invited us all on this journey, solo or as a group. I'm eternally grateful for this wisdom and the invitation to reconnect with 'global sisterhood.'"

— **Oneika Mays**, healer and star of TBS' *Lost Resort*

"Abiola invites us all to embrace the divine feminine energy within that is needed to nurture the planet at this time, and she takes us on a healing journey passed down from our ancestors to go within and activate our most authentic selves while removing limiting beliefs that hold us back from expressing who we truly are."

— **Koya Webb**, author of *Let Your Fears Make You Fierce* and star of Z Living series, *Yoga Girls*

"One of the most important contemporary books on the transformational power of ritual, and the journey to awakening the Divine Feminine in ourselves, Abiola Abrams has generously gifted us with a profound body of work inviting us into the sacred spaces and rituals of her spiritual ancestry—the extraordinary rich world of African goddess magic and mysticism. This book is pure alchemical magic. If you're called to open its pages, it offers nothing less than a fierce, loving, and timely initiation to awaken the Goddess within. More importantly it fills a great gap in our collective soul as the author reclaims the mystical power of her ancestors and firmly restores it to its rightful place. African Goddess Initiation is a living map to an inclusive unified world where we all are valued."

— **Colette Baron-Reid**, oracle expert and best-selling author of *Uncharted*

"Abiola blesses the world with the knowledge of her spiritual ancestry, inviting all women to wake up to their divine power. Read this book from cover to cover or close your eyes and trust as you open a page. You'll find wisdom and rituals to nurture your spirit on every page."

Jessica Ortner, *New York Times* best-selling author and co-creator of the Tapping Solution app

"Women are awakening to our sacred feminine power, and it has been a long time coming. At the forefront, beating the drum and clearing our path is Abiola Abrams. Abiola has held sacred space and hosted goddess circles for just over 20 years now, and it has culminated in her latest offering African Goddess Initiation. In this book, Abiola joins forces with our powerful goddesses, ancestors, and spirits to guide us through a divine feminine initiation and rebirth into our capital 'S' self. With the warmth of your best girlfriend and the wisdom of the ages, Abiola walks us through nine key inner temples we must face to awaken the goddess, the divine feminine, within. Goddess rising is an energy that can no longer be contained. Abrams invites us to answer the whisper of the goddess rising. Will you say yes?"

— **Nikki Woods**, best-selling author, leading media strategist, and former executive producer of the *Tom Joyner Morning Show*

"When it comes to self-love and self-care, sacred rituals have the power to transform the relationship you have with yourself and deepen your understanding of what love can be. The way Abiola shares African rituals is powerful, sensuous, and connected. African-based spiritual tools through a womanist (or feminist) lens are necessary, now, more than ever. My hope for this book is that it is in the home of every woman of color in the world."

— **Dr. Jeanine Staples**, anthropologist, sociocultural literacist, and author of *The Revelations of Asher: Toward Supreme Love in Self*

AFRICAN GODDESS
INITIATION

ALSO BY
ABIOLA ABRAMS

Books

Dare: A Novel

The Sacred Bombshell Handbook of Self-Love:
The 11 Secrets of Feminine Power

Card decks

African Goddess Affirmation Cards

African Goddess Rising Oracle Cards

Sacred Bombshell Self-Love Journaling Cards

Womanifesting: Fertility Goddess Oracle Cards

AFRICAN GODDESS
INITIATION

Sacred Rituals for
Self-Love, Prosperity, and Joy

ABIOLA ABRAMS

HAY HOUSE, INC.
Carlsbad, California • New York City
London • Sydney • New Delhi

Copyright © 2021 by Abiola Abrams

Published in the United States by: Hay House, Inc.: www.hayhouse.com® • *Published in Australia by:* Hay House Australia Pty. Ltd.: www.hayhouse.com.au • *Published in the United Kingdom by:* Hay House UK, Ltd.: www.hayhouse.co.uk • *Published in India by:* Hay House Publishers India: www.hayhouse.co.in

Project editor: Melody Guy
Indexer: Joan Shapiro
Cover design: Chelsea Hunter
Interior design: Julie Davison
Interior photos/illustrations: Destiney Powell

Spiritpreneur® is a trademark of Abiola Abrams. All rights reserved.

Cataloging-in-Publication Data is on file at the Library of Congress

Tradepaper ISBN: 978-1-4019-6294-4
E-book ISBN: 978-1-4019-6295-1
Audiobook ISBN: 978-1-4019-6296-8

10 9 8 7 6 5 4 3 2 1
1st edition, July 2021

Printed in the United States of America

We pour honey . . .

This book is dedicated to
All those who still live with me
And those who still live within us.

For my Creator.

For Norma, who birthed me.
For Eve, who birthed Norma.
For Ma Catherine, who birthed Eve.
For Adonis, who birthed Ma Catherine.

For Beryl, who birthed my Daddy.
For Tamar, who birthed Beryl.
For Alice, who birthed Tamar.
For Mariah, who birthed Alice.

For Matilda, who birthed Grandfather.
For Betsey, who birthed Matilda.

For Missy, who begat us all.

For my sister Damali.
For my aunties Wendy, Ruby, Pearl, Vanny, Bobsie, and Joy.
For Adana, Michelle, Jonnelle, Nickeola, and all of my my goddess sister-cousins.
For my sisters in magic, Kristal and Patranila.

For Tesha, Akiela, Ariella, and Maya;
And for Miss Ava Renee Silvy, all of my nieces, and the next generation of
goddesses who will show us the way.

"i found god in myself
and i loved her /
i loved her fiercely."

—NTOZAKE SHANGE

CONTENTS

Foreword xv
Declaration: You Are Sacred xix
Introduction: Getting Started 1

1. The Threshold: Sankofa 12

Nana Buluku (Benin) 14
Traditional New Cycles Ritual: Recording the Sacred
Your New Cycles Ritual: Goddess Soulbook and Initiation Contract

Mawu-Lisa (Benin) 20
Traditional Cosmic Power Ritual: Altars and Shrines
Your Cosmic Power Ritual: Goddess Altar and Womb Bowl

⁕ Congrats! You have completed the Threshold. 28

2. The Temple of Ancestors: Your Soil Energy Channel (Amadlozi) 29

Sawtche (Khoekhoen/South Africa 36
Traditional Grounding Ritual: Milk Tree Initiation
Your Grounding Ritual: Mother's Milk Miracle Floor Wash

Tituba (Barbados/Guyana/Salem) 44
Traditional Feeling Safe Ritual: Pouring Libations
Your Feeling Safe Ritual: Ancestral Protection Ceremony

Mbuya Nehanda (Shona/Zimbabwe) 51
Traditional Rebirth Ritual: Catching Komfa
Your Rebirth Ritual: Ancestral Altar

Sara la Kali (Romani/Egypt) 59
Traditional Divine Lineage Ritual: Mo'juba Ancestral Prayer
Your Divine Lineage Ritual: Ancestral Tribute Prayer

Marie Laveau (New Orleans) 66
Traditional Abundance Ritual: Gris-Gris Bag
Your Abundance Ritual: Gris-Gris Bag

⁕ Congrats! You have completed the Temple of Ancestors. 75

3. The Temple of Conjurers: Your Creation Energy Channel (Heka) 76

Ngame (Ashanti/Akan) 84
Traditional Desire Ritual: Kunkuma Menstrual Broom
Your Desire Ritual: Yoni Art Masterpiece

Modjadji (Balobedu/South Africa) 91
Traditional Manifestation Ritual: Raindancing
Your Manifestation Ritual: Water Whisperer

Ma'at (Egypt) 98
Traditional Giving and Receiving Ritual: Ethiopian Healing Scrolls
Your Giving and Receiving Ritual: Goddess Intention Incense

Tanit (Tunisia) 104
Traditional Pleasure Ritual: Erotic Binding Spells
Your Pleasure Ritual: Sacred Erotic Magic

The Seven Sisters (New Orleans) 110
Traditional Creativity Ritual: Fertility Dolls
Your Creativity Ritual: BMGV Vision Doll

• Congrats! You have completed the Temple of Conjurers. 116

4. The Temple of Warriors: Your Power Energy Channel (Àṣẹ) 117

Oya (Yoruba/Nigeria) \ 124
Traditional Storms Ritual: Protection, Binding, and Blocking
Your Storms Ritual: Calling in Rapid Lightning Change

Atete (Oromo/Ethiopia) 130
Traditional Worthiness Ritual: Jebena Buna Coffee Ceremony
Your Worthiness Ritual: Goddess Coffee Ceremony

Sekhmet (Egypt) 136
Traditional Wounded-Healer Ritual: Capoeira
Your Wounded-Healer Ritual: The Sun Rises Disc

Asase Yaa (Ashanti/Ghana) 142
Traditional Joy Ritual: Renewal at Souvenance
Your Joy Ritual: Tolerations and Happy List

Sitira (Guyana) 148
Traditional Brazen Ritual: Kwe Kwe Celebration
Your Brazen Ritual: Liberation Dance

• Congrats! You have completed the Temple of Warriors. 156

5. The Temple of Shadows: Your Inner Monsters (Jumbies) 157

Long Bubby Suzi (Garifuna/Central America) 163
Traditional Shame Healing Ritual: "Keeping Kumina" Ceremony
Your Shame Healing Ritual: Body Map

Aunt Nancy (Diaspora/Akan) 170
Traditional Betrayal Healing Ritual: Energy-Clearing Incense
Your Betrayal Healing Ritual: Clearing Life Clutter

Soucouyant (Trinidad/Diaspora) 177
Traditional Scarcity Healing Ritual: Sous Sous
Your Scarcity Healing Ritual: Goddess Superhero You

Gang Gang Sara (Tobago) 185
Traditional Resistance Healing Ritual: Afro-Caribbean Masquerade
Your Resistance Healing Ritual: The Mask That Grins and Lies

Medusa (Libya) 193
Traditional Rage Healing Ritual: Temple of Pythons
Your Rage Healing Ritual: Rewrite Yourself

• Congrats! You have completed the Temple of Shadows. 201

6. The Temple of Lovers: Your Love Energy Channel (Ubuntu) 202

Oshun (Yoruba/Nigeria) 207
Traditional Revolutionary Love Ritual: Ancestral Aphrodisiac Incense Parfum
Your Revolutionary Love Ritual: Self-Love Sweetening Jar

Qetesh (Egypt) 214
Traditional Sacred Sensuality Ritual: Sacred Sexuality
Your Sacred Sensuality Ritual: Cleopatra's Aphrodisiac Bath

Erzulie Dantor (Haiti) 221
Traditional Energy Cords Ritual: The Okra Slip
Your Energy Cords Ritual: Cord Cutting and Clearing Wash

Mbokomu (Bantu) 228
Traditional Soul Forgiveness Ritual: Step on the Egg
Your Soul Forgiveness Ritual: Carry the Stone

Ala (Igbo/Nigeria) 235
Traditional Grief Ritual: Mbari Temples
Your Grief Ritual: Grief Release Circle

• Congrats! You have completed the Temple of Lovers. 242

7. The Temple of Griots: Your Voice Energy Channel (Akoben) 243

Mami Wata (Diaspora).. 249
Traditional Emotionally Naked Ritual: Hydromancy
Your Emotionally Naked Ritual: Water Gazing in the Hidden Lake

Yasigi (Dogon/Mali).. 255
Traditional Self-Expression Ritual: Sisters of the Mask
Your Self-Expression Ritual: Vision Mask

Mama Djombo (Guinea-Bissau).. 261
Traditional Shine Ritual: Oríkì Praise Poetry
Your Shine Ritual: Goddess Self-Praise Poem

Mame Coumba Bang (Senegal) 268
Traditional Speaking Up Ritual: Inkulisela Voice Power
Your Speaking Up Ritual: Goddess Mission Statement

Nunde (Benin) 274
Traditional Truth Ritual: Ash Circle
Your Truth Ritual: Awkward Conversation Challenge

• Congrats! You have completed the Temple of Griots. 279

8. The Temple of Queens: Your Insight Energy Channel (Chi) 280

Queen Nandi (Zulu/South Africa).. 289
Traditional Intuition Ritual: Momone Community Cleansing
Your Intuition Ritual: Mirror Gazing Meditation

Queen of Sheba (Ethiopia).. 297
Traditional Divination Ritual: Throwing Bones
Your Divination Ritual: You Are the Oracle Cards

Queen Mother Nanny (Maroons/Jamaica) 304
Traditional Dreams Ritual: African Dream Root
Your Dreams Ritual: Dream Traveling

Queen Nefertiti (Egypt) 310
Traditional Alchemy Ritual: Baby Naming
Your Alchemy Ritual: Choose Your Goddess Name

Queen Yaa Asantewaa (Ashanti/Ghana).. 316
Traditional Quantum Leap Ritual: Iboga Ceremony
Your Quantum Leap Ritual: Burn-and-Release Visualization

• Congrats! You have completed the Temple of Queens. 322

9. The Temple of High Priestesses: Your Ecstasy Energy Channel (Umbilini) 323

Yemaya (Yoruba/Nigeria) 328
Traditional Awakening Ritual: Lave Tet Head Washing
Your Awakening Ritual: Coconut Head Wash

iNkosazana (Zulu/South Africa).. 335
Traditional Alignment Ritual: Rocks, Stones, and Crystals
Your Alignment Ritual: Umbilini Mantra Meditation

Ayizan (Haiti) 343
Traditional Miracles Ritual: Spraying Money
Your Miracles Ritual: Manifesting Miracles Rice

a-Bol-Nimba (Baga/Guinea)... 351
Traditional Harvest Ritual: The Yam Festival
Your Harvest Ritual: Womanifesting Womb Awakening

Iset (Nubia/Egypt) 360
Traditional Spiritual Surrender Ritual: Anointing
Your Spiritual Surrender Ritual: Anoint Thyself

◆ Congrats! You have completed the Temple of High Priestesses. 370

Conclusion: The Ascent: Moving Forward 371
"I Am a Goddess" Manifesta 372
Goddess Empowerment Resource Guide..373
African Goddess Initiation Music Playlist 375
Goddess Directory 377
Endnotes...378
Index 387
Acknowledgments 398
About the Author 401

FOREWORD

My heart is a flutter as I begin to think of the possibilities afoot for the goddesses who are reading these words right now. Like finding an ancient treasure hidden in the depths of the sea, Abiola shares sacred wisdom and practices that have been secretly passed down from generation to generation in the African diaspora. *African Goddess Initiation* is the balm we need to heal our cultural wounds and reverse the effects of colonial demonization of ancient African traditions.

Abiola Abrams is not new to this movement. She has been sharing the glory of African goddesses within the community for decades. Years ago, I went to see Abiola speak in New York City. As she walked onto the stage, I could feel legions of ancestors behind her, giving her the courage to share her wisdom. Historically, descendants of Mother Africa have been persecuted and even killed for practicing these spiritual traditions, so Abiola speaking publicly about African goddesses carries an enormous spiritual burden and responsibility.

She has to contend with the fear from the community and the hatred from the oppressor, and transmute all of that energy into even more love for the African goddess. What is the fear from the community? There is both the fear of damnation and the fear of our sacred secrets being exposed. In Credo Mutwa's *Indaba, My Children: African Tribal History, Legends, Customs and Religious Beliefs*, he states in his introduction, "Much of what I shall reveal here will shock and anger many people—most of all my fellow Bantu, who resent having their doings and secrets exposed to foreigners."

Mutwa was considered a traitor to his people for revealing these sacred practices. But what about the children of Africa who have been cut off from the vast and colorful rituals that can quite literally save our lives? What about the children of the diaspora who have no other connection to this ancient wisdom? For us, Abiola is a courageous lighthouse, standing in the storm offering guidance and solace for those who are ready for this wisdom and transformation.

The call of the African goddess is deep and visceral. She stands you in front of the proverbial mirror of life and shows you your reflection. Your true reflection. Through tears, breakdowns, joyful dance breaks, rituals, contemplation, and meditation, we begin to see our true selves. Abiola has put together a divine guide to hold our hands during this journey. From rituals like the Coconut Head Wash for Yemaya of the Yoruba tradition in Nigeria to Choosing Your Goddesses Name with Queen Nefertiti of Egypt, each practice brings us closer to remembering who we really are.

The New Age spiritual movement has done its own damage in labeling "light" as good and "darkness" as bad. The darkness of the womb is where we were all created. The darkness of space holds our infinite possibilities. The darkness of the African Goddess holds deep compassion, love, power, and truth. Being held in the arms of THE ORIGINAL MOTHERS will heal us all. When I shared this sentiment with my colleague, Dinan Ra, she pointed out that Claire Heartsong, in *Anna, the Voice of the Magdalenes*, said, "While receiving this training I was introduced to the warrior goddesses—'the Dark Mothers.' . . . There was something about the energy of the 'Dark' Mother, the unconditional loving presence who is willing to descend into the hell realms where she finds her lost and suffering children and returns them . . . It was this capacity to love this much that I wanted to embody and practice."

Abiola's call to share the wisdom of the African goddess, the Dark Mother, is an ancestral one. While this call may be in many of our souls, Abiola answered it in creating this book: *African Goddess Initiation*. When we choose to answer our ancestral call, we are supported by countless generations of forebearers. For example, Dr. Velma Love, an expert on ancestral wisdom, shared with me the Ancestral Mathematics by Lyrical Zen: "In order to be born, you needed 2 parents, 4 grandparents, 8 great-grandparents, 16 second great-grandparents, 32 third great-grandparents, 64 fourth great-grandparents, 128 fifth great-grandparents, 256 sixth great-grandparents, 512 seventh great-grandparents, 1,024 eighth great-grandparents, 2,048 ninth great-grandparents. For you to be born today from 12 previous generations, you needed a total sum of 4,096 ancestors over the last 400 years."

In African spirituality, the role of the well of ancestors is great. These foremothers and forefathers stand with us, protect us, work with the goddesses, and conspire for our good. Can you imagine 4,096 people having your back?

On my journey in creating *Shallow Waters*, my novel about the African goddess Yemaya, I needed to heal my own ancestral wounds. Being a descendant of people who experienced chattel slavery, I had many traumas that spanned across the physical, spiritual, and emotional realms. By doing many of the rituals spelled out in Abiola's work *African Goddess Initiation*, I was not only able to connect deeper with Yemaya, I was able to heal many of my ancestral wounds.

That alone is MAGNIFICENT . . .

But the benefits to this work do not end there. Once we heal our past, we are brought into the present. Sensual rituals to Goddesses Oshun and Qetesh can heal our issues with pleasure and embodiment, thus creating flow in creativity and abundance. The words and lessons within this book are a gift that keeps on giving.

Can we work with African goddesses if we are not of African descent?

Do you do yoga, sage your home, or practice meditation? When we work with the wisdom of cultures different from our own, respect is a minimum (in the words of Lauryn Hill). Perhaps study the region from which the goddesses originated, or if you feel a deep connection or resonance with a certain deity, see how you can give back to the people in that country. Abiola has shared where each goddess is from, so half of the work is already done for you.

I bow deeply to Goddess Abiola Abrams for finding the courage to share her wisdom in her book *African Goddess Initiation*. May it be treasured for years to come, and may its readers find deep and true healing for ourselves, our ancestors, and our future generations.

Àse.

—Anita Kopacz, M.A., author of *Shallow Waters: A Novel*

DECLARATION
You Are Sacred

Sawubona, goddess—and grand rising!

Take a breath.

Welcome to the goddess circle. *Sawubona* means "We see you." Take a sip of fresh tamarind juice, my beautiful sister. This hibiscus petal–covered path was created just for you.

You hear that whisper? That is the sound of the goddess rising.

Rise, goddess, rise! Deep bow. You are the hero of this story.

Goddess rising is an energy that can no longer be contained. We are awakening en masse to our sacred feminine power, and it has been a long time coming. Actually, a long time coming back.

You are being called to bear witness to your own joy, magic, and power. Will you heed your own call?

Some of us have been hiding, shrinking, betraying ourselves, faking the funk, and playing small for so long that we believe that we *are* small. That shrunken self is not you. That shrunken self is a persona you created to survive.

Exhale. Leave your shoes at the gate. This is a barefoot journey.

This is where the invisible world meets the visible. The veil has been thin lately. Have you noticed?

We are a global sisterhood. Our goddess temple stretches around this magnificent cosmos. Take a moment to tune in now to your sisters who are joining you on this path. In your mind's eye, take the hand of the sister to the left of you in our great cosmic circle; perhaps she is in Atlanta or Rome. Now take the hand energetically of the sister to the right of you. Maybe she is in Harlem or Zimbabwe.

The quantum physicists say that time as we know it is an illusion. So maybe the sister to your left is in your past, and the sister to your right is in your future. Hold their hands and feel into their energy now as you hear the sound of your own breath.

Let the circle be unbroken. And may your initiation into the next phase of your life begin.

Goddess rising is you. Affirm it: *"I am goddess rising."*

Yes! You are goddess. Goddess. God-is.

Amen. A-women. Àse! And so it is.

Love, Abiola

INTRODUCTION
Getting Started

This book is a spiritual self-love initiation into awakening the divine goddess within and your sacred personal power, and a summoning to deepen your knowledge of self. All our lives, well-meaning folks said, "Just love yourself," but no one taught us how. As we learn our goddesses and ancient rituals, we learn ourselves. If your mother figure was not able to initiate you into this calling, it is because she did not know how. Your father figure could not initiate you because he did not know. You are not being initiated into any religion or spiritual sect.

This book is an invitation to a sacred healing adventure. You don't need to pack luggage or baggage for this trip; you already have it. This sacred self-love pilgrimage is about releasing that baggage.

This goddess circle is a sacred society of mystics, changemakers, starchildren, lightworkers, and indigo alchemists who know that we deserve more. We have existed for generations as a secret society, transmuting struggle into miracles. We are an inclusive community of lightbringers who acknowledge our own divine power. The sisters of this goddess circle recognize the spark in each other across countries, languages, ethnicities, religions, and cultures. We have been intending, praying, manifesting, banishing, binding, lighting, and putting out fires for a millennium and have been dismissed for far too long.

We are not here by accident. The sages predicted this time. We are out of alignment with Asase Yaa, aka Mama Nature. Life is out of balance. You see what is happening. There is upheaval in the atmosphere. Old systems are being dismantled, structures are breaking, and illusions are being exposed. The patriarchy is in shambles. This is the moment to summon the sacred within and step boldly into our sacred energies as queens, warriors, sorceresses, and lovers. We must nurture the goddess within to course correct.

You have been called to this goddess circle because somewhere in your bloodline there is someone who knows. She prayed for you before your grandmother's grandmother was a thought. She knew that you deserve better. She believed that you could have a life she could not fathom. She trusted in her sacrifices for you. We give thanks. Sawubona, great ancestress. We thank her and we see her. But this exploration, should you choose to accept it, is yours and yours alone.

Although there are other ways to use this book, this goddess rising initiation pilgrimage is a 42-ritual adult rite of passage. Our sacred goddess rituals are the path that illuminates the way. The word *spiritual* has the word *ritual* in it because we awaken our divine connection through the rituals we practice. I grew up in this world, but I also remember being a kid in Catholic, Southern Baptist, and African-derived spiritual churches and loving the rituals, divine symbolism, and ceremonies. Because my dad is a minister and spiritual mentor both initiated in our ancient African traditional religions and in Christianity, we also had services at home. Those were my favorite.

If the idea of ritual is scary to you, consider all of the rituals you already participate in. Ever blown out candles on a birthday cake? Have you opened a gift under a Christmas tree? Do you say "Bless you" when people sneeze? Did you put your hand over your heart to pledge allegiance? Ever painted Easter eggs? Do you kneel to pray or meditate? Did you dress up in a costume for Halloween and go trick-or-treating? Do you expect to see brides wearing white, flanked by bridesmaids? These are all rituals.

We pay little attention to the historical or spiritual significance of most of these rituals, but we do them anyway. Generally, rituals within a culture that we are part of seem normal to us. We are conditioned to see rituals and rites of passage outside of our own group as "weird" or "strange."

Accepted rites of passage in our modern society include Sweet 16 parties and quinceañeras, graduations, bar/bat mitzvahs, baby showers, bachelor/bachelorette parties, and retirement. Birth and death are rites of passage we all must participate in.

Ritual is the gateway to tap into your goddess energy. Surrender to your inner wise woman who knows your power. Meditate on your strength instead of believing lies of weakness. Would so many systems, governments, corporations, and ad agencies be so invested in trying to convince you that you are not powerful if that were the truth? The time is now to reclaim our magic, spiritual truths, and legends.

Relationship with the Divine is the key that begins to unlock who we were born to be. Some of you have been traveling a long time and may be further along than others. If you are newer to the circle, imagine being able to welcome goddess magic into your daily life to dissolve your fears, limiting beliefs, and shadow blocks. Allow yourself to consider how ancient rituals can help you to manifest and allow more joy, prosperity, and self-love.

So I ask again, Is this your journey? Only you can know.

If you have ever felt like you are not playing full out, then this is your journey. If you "followed their rules" and you are still unhappy, this is your journey. If you ever doubt your own greatness or feel like an impostor in your own life, this is your journey. And if you are not living the life you imagined, then you are in the right place.

Everything we are seeking on the outside is on the inside. All of the things we want to manifest—happiness, love, well-being, money—are on the other side of self-love, self-acceptance, and awakening your divinity. This goddess initiation is a rebirth into your womanhood and divinity, on your own terms. This is about your personal relationship with the Divine in you, as you.

This is a divine feminine initiation and rebirth into your capital "S" Self. I am your midwife in this sacred rebirth, with our powerful goddesses, ancestors, and spirits leading the way through transformational rituals, practices, rites, and ceremonies for your elevation.

Why African goddess magic? Well, why *not* African goddess magic? This is my spiritual inheritance that I was commanded to share with you. Again, you are not here by accident. We learned about the Roman goddess Venus and the Greek goddess Aphrodite in elementary school, but have you met the Guinea-Bissau goddess Mama Djombo, Yoruba orisha Oshun, Ashanti abosom Ngame, Egyptian goddess Ma'at, or Haitian lwa Erzulie Dantor? Our goddesses have ancient wisdom, healing magic, and transformational secrets to share.

Even as folks embrace Indian yoga, Japanese Reiki, Chinese Taoism and feng shui, Jewish Kabbalah, and mysticism from other cultures, ancient African religions, spiritual beliefs, and philosophy have been stigmatized, misrepresented, demonized, feared, and dismissed as backward, evil, savage, superstition, heathen, and primitive idol worship.

I was born into our traditions. I was named Abiola, a Yoruba name meaning "born into wealth," for a reason. The inheritance of our spirituality is my wealth. Guyana is the only English-speaking country in South America and considered to be Caribbean in culture. My mother is a devout Catholic, whose grandmother told her about her Ashanti and Fula roots. My father is a Spiritual Baptist minister. Spiritual Baptist is a syncretic Christian religion created by enslaved Caribbean peoples with our West African traditional spirituality at the foundation.

My father recalls being a teen and secretly attending spiritual worship meetings in people's houses because their church, songs, dances, traditions, and drumbeating was illegal. Illegal! That is psychological warfare. He remembers sneaking around to avoid religious raids from the authorities. All African spirituality was outlawed and considered evil . . . and this is in my parents' lifetime! This fight continues today in many places. So much of our history and culture was ripped away that it is an honor to be entrusted by the ancestors to document it for those to come.

There is no one African religious tradition, as Africa is a huge continent and her children are global. Mother Africa's spiritual history and beliefs stretch from Southern Africa, East and West Africa, and North Africa to the United States, South America, and the Caribbean—and beyond. I consider myself an African woman, American born, Queens/Harlem, New York bred, to parents and family who were born for generations in Guyana, all of us descendants of chattel slavery. That is a tremendous cultural inheritance.

When Africans were kidnapped, trafficked en masse, and brutally dragged in chains to work camps in the "New World," called plantations, we hid our deities and rituals in stories of saints, angels, and legendary characters. Our deities included a powerful cadre of orishas, abosom, lwas, álúsí, spirits, and god/desses. From South Africa to Egypt, Brazil to Cuba to even Indigenous Australia, we chant their names: Yemaya, Mami Wata, Atete, Iset, and Ala. Our celebrity artists like Beyoncé are awakening and paying tribute to the sacred feminine power of our deities. But this is not new. Beyoncé and others are now able to openly celebrate in the light what stars like Celia Cruz may have had to hide. Give thanks.

The ancestors told me to write this book. I was not given a choice. Then I had to get their permission to share specific pathways and teachings with you. These are our living cultures. We inherited the fears, challenges, and issues of our ancestors but not their solutions, which exist in our rituals, rites, and ceremonies.

Take a breath. This is not New Age or a trend. We have been doing this since time began.

Right before the pandemic hit, I was thrilled to be offering my first large-scale American spiritual retreat at the Omega Institute in Rhinebeck, New York. I had 500 seats reserved for you for the Goddess Unmasked Retreat. But as we know, we plan and God/dess laughs. The day before our launch event in March 2020, we were canceled as New York State shut down everything on the calendar. I was so looking forward to doing this work with 500 of you in person and to get to break bread, laugh, sweat, and cry together to shift energy. But God/dess said "bigger" and made space for me to birth this sacred medicine for you in this way.

So how does this path unfold? Nine goddess temples (chapters) hold 42 goddess sanctuaries (sections) and rituals. Each goddess temple is a rise through consciousness. You will also see the stories of Goddess Temple Circle sisters throughout.

You may be feeling excited, nervous, or even scared. Or you wandered in the wrong door and find this ridiculous. Whatever you feel is whatever you feel. This is your goddess initiation. These are your goddess rituals. This is your soul journey.

So, when did I start sharing these teachings? At the close of the '90s as a recent college grad, I stood on stage at the Schomburg Center for Research in Black Culture in NYC with my girls in our three-woman show, *Goddess City*. My creative sister Goddess Antoy Grant stood to my left as the Goddess of Fever. Our current Goddess of Truth stood to my right, and I stood in the center as the Goddess of Nerve. *Goddess City* is recorded in history as the first hip-hop theater piece ever, so folks were all kinds of confused as we declared, "The stage is our altar." The late Great Ancestress Ruby Dee and Mr. Ossie Davis were in the front row as afterward we opened the town hall goddess circle.

I have held sacred space and hosted goddess circles for just over 20 years now. Some have been living-room gatherings of 10 people, workshop sisterhoods of 40 people, or international retreats from Bali to London. Others are digital sister circles with private online groups and courses. But whether there are 10 people or 10,000, whoever needs to be there is there.

There is one thing those who are called to this path have in common: we all know that Spirit is calling us higher to a greater purpose. Here is a path forward. It's your time to rise and to shine. You are sacred power and magic, fearlessly made.

So much of self-help is about sanitizing spirituality and making it palatable. We've tried to take the sacred out of our rituals—and ourselves. Good vibes and bad vibes are really about good spirits and bad spirits. Meditation and breathwork are about aligning with the power of Spirit. Setting an intention is prayer. Manifestation is casting spells. A vision board is a visual prayer quilt. The essence of yoga is spiritual union. I hold no judgment of anyone else's practice. I share that only to say you've already been doing this.

Are you ready? When you came into the circle, I greeted you with, "Sawubona." *Sawubona* is an isiZulu greeting. It means "We see you," but who is "we" for each of us? My "we" is me, my Creator, my ancestors, my descendants, my community, and everyone I have ever been or will ever be.

Call all parts of you back home now. That part you left on the bottom of that person's shoe. The energy that other one sucked right out of you. The selves stuck to those incomplete projects. That little self who didn't get what she needed from those well-meaning grown-ups. Call those parts back to you now. You will need to be fully present for your courageous expedition.

HOW TO USE THIS BOOK

There are nine key inner temples you must face to awaken the goddess, the divine feminine, within. For the full goddess initiation experience, start at the beginning and spend as long as you need with each goddess and ritual as you ascend through the nine temples (chapters). Each temple corresponds to an area of your life, consciousness, and body.

The nine temples of this initiation are:

1. The Threshold (Sankofa)

2. The Temple of Ancestors: Your Soil Energy Channel (Amadlozi)

3. The Temple of Conjurers: Your Creation Energy Channel (Heka)

4. The Temple of Warriors: Your Power Energy Channel (Àse)

5. The Temple of Shadows: Your Inner Monsters (Jumbies)

6. The Temple of Lovers: Your Love Energy Channel (Ubuntu)

7. The Temple of Griots: Your Voice Energy Channel (Akoben)

8. The Temple of Queens: Your Insight Energy Channel (Chi)

9. The Temple of High Priestesses: Your Ecstasy Energy Channel (Umbilini)

Each chapter is the sanctuary of five goddesses, ancestors, or spirits from the global African diaspora. "Chak moun ki rive, vini ak moun pa li." That is a Haitian proverb meaning "Each person who arrives, comes with a person of his own." As is our cultural tradition, those you invite bring friends. So when I opened the door for the goddesses, they brought divine ancestors, ancient queens, and other spirits with them. You will meet each one and receive her wisdom gifts and lessons. Then you will be given a transformational ritual based on a traditional practice related to her key principle.

As an alternative, you may also choose to use this book as a reference guide. For example, if you need a grief ritual, you can find Goddess Ala and use the grief ritual immediately. If you feel ready to deal with the wounded healer in you, locate Goddess Sekhmet. Goddess Tanit is who you need if you want to turn up your pleasure practice. Go directly to the Temple of Shadows if dealing with your shadow self is your focus.

WHO IS INVITED AS AN INITIATE?

This is a sacred feminine quest. Spirit chooses who should enter the circle. The language I use includes the terms *woman/women, sister, daughter, goddess,* and the pronouns *she/her.* I address all readers as "goddess." This is a divine feminine-energy pathway, but we all have both sacred masculine and feminine energy. I also speak of the yoni and energetic womb. If this language feels like home to you, you are welcome here.

Some of the deities who showed up are from closed practices. If that is the case, I will let you know the honorable way to proceed.

When I was younger, I remember being annoyed about someone inserting themselves in a closed spiritual practice. It felt disrespectful, although it wasn't my ceremony. I thought, *We have so little, we must protect it.* Then Spirit told me, "We can take care of ourselves. Just share what we ask you to share." They commanded me to shift my worldview from "but we have so little." They said, "You are wealthy. You are an heiress. You have so much. We choose who shows up." And that clarified it for me.

This spiritual self-love initiation is a paradigm shift. The human part of you will do anything to hold on to your identity, your perception of self. This is why sometimes traditional self-help falls flat.

They told us that to be a girl is to be less than. The opposite is true. You are fertile with everything we need for a better tomorrow. You are fertile whether you ever give birth to another human. On this path, we speak with reverence about the energetic womb and yoni because many of us were taught that our bodies' natural parts and functions are dirty and shameful, so we need to cover up with sugar and spice and everything nice. Women-identified people give birth to society's dreams. Knowing this is goddess rising.

Please note that this is a "first do no harm" spiritual healing passageway.

ABOUT THE ENERGY CHANNELS

When I was a kid, I loved jumping Double Dutch, hula-hooping, and roller-skating. The magic of jumping between two ropes, balancing circles on my hips, and walking on wheels was also an initiation to the magic and paradoxes of Black womanhood. When you are called to deliver sacred medicine, which is what I consider this book to be, you bring all of yourself to it. So you, dear reader, get bamboo-earrings (at least two pairs) me, yogini-meditation me, weirdo-whose-family-had-chickens-in-an-NYC-backyard me, and braids-beads-barrettes and eating-messy-mangoes me.

You get the me who was a teen rapper in a group named Females Beyond Control and the me who studies chakras.

Because the power of chakra work and similar systems are the foundation for many of the healing systems I channel and create, I use that as a foundation here too. I didn't want to confuse or overwhelm readers with the ancient African and Indian spiritual systems, so I created a chakra-based system that is distinctly African. But it is important for me to acknowledge lineage. For those who find it helpful, the lower three temples here mirror the lower chakras, and the upper four temples mirror the upper chakras. However, you don't need to know any of that for this experience.

You will learn to use the elements in the first chapter, "The Threshold," in Mawu-Lisa's section.

HOW TO CREATE A GODDESS GROUP

You may take this goddess initiation adventure solo or with a goddess circle. A goddess circle or sister circle is a group gathered for the purpose of personal evolution. You can have 3 or 30 vibrant souls in your group. Invite only those who are positive and excited about evolving together. If you have to drag or convince anyone, then they are not a good fit (currently) for your group.

Have a reading schedule like a book club and then come together to share your thoughts and ritual experiences. For example, you could decide to jointly read one goddess section per week. Have a regular meeting time, weekly, biweekly, or monthly. Be sure that everyone is given equal time to participate. One person can be the organizer and leader, or leadership can rotate.

Your meetings can be virtual or in person. You will find additional resources in the back of this book to enhance your experience.

HOW TO PREPARE YOUR RITUAL SPACE

You will see the words "Prepare your ritual space" at the start of almost every one of your goddess rituals. This will mean something different for each of you. Those words are an invitation to do some or all of the following things: set an intention, pray and/or meditate, cleanse the space, take a shower or bath, dress and light your candles, burn incense, go to the altar, make a sacred offering, turn on music, and/or invite in Spirit. Follow your own inner guidance.

Please note: Traditionally, the word *work* is used to describe ritual in most global African practices.

WHAT IS SACRED WATER?

Some rituals will ask you to use a holy or sacred water of your choice. Of course, holy or sacred water can be blessed by a spiritual figure. Sacred waters may include rainwater, moon water, and sun water. Each is created by setting your intentions with the water and charging it for at least 90 minutes in the corresponding element. Ocean water is also a sacred water that can be replicated by adding the salt of your choice to water. Coconut water can be used as a sacred water as well. You can also purchase sacred "waters," colognes that have been used for ritual work for generations, including Florida Water and Kananga Water. Kananga is a holy ritual cleansing water made with ylang-ylang. It's like Florida Water for the Caribbean. Feel free to create your own sacred water by charging water on your altar and praying over it.

WHAT IS THE CROSSROADS?

In many rituals, you will see the note "dispose at the crossroads of your own understanding." Leaving something at the crossroads means releasing that which no longer serves you. Natural items, such as herbs, take on the energy of the spiritual work you do with them. If you are using them in a ritual to release negative energy, for example, the energetic residue will be in the herbs.

Crossroads are spaces of highly transmutative energy. In an ideal situation, we would have access to a real four-way crossroads, but most of us don't. Decide what represents the crossroads for you. It could be your backyard or your garbage disposal. Just come from an energy of reverence and gratitude and all will be well.

WHY INCLUDE DIVERSE CULTURES?

For those of you who take issue with goddesses and spirits from different diaspora traditions and pantheons working with us together for our evolution, note that for many of us, this was our ancestral experience. We suddenly found ourselves side by side with our sisters and brothers who spoke different languages and venerated different deities. So this is how the goddesses showed up in my ancestral memory. Together.

This is not a new thought movement. It's an ancient thought movement. We are not new to this. We are true to this.

The African Goddess Creed

Africa is far from a monolith. There are over 54 nations in Africa and thousands of African cultures. Most of the map lines on the continent cross tribal delineations because we did not create those borders. Plus, African people and our spiritual traditions stretch across the globe. For those of us in the diaspora, we were forced to leave our land, but our land didn't leave us.

As a result, this feminine energy initiation not only includes deities, spirits, and ancestors from continental Africa but also from diasporic countries and cultures with African retention such as: Haiti, Cuba, Barbados, Trinidad and Tobago and Jamaica in the Caribbean, Guyana, Suriname and Brazil in South America, the Garifuna communities of Central America, Louisiana and the Gullah Geechee Corridor in the United States. The horrors of the global African holocaust known as slavery's Middle Passage left people of African descent physically scattered. Our spiritual traditions have helped us to remain whole.

Global African spiritual traditions and spiritual philosophies include Ifá/Òrìṣà, Odinani/Odinala, Akom, Vodun, Obeah, Shango, Hoodoo, Juju, Conjure, Komfa, Winti, Kumina, Santeria/La Regla Lucumi, Candomblé, Spiritual Baptist, Palo, Macumba, Muthi, 21 Divisions, Umbanda, Rastafarianism, and yes, Christianity, Islam, and Judaism. Some traditions are Yoruba, or Fon derived, others are Bantu rooted, some practices are Akan in nature, plus the original traditions, and so much more.

If you are familiar with any of the African spiritual traditions, you may have learned a particular practice, goddess story, or ritual another way. There are variations in the oral literature, stories, practice, and even in the spelling of many of the names of goddesses, rites, and rituals. That makes sense. These are living traditions and we are all in this together. Imagine how someone might share your story globally in a thousand years. There would be different aspects and interpretations.

Although these practices have key cultural differences and deities, common foundational beliefs run through most of them. These make up our African Goddess Creed for this initiation.

These are the 10 beliefs common across most African religious traditions and spiritual belief systems you will find in this book:

1. **God/dess.** There is one Most High Creator, Supreme Being, who is immortal, all-seeing, omnipresent, and omnipotent. You will find different names in different cultures and languages. I will refer to the Supreme Being as Spirit, God/dess (meaning God or Goddess of your understanding), the Most High, God, Goddess, the Creator, the Divine, the Universe, and Guidance interchangeably.

2. **Guidance.** The Creator's divine team (pantheon) includes deities and spirits—divine energies that can be intercessors on our behalf. Angels or saints may be helpful as a reference. These orishas, lwas, abosom, álúsí, and others are all deified energies, manifestations of the Most High Creator, faces of God/dess.

3. **Ancestors.** Our ancestors are holy. Veneration is the practice of honoring those who have transitioned. They have power in our lives and the ability to intercede with the Divine on our behalf.

4. **Elders.** We have reverence for our elders. We honor the wisdom of those who come before. We have a duty to pass on their knowledge and pay it forward.

5. **Soul.** We are Divine within. Our life-force energy is God/dess. This is the power of the soul and the reflection of the Most High.

6. **Spirit.** Spirit is present in everything. We respect the power and wonder of nature. We are able to communicate with the ever-present Spirit world. There is no secular (non-spiritual) world.

7. **Community.** The collective is holy. We are all in this together.

8. **Signs.** Divination is a sacred gift to communicate with the Divine and deepen our knowledge of self.

9. **Miracles.** We believe in the Creator's magic and the ability, with the support of the Divine, to co-create our reality.

10. **The Circle.** Let the circle be unbroken. The circle is sacred. The circle recurs in our dances, prayers, divination, and lives.

1

THE THRESHOLD
Sankofa

BLESSING OF THE THRESHOLD GUARDIANS

Dawn awakens;

You are at the threshold.

This is the bridge, the door, the passage, the gateway;

The path to the rest of your path.

It has taken you a lifetime of experiences to get here.

May your joy know no limits.

May you be loved wholly.

May your calabash overflow with riches.

May pleasure and creativity pursue you.

May you be brazenly fearless.

May your mind and heart be open.

May you be you.

This is the goddess blessing of the threshold.

Blissful greetings, gorgeous!

Take a breath. An initiation begins with an entryway. Power is ignited at crossroads. You are at the opening of the gate, the opening of your life. This threshold is named <u>Sankofa</u>. *Sankofa* means "Go back and get it." There is a you who existed before life taught you your limitations. You are going back to get your very Self.

We knock nine times and ask the spirit of the crossroads if we may proceed.

Who knocks?

Your daughters. Please open the gate.

We are granted entry by our Threshold Guardians, the ancient ones, Nana Buluku and Mawu-Lisa of Dahomey. You now stand before the goddesses who are here to guide you in. The Guardians are protective guiding goddesses at the crossroads of your life. Their energetic color frequency is hot pink, and they show up when important choices must be made. The sacrifice that is required is the death of the old, the leaving behind of our comfort zones, releasing who you think you are.

Give thanks. They each have gifts for you. They have been the keepers of this guidance from time immemorial. You must choose to drink their wisdom. Should you accept their gifts, life will never be the same. Your threshold rituals will give you foundational support tools for your goddess initiation adventure.

Do you dare to enter?

Congratulations. If you are still here, you have committed.

NANA BULUKU

Goddess of New Cycles
Benin
Goddess Soulbook and Initiation Contract Ritual

"I am limitless."

NANA BULUKU'S MESSAGE

Ób'ókhían! Welcome home, daughter. I have been waiting for you. You have been waiting for you too. Don't be in a hurry. There are no shortcuts on this trip. Allow yourself to become present, maybe for the first time. You have entered a new cycle that is very old. Many have held the door open for you.

NANA BULUKU'S STORY

Great Goddess Nana Buluku, we say your name.
We honor you.

She is the guardian. Her face is covered with a veiled curtain of cowrie shells because you need not look her in the eyes.

We must go back to the beginning to move forward. When it all began, she was there.

Nana Buluku is the Most High, Supreme Being, primordial mother, grand-mother of all the orishas (deities), and Creator of all we see for the Dahomey. Before Dahomey became Benin, she gave birth to the first deities, a woman and man, twins, Mawu and Lisa. Together they formed one of the first spiritual trinities. Then all of that world birthing wore her out! And she went to go rest and enjoy her praise and her creation.

Nana's attitude shifts from nurturing to fearsome between cultures. She is so revered among some that her name is never spoken. She is so feared among others that when her name is spoken, all must throw themselves to the floor in prayer position. Nana is no joke. Come to her humbly and honestly. She has been miscategorized as bitter, angry, crone energy. The truth is that she is a fighter who protects women and has time for nobody's bull. She aids the reincarnated souls in being ready to be reborn.

At times Nana is both masculine and feminine energy. But her energy is always matriarchal as she mostly works with priestesses. Nana, goddess of the muddy waters, carries an ibiri, a magical scepter made from the stalks of palm leaves and shells. Her ibiri cannot be held by men. She is a wise woman and herbalist with healing energy that predates the orishas and the Iron Age.[1] That's why you won't use iron knives when you work with her. She prefers simple wooden knives made of bamboo.

Hear us, Nana! Nana is revered for her strength. In 1890, a Brazilian ethnologist noted that enslaved African people would sing when one of them was being violently punished. The enslavers found it strange and took it as further proof of the inhumanity of Black people. They didn't know that the African people were singing their prayers for protection during horrific whippings and torture.[2] The songs were Candomblé chants to Nana and other orishas, abosom, and álúsí to support the person being tortured. They petitioned Nana to lift the abused person up and take the pain for them. In the prayerful lyrics from old-school Brazilian sambista Sidney da Conceição's song, "Nanaê, Nanã Naiana," he sings about Nanã Buruke taking the blows and the pain.

There are endless stories of Nana Buluku, as everyone wants to claim her. Nana is claimed by the Fon, Yoruba, Ewe people, and many more. So you will find her not only find her in Benin, Togo, Ghana, Nigeria, and other African countries but also in the African religions of her children transmitted throughout South America, the United States, and the Caribbean.

Saluba, Nana!

Let's Talk New Cycles

This moment initiates a new cycle. Are you ready for a new beginning? Newness is both titillating and terrifying. When we choose a new path that will evolve who we have been, we are ripe for self-sabotage. This is the power of identity. The reptilian part of our brains would rather be in sync with what we think of ourselves than grow. Goddess energy is moving from the brain to the Spirit.

Whenever goddess sisters are signing up for my sacred retreats and programs, I always tell them that they can look forward to something else popping up that suddenly needs their attention. A life test often rears its head saying, "Don't do that new life-changing experience now. Do this instead." It could be something as important as your family, job, or business suddenly needing you or you realizing you don't have the time or money to spend on yourself. Or worse. Fear grips you after you have invested, and you drop out on yourself. People pay in full for a VIP ticket to international retreats and then don't show up. It happens every year. Change can be terrifying.

So I want to alert you now of the same thing. Yes, life happens. And of course we leave room for that. But be aware of the difference between potential emergencies and self-sabotage that would mean you delaying this empowerment mission for yourself.

When the commitment test pops up, stay the course.

Your time is now.

HOW TO HONOR GODDESS NANA BULUKU

When you honor Goddess Nana Buluku, you honor the part of you that embraces new cycles and is always birthing the next moment. You may choose to honor this energy inside yourself or invoke her energy according to your own tradition.

To honor the goddess in you: Keep it simple if you have not been initiated into her energy. Her shrines are mounds called Nana Buuken, traditionally built outside because of the overwhelming sacred, potentially volatile power of her energy. If you are not connected with her, honor her by getting in touch with your own wise-woman herbalist within. How can you better nurture yourself? What natural foods and herbs will cradle you with the love of grandmother energy?

Symbols: The moon, mud, leaves, birds, moonstone, black opal, and agate; palm frond– or raffia-covered mounds for her shrines

Colors: Her colors are purple, dark indigo, black, white, green, and red. She doesn't like metallics.

Auspicious times: Monday and Saturday are her days. July 26 is her feast day.

Music: "Nanaê, Nanã Naiana" by Sidney da Conceição and "Cordeiro de Nana" by Thalma de Freitas

Suggested offerings: Whiskey, rum, tobacco, coffee, shrimp, or tomatoes. She also enjoys garlic, juniper, marshmallows, and mint.

Alternate names: Nana Bukuu, Nana Buruku, Olisabuluwa, Nanamburucu, Nanan, Nanã Buruke

Traditional New Cycles Ritual: Recording the Sacred

We record our knowledge so that even when life begins a new cycle we are building on what came before.

Traditional African religions have an ancient tradition of recording their knowledge through oral and written literature. We will meet the griots, the storytellers, later, but the literary corpus of Ifá texts is the scripture of the Yoruba people that was passed down orally. Ifá is used for divination but also includes sacred verses, spiritual magic and rootwork, genealogy, history, medicinal treatments, philosophy, and psychology.

In Ethiopia, magical healing scrolls have been prescribed for 2,000 years by debteras.[3] Debteras, also called dabtaras, are a combination of priests, healers, and magicians. The scrolls, regarded as magical medicine, included art, prayers, poetry, and astrology.

The Timbuktu manuscripts also contained geomancy divination secrets, spellwork, astrology, incantations, and wizardry.[4] Timbuktu, in Mali, was a revered center of learning founded in the 1300s.

Ancient Egyptians had the Ebers papyrus of herbal knowledge for the living. Then their Book of the Dead contained declarations and prayers for the afterlife.

South Africa's rock art includes paintings, engravings, and drawings that are over 3,000 years old.[5] I'm sure if we were able to properly interpret them, we would probably find spiritual knowledge and teachings as well!

Your New Cycles Ritual:
Goddess Soulbook and Initiation Contract

Ritual intention: To create your Goddess Soulbook, a sacred place to record your personal magic. Then you will awaken it with a soul contract.

Like Queen Nefertari of Egypt, you are your own scribe. As you embark on this experience, you will need a sacred book to record your goddess profiles, ruminations, spiritual knowledge, dreams, affirmations, herbal recipes, prayers, meditations, rootwork, spells (yes!), and magical ritual practices. Add sketches and glue in images representing goddess wisdom, along with your ritual modifications and results, as a reference book. Record what is valuable to your goddess path. Someone sacrificed so that you can tell your story and your truth. You should also have a separate notebook for long-form journaling.

You will need:

- Goddess Soulbook (magical book of your own choosing or design)
- Initiation journal (plain lined journal)
- Special writing utensil

Special note: I recommend that you use both a Goddess Soulbook and a regular notebook or journal for this process. Your Goddess Soulbook is more like a visual magical reference book that you are creating, similar to a Book of Shadows. Your initiation journal is where you will delve into the many long-form self-illuminating questions and assignments I've included throughout this book. I will tell you which to use for each practice. You may choose to share and pass down your Goddess Soulbook, but your journal is private.

What to do:

Part 1: Your Goddess Soulbook

Acquire a blank book. The best books for this practice are unlined, thick, and can stay open on their own during rituals, but use what you have access to.

Prepare your ritual space, as explained previously in the "How to Use This Book" section.

Design your Goddess Soulbook to your liking. This step is not required if you bought a predesigned book. Some will use stampers, stencils, calligraphy, tea stain, and painted text; some prefer all one-color handwriting. There is no wrong way to do this.

Bless, dedicate, and cleanse the book. You may choose to use a clearing incense and say your own prayer to bless the book. A simple consecration blessing is to close your eyes, hold the book to your heart, connect with Spirit, and say, "Please bless this Goddess Soulbook to hold Your wisdom and mine."

Write your name on the front with your special writing utensil. Some people use colored pens, paint, or special inks.

Sleep with your book so it gets your energy. You can put it under your bed. If you put it on the bed or under your pillow, the pages may become creased.

Don't be too intimidated to use it!

Part 2: Your Goddess Initiation Contract

Copy this simple contract into your new Goddess Soulbook. Feel free to modify and embellish it as your own spirit commands. Read it out loud and then sign it.

O Great One, God/dess of All That Is!
I commit now to awaken my true goddess within.
All I have been searching for is within me.
I am willing to know my own power.
And for this, I am so grateful.
I choose the goddess way.
Let my path be blessed.
Let the path of all those on this journey be blessed.
Let the path of all those not on this journey be blessed.
I honor the goddesses who I will learn from on this quest.
These are my words, and I have spoken.
Goddess rising!
Àse.

MAWU-LISA

Goddess of Cosmic Power
Benin
Goddess Altar and Womb Bowl Ritual

"My power shines forth from within."

MAWU-LISA'S MESSAGE

Kóyo! Welcome, daughter. It is with great anticipation that I greet you today. You are in the right place. Things may seem uncomfortable until you get your bearings, but you will. That feeling you have always had of being different is real. You are sacred. You are magic. Now that you know this, stop pretending not to.

MAWU-LISA'S STORY

Great God/dess Mawu-Lisa, we say your name.
We honor you.

Mawu was the moon and the night sky. She, the divine feminine, lived in the west. Lisa was the sun and the daylight. He, the divine masculine, lived in the east. They came together during an eclipse to create cosmic power. Supreme Being

Nana Buluku, their mother, birthed them as twins. In many traditions, they are the Supreme Being. Their energy helps to birth new creations. We all have the divine feminine and masculine within us.

Mawu-Lisa is a powerful dual deity who is the literal representation of "Mother-Father God." Mawu is a moon goddess in her own right. Lisa is a sun god in his own right. Together they make up the singular Fon god/dess with the power of the sun and the moon, Mawu-Lisa. The proverb goes, "When Lisa punishes, Mawu forgives."

Mawu's power is inward, cool, healing, intuitive, emotional, and wise. Lisa's power is outward, hot, action-oriented, linear, firm, and adventurous. With the merger of those energies, they created everything that we need. They represent in equilibrium a unity of duality. Even though they are equal and opposite energies, they are oneness. They either appear separately or as one entity with two faces. They are different aspects but one spirit. This is the rhythm of life.

After creation, Mawu-Lisa needed a way to hold the world together, so they created the mighty Ayida-Weddo, the rainbow serpent. Ayida-Weddo coils around the globe with her husband, Dan/Damballah, the snake god, Mawu-Lisa's son. Together they connect the lands and the seas.

The Book of Fa (Ifá in Yoruba), determiner of our destiny, is Mawu-Lisa's messenger. Keeping everything in universal order, Mawu fashioned us from clay. She likes to recycle materials, so that's why we look like our relatives. When someone dies, their soul is returned to Mawu-Lisa and gifted to a newborn in their lineage. Mawu is a portal for channeling our dreams into abundance. The name *Mawu*, meaning "God," is often invoked to refer to both energies. When the Fon people say, "I swear to God," they say, "N'xwlé Mawu."

Like the principles of yin and yang, divine feminine and masculine, we have Mawu energy and Lisa energy. "Awaken the mother mind within every one of you human beings," commanded the great Zulu philosopher and sangoma (healer) Credo Mutwa, as the way to save the world. He called Mawu energy the "mother mind." The Zulu believe that every human has two minds, a feeling mother mind and a linear warrior mind. The mother mind, Baba Credo said, looks at a tree and feels the living entity and looks at a stone and sees "the future lying dormant in that stone."[6]

Awaken your Mawu power!

Let's Talk Cosmic Power

The balance of power in our world has been off for generations. So many of us are attuned with our divine Lisa energy, which says move forward; take action; be direct; go, go, go only; and we are starving for our Mawu energy. The being, loving, receiving Mawu energy is at a deficit.

We are over-Lisa'd and under-Mawu'd. That is why you are here. Like Mawu-Lisa, you have come to heal, reflect, and shine.

Your true power has nothing to do with external gains. You were created by the same force that birthed the sun and the moon. How magnificent you must be! That is cosmic power, the kind of power that cannot be destroyed or lost. You are courageous to be here. It is scary to go against the norm.

So what happens if you keep refusing the call to your true power?

Ma, my maternal great-grandmother, was a midwife and the equivalent of a women's fertility healer in Guyana, South America. Ma could be seen all hours of the day and night putting on her boots and grabbing her bag to go "catch babies." She knew exactly which herb to use for which ailment. To counteract her own bad eyesight, she used "young okra" as eye drops. This woman, born in the 1800s, somehow knew what science is telling us now, that okra contains vitamin A, which is good for the eyes.

Ma also felt the calling from Spirit to be a spiritual leader. Alas, this was not a calling that Ma wanted. Spirit would tell her what to eat and what not to eat to have a clear channel to receive guidance. Ma, apparently a contrarian like her great-granddaughter Abiola, would do the exact opposite of what her spirit guides told her on purpose. They told her not to eat pork, so she ate it in abundance. These were not gifts that she wanted.

My mom says that my sister, Damali, with her healing hands and doula energy, is the current incarnation of Ma. She is walking in Ma's cosmic power. We are Ma's legacy. Spirit wanted her blood in this game. Now over 100 years after Ma's birth, Goddess Damali and I are not her only healer descendants. There is my cousin Michael, who travels the world helping people; my cousin Tristan, who focused on helping others get healthy after his horrible bout with coronavirus; my cousin Goddess Adana Collins, who knits with beauty and paints love on skin with henna; and my cousin Goddess Nickeola Marshall, an empowerment coach who doesn't let lupus stop her; to name just a few.

Ma's refusal of the call is not so different from so many of us sabotaging our-selves out of the things we claim we want. Your Mawu energy wants to be adored, and your Lisa energy wants to be respected. You are worthy and deserving of both. But are you both adoring and respecting yourself?

Write in your Goddess Soulbook: *I am adored. I am respected.*

Journal question: What are you doing to block or receive your gifts?

HOW TO HONOR MAWU-LISA

When you honor God/dess Mawu-Lisa, you honor the part of you that is cosmic power. You may choose to honor this energy inside yourself or invoke their energy according to your own tradition.

To honor the goddess in you: Mawu-Lisa is in charge of the soul. Embrace your sun energy and your moon energy. There is a sacred ceibo tree at Souvenance in Haiti called Mapou Lisa. Find your own sacred tree to share your victories and sorrows with. Mawu's themes are birth, motherhood, creativity, divination, and abundance. Lisa, like the Lisassi wives of Lisa, in Benin, is fiery and tough. Allow yourself to be a receiver as well as a giver, to "be" as much as you do.

Symbols: The moon, the sun, palm kernels, rain, clay, elephants

Color: Their color is white.

Auspicious times: All celestial activity, including sunrise, sunset, full moon, moonrise, and moonset

Music: "Eshou/Mawu-Lisa" by Oxaï Roura and "Mawuse" by Petit-Pays Oméga

Suggested offerings: Drumming, palm kernels, clay, soil, seeds, moon water, sun water

Alternate names: Mahu-Lisa, Maowu-Lisa, Mahou-Lissa, Lusa, Leeza, Leza, Seboulisa, Yehowa-Liza, Mawuga Kitikana

Traditional Cosmic Power Ritual: Altars and Shrines

Altars, temples, and shrines are a consecrated space for divine power. These practices are as old as time. Shrines are usually places of honor and veneration, whereas altars have the added responsibility of being places for spiritual work. Traditionally, the shrine is where the deity lives, like the Osun-Osogbo Sacred Grove in Nigeria.

Altars can be tiny or huge. In college I hid my altar in my desk drawer. I believe that when we look at the care that Afro-Caribbean women put into the practice of dressing their dresser tops, we are seeing the remnants of altar-keeping.

In ancient Egyptian temples, altars were either portable tables or immovable and made of stone. The smaller altars had space for food, flowers, a libation bowl, and an incense dish. Larger altars often faced east. There were also private domestic altars behind closed doors.

I grew up in a home that always had altars. This was incredibly embarrassing as a kid. The spiritual practices of the families of my childhood friends were safely tucked away in their churches under the guardianship of a gatekeeping pastor. Their altars were there as well. In my family, our altars and relationship with the Creator were personal.

When my friends asked, "What is that table with the oil and candles? Why is there incense burning? Why don't y'all eat pork? Why do I have to take off my shoes in your house?" I didn't have the language to explain any of it. I just shrugged it off. But the truth is that our altars made me feel protected.

I encountered altars again outside of religious spaces in Black theaters in New York City. After graduating from college, I was a part of the Black theater and spoken-word scene with my three-woman show, *Goddess City*. Back then, when you walked into the National Black Theatre in Harlem, the La MaMa Theater Club or Nuyorican Poets Cafe in the East Village, they had gorgeous, elaborate altars somewhere in the space.

An altar is simply a place of consecrated spiritual energy. There are all kinds of altars: ancestral altars, devotional altars, love altars, protection altars, prosperity altars, and more.

Your Cosmic Power Ritual: Goddess Altar and Womb Bowl

Ritual intention: To create or awaken your altar practice by creating a goddess altar.

Altars are incredibly personal. Many people will have lists of dos and don'ts, but let your Guidance speak to you. If you already have an altar, refresh it for this ritual. Your intention matters most. Your altar can be inside or outside. Put your altar in a private place if possible. I create temporary mini altars when I travel.

A goddess altar is an altar of birth, creativity, sensuality, nurturing, and abundance. Get clear on your own goddess altar's purpose. Will you be praying or meditating here? The altar that speaks to me will not necessarily speak to your goddess altar rituals. You may wish to do this practice at night or in alignment with your moon time. If you are further along in your goddess experience, you might decide to dedicate your altar to a specific goddess.

You will need:

- A flat surface
- Altar cloth
- Goddess element (representative)
- Moon element (representative)
- Chalice, glass, or vessel for moon water
- Water
- Elements of earth, air, fire

What to do:

Part 1: Set Up Your Goddess Altar

Prepare your ritual space.

Choose your altar base and cleanse it. You never want to use any spiritual items without clearing the previous energy. Whether it is a table or a windowsill, approach it with reverence, love, and respect.

Add an altar cloth. Choose a color to represent the deity or energy of the altar. Use a white cloth if you are unsure. A silver cloth represents the moon.

You may choose the direction of your altar. In many cultures, altars face east, the direction of the rising sun. In some traditions, altars face north, the direction of the earth element. Trust your guidance to decide what works for you.

You may set your intention based on the phase of the moon. The new moon is the start of the lunar cycle and the perfect time to initiate projects. It's the energy of new beginnings. The waxing moon represents growth and expansion. The full moon is a great time to reflect and release. The waning moon is about letting go.

Represent the goddess. You may choose to have a statue, doll, or spiritual symbol like an ankh to represent goddess energy or a specific goddess. You may want to add yoni art or symbols and represent moon blood. This could be a sacred vessel or something red to represent menstruation.

Represent the moon. The moon is sacred feminine energy. Crystal balls and spherical elements reflect the moon. So do cutouts of the moon or white and clear stones and crystals like selenite and moonstone. Botswana agate is especially pleasing to motherland goddess energy.

Represent the four elements on your altar: earth, air, fire, and water.

Represent the earth. Earth (or "Bush" as we call it in the Caribbean) representations include soil, rocks, crystals, salt, seeds, plants, gold, silver, iron, magnets, bones, fruits, vegetables, flowers, brown items, and earth imagery.

Represent air. Air representations include incense, feathers, bells, fans, wands, swords, birds, clear items, or air imagery.

Represent fire. Candles most easily represent fire. Prepare your candle by dressing it. If all you can do is cleanse and bless it, that's fine. Anoint the candle by rubbing a pure oil relevant to your purpose on it. Fixed candles are enclosed in glass. If your candle is not enclosed in glass, you can carve an intention onto the candle, draw a relevant symbol, and/or prepare it with crushed herbs in accordance with your purpose. Of course, heed all safety instructions. Some herbs and oils are highly flammable. Fire, red items, fire spirit imagery, and spicy foods can represent your fire element as well.

Represent water. Water representations include water, rainwater, sun water, moon water, seawater, fresh water, cowrie and other seashells, coral, mirrors, ankhs, fish, sea plants, blue items, wine and other liquids, water and water creature imagery.

Add your personal sacred items. These could include photos, art, affirmation or oracle cards, prayer beads, gifts from a maternal energy, stones, cultural totems, jewelry, sacred books, or spiritual text.

Arrange the items in a way that feels pleasing to your soul. Think in terms of a circle. Either before or during the altar ritual, put your glass of water out in the moonlight to charge. Also put out any sacred items you want to charge.

Dedicate the altar with an offering and libation. Start the dedication by giving thanks. Pray or meditate according to your practice. What would you like to offer the divine goddess? You will learn more in the cycles ahead. For now, trust your intuition.

Sprinkle your home with moon water.

Clean and maintain your altar as a sign of respect.

Alternative elements: Earth (bush), air, fire, and water are a foundational universal elemental system. You may wish to use an alternate system. The five elements for the Dagara people of Burkina Faso are earth, fire, water, nature, and mineral. In the Winti spiritual philosophy of Suriname, the four elements are earth, air, water, and bush. Bush, meaning plants and herbs, is what we use for medicine, as in "bush tea." The Bush is also where Maroons hid after escaping slavery in Suriname, Guyana, and throughout the Caribbean.

Part 2: Create a God/dess Womb Bowl

Ritual intention: To release your issues to the womb of Spirit.

You will need:

- A bowl
- 28 small pieces of paper
- Writing utensil

What to do:

Prepare your ritual space.

Creating a god/dess womb bowl is a method of active prayer. Find a sacred bowl to represent the pelvic bowl or womb space of the Divine. The pelvic bowl is a sanctuary of creation and pleasure. Fishbowls are wonderful for this, but you can use a regular bowl. Clean and bless it. Decorate the inside or outside if you wish. Add the bowl to your goddess altar.

You will put issues and challenges into the bowl that you wish to release to God/dess. Start with 28 small pieces of paper. They could be any size, color, or shape that makes sense to you. The paper could be relevant to the issue, such as bill envelopes or love letters.

No item is too big or too small to release to Spirit. Take each piece of paper and write the succinct issue you are letting God/dess handle. Surrender the issue, then give thanks that it is done and put it in the bowl.

To keep the energy active, each day at the same time, go to your goddess altar, pick an item from the goddess bowl, and read it out loud and give thanks with joy. If the item you choose has been fulfilled, burn, bury, or dispose of it.

Ultimately, you can add as many items as you want. There is no limit to how much we can release to Spirit.

Congrats! You have completed the Threshold.

Threshold Mantras

- *I am limitless.*
- *My power shines forth from within.*

Threshold Journal Questions

- Who am I today?
- Who do I want to be?

Threshold Embodiment

- Add something personal to your altar to celebrate awakening your goddess power.

Threshold Integration

- Add the Threshold goddesses and your experience with the Threshold rituals to your Goddess Soulbook.

2

THE TEMPLE OF ANCESTORS: YOUR SOIL ENERGY CHANNEL

Amadlozi

BLESSING OF THE ANCESTORS

Look for us amongst the oryx gazelles in the Kalahari Desert,

Hear our guiding whispers in the Tengzug Shrine,

Smell our fragrance in the dew drops near the Zambezi,

Taste our laughter in the guavas of the Land of Many Waters,

Sense our embrace beside the Sudanese pyramids.

We see you

Laughing.

We hear you

Crying.

We feel you

Breathing.

We love you

Being.

We walk with you,

And we are well pleased.

Blessings and blissings, goddess!

You are entering the Temple of Ancestors in the soil energy channel. The five great ancestresses, amadlozi, here just for you, represent roots, grounding, feeling safe, abundance, rebirth, and divine lineage. Mbuya Nehanda, Sawtche, Tituba, Marie Laveau, and Sara la Kali have been the keepers of this guidance from time immemorial. You now stand in an elevated circle of ancestors who are here to guide you in your shift from surviving to thriving.

Sit in the center and take in their wisdom. They each have gifts for you. Should you choose to accept their gifts, you will strengthen the foundation for your life-force energy. To finish this temple, complete their five rituals.

ABOUT THE TEMPLE OF ANCESTORS

The Temple of Ancestors is the soil energy channel. The soil energy channel governs our basic human survival needs such as food, clothing, shelter, and sleep. This energy channel is all about you feeling safe and grounded in your body and your life. This is what your ancestors want for you.

Ancestral veneration is a key part of all African traditions. Our dead have not left us. Life continues after physical death. Our ancestors, who can be blood related, culturally connected, or spiritually adopted, hold our greatest power and connection to the Divine.

Amadlozi is the Zulu word for elevated ancestral spirits and the term we will use in this practice. For the Igbo, the ndichie are esteemed ancestral spirits; for the Yoruba, the realm of the ancestors is the Egun; for the Ashanti, our ancestors are the Nsamanfo and their realm is Asamando; and for the ancient Egyptians and in Kemetic Orthodoxy, the blessed ancestors, akhu, reside in the Field of Reeds. Different languages and cultures, same energy. Those who have transitioned continue to take care of us from the realm of the ancestors, and we must take care of them.

Your amadlozi can be invoked for guidance, support, protection, or veneration. Like angels and saints, they can be mediators between us and the Creator. Their guidance comes in the forms of dreams, signs, divination, coincidences, mediums, and direct communication.

Each of us is made of hundreds of ancestors. Some of them you may know of; most you will not. My sister, Goddess Damali, and I both have had gifted seers tell us separately that they see us walking with a heavyset grandmother. None of our known grandmothers or great-grandmothers were heavyset. But we have hundreds of ancient ancestral grandmothers going back.

My goddess sister, as I write this, I feel so charged up with the greatness of those who came before us. You are not walking by yourself. I feel my maternal ancestors—primarily the women—the most, but lately the divine masculine have been making themselves known!

Write in your Goddess Soulbook: *I stand on the shoulders of giants.*

My dad came over to help me with some handiwork. I have a great handyman, but in addition to being a minister, journalist, precious metals expert, and professor, my dad worked with his dad as a carpenter. While we hung shelves, my father shared that when he did woodwork as a teen, he made $10 a week in Guyana. And he was able to make that much because of the special journeyman skills he had. Apprentices made only $2 a week. Then his father said something to him that changed everything.

As they were building a stool, my grandfather said, "This is not for you. Go to school and do bookwork." My grandfather had never made it past elementary school, but he had a different intention for my father.

I handed my dad some nails. I looked down at my hand and his hand. Our hands were identical. After his father's command, my dad ended up getting his education on three continents. He worked his butt off to attend school in the UK and then in New York City. That's where he met my mom, who was from the same Guyanese village, and then they had me. By then, my grandfather was no longer in the land of the living.

Granddad often told my father, "Don't talk about me when I am gone." Now here we were, talking about him, using his carpentry skills, and reaping the benefits of the "bookwork" intention he set for my dad. My recent ancestor, this grandfather, changed the trajectory of my life and I never even met him. I always knew I could be an author because my dad is. If not for this grandfather's advice to my dad, maybe you wouldn't be reading this.

With your life, you stand on the shoulders of your giants who came before you. If you feel like you don't have an ancestral connection, that's okay. You can claim your cultural ancestors. For example, you cannot tell me that Mama Josephine Baker, Mama Harriet Tubman, and Mama Zora Neale Hurston are not my blood. They are my energetic and cultural ancestors. This is why we erect statues. You are a conduit and channel for spiritual energies. You have access to all the energy that came before you and all the energy that will come after you.

With the Internet, you and I are able to connect through time and space, right? Well, your àse (life-force energy) is a force that is greater than Wi-Fi. As our Goddess Temple Circle sister Goddess Channita says, tune in to "the ancestor-net." The ancestors will rarely impose their guidance on you. You must connect.

Even if some of your ancestors were not the most upstanding people in life, they can guide and protect you now. The truth is that my paternal grandfather had a notoriously difficult personality. He was famous as the town bully. I'm not kidding. People we do not know have written about him! But it's okay, because we understand that people have issues, and he has transitioned and moved on up. I have been blessed to begin to get to know him now in a different energy. I love you, Granddaddy Alec, and I am proud of you.

I share this because so many sisters in our circle tell me that they have a difficult or nonexistent connection with their family members. Or maybe their ancestors were not the greatest people. People wonder how they can honor ancestors they don't know.

Get rooted with your ancestors. As the late Great Ancestress Toni Morrison wrote, "Ancestors are not just parents, they are sort of timeless people."[1] Tune in to the ancestor-net and bask in the vibration of those who walked before you.

Start with your blood ancestors if you have access. But you don't have to be blood to be kin, okay? If you were adopted, for example, your ancestors include your blood relations and the ancestors of the family who raised you.

The first way that we honor our ancestors is to speak about them. Then light a candle and set a place at the table for them on special days. Make offerings or sacrifices to them according to your personal tradition. That's why we "pour some out" for those who aren't here. Libations honor our ancestors. Exalt them on altars, in shrines, and in temples.

Declare yourself to be the daughter of your ancestors. Even our giants stand on the shoulders of their giants. Who are your ancestral giants?

WHAT IS YOUR SOIL ENERGY CHANNEL?

Soil is the foundation for everything. The soil energy channel is rooted under us just as it was rooted under our ancestors when they were here in physical form. The soil energy channel is our foundation for wholeness, healing, and goddess energy rising.

You cannot be initiated into your own power if you are ungrounded. Your ancestors and your soil energy center are your foundation. The color associated with this energy channel is red, and the body parts it houses include the pelvic floor, lower back, hips, booty, legs, and feet.

So what do you need to feel safe and stable? It begins with the fundamentals of your physical needs: water, food, clothing, shelter, and the resources to acquire them with. You also have fundamental emotional needs, too, beginning with feeling safe and protected. I cannot talk to you about enlightenment and transcendence if your basic human needs aren't met.

The sacred Temple of Ancestors and soil energy channel also connect us to our beautiful planet Earth. Our soil energy channel must be solid and rich for us to prosper. Let's take it back to the farms of my grandparents. What kind of soil do you want to plant your life in? If the soil is nutrient-rich, life prospers. If the soil is dry and deficient, life is a struggle.

This is the base for our life-force energy. Life-force energy is called "àse" (pronounced "ah-shay") by the Yoruba of West Africa, "prana" in Hindu culture, "qi" in Chinese medicine, "nyamam" in Dogon thought, and "sunsum" in the Akan philosophy of Ghana. Your àse affects every part of your life and body. The soil energy channel is the base for our àse, vital life-force energy.

Right now, we are all witnessing global birth pains. Some call it a worldwide dark night of the soul. But what comes with birth pains? Birth and rebirth, ascension and rising higher. What comes after night? Morning. The reset is real. We are here to be put back together, not for a new normal, or any kind of normal, but to be more in sacred alignment. We are here to be reset.

Write in your Goddess Soulbook: *I am in sacred alignment.*

So many of us have figured out how to live life while feeling unsafe; as women, as Black people, as gay people, as trans people, as people with disabilities, as Indigenous people, as Latin people and people of color, as poor people, as immigrants, people with mental health issues, and disenfranchised peoples across the board.

I am choosing to believe that things are getting better because we are saying no more. Feeling like a second-class citizen in your own life is no longer acceptable. No more saying that you're not worthy, no more feeling like you're not enough, no more watering yourself down to make other people feel safe. No more not living up to your own dreams and full magic. No more.

This is a circle of healers, creators, artists, sorceresses, and lightworkers. We are choosing right now to say, "I deserve better, and so do my sisters and brothers." And we're seeing it reflect and begin to ripple. Evolution happens like a groundswell.

Write in your Goddess Soulbook: *I'm choosing to believe that things are getting better. I'm choosing to believe that I am making a difference.*

So what are we saying yes to? We are saying yes to the fact that we are worthy. Stepping into your fullness means something different for each of us. But to heal the world, we must first heal ourselves.

Write in your Goddess Soulbook: *I now dare to step into my fullness.*

"I am." As we know, those are the most transformational, spellcasting words we can speak. So what are you speaking over your life right now? If you're speaking fear, desperation, or scarcity, then that is what you are calling forward. Speak love over your life. Speak abundance into your life. Speak healing so that if you are on the front lines of a protest or a city council meeting, you are going in fully armored in your goddess power, truth, and strength.

And if you are not on the front lines on the street, but maybe you are on the front lines as a prayer warrior on your meditation pillow, you are beaming strength and healing to everyone who is out there. Or you are healing your household and armored with love, the greatest force there is.

Declare it: *I am full. I am worthy.*

HOW TO KNOW IF YOUR SOIL ENERGY CHANNEL IS BLOCKED

Do you feel secure in your body and your life? Can you trust that your needs are taken care of? Do you have what you need to survive? Were your primal survival needs met as a child? Was there order or chaos?

While I am writing this, we are going through a global challenge. Many of us feel uprooted, uncertain, and ungrounded. During the pandemic, we have felt unsafe in our bodies and health, feared for the well-being of our loved ones, been concerned for our elders and our children, and experienced financial upheaval. The idea that anything was certain was pulled from under us as in the midst of it, non-Black people started waking up to the generations of racial brutality and injustice we have been subjected to at the same time. Someone asked on social media what was happening cosmically, and I replied, "Awakening. Cleansing. Rebirth. Critical mass rage and grief for lifetimes of horrific injustices plus ancestral rage, grief, unprocessed trauma. Old systems, structures, and status quo are grasping by reinforcing false power with physical, emotional, psychological violence and terror."

People ask me often about ancestral and generational curses. The most powerful ancestral or generational curse we face is our unhealed trauma. I was putting together some journal questions for you, and an inner voice said loudly, "You are not betraying your ancestors by healing your trauma." It knocked the wind out of me. I didn't even know it was a belief or fear I had. But we are attached in so many ways to our identities. It makes sense that we would fear that if we heal our trauma bonds, we are betraying our collective. No, our ancestors want us to heal the bloodline. That is evolution. That is why you were born.

These fears are all blockages in the soil energy channel. So how can we ever be completely safe? Safety is an internal job. And it starts with being planted, grounded, rooted on solid soil.

Luckily, no matter what is happening, our ancestors always have our back. The five ancestors here showed up to help you create a foundation for your personal power. Great Ancestresses Sawtche, Tituba, Mbuya Nehanda, Sara la Kali, and Marie Laveau, our sacred rebels, are here to support you.

You may join each ancestor in her goddess sanctuary now.

SAWTCHE

Goddess of Grounding
Khoekhoen/South Africa
Mother's Milk Miracle Ritual

"I am firmly planted and deeply rooted."

SAWTCHE'S MESSAGE

Halau, daughter. You did the best you could under the circumstances. Your heart is your own. Your body is your own. Your mind is yours. Your truth, your story, your own. Be grounded in that knowledge. Be rooted in your truth.

SAWTCHE'S STORY

Great Ancestress Sawtche, we say your name.
We honor you.

You may know Great Ancestress Sawtche by the name Sarah Baartman. Under that name, she was forced to perform as the "Hottentot Venus," a circus-style act in

London. But before she was Sarah Baartman, she was Saartjie in South Africa. Before that she was Sawtche, a Khoekhoen (Khoikhoi) girl.

Sawtche's people were once the largest group of people on the planet. They have a heritage as nomadic hunter-gatherers and considered themselves to be people of the moon. Women gathered berries and tubers. Men hunted and herded mostly cattle and sheep.

Sawtche was born in the 1770s along the Gamtoos River in what is known as the Eastern Cape in the Cape of Good Hope. When she was born, her mother most likely buried her placenta on the family plot for protection and grounding. Her mother died soon after, leaving Sawtche in a time of war and uncertainty. Sawtche was promised a new life when she moved with her father to Cape Town.[2]

Sawtche's rite of passage into puberty was celebrated with a tortoiseshell necklace. She would keep it all her life. In 1779 her family moved as laborers to one colonialist farm and then to another. About 17 years later, she was sold as chattel and enslaved by a Dutch farmer. She worked as a washerwoman, wet nurse, and nursemaid. And then two strangers promised her a new life. She was contracted to leave for England and told she would be able to return home in five years.

At 225 Piccadilly in London, they advertised the African Venus, naming her after the Roman goddess of love. Evidence shows that love was most likely scarce. At the "freak" show, her ample backside was the main attraction, along with her elongated labia from her puberty initiation. Sawtche was put on display in a cage with a crimson curtain and threatened with a cane to perform. People were allowed to touch and prod her, much like at a petting zoo.

Sawtche's body was regarded as obscene, but clearly the obscene people were in the audience. They were simultaneously obsessed with and repulsed by her kind of beauty. Her body was different from European women, the standard for true womanhood. They regarded her body as unmistakably sexual, which meant animalistic for a woman. With her brown skin, tightly coiled hair, and ample backside, she was the exotic other.

Next, the showmasters sold Sawtche to an animal trainer in Paris, where the science of the day classified her as a different species. She was again promised a new life. Women and men attended shows where she was featured, paying extra to touch her "strange" butt, genitals, and hair. Viewers had paid two shillings in London, but they paid three francs in France.

Sawtche, still a young woman, died in France of disease and broken promises. But even in death, the dishonor continued. Her body was dissected, and her brain and genitals were pickled. A plaster cast of her body was displayed with her skeleton and body parts until 1974.[3]

When Nelson Mandela became president, he fought for Sawtche's remains to be returned home so that she could be honored with a proper burial. At less than four feet, seven inches tall, this woman was a giant. On August 9, 2002, South African Women's Day, she finally received a proper homegoing and burial. Sawtche's people, the Khoekhoen are now considered Khoisan. Her full, true name has been lost to history with only sporadic accounts referring to her as Sawtche. We take this name to honor her, to represent what has been lost over the names given to her by her oppressors.[4]

Sawtche is reborn, as a queen, as a goddess.

We see her. We feel her. We are her. We are daughters of unspeakable crimes. We are daughters of unbridled joy. We were promised a better life and we claim it.

Great Ancestress Sawtche, we will never forget.

Let's Talk Grounding

All of your power is in the present moment. Grounding is the process that helps keep us in the present. Trauma, stress, feeling run-down, anxiety, and fear all take us out of our bodies. Being grounded is important for the soulwork you are doing here.

If you feel disconnected or are worrying about the past or future, you are ungrounded. Sometimes when we are knee-deep in soulwork like this, we forget that we are in the land of the living. We have a body and earthly duties that need to be attended to. That, too, is a sign of being ungrounded.

If you are a person who gets overwhelmed or has anxiety, learning how to ground yourself is important. Grounding yourself is also key if you are an empath or empathic person. Chances are if you're reading this, you fall into one of those categories. As empaths, we are more porous to the environment around us. So being grounded is not only a spiritual practice, but it is a key for our mental health and vibrancy.

Grounding techniques were an important part of me beginning this book. I have attention deficit challenges, anxiety, and I am an empath. So it's easy for me to become overcome by my environment if I am not grounded. The first thing I do when I am channeling a big project like this is freewrite journaling every morning when I wake up to clear my mind. This helps me come back to the land of the living from my dreamtime and gets me present for the day. You can read about this daily morning pages ritual in *The Artist's Way* by Julia Cameron.

When you feel unsettled, first come back to your breath. Meditation and breathwork are grounding. The easiest way to begin is with box breaths. Breathe in four counts. Hold for four counts. Exhale for four counts. Repeat four times. If you can do this in fresh air, go for it.

Then try earthing. Earthing is connecting your feet to the soil of Mama Earth. I live in Manhattan, so reconnecting to the earth physically is not always possible. If you don't have access to soil, see a golden light shooting up from the center of the earth and through your body. Clapping, stomping, and rubbing your hands together are also grounding techniques.

Using ancestral rocks like South African bloodstone or your favorite crystals as worry stones can also be helpful for grounding. Using rocks you find in your present location is great because they are charged to the energy of your current coordinates. Stones hold on to energy. Close your eyes, hold the stone in your right hand, and direct your stress and worries into it. Tell it your problems. Then either dispose of the stone in nature or cleanse it in sunlight, the full moon, ocean water, or salt water. South African bloodstone is self-cleansing, so it doesn't need to be disposed of.

Scents also promote calm, concentration, and feeling grounded. Sandalwood, frankincense, citrus, cinnamon, jasmine, African rosemary, and wild water mint are all ancestral scents that get the green light for aromatherapy grounding. Eating mindfully brings us back to the present. No TV or phone, just eating in gratitude and feeling the love, nourishment, and preparation in every bite.

Plus, you can always just bring yourself back to gratitude. If you don't know what you're grateful for, start with the fact that you are breathing. Know that in this very moment, all is well.

HOW TO HONOR GREAT ANCESTRESS SAWTCHE

When you honor Great Ancestress Sawtche, you honor the part of you that is grounded. You may choose to honor this energy inside yourself or invoke her energy according to your own tradition.

To honor the goddess in you: Ground yourself daily. Give yourself a stable foundation as a gift. Celebrate the power of choice in your life. While you have breath and the ability to make new choices, you can be who you were born to be. If you have experienced life-altering trauma, honor yourself by working with a trauma specialist.

Khoisan healers were the founders of what has been rebranded as "shaking medicine," the power to heal the body and align with ecstatic states through tremors and shaking. Get your shake on to a drumbeat for a rooted state.

Symbols: Sawtche wore her native tortoiseshell necklace for most of her life. There are beautiful faux alternatives that could be a special way to honor her.

Colors: Her colors are green and gold.

Auspicious time: Celebrate her on August 9. On that date in 2002, Sawtche was finally buried in South Africa.

Music: "For Sarah Baartman" by Nitty Scott and "Welcome Home—Sarah Baartman" by Robbie Jansen and Alou April

Suggested offerings: You might drink or pour libations with honey wine. Khoisan people perfected honey mead, one of the world's oldest alcoholic beverages.

Alternate names: Sarah Baartman, Saartjie Baartman

Traditional Grounding Ritual: Milk Tree Initiation

In Zambia, the N'kanga girls' puberty initiation takes place when a girl starts to develop breasts. Each girl enters womanhood one at a time. As a part of the ritual celebration, the novice girl is grounded and wrapped in a warm blanket at the foot of the mudyi sapling tree. The mudyi, which exudes a white latex similar to milk, represents the Great Ancestress.[5]

In this traditionally matrilineal culture, the mudyi tree is called "the tree of mother and child." As the girl lies at the base of the tree with the "milk" coming out, it is as if she is being breastfed by the tree. She is feeding from the knowledge, safety, and protection of generations of great ancestresses. Men are circumcised under the same tree.

The women of the community dance around the girl and tree and sing. This is a mother-centered culture, but the mother of the girl being initiated is not allowed to sing or dance. She exchanges clothes with her daughter. She is symbolically mourning the loss of her child. The milk represents nurturing, but this is also a gateway to sexual awakening. The girls are grounded in the present moment, reminded of mother love and ready for the next life phase.[6]

Your Grounding Ritual: Mother's Milk Miracle Floor Wash

Ritual intention: To feel grounded in your space, clear the energy, bless your home, and infuse it with magic.

Baptizing your floors, as I like to call it, is an important magical ritual. Spiritual floor washes are a key part of most of our cultures worldwide, including the African American Hoodoo tradition, throughout Yoruba-based practices, and in the Spiritual Baptist Afro-Caribbean tradition. Whenever I ask older relatives what my maternal great-grandmother Ma was like, they say, "She was serious, always sweeping, wiping down the yard, and sprinkling water." Cleaning, cleansing, and clearing is a magical art in itself.

You will need:

Use your guidance to choose the right amount of each ingredient. Fresh plants are preferred for this ritual, but work with what you have available.

- Milk of your choice
- Holy water of your choice (suggestions: rainwater, moon water, sun water, Florida Water, or Kananga Water)
- Abundance herbs and spices: cinnamon, basil, rosemary
- Miracle plants: hyssop (can substitute mint), pine (pine needles, pine oil, or pine cleaner; if using Pine-Sol, add after boiling the rest of the ingredients)
- Clearing fruit: lemons or limes
- Pinch of salt of your choice

What to do:

Part 1: Create the Floor Wash

Prepare your ritual space.

Mix everything together in a big pot. As you chop the ingredients and add them, do it with love. Speak words of safety, protection, and health for your home and family. Speak on the miracles you are welcoming in:

- As you add the holy water, say, "Thank you for keeping me safe. Thank you for keeping my beloved safe. Thank you for keeping my loved ones safe."

- As you add the sacred milk, say, "Thank you to the mothers who have loved me and who continue to love me. May continued blessings rain on all those whom I have mothered and mother now."

- As you add the miracle plants, say, "Thank you for the miracles that have happened, are happening, and are to come."

- As you add the abundance herbs and spices, say, "Thank you for the riches. Thank you for the prosperity. Thank you for the abundance."

- As you add the clearing fruit, say, "Thank you for clearing all blocks now."

- As you add the salt, say, "It feels good to be safe. It feels good to feel good."

Boil the floor wash for 20 minutes, then simmer for 20 minutes. Turn off the stove. Steep for at least 3 hours. Strain out solid ingredients. They should be properly disposed of later at an available crossroads of your understanding.

Close your eyes over the pot. Imagine white protective light shooting from the center of the Earth, through the pot, and through your body. See roots coming from the center of the Earth through the wash and through your body. Give thanks for being safe and grounded. Give thanks for all the miracles.

Depending on your spatial needs, pour the wash into your cleaning bucket and add a gallon of water. You may choose to wash the floor for 1 day or 3 days in a row, at the same time each day.

Use the entire mixture within 28 days.

Part 2: Baptize Your Floor

Do a house cleaning first. You may clean the room with your altar and your entryway or your entire space. Prepare your ritual space and pray according to your tradition. Wash the floors from the top floor down to the bottom. Wash down windows, walls, doors, and doorways. Porches and decks are considered rooms. Continue to speak your gratitude and intentions.

Wash outward to flow negativity out. Clean your home from the back to the front entry, wiping away from you. Do the reverse to invite miracles and prosperity in. Clean from the front to the back, and wipe, pulling the miracle energy toward you.

Open the windows if the season allows it. Allow the floor wash to air-dry. You may put unused wash in jars behind the doors for seven days. Dispose of the used wash and strained ingredients safely at the crossroads of your choice (for example, your garbage, a field, etc.), say, "Thank you. Good-bye," and don't look back. Be careful if handling chemicals.

(Alternative: If you have carpets, you can either pour the mix in the corners and center of the room or dip the broom tips in the floor wash and sweep the rug.)

TITUBA

Goddess of Feeling Safe
Barbados/Guyana/Salem
Ancestral Protection Ritual

"I am safe. It is safe to be safe."

TITUBA'S MESSAGE

Good morrow, daughter, how do you fare? You have wandered through a dark night. Your trip has been long. Know this. There is light ahead. Your liberation is apparent. It is finally safe to be you.

TITUBA'S STORY

Great Ancestress Tituba, we say your name.
We honor you.
She said, "I am blind now. I cannot see."
Great Ancestress Tituba was an enslaved Caribbean woman who was the first person accused of witchcraft at the 1692 trials in Salem, Massachusetts. She was most likely kidnapped from the Guyana region in South America and then sold

through a Barbados plantation into Salem, Massachusetts. Poet Henry Wadsworth Longfellow describes Tituba's father as an "obi man." Obeah is a demonized African spiritual practice in Guyana and throughout the Caribbean. My mother's grandfather David originally came from Barbados to Guyana, so I have long related to Tituba as a cultural ancestor.

The common theory of the Salem "hysteria" is that Tituba's Vodou or obeah storytelling frightened the young women in her charge and sent them into a frenzy. The truth as we know it is that Betty Parris, 9, and her cousin Abigail Williams, 11, were experimenting with a divining technique called the Venus glass. This was common crystal ball–style fortune-telling of the time. To create a Venus glass, you suspend an egg white in water. The resulting shapes reveal your message. The girls' intention was to predict their future husbands and social status. Instead of seeing husbands in the glass, the girls saw a coffin.

These girls and others in the area then began exhibiting strange behavior. They were forgetting things, convulsing, experiencing fits, feeling like they were being pinched and at times unable to speak. The local doctor diagnosed Betty as being afflicted by the "evil hand." They prayed over the girls, and they had violent reactions. The community fasted to bolster their spiritual strength. Witchcraft was the only conclusion. Most people practiced some degree of "folk magic," like the Venus glass, but witchcraft was viewed as evil.[7]

A family member of the girls then approached their caretaker Tituba and her husband, John Indian, also enslaved, and asked them to make a witch cake. A witch cake mixed rye meal with the urine of an accused person. When this cake was fed to a dog, the dog's bark would supposedly sound like the name of the guilty witch.

Reverend Parris, Betty's dad, was furious when he learned his family member did this. He pressed Betty on who her bewitcher was, yelling, "Who torments you?" Betty pointed the damning finger at Tituba. Tituba was arrested to be hanged for being a witch. Abigail also implicated local women Sarah Good and Sarah Osborne, easy targets because one was mentally ill and one was semi-homeless. It was indicated in legal papers that one of them rarely attended church.

Formally accused of witchcraft, Tituba was called to testify in court on March 1, 1692. The courtroom scene was dramatic. Betty and Abigail started throwing fits at the sight of the three women they accused. Both Sarahs denied the charges. Tituba, however, had been violently beaten and threatened by Betty Parris's dad, the good reverend.

Tituba testified for two days. She pleaded guilty and said that she had participated in witchcraft as the "devil's servant" against the children with the two Sarahs. Tituba's story was embellished with Native American, English, and African occult magic. She shouted, "The devil came to me and bid me serve him."[8] In her elaborate confession, she claimed to have seen apparitions of talking animals, and other people involved in the crimes that she did not know. She confessed to signing the devil's book and gave the first account of witches supposedly flying on sticks.

History is torn on whether Tituba was of Amerindian Arawak or African descent. We honor her without parsing her genealogy. Perhaps she was both Afro-Taino and Arawak. Sugarcane slavery using the labor of trafficked Africans started around the 1640s in Barbados and the surrounding region. At the time, record keepers were not concerned with properly identifying the cultural background of enslaved peoples. They described many Native people as Africans and vice versa.

At the end of her testimony, Tituba claimed, "I am blind now. I cannot see." She said that the devil blinded her. This way, she could not be forced to identify and accuse anyone else. Tituba never named anyone that the girls had not already named.

After charges against Tituba were dropped, she remained in prison as she had no money to pay for her shackles, chains, and other prison charges. Magically, an unknown stranger is believed to have come forward to pay Tituba's fees, and she was released.

Sarah Osborne died in jail in May 1692. Sarah Good was hanged in July the same year. This was just the beginning of the Salem Witch Trial fervor and mass panic. Eventually there were at least 150 people accused. Thirty were found guilty, nineteen people were hanged, and one man was pressed to death for refusing to confirm or deny his affiliation with witchcraft.

Tituba, cultural shape-shifter, accused, survivor, vanished.

Let's Talk Feeling Safe

Do you feel safe in your body and in your life? Right now I am at home in my beautiful environment, so I feel completely safe. But as a Black woman living in a major city, some days I begin to feel unsafe the moment I step outside—or the moment I go online. It was important for me to learn how to feel safe in my body because, increasingly, people who should make me feel safer terrify me.

"I am safe. It is safe to be safe" is one of my favorite affirmations because many of us didn't even know that feeling safe was a possibility. If the environment you grew up in was emotionally, spiritually, or physically unsafe, you may relate.

Feeling high internal stress was normal to me. If you were raised in any kind of chaotic situation, this may be true for you too. Because stress was my normal, the absence of these stressful feelings made me uncomfortable. I would think that certain guys I dated were too nice, for example. I had to reset my default settings to a healthier vibration. In addition to the rituals you are learning on this journey, EFT (Emotional Freedom Technique) tapping—which involves tapping points on the body to restore balance in your energy system and relieve physical and emotional pain—is a modern-day ritual that I use and teach as a feeling safe technology. (Find free EFT tapping videos on my YouTube channel and Woman-ifesting.com/eft).

Food has been an unhealthy way that I unconsciously made myself feel safe. As I type this, I gained 20 pounds during the pandemic and racial disturbances and injustices. I quarantined with my parents for six months, after thinking I'd be there for a couple of weeks and the whole virus thing would "blow over." I lost neighbors and friends. Extended family members died. Many people I know lost parents. Some folks have gotten sick and have not fully recovered. I love and accept myself—and I am also aware that, for me, extra weight has meant a cloak of safety in the past. As I am shifting back from the energy of fear to love, my body is naturally moving back into a state of health.

In emergency situations the goal becomes surviving, not thriving. And that is okay. It is okay temporarily not to be okay. Being able to sit with uncomfortable feelings and emotions when they come up is healing. This is holding space and creating a safe container for yourself.

One of my unguilty pleasures is watching the *Real Housewives* reality TV series. On a recent show, one of the cast members pummeled another, beating her on the back of her head. It felt disgusting even to be a part of it, watching these women fight as a spectator sport. Watching Black people's bodies abused and murdered on the news is already white noise to many people. It is definitely not my choice as entertainment.

The woman who pounded the other woman in the head said something like, "If you keep talking like that, you want to get hit." That is classic abuser-speak. She felt like the other woman's words instigated her violence. In that moment, she took no responsibility for herself as an adult. Know this: No one can make you do anything with their words. You choose your own actions.

The cast member that was physically beaten expressed feeling post-traumatic stress disorder. The lack of compassion for her, in addition to the number of women on social media who sided with the abuser, was even more upsetting. We don't even have tenderness and compassion for our own humanity. People felt that because the woman who was beaten was a rude loudmouth, she deserved it. They felt that she was crying victim because she said that she felt unsafe. I found myself asking, Who have we become that displays of humanness and vulnerability seem to people like self-victimization?

Then I remembered that most of us live with post-traumatic stress daily. We have little compassion for someone in the aftermath of abuse because many of us are living in the aftermath of generations of abuse. You can't ask people to have love and compassion for others when we lack love and compassion for ourselves. If you asked any of the women in the audience if they loved themselves, they would say, of course. But if you believe that if you say the wrong thing, you deserve to be physically struck by another adult, you cannot love yourself. You are your sister's keeper, even if you don't like her.

Maybe we don't know what feeling safe is. Feeling unsafe and traumatized is normal to too many of us. Feeling safe is trusting your path. Feeling safe is feeling free around the people you love. Feeling safe is feeling at home in your body.

Set an intention to feel safe and reconnect to your body now. Feeling safe is believing that the sun will rise again.

HOW TO HONOR GREAT ANCESTRESS TITUBA

When you honor Great Ancestress Tituba, you honor the part of you that deserves to feel safe. You may choose to honor this energy inside yourself or invoke her energy according to your own tradition.

To honor the goddess in you: In Tituba's time in Barbados and Guyana, Atabey (Arawak/Taino) and Asase Yaa (Akan) were the Mother Earth protector goddesses of women like Tituba, you, and me. The Indigenous people were Arawak, Taino, Kalinago/Carib, and Warao. Almost all of the Africans brought to Barbados at the time were from Ghana and the Gold Coast, and the majority of the Africans brought to the Carolinas in the United States were transported from Barbados.

Close your eyes. We see Tituba filled with the maternal love of the great foremothers of her land, Atabey and Asase Yaa. We feel Tituba filled with the loving, fertile energy of Atabey, Moon Mother of safe childbirth. She is cleansed by her cool water. We feel Tituba safely wrapped in the joyful, protective energy of the upholder of truth, Asase Yaa. She is loved by her tight embrace. By lifting her up, we uplift ourselves.

Color: Her color is violet, in honor of her daughter.

Auspicious time: March 1 is a beautiful day to show Tituba love as she was first interrogated on that date in 1692.

Music: "Bruja" by La Perla and "Diamonds" by Rihanna

Suggested offerings: Mammee apples, mangoes, and sugarcane

Traditional Feeling Safe Ritual: Pouring Libations

Libation in all African traditions is a liquid offering or sacrifice poured out for an ancestor or deity. It is such an act of love to pay tribute to those who came before. You generally pour liquor, water, perfume, or wine, and you can also pour milk, holy water, Florida Water, Kananga Water, moon water, or whatever you have access to. Intention matters most. You are honoring and awakening the ancestors. You can pour the libation directly onto the ground, into a plant, or into a bowl or vessel. In some practices, libations are sprayed from the mouth. Libations can be an opening for another ritual or celebration. You have awakened the ancestors. Now what?

As you pour libations, you should express gratitude to the ancestors for safekeeping, wisdom sharing, and anything else that matters to you and them. They are so happy to hear from us. Speak with love, humility, and reverence. If you have any requests, present them only after your gratitude and acknowledgment. You can request illumination on a specific issue. You can also request support, blessings, protection, or something else.

In a group, give an elder the honor of pouring libations. Close with a confirmatory declaration such as "àse" or "àse-o," which means "life-force energy" in the Yoruba tradition, or some other acknowledgment that works for you. Other confirmatory responses include "so be it," "amen," "a-women," "aho," and "so it is."

I don't recall if I ever connected the big brothers on my Queens block pouring "some out for the brothers that's not here" with the libations my father poured for the ancestors. Same gesture, similar words, same intention. When the big brothers did it, it was usually with a snicker, unless we had recently lost someone in the neighborhood. We did the same in college. And I love that while we were cracking 40s, Mad Dog 20/20, and wine coolers (yes!), we were on a sacred continuum, connected to an ancient gift that survived from our ancestors.

Your Feeling Safe Ritual: Ancestral Protection Ceremony

Ritual intention: To request the guidance and protection of your blessed ancestors.

Oftentimes we feel unsafe and unprotected because we believe we are alone. Our ancestors, who can be blood related, culturally connected, or spiritually adopted, hold our greatest power and connection to the Divine. In this ritual, you will pour libations to awaken and honor them and request guidance and protection. Feeling safe in the protective and blessed arms of those who came before is powerful. Pour libations in love, reverence, and gratitude.

You will need:

- Your libation vessel
- Your libation liquid (water, liquor, a holy water, or perfume)
- Sacred items or altar (if at an altar)
- Incense (not necessary, but it may help to invoke ancestors)

What to do:

Prepare your ritual space and your libation. You can do this ceremony at an ancestral altar, shrine, or in an outdoor space. Light candles or play music the ancestors would enjoy. You can even prepare a meal for them.

Light incense if you wish. An ancestral incense like imphepho, myrrh, or frankincense may feel in alignment. Imphepho can help induce trance states and call in ancestors. Muhuhu, high-vibrating African sandalwood oil, may be hard to find, but sprinkling some in the corners is quite potent. Muhuhu is also good for spiritual connection.

Call in the ancestors. Is there a specific family member or group of ancestral family members who have transitioned that you wish to connect with? Is there a cultural ancestor or goddess that you want to pay tribute to?

Pour your libation and say their names to awaken and "feed" them. If you don't know their names, you can use their titles, like "my sacred grandmothers."

Express gratitude. Are you grateful for their loving energy? Their sacrifices? Let them know. Request their guidance. You can be specific or general.

Request their protection. Is there a specific place in your life where you feel unsafe? Allow your ancestors to have your back.

Thank them for their guidance and protection as it has already been granted. Give thanks for them interceding with the Creator on your behalf.

Use this time to communicate with your ancestors. Messages, guidance, sudden phone calls, or e-mail with opportunities may pop up. Write down any guidance you receive and take inspired action.

Answer in your Goddess Soulbook:

- *Who did you pour libations for?*
- *What are their traits that you admire?*
- *What traits do they have that you see in yourself?*
- *What guidance did you request?*
- *When do you need their protection most?*

MBUYA NEHANDA

Goddess of Rebirth
Shona/Zimbabwe
Ancestral Altar Ritual

"Still I rise."

NEHANDA'S MESSAGE

Mhoro, my child. You can choose at any moment to be reborn. You don't have to struggle so much. Your power goes back generations before generations. Yes, like the sun, you rise.

NEHANDA'S STORY

Great Ancestress Mbuya Nehanda, we say your name.
We honor you.
"My bones shall surely rise again!"

Grandmother Nehanda gives life to Great Ancestress Maya Angelou's prophecy, "Still I Rise." At her birth around 1840, Prophetess Charwe Nyakasikana was known to be a connector between the spirit and material worlds. She went on to be one of the most radical political figures of her time in Mashonaland, present-day northern Zimbabwe, the breadbasket of Africa.

Charwe channeled an ancient spirit named Nehanda, who has been incarnated by several revolutionary Shona women during history. The Nehanda spirit that guided Charwe had possessed women for at least 500 years. Her spirit is channeled by women, especially revolutionaries or leaders. The first Nehanda was Princess Nyamhita, circa 1430.

The Nehanda spirit is a mhondoro, meaning a royal lion spirit. Spirit mediums of the Zezuru Shona people who channel mhondoro spirits are known as svikiro. There have been many people throughout history, even today, who claim to be possessed by the spirit of Nehanda, but impostors are unable to pass the secret tests.[9]

Called Mbuya Nehanda (Grandmother Nehanda) as a sign of respect, she performed sacred ceremonies and supported her community. The Shona had built a strong economy. Then British colonizers invaded in 1880, confiscating land, taxing people, and forcing them into hard labor.

King Lobengula signed an agreement that he did not realize gave the British unlimited access to exploiting the natural resources of his land. In their belief system, you could not own land. Even the king was only considered a custodian and guardian of the land. They saw all land as the property of Mwari, the Most High God.

Nehanda and others initially welcomed their soon-to-be occupiers.[10] The region had dealt with the Christian missionaries for a while. The missionaries fused Mwari to the God in the Bible to more easily convert the people. They also had a successful trading relationship with the Portuguese in Mozambique and assumed that these Europeans would be like those.

The contract terms turned out to be brutal. When the king realized what he had signed, he sent emissaries to speak to Queen Victoria about getting out of it. She made his men wait for days and then refused to see them. The foreign language agreement that Lobengula signed was irrefutable. The British created a new government on their land with no recognition of pre-existing ruling structures.

The Indigenous Africans became tenants who could be evicted at any time from their own ancestral land. They were forced to relocate from the most fertile areas where they grew their crops. Hunting, which was their way of life, became illegal poaching. Their natural resources, like minerals and metals, such as gold, all now belonged to the British. They suddenly owed taxes to the new settlers, which they had to pay with their own livestock or labor. Local wealth was redistributed to the foreigners in some cases at 3,000 acres apiece, leaving the Indigenous people destitute.

Mbuya Nehanda was guided to rise up and protect her people. The fact that she was a woman over age 55 who had never been to war was of no consequence. She waited for the opportune moment. Two other well-known spirit mediums joined her. God had decreed that these colonizers had to be driven out. This has become known as the First Chimurenga, uprising and rebellion.

In 1889 Mbuya Nehanda and her spiritual husband, medium Sekuru Kaguvi, led a revolt against British colonization of Zimbabwe. The freedom fighters wore their customary black beads and dark ash camouflage. The army loved Nehanda and was grateful for her leadership and support. But they were outmatched by the Europeans with firepower and resources. Nehanda decided that turning herself in would mean less loss of life for her people.

Nehanda was tried in the case of "The (British) Queen against Nehanda."[11] She was convicted along with Sekuru Kaguvi and sentenced to death by hanging. A Catholic priest attempted to convert her to Christianity on the day of her execution. She refused.

Mbuya Nehanda declared, "My bones shall surely rise again!"

They say that the executioner hung her twice and she just refused to die. Then a villager suggested they remove her tobacco pouch, aka mojo bag. She died by hanging, but that was only one lifetime. Mbuya Nehanda will rise again.

Nehanda's head was taken to Queen Victoria as a war trophy. The men who created the agreement exploiting Zimbabwe were knighted. Nehanda's head, along with others from the war, was placed on display.

As I write this, Mbuya Nehanda and Sekuru Kaguvi's remains are at Westminster Abbey and the British National Museum. In 2020, a delegation was dispatched from Zimbabwe to repatriate Nehanda and the remains of at least 13 others. Zimbabwe is demanding the return of 13 skulls and a sacred talking stick.[12] Mbuya Nehanda's people would like to give her a proper burial. Hopefully by the time you read this, it has happened.

Let's Talk Rebirth

Rebirth is the ancient Egyptian principle of Bennu, the soul of the sun god. Bennu was a bird who, as the sun's soul, was a fertile force. Bennu gave birth to itself daily and had the capacity to rise daily and be endlessly reborn. Just like you.

Ilu uwa, translated as return to our world, is the Igbo principle of reincarnation in the Odinala (also called Odinali) religion. The Igbo believe that you reincarnate four to eight times, usually into the same family you came from. You are reborn after this life.

That is divine, but let's talk about how to have a conscious rebirth or restart while you are still here. We will need to start over and make comebacks many times in our lives. Life is about transition and change. It's not linear. You will fall on your face, change your mind, and need to make a "comeback" again and again.

So how do you do that? Start by releasing the idea that you messed up if things weren't perfect. Release the illusion of perfectionism. In American public school education, a bell rings and it tells us it is time to go. You respond to the bell and you are rewarded. You raise your hand if you've got the right answer. You are rewarded for following the rules. The closer you are to perfect, the better for everyone else. The system doesn't care what you've got to do to be close to perfect. Or whether this makes you happy.

Perfectionism is tyranny against the self. Blindly following the rules is self-destructive. Sure, some rules will work for you. Take what works and release the rest. Trying to be perfect will keep you stuck because it's not possible. Look at a field of flowers; they are wild, weedy, and messy. Fruits grow in odd colors, shapes, and sizes. They're weird, fun, and messy. The messiness is the beauty. Embrace it. If you need a reset and you are trying to be perfect, you're just creating another box to free yourself from.

Your happiness is your responsibility. We can't always choose what happens to us, but we can choose how we react. Don't make another person, institution, or system responsible for your happiness. Reach for daily bursts of pleasure, joy, and fun. (As someone who has chronic anxiety, I'm talking about when your brain is healthy and balanced. If you have clinical depression or another mental health challenge, please consult with a medical team to find what works for you.)

Someone left a trolling comment on one of my YouTube sound healing meditations: "She was a dating coach and now she's a spiritual teacher?" Yes, I was a spiritual teacher when I was afraid to come out of the spiritual closet as a dating coach—and when I worked in a shoe store as a teen. My gynecologist was once a waiter. Poet laureate and Great Ancestress Maya Angelou was a calypso singer and dancer. Evolving means that we are reborn in many different incarnations. Some people will be uncomfortable with your evolution because they are uncomfortable with their own.

You can't live for other people, even people you love. If you are going to make a comeback, restart or rebirth, you don't want to sing, "I did it their way." You want to do it your way. Stop polling everyone to know what they think about how you should live your life. Stop waiting to be ready.

Decide your way out of stuckness. There may be decisions that you need to make to get you unstuck. Decision helps you move from limbo-land. Declare what you want and then figure it out.

Who do you want to be in this world? How do you want to show up? Declare it, now. That is how you make a conscious rebirth.

HOW TO HONOR GREAT ANCESTRESS NEHANDA

When you honor Great Ancestress Nehanda, you honor the part of you that is reborn again and again and again. You may choose to honor this energy inside yourself or invoke her energy according to your own tradition.

To honor the goddess in you: We know that Mbuya Nehanda will rise again. She was/is a lion spirit. See yourself in this energy. Decide to be consciously reborn. Making new choices helps you continue to rise.

Originally, the Shona god Mwari was both and neither male or female, simultaneously the representative of light and dark. Perhaps Mwari kept Nehanda strong. Connecting to your ancestors and leaving room for the power of positive spirits to move through you would be a great tribute.

Symbols: Nehanda was a member of the Shona Mhofu clan, making a key totem the eland antelope. Other related symbols include Ngoma drums, the Zimbabwe bird, and sorghum.[13]

Color: Her color is brown.

Auspicious time: Celebrate Mbuya Nehanda on Zimbabwe's Heroes' Day, the second Monday in August.

Music: "Mbuya Nehanda" by the Harare Mambos and "Still I Rise (Caged Bird Songs)" by Maya Angelou, RoccStar, and Shawn Rivera

Suggested offerings: Flame lily flowers, ostrich meat, Nhedzi mushroom soup, whawha (maize beer), and porridge

Traditional Rebirth Ritual: Catching Komfa

In our traditions, those who have transitioned from this life are never gone. In my family's country, Guyana, there is an "African wok" ceremony called Komfa where the spiritual community invokes and celebrates with seven ancestral "tribes" of spirits. To "ketch Komfa" is to be mounted by Spirit. The practice changes in different locations, but this is how my family's village has done it for generations.

In a Komfa ceremony, you create a sacred container for the ancestors and call upon them to come down and be celebrated by us. We do this with drumming, dance, song, and ritual trance/possession. The name Komfa, also spelled Comfa, is rooted in the Akan word *Okomfo/akomfo*, meaning "traditional soothsayer, diviner, or priest." We have strong Akan roots in Guyana.[14]

Komfa was traditionally an outside ceremony, which would usually be held at the home of the medium. Back in the day, they started the ceremony with drums at the burial ground, walking out "by our back" to invite the spirits. A chicken, goat, or lamb must be sacrificed. Eggs are also broken in a huge circle to prepare the space. The ancestral spirits may come down on one medium; most people present "ketch Komfa." Walk in backward to make room for the spirits.

Some folks consider Komfa a religion. Most practitioners in my family's village didn't call Komfa a religion as they also went to church. Spiritual teacher Dr. Michelle Yaa Asantewa, author of *Guyanese Komfa: The Ritual Art of Trance*, told me, "I don't define Komfa/Comfa as a religion. I refer to it as an African-derived spiritual practice. The practitioners are 'spiritualists.'"

Komfa was originally a ceremony for Mami Wata, known as Watra Mama/ WatraMumma in the Guianas. "Oh blackie water mama, a stranger dance a ganda . . ." As I learned from my family, some of our songs celebrate her, like "Open ganda, mermaid a come, open ganda, mermaid a come, open ganda, mermaid a come."

The ganda circle is the ritual altar space in the center on the ground. My dad recommends using colorful, cultural fabric as the foundation. Here is where you put your offerings for the spirits in a calabash and around it. When the spirits come down they go straight to the ganda to seek their nourishment. Every ganda is unique. You may want to put into the calabash items like high wine, fufu, ancestral perfumes, and cloves. In addition to calabashes of food, for the ganda circle you may include an ankh, rainwater or river water, a pointer broom, and plantain leaf. Some items I recommend are cowrie shells, items to represent the various cultures, items to represent your personal ancestors, and palm leaves or trees.

The Komfa drummers set the tone. Libations are poured, beginning with the four corners for protection and gratitude. Guyana's famous Demerara rum or high wine would be ideal, but people use what they have. When attending, you may want to bring an offering for the ancestors. Money, food, fruits, and alcohol are welcome. Everyone should wash their hands. You can cleanse with Kananga Water.

Guyana is the land of many waters and six peoples. The Komfa spirits reflect the cultural ancestors of Guyana. The host spirit invites the others. Tribute may be paid to each, beginning with our Amerindian, African, East Indian, mixed race, Chinese, and European (Portuguese/Dutch) ancestors. You must include the favorite foods of the ancestors you will invite. My dad said to remind you that the African ancestral spirits are also from vastly different cultures themselves—from Yoruba to Ashanti.

According to my dad, Ovid Abrams, Sr., author of *Metegee: The History and Culture of Guyana*, "You need someone who is a master at Komfa to conduct the ceremony. Once the spirit takes possession, they ask for their favorite food, which of course has already been prepared. The spirit also drinks their favorite liquor and dances to the rhythms of Komfa drums. Spirits also bring messages from the other side."[15] People interact with the spirits who are speaking through individuals present.

The ceremony ends promptly at 3 A.M. and everyone must return home before dayclean (daylight). All leftover food or liquor is tossed in the ocean or a trench. The day after Komfa, participants return to the cemetery. Bring only rum to pour at the four corners, no drums. You thank the spirits, your friends, and relatives, who celebrated with you the night before. This time you are leaving the spirits in the cemetery, so there is no need to walk backward. Face the road and walk through the gate.

Your Rebirth Ritual: Ancestral Altar

Ritual intention: To honor familial and cultural ancestors with an ancestral altar.

You have already created a goddess altar to honor the divine feminine. This is an ancestral altar to honor those who came before. You can create this ancestral altar in addition to your divine feminine altar or in place of it, but they are two different altars.

Our ancestors pick up on the vibration of our intention. If your energy and intention is positive and good, that is what is going to be vibrated. There are people who will try to spiritually shame and say, it must be done this way. We're not talking about what we can imagine with our human minds. Energy reads energy.

You will need:

- List of familial ancestors (if available)
- List of cultural ancestors (if you choose)
- Ancestrally connected items
- Altar space
- Cloth in white or patterns and colors they connect to
- Representations of the earth, air, fire, and water elements
- Libation
- Music of your ancestors
- Food of your ancestors

What to do:

Part 1: Prepare Your Altar

Prepare your ritual space. Set up your altar. You can use a tabletop, the floor, or many other options. The floor may seem shocking, but traditionally in many cultures we use the ground.

For a basic ancestral altar, create an altar as you did in Mawu-Lisa's sanctuary (Chapter 1). This time, instead of representations of the goddess, you will include representations of your relatives and cultural ancestors. Do not include photos of living elders here. This space is only to pay homage to those who have transitioned. Be sure to include the four elements, following the previous instructions.

Feel free to get creative with your ancestral altar. If you have a small space, create an ancestral shrine on a wall or your refrigerator door. You can create shrines and altars on shelves. Just make sure you properly clean and purify each ritual space. My sister, Goddess Damali, loves to make Pinterest board altars and shrines. You can include images of the elements, cards, beautiful pieces of paper, photos, and loving words. Go for it.

Part 2: Salute Your Ancestors

Write a letter telling your ancestors what you want them to know. Roll it up as a scroll. You can seal it by dripping wax from a candle on their altar over the note. Tie it and put it on the altar. Put food on the altar for them. If you have mixed cultural roots, as most of us do, prepare the favorite foods of the different ancestors in your inherited or chosen lineages.

Add the ancestors' photos, favorite objects, or objects that make you think of them. Play your music that they would enjoy.

Invite friends for an ancestral celebration or celebrate on your own. Pour libations and give thanks.

Receive any communication. Messages, guidance, sudden phone calls, or e-mail with opportunities may pop up. Write down any guidance you receive.

Record this ritual and experience in your Goddess Soulbook.

SARA LA KALI

Goddess of Divine Lineage
Romani/Egypt
Tribute Prayer Ritual

"I am my sister, and my sister is me."

SARA LA KALI'S MESSAGE

Sastipe, daughter! The holy grail is you. You thought yourself to be rejected, lost at the crossroads of fate and free will. You were treated like a stranger. But you were home all along. Be present. Connected. The sea holds your secrets. You don't need them anymore.

SARA LA KALI'S STORY

Great Ancestress Sara, keeper of mysteries,
We see you. We say your name.
"If you bring forth what is within you, what you bring forth will save you."
Sara la Kali is the patron saint of the Romani people. Oral tradition says that she was from Egypt. Sara la Kali means "Sara the Black." I invited the Black Madonna to

our circle, and she introduced me to Sara. Sainte Sara is the Romani's Black Madonna and her very own goddess.

On May 24, almost 40,000 Romanis, Gitanas, Sintis, Manoushes, Tziganes, and people throughout Europe will travel to the southern seaport as they have done for hundreds of years. These pilgrims will arrive in Saintes-Maries-de-la-Mer, a small fishing village in southern France, for Sara la Kali's annual pilgrimage. Saintes-Maries-de-la-Mer means "Three Marys of the Sea."

The pilgrims will camp in streets, parks, and beaches, all to venerate their saint. Then, at the appointed hour, candles in hand, solemnly singing and praying, their procession will carry the statue of Black Sara to the sea. This is the annual recreation of the welcoming of the saints.

Sara la Kali is accompanied by guardians on majestic white horses. Her sacred statue is dressed in jewelry and seven layers of luxurious gowns and robes. She deserves nothing less. The devotees offer praise and make prayer requests. When the hem of her garments touches the water, disciples throw themselves into the Mediterranean.[16] Divination tools, like oracle cards and crystals, are also dipped into the sea to be blessed at the exact moment that Sara touches the water.

The atmosphere is frenzied. Believers cry and the lucky get to touch her skirts. Devotees make offerings. Items belonging to the sick are presented in hopes that loved ones will be healed. Then they parade back to the church, cleansed, happy, singing hymns, chiming bells, shouting, "Vive Sainte Sara."

So who is this mysterious saint aligned with the Dark Mother? This protector of nomads and caravans, this path blesser . . . Her story is a controversial one.

Oral tradition remembers young Sara as a beautiful Black Egyptian princess or noblewoman. In 1521, Vincent Philippon refers to her as a "charitable woman that helped people by collecting alms."[17] In Sara's time, there was an annual spiritual procession where a statue of the goddess Ishtar was carried to the sea.[18] Sara would have recognized Ishtar as Goddess Tanit, originating in Carthage. (You'll meet her later.)

Sara was a prophetess with gifts of divination. She had her own sect. Then one day she had a disturbing vision. She saw three holy women arriving by rough seas in a boat with no sails, rudders, or oars. They were having a difficult time on the water, and it was possible they would not make it.

Unbeknownst to Sara, at that time in the year A.D. 42, the three Marys—Mary Magdalene, Mary of Clopas, and Mary Salome—were trying to escape religious persecution from the Romans. These are the same three Marys that found the tomb of

Jesus empty after the crucifixion. Mary Salome was the aunt of Jesus, sister of his mother Mary. For their safety, they crossed the Mediterranean for Gaul.

At the vision of these women in distress, Sara got into her own small boat and rushed to find them. She saw them up ahead, but the waters were indeed rough. The waves almost pulled Sara in and capsized her tiny vessel. The women called out to her, and as an act of desperation, Sara tossed her coat into the water. The coat miraculously turned into a raft, and they were all able to make it safely to shore.[19] The holy delegation lived in the village until their deaths.

There are other magical stories and beliefs around Sara. In one version of the story, young Sara was the Egyptian servant girl of Mary Salome and Mary Jacobe. In another version, Sara la Kali is the daughter of Jesus and Mary Magdalene. In yet another, Sara walked on water! Some even wonder if Sara is the goddess Kali, but *kali* here just means "Black."

Although Sara la Kali has never officially been conferred sainthood by the Catholic Church, we see you, Sainte Sara. We honor you. We say your name.

Let's Talk Divine Lineage

Spirit was your first ancestor.

Gentle reminder, in case you needed it today. You are not alone. However you define the God/dess of your understanding, they birthed the first people, right? And as a human being, you trace your lineage back to those first people. So, the Most High is your first ancestor. Your DNA is holy. Your lineage is divine.

Unbury your ancestors. We have so much history that we don't have access to, so let us exalt in the parts we know. When I first started on this journey, I was a self-esteem and relationship coach. I used to go to clients' homes, and one goddess had no personal photos on display. She revealed that she had generations of her beloved ancestors' photos buried in a dusty closet. She was experiencing major personal blocks—and no wonder!

I used to feel so jealous when friends would be like, "Here's my picture of my great-great-grandfather." I don't even have pictures of my parents before they came to the U.S. as adults because in Guyana it was an expensive luxury to take photos. What gifts of your divine lineage are you taking for granted?

The spirits of the people you love want to be unburied. If you have photos, create a beautiful ancestral wall or space where they can feel appreciated. Honor those who came before with an altar wall or shrine. If you don't have photos, use your imagination to honor them. We are all connected, and your people want to be acknowledged.

Have you ever heard of Inzalo Yi'langa aka "Birthplace of the Sun" in South Africa? The Blaauboschkraal stone ruins created by the BaKoni society are based in the town of Mpumalanga overlooking the Barberton Valley. These ruins were most likely the site of ancestral rituals. The great Zulu sanusi (healer) Baba Credo Mutwa, who defined himself as a "priest diviner of the great earth mother," says that he had his initiation there almost 100 years ago, as the energy connects us to the ancients.[20] The name *Mpumalanga's* direct translation from Xhosa as "the place where the sun rises" makes sense as this region is home to some of the oldest known rocks. The stone-walled and circular ruins, nicknamed the South African Stonehenge, are the subject of much spiritual and scientific debate.

People have noted that these structures look similar not only to Stonehenge in England but also to structures in Sardinia, Gobekli Tepe in southeast Turkey, and the Cult of Upright Stones in Senegal. In Senegal the stones weigh a ton each and the openings face east.

How incredible that we can visit structures beyond human memory and connect energetically to generations of people whose names we will never know. How magical that structures built in totally different geographical areas could be so similar. We share divine lineage and are all connected through time and space.

Put your hand over your heart and say aloud, "I am not alone." Your ancestors walked before you, and we, your sisters on this cosmic quest, walk with you. No matter what you are going through, know that right now there is someone somewhere who feels exactly as you do. She may be reading these words now too. Think about this the next time you feel alone.

HOW TO HONOR GREAT ANCESTRESS SARA LA KALI

When you honor Great Ancestress Sara la Kali, you honor the part of you that is fully connected to your divine lineage. You may choose to honor this energy inside yourself or invoke her energy according to your own tradition.

To honor the goddess in you: Sara la Kali's devotees lay their heads on her statue's feet to feel their connection to her. Touch your head to the earth. Close your eyes and send love to those you feel connected to who came before you. See yourself beaming love to them while they beam love right back. What can you do today to be a great future ancestor?

Symbols: Sara la Kali's symbol is the Camargue cross.

Colors: Her colors are blue and gold.

Auspicious times: Her feast day is May 24. October 22 and 23 are also key days for her devotees worldwide. These are the feast days of Mary Salome.

Music: "Sara la Kali" by Dani Caracola & La Banda de Ida y Vuelta and "Mary Magdalene" by FKA Twigs

Suggested offerings: Throw flowers, head into the ocean, dance, or make your own pilgrimage to her major shrine in Saintes-Maries-de-la-Mer, France. Small satchels of earth are placed at Sara's statue's feet. She loves shiny things and things from the sea. One of her favorite offerings is jewelry.

Alternate names: Sara la Negra, Sara the Black, Sainte Sara, Black Sara, Black Madonna

Traditional Divine Lineage Ritual: Mo'juba Ancestral Prayer

Mo'juba prayer is used in Yoruba traditions as a divine invocation to call the spirit. *Ajuba* means "salute." There are many different Mo'juba versions, but they all give reverence to the Most High, to your personal ancestors, to renowned community ancestors, to the earth and nature, to your parents, and to your ascended masters and spiritual guides. Mo'juba changes based on country, religion, lineage, spiritual house, etc. This prayer creates a sacred space of connection for the àse, life force, to be manifested here in the material world with us.

The Mo'juba traditionally follows the libation or is a part of the libation. *Mo'juba* means "We give reverence to." *Iba* means "I give reverence to," "I salute," or "I pay homage to." You may find in some traditions they will say "iba se" and in others they will say just "iba."

Some include giving reverence to the dawn, the dusk, and every natural blessing in between. If you have spiritual godparents, please include them. I love the beauty of Mo'juba. In my humble opinion, this is where we inherited the hip-hop and dancehall traditions of giving shout-outs.

Here is a simple version of Mo'juba:

Iba Olodumare (I give reverence to God).

Iba Orunmila (I give reverence to the gift of Odu).

Iba Ori (I give reverence to the spirit of my head).

Iba Iya (I give reverence to my mother).

Iba Baba (I give reverence to my father).

Iba Irunmole (I give reverence to the primordials).

Iba Orisha (I give reverence to all of the orishas; you can then get specific).

Iba Egungun (I give reverence to my personal ancestors).

Iba _____ (I give reverence to my cultural ancestors).

Iba _____ *(I give reverence to my elders).*
Iba toto mo'juba (I give respect to all).
Àse-o, àse-o, àse-o.

Your Divine Lineage Ritual: Ancestral Tribute Prayer

Ritual intention: To connect with ancestors through a tribute prayer.

You will need:

- Your Goddess Soulbook
- Names of your women ancestors (if you don't know names, you can say great-grandmother, etc.)
- Names of your ancestral men (if you wish to include them)
- Names of goddesses you are connected to (if you wish to include them)
- Libation

What to do:

Part 1: Write Your Ancestral Tribute Prayer

Prepare your ritual space.

Make a list of the women ancestors you want to pay tribute to, your own family lineage and cultural lineage. Make a list of the goddesses and ascended spirits you want to give reverence to. Make a list of the elements in nature you wish to pay homage to.

Put them in the order you wish, using affirmative statements such as "I honor you," "I thank you," "I give reverence to," "I salute," and so on.

I like to get specific on their gifts, such as:

"I give reverence to my Great Ancestress Aunt Silvy, for loving us, being the best cook, and making us feel protected."

You may choose to use the Mo'juba prayer as a guide to create your own in your tradition, or not. Add your prayer with your ancestral names to your Goddess Soulbook. You may choose to write it on a piece of paper first and then add to your Goddess Soulbook when complete.

This prayer is just for the divine feminine. You can do another including the energy of the divine masculine you wish to tribute.

Part 2: Salute Your Ancestors

Prepare your ritual space. Go to your ancestral altar. Pour libations.

Read your ancestral prayer. You may decide to scroll it (or not) and add it to your altar.

Part 3: Sit Quietly and Receive Your Ancestors

You have invited them in, and they have guidance to share. Close your eyes and see yourself in circle with them. Who comes up to speak to you and why? What do they want you to know?

Sit for at least 20 minutes. Open your eyes and take notes in your journal. If you have a divination practice like oracle cards, this is a good time to do a reading to download their guidance. It may be helpful to look at each name in your prayer and write down the first thing that comes to mind.

MARIE LAVEAU

Goddess of Abundance
New Orleans
Gris-Gris Bag Ritual

"All I do is win."

MARIE LAVEAU'S MESSAGE

Bonjour, daughter! Ooh! You are divine. You are rich. You have good juju as you have inherited the greatest inheritance there is. You have the power to shift worlds and bend them to your will. Accept your ancestral inheritance now. You are heiress to a rich heritage of divine prosperity.

MARIE LAVEAU'S STORY

Great Ancestress Marie Laveau, keeper of mysteries,
We see you. We say your name.

Great Ancestress Marie Laveau made history as a legendary "voodooienne" in New Orleans. It is unclear whether she was born in 1794 or 1801. But if she wanted us to know, we would. Marie was born a free person of color in the French colony of

Louisiana. Her mother was a formerly enslaved woman, and her father was a multi-racial businessman, who some say was from Saint-Domingue.

Her first husband, Jacques Paris, was a Creole man from Saint-Domingue, which became Haiti. He had arrived in New Orleans fleeing the Haitian Revolution, along with over 25,000 other people, beginning in 1791. Can you imagine the energy of trauma in the air? Marie and Jacques had two children together, and then Jacques mysteriously disappeared in 1824.

Marie took to calling herself the Widow Paris. An astute entrepreneur, the "Voodoo Queen" first built a thriving business as a hairstylist. Then she parlayed that into a prosperous business built on her spiritual gifts. In her enterprises, Marie served clientele of every race and gender, and her wealthy clients gave her access to their hair, mansions, and secrets. Some claim she used those secrets to leverage her own fame and fortune. Who's to say?

Marie went from doing the hair of aristocrats in the Big Easy to becoming a socialite herself. One of her powerful companions was Père Antoine, the head chaplain at St. Louis Cathedral. This afforded her uncommon political and spiritual leverage. It also gave her access to do good community works, such as visiting with and praying for prisoners.

Marie was strikingly beautiful and wore a tignon, a version of the West African gele (headwrap). In 1786, the Louisiana Tignon Laws were passed, mandating that Creole women keep their hair covered. Their beauty was seen as a threat to social order.[21] An unexpected side effect was that the tignon made beauties like Marie stand out more.

Oral tradition reveals that Marie inherited spiritual gifts and teachings, and she was taught Voodoo by the Senegalese Dr. John Montanee.[22] He was considered the father of New Orleans Voodoo and the gris-gris king himself. Some say that she also learned Voodoo from her mother and first husband. There is a dispute about whether she was initiated into Voodoo or practiced Hoodoo. All of the above is most likely true.

Voodoo already existed in Louisiana before the new Haitian population arrived, and then it was buoyed and reinforced by their influx. Haitian Vodou and Louisiana Voodoo have more differences today than they had during Marie Laveau's time. Here are the similarities: Although spelled differently, both Haitian Vodou and Louisiana Voodoo originated from Vodun in the former Kingdom of Dahomey, West Africa, and crossed the oceans with enslaved people. *Vodun* means "spirit" in the Fon language. Both Louisiana and Haiti were colonized by the Catholic French, bringing similar syncretization to each region. Louisiana Voodoo also incorporates elements of Native American spirituality.

If folks doubted Marie's prowess, they no longer did after everyone started gossiping about Marie and the judge. A wealthy European man came to her, desperate and inconsolable. His innocent son was being accused of rape or murder. He promised Marie that if she could use her gifts to free his son, he would gift her a house.

Marie is said to have performed the following ritual: She prayed at the altar of St. Louis Cathedral, asking for the support of the Divine. Some say she brought her snake Zombi, the incarnation of Damballah Weddo, with her. Then she made the defendant one of her famous mojo bags. She put three superhot Guinea peppers, also known as grains of paradise, under her tongue the day of the trial as a sacrifice. Grains of paradise are used for protection and success. She placed the same peppers under the judge's chair. Guess what? The man's son was acquitted, and the gentleman handed over the keys. Some say she already had sway over the judge. Either way, she won.

After her first husband's disappearance and presumed death, Marie entered a domestic partnership with Christophe Dominick Duminy de Glapion, a Frenchman. They raised 15 children together, although many of that brood may include her grandchildren.

It is said that Marie's Sunday ceremonies in Congo Square were the place to be for rituals and celebrations. Zombi the snake was most certainly in attendance, and she often served gumbo during Voodoo rites.[23] Upon her death, Marie's official bio was that she was a devout Catholic, a caring nurse, and was "skillful in the practice of medicine and was acquainted with the valuable healing qualities of indigenous herbs."[24] All of that was most likely true, but those in the know also remembered Marie for her wild parties. They say that the emperor of China and Queen Victoria sent her gifts.

Over 200 years after her birth, her name is still synonymous with magic. Gamblers shout her name before throwing dice. Her name had such sway that Marie Laveau's daughter continued to use it in the same business after her death. However, she was more known for her thriving brothel. In the fall of 1928, Hoodoo doctor Luke Turner (aka Samuel Thompson), who claimed to be Ms. Marie's grandnephew, initiated writer Zora Neale Hurston.

Marie's gravesite at St. Louis Cemetery No.1 attracted so many fans hoping that she would grant their wishes that there is only restricted access. There is a mini ritual that visitors say will invoke Marie's energy to grant your desires. It is said that you must draw an X on Marie's tomb, turn around three times, knock on the tomb, then yell out your wish. You then release your wish, pay close attention, and go on with your life. After your wish is granted, you must return in gratitude to Marie's grave, circle your X, and leave her spirit an offering.

Shhhhh . . . People say you can still see her walking down certain streets.

Let's Talk Abundance

Marie had good juju. She created and attracted wealth wherever she went, and so can you. One of the groups of incredible women I have been blessed to hold space for are the lightworkers that I call Spiritpreneurs. I created the term *Spiritpreneurs®* to mean spiritual women entrepreneurs: healers, masseuses, coaches, yoginis, psychics, astrologers, and teachers who want to build businesses around their wellness and healing practices. I created a safe container to support other women in spiritual business in part because of the fears and blocks that I had around finances, being seen, and creating a spiritual business.

Most of us are already programmed with the beliefs that it is not spiritual, feminine, or creative to charge money for your services. This becomes an issue when you don't feel that your call to service is a hobby or something you do in your spare time. For most of us, if the need for money disappeared tomorrow, we would gladly keep doing the same work that we are doing. We are passionate about this work. But we live in a capitalist society, so we become de facto or reluctant entrepreneurs. And if we believe that money is dirty or negative, we end up overworked, underpaid, and destitute.

People always point to an idyllic view of the healers of old, who didn't seem to need money—at least in our present-day imaginations. A breakthrough came to me when I reconnected with the spirit of my late great-grandmother Ma, who was born in the 1800s. In our present-day language, she was an herbalist, midwife, and women's fertility healer. The community loved her. People paid her generously in chickens, crops, coins, and whatever they had. Her Bajan husband, my great-grandfather David, was decapitated in a mining accident, so she was raising six daughters on her own. She never turned anyone away, so she also took in the laundry and did ironing for hire. By all accounts, she was most likely exhausted.

We say old-school healers didn't need money because the community supported them. This is true; Ma took care of her community, and her community supported her. But how do we think the community supported healers like Ma? They took care of them with the equivalent of money. The goats, chickens, and crops that people brought were currency. Those were money in their village.

The equivalent of a "thank you goat" for a healer living in Chicago is someone swiping their bank card for her services. I love paying abundantly to work with people who are making my life and the world a better place. When you can pay others abundantly with joy, you are making space for others to do the same for you.

Is answering your calling only for rich people? Are you meant to struggle by doing the work you were called to do only part-time? Of course not.

Abundance is the way of the Universe. Walk by a field and notice how many kinds of flowers and insects there are. Don't you want your children to be abundant? Don't you think that your Creator wants you to be abundant too?

Our Goddess Temple Circle sister Anna Jae Fit is a weight-loss coach, personal trainer, and nutrition specialist. In her spiritual business, she helps women who are dealing not only with mental health challenges but also with body image issues. Her personal practice is ancestral, influenced by Mississippi Voodoo. Anna is also a single mother to a 4-year-old and an 11-year-old. Doesn't she deserve to have a prosperous and thriving business?

Luckily, Goddess Anna inherited positive views on abundance and good juju amid the messages she also received of pain and struggle. She describes her business as flourishing.

Goddess Anna comes from a long line of "Mississippi Voodoo Queens." She says that "Voodoo and Hoodoo seem to automatically be associated with Louisiana," but the heritage is rich in the "Mississippi Delta where the flat land and the climate [were] ideal for cotton growing." All the women from her great-grandmother going back were in tune with the Voodoo tradition that had been passed down. Her own grandmother was the first generation in her lineage to believe that their African ancestral beliefs were evil.

Anna connected spiritually with her late great-grandmother Odessa, born in 1898. Miss Odessa was a known Voodoo queen and was feared due to her powers. Anna's father was the only child in the family who had a true relationship with Miss Odessa. Growing up, his family stopped the 16 grandkids from going to her house. They dismissed her as a "voodoo witch" dabbling with dangerous witchcraft. But Anna's dad spent countless days at Odessa's house because "she had the best fried chicken."

Her father went out to the fields daily with Miss Odessa as a child in the early '60s to help her pick cotton. Miss Odessa always engaged in a morning ritual first. She told her grandson that it was for their protection "from the white man and the snakes in the cotton fields." Miss Odessa would burn 11 candles that had family names carved into them and chant. He never figured out what she was saying or what language it was, but he knew it was not English.

Out of 16 grandkids, Goddess Anna's dad is the only one who was able to walk in his abundance. He traveled the world, has significant academic achievements, built wealth, and had a successful career. Anna's family is convinced that he was the special one because there was something in Odessa's fried chicken.

Every new moon Goddess Anna pays tribute and welcomes in more abundance. She expresses gratitude to the moon and meditates directly in the moonlight. Then she writes down one thing she wants to release and how releasing it will allow her to reach new heights. Before her conjure herb bath, she drinks a hot cup of "Voodoo cleanse tea" she makes with jasmine, pansy, peppermint, lavender herbs, and sea moss gel.

Yay for making space for generational abundance! Call in all of your money now. Call all of your ancestor's money back to you now. You have good juju.

Write in your Goddess Soulbook: *I have good juju. Abundance, wealth, and prosperity flow to me easily always in all ways.*

HOW TO HONOR GREAT ANCESTRESS MARIE LAVEAU

When you honor Great Ancestress Marie Laveau, you honor the part of you that is in alignment with your abundance. You may choose to honor this energy inside yourself or invoke her energy according to your own tradition.

To honor the goddess in you: Marie's lifestyle embodied the idea that living well is the best revenge. How can you unabashedly claim your own abundance and good juju? Marie allowed herself to have a voice and shine, which was revolutionary. She thrived as an entrepreneur, and although she had loving husbands, she owned herself.

Symbols: Madame Marie's cherished snake, Zombi, is one of her symbols, as well as gris-gris bags and the Christian cross.

Colors: Her colors are purple, green, and gold.

Auspicious times: Her recorded birthday is September 10. She is celebrated on St. John's Eve on June 24.

Music: "Marie La Veau" by Papa Celestin's New Orleans Band and "My Power" by Beyoncé

Suggested offerings: The cross, champagne, red beans, Guinea peppers, beautician's tools, and dolls

Alternate names: Marie Laveaux, Marie La Veau, Marie Leveau, The Widow Paris

Traditional Abundance Ritual: Gris-Gris Bag

Gris-gris bags, used throughout the diaspora, are best known in North America in relation to both the African American Voodoo and Hoodoo traditions. Gris-gris bags are a sacred container for a spirit or a prayer in a bag. Other names for gris-gris include mojo bags, hands, mojo hands, and more. A gris-gris bag is a bag filled with specific herbs, oils, stones, seeds, beans, powders, bones, and natural ephemera and other charms in order to create a magical outcome for the wearer. Some traditions say to use an odd number of less than 13 ingredients only.

Traditionally, a gris-gris bag is prepared by a healer, priestess, or shaman at an altar, shrine, or other ritual space. Every item in the bag, including the bag itself, is part of the spell. Gris-gris can be worn on your body or placed in your home or office, depending on the issues and the prescription. Most should be worn against the naked body. Some trace the word *gris-gris* back to the Yoruba word *juju,* meaning "talisman." They have different names in different cultures. For example, resguardos in Santeria are often made with consecrated herbs, blessed beads in the attending orisha's colors, and cowrie shells. A gris-gris in some traditions can also be a doll.

In Kongo spirituality, nkisi is an object that is inhabited by Spirit. The word *nkisi* is used to describe the spirit as well. These nkisi containers were bags, bundles, gourds, shells, and other vessels. The magical elements added were considered medicine. In Jamaica, Guyana, or Trinidad the obeah man might make you a personal "wish bag."

When the British first tried to execute Shona freedom fighter and svikiro (spirit medium) Great Ancestress Mbuya Nehanda, she wouldn't die until they reportedly removed her pouch. In Ethiopia, debteras prescribe spiritual leather amulets that are worn on the body containing herbal ingredients. They also may prepare small prayer scrolls or silver protective amulets to be worn against the body.

Great Ancestress Marie Laveau was a gris-gris queen. Her grandnephew Luke Turner taught writer Zora Neale Hurston her secret Hoodoo petition and response and mojo hand (gris-gris bag) ritual for good luck: Start with a whole nutmeg of The Indies (Grenada) and bore a hole in it. Pour in argentorum (liquid silver). The original instructions say to also pour in quicksilver (mercury), which is now known to be toxic. Use either liquid aluminum or add a tiny piece of aluminum foil as a substitute. Seal the nutmeg with fresh pine tree blood (sap). Add Wish Beans (St. John's beans), Wonder of the World (ginseng) root powder, frankincense, and myrrh.

A key ingredient is Powder of Attraction, for which you can use High John the Conqueror root. High John the Conqueror represented the spirit of freedom for Black Americans. He was said to have been an African prince who was enslaved. It was said that when enslavers were whipping an enslaved person, High John the Conqueror would lessen the pain. His spirit is in all forms of the John the Conqueror root.

In Mama Marie's method, you then put each ingredient in a pure chamois leather bag while praying, "Oh, good Lord, let my words be hearkened to. Oh, good Lord, drive the evil spirits from me. Oh, good Lord, give me success. Oh, good Lord, let me hold all of these things into this bag." Then sew it up tightly. Mix geranium spirits (gin) and cinnamon essence and rub them on the bag. Keep the bag next to your body so you feel it first thing in the morning. This is "the bag of many lucks which will make your mind clear and your heart stout so that you cannot fail."[25] So be it.

Your Abundance Ritual: Gris-Gris Bag

Ritual intention: To create a money magnetizing gris-gris bag.

Feel free to substitute ingredients. Adjust according to your guidance. Remember that our ancestors used local items and whatever was available. You know more than you think you know! Notice that you have been building your relationship with your ancestors, caring for them and feeding them before this step.

In a traditional African American Hoodoo gris-gris bag, you use 3 to 13 items, with an odd number of items.

You will need:

- Abundance herbs (dried): basil, bay leaf, cinnamon, rosemary
- Money drawing oil: palm oil (very important in West Africa)
- Dry black-eyed peas
- Frankincense resin or oil
- Ancestral stone: African citrine or Zambian aquamarine (or crystal of your choice)
- Magnetizer: lodestone or another type of magnet (you can use a lodestone oil as well)

- Shell (cowrie shell would be ideal)
- Beautiful mini bag or 7 x 7–inch square of cloth and tie string (red, green, gold, or silver are preferred; flannel was traditional)
- Currency: $1 paper money or representation of money or silver coin
- Magical writing utensil

What to do:

Prepare your ritual space. Cleanse each item according to your practice. This is a great new-moon ritual, and charging these items in new-moon energy is powerful. You can also charge them on your goddess altar.

Come to this ritual with the energy of joy and gratitude. You never want to approach abundance work with the energy of desperation.

Pray over the ingredients. Touch each item, make friends with them, and let them absorb your àse. Gris-gris is a spirit. Present the energy of palm oil as an offering to the gris-gris and the herbs. Address each item and speak words of abundance, prosperity, and riches into them. You may use mantras, affirmations, or declarations. Tell each item what they are here for.

Rub the oils on your hands. Begin with putting the dried black-eyed peas into a bowl. Black-eyed peas represent the spiritual force, fortitude, and the eye of the Creator.

Add the abundance herbs: basil, bay leaf, rosemary, and cinnamon.

Add 7 drops of frankincense resin or oil. Add 7 drops of palm oil.

Add and feed the lodestone or other magnet. Lodestones are naturally occurring magnets used in the Hoodoo tradition to magnetize your desires to you. You must baptize it and give it a name before use. You feed it with prayers, magnetic sand, and a little liquid.

Add the sacred stone of your choice. You can add ancestral crystals such as African citrine or Zambian aquamarine. You can also add a piece of jewelry or a found rock from a key geographical location.

Fold the money up toward you if it is paper money. Some prefer to fold the money around the stones or other items. Trust your Guidance.

Sew the bag or tie it closed. Knot the string over it three times. Inhale and exhale with the energy of abundance. See money and gold coins falling around you. Blow on it to activate it. Yes! You just gave it life. Now what are you calling in? Close your eyes and see it. Feed the gris-gris bag with more palm oil.

You can keep the bag against the left side of your body, on your altar, in a doorway, or in your home, car, business, or bag.

Congrats! You have completed the Temple of Ancestors.

Temple of Ancestors Soil Mantras

- *I am firmly planted and deeply rooted.*
- *I am safe. It is safe to be safe.*
- *Still I rise.*
- *I am my sister, and my sister is me.*
- *All I do is win.*

Temple of Ancestors Journal Questions

- What makes me feel safe?
- What beliefs did I inherit?
- What do my ancestors want for me?
- What ancestral traumas am I willing to release?
- How can I ground myself daily?

Temple of Ancestors Embodiment

- Add something to your altar that represents feeling rooted in your goddess power.

Temple of Ancestors Integration

- Add the Temple of Ancestors goddesses and your experience with these rituals to your Goddess Soulbook.

3

THE TEMPLE OF CONJURERS: YOUR CREATION ENERGY CHANNEL

Heka

BLESSING OF THE CONJURERS

Sewing, tacking, molding, weaving,
Bending the order of time.
Spinning, knitting, stitching, dreaming,
Bending the meaning assigned.

You see it, you feel it, you be it;
Shift the months from conception to birth.
Place the clock's numbers as needed.
Spin, weave, dance, shift.
Do you trust what you see?

With my little I, eye spy
You.
You create,
You deserve,
You receive,
You deserve,
You are fertile,
You are ready.

Enchanted dawning, sacred one!

You are entering the Temple of Conjurers in the creation energy channel. The five goddesses, here just for you, represent creativity, manifesting, emotions, and birth. Ngame, Modjadji, Ma'at, Tanit, and the Seven Sisters have been the keepers of this guidance from time immemorial. You now stand in an elevated circle of goddesses who are here to guide you in your shift from surviving to thriving.

Sit in the center and take in their wisdom. They each have gifts for you. Should you choose to accept their gifts, you will ignite your ability to manifest your life. To complete this temple, complete their five rituals.

ABOUT THE TEMPLE OF CONJURERS

The Temple of Conjurers is all about you creating your world through the art of creativity, manifestation, and your fertile sexual magic. Our traditional African spirituality term for this temple's principle is *heka*, the ancient Egyptian word for the art and science of "magic." Divine manifesting is collaboration with God/dess energy to mold our lives for the highest and best good of the collective. We are all manifesting our lives, albeit unconsciously for most people.

Throughout the diaspora, we have countless traditions to wield the wand that commands life to bend. Conjure is an African American spiritual practice, originally created and nurtured by those with deep roots in the southern United States. Conjure teaches us that the power is in our hands. A traditional conjurer wields the power of magic but is so much more than a magician. These sorceresses are able to harness the power of the Divine for evocation, manifestation, and transformation. This temple is named in their honor.

Goddess alchemy is learning to see through this dimension into the next and welcome in what you are seeking. Healers, priestesses, and brujas of African descent have used magic for access to healing, protection, and joy since time began. We will continue to tap into this magic as we started with the ancestors in the last temple.

Mini ritual: Close your eyes and do a Kegel. I know, I'm giggling too. Go ahead. Okay good, now do another Kegel, and this time imagine your pelvic muscles pulling in from the ether all of the happiness you deserve. Yes! You just cast a manifestation spell.

Conscious manifestation requires being in tune with your intentions and intuition, knowing how to access your goddess power, and finding alignment. This is alchemy.

You have a right to feel passion. Basic surface manifestation, like parlor tricks, can be taught to anyone. In the Temple of Conjurers, you will be initiated into your own gifts of magical creation.

Write in your Goddess Soulbook: *I am magic.*

WHAT IS YOUR CREATION ENERGY CHANNEL?

Our creation energy channel is about our emotions, fertility, creativity, pleasure, manifesting, and sexuality. Creating something from nothing is magic, whether you are manifesting a baby, a book, or an orgasm. This energy channel is associated with the color orange and governs your lower abdomen, uterus, ovaries, sexual organs, large intestine, kidney, and bladder.

I had overwhelming resistance in downloading the messages from Spirit for this energy channel. I have had so many challenges around birth—fertility issues, failed in vitro fertilization attempts, and miscarriages—that I wanted to avoid it altogether. But Spirit kept nudging me, then shaking me. First, I started to receive a bunch of misdirected birth-related mail that was for my neighbor, who was pregnant, then the baby ads, then random e-mail messages about birthing centers. What we resist persists. So I finally did the rituals our goddess conjurers in this temple requested, and here we are.

You are a creative force. You are co-creating this planet right now. You are fertile whether or not you ever give birth to a human. Everything around us first existed in someone's thoughts. Fertile imaginations and creative power brought forth everything from peanut butter to traffic lights. As author and spiritual teacher Esther Hicks says, you are the energy that creates worlds. (Esther Hicks channels a group of positive spirits called Abraham-Hicks, so she would know!) I'm laughing now because I got my period the moment I started to write these words to you. These teachings needed to come from the flow.

Take a deep breath. Let it out. This time, I want you to take a birth-energy breath. Take a breath from the depths of Mother Earth's womb energy. Take a deep breath from the creation energy of all of the wombs that birthed those who birthed you, an ancient, ancestral, eternal breath.

Let's do it together. Inhale. Hold. Exhale.

Yes. I felt that, goddess. I feel your womb energy. It doesn't matter if you have never had a physical uterus or if you no longer have one. I feel your spiritual womb energy. This is the Mawu energy that we have been hungry for, the goddess energy that the planet is starving for. Birth is not sanitized and orderly. It's messy, loud, and bloody. So is creation.

Want to manifest and create and have a sexy, fertile dance with life? Let's begin at the beginning. Take a moment. Send a blessing to your spiritual womb.

A year and a half ago, I had uterine surgery, and it was a difficult experience, to say the least. I had a massive asthma attack under the anesthesia. You know you need to be scared when your doctors are scared. I woke up with them yelling at me, "Why didn't you say that you had asthma?" It was so bad that the hospital alerted my emergency contact.

I hadn't had any signs of asthma since I was 16. And I had never exhibited any signs before about age 12. Because I no longer needed an inhaler from the time I went away to college, I came to believe that I had never had asthma. I thought that maybe my anxiety attacks had been misdiagnosed. So asthma has not been on any of my medical forms since I was a teen.

The healing from this surgery was brutal. Mentally, physically, emotionally, and spiritually. I left the hospital and went straight to my parents' couch. My apartment was in a Manhattan walk-up, and my body just couldn't do that. My bones hurt. My chest felt like there was an elephant chilling on it. I couldn't speak and could barely move. I stayed on my parents' sofa because I couldn't make it upstairs or downstairs. I came in the front door and that was as far as I could go.

The day after surgery, I attempted to do my weekly livestream with my group-coaching clients. I was still kind of delirious because anesthesia remains in your body for a while. I posted a notification that I was broadcasting live. Thank the goddess for sisterhood. Our Goddess Temple Circle sister Tracey Bryant Swint, founder of Love My Womb Academy, wrote back, "NO. Get off the interwebs and go heal your womb. Get out of here."

And that was absolutely the right advice. The creation energy channel houses our reproductive organs. Uterine surgery may clear your womb physically, but it does not heal your womb spiritually or emotionally.

We all need womb-energy healing. Again, it doesn't matter if you have never had a physical uterus or if you no longer have one. Your spiritual womb is the center of your goddess energy, creativity, fertility, emotions, and pleasure.

Write in your Goddess Soulbook: *I have the energy that creates worlds.*

You have the energy that creates worlds. This knowledge that lives deep in your rememory can be so secretly terrifying that we intentionally sabotage and block it. I say "rememory," a Toni Morrison *Beloved* term, because I mean our connected primal, ancestral memory that started before this life. It's more emotionally safe to focus, fear, and complain about the things that we can't do. But it's time to focus on the things that we can do. This is how we turn the terror zone of "can't" into a sacred, creative, fertile zone.

You *can* easily and effortlessly secure the bag because the bag is within you. We had a Law of Manifestation challenge in my virtual Goddess Temple Circle, and so many manifested magical things. One person manifested a baby; people manifested money and jobs. But many folks didn't manifest what they wanted because they had blockages. They wanted to call in love but called in money instead because they had love blockages, or vice versa. So you will need to release and clear those blockages so you can magnetize from your goddess power. You have the power to create worlds.

Write in your Goddess Soulbook: *The bag is within me.*

Now this next declaration is going to be a bit controversial. We must heal our relationships with maternal energy, the queen of your childhood.

Write in your Goddess Soulbook: *I am willing to heal my relationship with my maternal energy.*

This could be your birth mother or the maternal energy that raised you. For some people that may be your grandmother or an aunt. Or you may not have had maternal energy present in your household at all. Some of our goddess sisters shared with me that they had a mother figure who was narcissistic or sociopathic. That is a person who is inaccessible to healing. That is not a healthy energy to seek in-person connection with. Or your mother may have transitioned and is no longer on this earth plane.

The beautiful news is that you don't have to interact with somebody physically to heal your relationship with them. In fact, you can have more powerful relationships with some people energetically than physically. Meet with them on the astral plane in a visualization, express your feelings, and hash it out.

My mother came with us on my goddess retreats to Belize and Paris, and it was wonderful to heal that sacred umbilical cord relationship. If we have anger and unforgiveness toward the maternal energy we are connected to, it affects us. And yes, you are still connected to that primal-source energy. You cannot hate your mother and love yourself completely. This does not mean that you are obligated to have any contact with her whatsoever. You need not expose yourself to harm in the name of healing. Give thanks for the womb that birthed you. Give thanks for the goddess energies that raised you, perfectly imperfect though they might be. Consider the Kikuyu Kenyan proverb "Kũngũ Maitũ na Hunyũ Wake," meaning "Hail Mother with all her warts and dirt."[1]

Our mother energy is not only that goddess whose womb you came through or who helped to raise you or who was a mother figure for you, but also the Mother

Earth of where you were, where you are, and where your lineage came through. That's why we say mother tongue, mother country, and motherland. So we have our beautiful physical mother and womb that we came through, plus the mothers who raised and cared for us, but there is also the earth mother coordinates of where you and your people came through on a physical plane.

For me, that means Guyana where my mother and father were born, Barbados where my great-grandfather was born, and West Africa from which my ancestors were enslaved. My people were there for centuries before being in this hemisphere. My ancestors' history did not begin in 1502, 1797, 1808, or whatever years they were kidnapped. I have only taken one trip so far to West Africa, but it's still my motherland. Nigeria, Ghana, Togo, and Benin are still a womb and umbilical cord for me.

A couple of months ago, I watched a video of a strikingly dignified community elder in Ghana apologizing to African American and Afro-Caribbean people for his ancestors' role in the slave trade. He apologized for their role in selling us. I burst out crying and bawled like a baby. I had no idea that this was an apology I needed, but in that moment my soul felt it. No wonder my abandonment issues were so deep. I had been being rejected before I was born. This was ancient pain. There was a feeling of primal rejection and betrayal, an umbilical cord that had been severed. There are many historical records of African chiefs making deals with Europeans to traffic other tribes, not their own. Of course those deals were not kept, and to their shock, the chiefs would find their own people, family members in some cases, kidnapped and trafficked. This elder attempting to make amends looked like my family. And maybe was.

I have seen disparaging comments on social media toward my fellow African American and Afro-Caribbean people throughout the diaspora. People saying things like, "They're wearing beauty shop dashikis," or "They're grasping at straws because they don't know anything about Africa." Listen, we get our healing the way we need to. And if I put on a beauty shop dashiki, it's because that is what I have access to. And I will rock it—proudly—and be connected to my motherland and my Source in the way that my womb energy tells me is connective for me.

I've had motherland-born African family tell me I don't have a right to my Africanness because my ancestors were sold. I have had multigenerational African American family tell me I don't have a right to my Americanness although I was born and raised on Black soil in the U.S. of A. I have had Guyanese family tell me I don't have a right to the culture that birthed my parents, grandparents, and their great-grandparents because I am a "Yankee." For all these folks, I am an orphan. But that's their problem, because only I get to define me, and I own all of my spiritual, cultural, geographical, and genetic DNA. I have access to the energy that creates worlds.

A woman contacted me and asked if I could connect her with someone "exactly like [me] who is Syrian." She wanted a Syrian spiritual mentor, teacher, and healer as she was Syrian. She was apologetic and didn't want me to be offended. I wasn't offended at all. Do what works for your own healing.

One of the sisters in our goddess circle said she was healing her Celtic roots and folks told her, "No, that's not what you should be doing." I had the same experience when I was working with rune stones. Someone said, "That's not African; you shouldn't be reading runes."

Do you. What is healing for you? Ask your ancestors, your Creator, your spirits, and your womb. Feel free to claim all of you in the way that works for you. It may not look right for somebody else. Tell them, "I'm following what my womb is telling me." And that is greater than any other human's opinion.

Consider also healing the geographical Mother Earth energy connection of your current location. I am a New Yorker, born and raised. I grew up on New York City tap water in Southeast Queens, on the border of Long Island. Belmont Raceway, Green Acres Mall, Jamaica Ave, and the Colosseum are all in my blood. Then I lived in Harlem for over 20 years. People move and they never look back. Heal that geographical mother energy.

You are eternal and ancient. You are a conjurer. You have a right to your sacredness. You have a right to your fertile creativity. You have a right to your pleasure.

HOW TO KNOW IF YOUR CREATION ENERGY CHANNEL IS BLOCKED

Does your creativity feel blocked? Are you pregnant with creative projects but then can't quite birth them? Do you feel jealous or compare yourself to others often? Does pleasure have to be earned for you? Is feeling sexually free challenging?

This is an energy center that is blocked for many of us. These blocks may turn into dysfunctional relationships. They may show up as tumors and uterine issues. They may manifest as communication issues.

These blocks show up as sexual issues, too, because so many of us have sexual traumas. For years I wrote a sexual self-esteem advice column for *Essence,* and so many readers wrote to me about their sexual traumas. This is also generational. It may not even be your trauma that you're carrying. As a sacred container, the womb can carry and nurture a human baby, and it can also hold on to all our "stuff." If we are not doing sacred healing processes to heal our womb energy, then we are carrying generational womb trauma energy. And I don't know about you, but I'm willing and ready to let all of that go.

When your 10-times-great-grandma was born, she held all of the eggs her body would hold in a lifetime. That means she held a kernel of you. That means you have her stuff and everyone in between.

We have deep-rooted ancestral traumas in this area. As just a "small" example, Black and Native American women were given hysterectomies against their will for a major part of American history. This is not ancient history. In the late '70s, after she had already had my brother and me, the doctor told my mother that she had to have a hysterectomy. The doctor gave her no formal diagnosis of anything. He saw a young, Black immigrant woman and decided that her uterus needed to be removed, no questions asked. The day of the surgery, my mother jumped up from the bed when the doctor stepped out, ran from the hospital, and never looked back. Thank goodness! Because she had a healthy pregnancy and gave birth to my sister about a year later.

Again, if this energy channel is blocked, you may also have unhealthy attachments, co-dependencies, and negative relationships. Remember the womb is a container. Emotions and experiences that you do not release—from resentments to traumas—remain energetically contained there. So heal what cries out to be healed, birth what needs to be birthed, dissolve what must be dissolved. Release what no longer serves you. Lovingly let go.

It is time.

Goddesses Ngame, Modjadji, Ma'at, Tanit, and the Seven Sisters welcome you to the Temple of Conjurers. These goddesses are working together to help you turn up your creativity and fertility and manifest your power.

You may join each goddess in her sanctuary now.

NGAME

Goddess of Desire
Ashanti/Akan
Yoni Art Ritual

"What I desire desires me."

NGAME'S MESSAGE

Maaha, daughter of Mama Moon! You are a cosmic creatrix. Your desires are fulfilled.

NGAME'S STORY

Great Goddess Ngame, keeper of mysteries,
We see you. We say your name.
The herald of Ngame plays a flute; his music signals her arrival.[2] "None greater in the universe than the Triple Goddess Ngame!" he declares. We are all children of the moon.

Ngame and her lunar sisters hold hands to welcome us on a moonlit night. She has invited the moon goddesses to witness you. Yes! Goddesses Ngame of the Ashanti, Libyan Neith, Tanit of Carthage, Dahomeyan Mawu, and Atabey of the

Arawak/Taino are here. Yes! Dinka Goddess Abuk, Ala of the Igbo, and iNyangu of the Zulu are gathering.

The moon goddesses clap now, singing the Ghanaian adage, "The moon moves slowly, but it gets across the village." From new to full, each takes a turn as a different phase of Luna. The heavenly bodies dance in the moonlight, singing your name. Tell them in their newness what desires you are calling in. Tell them in their fullness what blocks you are releasing.

The wise moon mothers chant in the tongue of the Akan: "Osram mmfiti preko nntwareman." ("It takes the moon some time to go round the Earth.")

Ngame is the triple-moon goddess of the Ashanti. Every new day, this mother goddess rebirths the sun. When we were born, she shot life into us with her new moon bow. Her lunar rays give each human a soul as she stands with one foot in water and one foot on dry land.

Yes, Ngame is also the goddess of the soul, known as our kra. So, our soul is connected to the moon. If a baby is born on the full moon for the Builsa people of Ghana, an iron amulet of the moon and the moon's horns is made for the baby for luck. The horns of the moon represent in part the two crescent moons with the full moon in the middle—the triple goddess, Ngame.

When we are in tune with Mama Moon, our emotions align with and reflect hers. You must be in touch with your emotions to be in touch with your powers of creation. Opening ourselves to the moon opens us to our greatest priestess, the one inside.

If you have a moon time, pay attention to how your menstrual cycles align with Ngame, the Shining One. Do you have new moon or full moon periods? If you don't have moon time, align your energetic menstrual periods with the moon. Your energetic moon time (menstrual period) if you do not have a biological one is four to seven days beginning the first day of the new moon.

Trust your moon mind, Ngame's daughter. What does your guidance instruct you to release on the full moon? What does your guidance ask you to allow in on the new moon? Intuition is also key for conjuring. And knowing how to play and work with Mama Moon can accelerate our manifestations. You can also use your intuition for discernment. Which of the things, people, and/or experiences that you desire are really in alignment with you?

The guidance of the moon was and is key in Indigenous African cultures. Many African nations used lunar calendars, and most harvest festivals are planned around the moon. On the Akan calendar, the bosome, or month, is 28 days. Yorubaland and Igboland also had calendars based on the moon. Before their solar calendar, the ancient Egyptians also used a moon calendar. When the waning crescent moon disappeared, the new month began.[3] They called the days of a lunar month a "temple month."

Every Akan queen mother is an incarnation of Ngame.[4] All girls aspire to be like the queen mothers as soon as they enter womanhood. When Ngame's daughters have their first period, it is cause for great celebration. The six-day Bragoro must be planned! A daughter is being initiated into womanhood. A diviner is consulted to make sure the timing is right.

The girl begins with a bath, and then she sits on a stool outside her home or in a town square if there are other initiates, embodying the energy of a queen. A brass basin with adwira leaves, eggs, and dried okra fruit is placed beside her. One egg is placed in front of her, and one is placed behind her. She sits under a white or colorful umbrella to hold court. We welcome her with love into womanhood.

Let's Talk Desire

Close your eyes and think about something that you truly desire. It feels good to desire, doesn't it? You've been taught, in so many ways, that your desires are taboo or selfish. How dare you want more than what you have? But our desires cause the world to evolve. It was someone's desire that created my laptop through which I am transmitting this love letter to you. Desire birthed everything from potato chips to pacemakers. Manifesting, creation, has to start with a desire, a want, a need.

The Law of Manifestation is that you are co-creating your life with the Divine, based on your desires. There are desires we have that come from the energy of fear. The manifestations that come from those desires will usually keep you safe and small. Then there are the desires that come from the energy of love. Those will expand your consciousness and your life. When you have a desire, ask yourself if it is coming from love or fear.

You don't have to believe in the Law of Manifestation in order for it to work; that's a great thing. I can say I don't believe in gravity, right? But gravity doesn't care if I believe in it. You're not going to just start manifesting now. You're already doing it. Desire is a force for consciously manifesting and co-creating.

So begin with one desire, a desire that feels like it's the next step for you. What do you desire to manifest? Is it a small desire or a goddess desire? The word *desire* itself comes from the Latin *de sidere*, meaning "from the stars." Your desires are God/dess force in motion. It's okay to want big and small things. When I say a small desire, I'm talking about what I call LAVB, Lying Ass Vision Boards. As you most likely know, a vision board is a spiritual tool that uses images to help you manifest your desires. Many of you put together these beautiful vision boards of the material things you want. Then you present these gorgeous boards filled with wonderful things for approval.

But it's all B.S., and I call them LAVB because these things are not what you really desire. An LAVB is filled with safe objectives and surface-level goals that won't make you (or your loved ones) uncomfortable. Desire can feel scary. It is vulnerable to express desire and potentially get your heart broken when your desires aren't fulfilled. So we choose safe, puny surface-level wants.

Your true desires should turn you on, give you a juicy tingle between your legs, excite you and stretch what you believe is possible. Give the Divine the opening to dream the biggest dream for you by dreaming the biggest dream for yourself.

So what do you really desire? What's your big magical goddess vision? I was inspired by the term "BHAG" or "Big Hairy Audacious Goals" from the book *Built to Last* to call our real desires our BMGV, Big Magical Goddess Vision. In this book, business growth experts Jim Collins and Jerry Porras introduce the concept of BHAGs as a way to align with your highest purpose.

So what is your BMGV for your life? Your BMGV should titillate you. It should also scare you a little and make you feel uncomfortable. Allow yourself to stretch what you believe is possible for you.

If there was a movie of you enjoying the success of your BMGV, what would we see? Imagine a scene from your desire turned manifestation. Describe it in detail. Pick one scene. Maybe it's you buying your dream house, giving birth, making a speech, or opening a shop. If, for example, you desire a soul mate relationship, what do you see in your movie? Maybe it's you and your partner, happy on a beach, having the best convo ever.

Use your imagination. Our imagination is where we create and envision. See your BMGV movie clip (visualization) and go through your senses: seeing, hearing, smelling, feeling, and tasting. *Do you see someone handing you keys? Do you hear people clapping for you? Do you smell newborn baby poop? Do you feel a hug from your estranged relative? Do you taste breakfast made by your beloved?*

Let's switch perspectives on your BMGV movie clip of your desire. Now see it from your point of view. Don't see yourself in the movie. See it through your eyes as you live it. When you think of a memory, unless you're watching a video, you don't see yourself. See the scene from your POV as a memory that already happened.

Answer in your Goddess Soulbook:

- *Describe your BMGV movie scene. Make it detailed and juicy.*

- *Why do you desire this? Be specific.*

- *How do you want to feel when your manifestation is a success?*

- *Why do you believe this is possible?*

HOW TO HONOR GODDESS NGAME

When you honor Goddess Ngame, you honor your own desires. You may choose to honor this energy inside yourself or invoke her energy according to your own tradition.

To honor the goddess in you: "Like the moon, we go through phases," as the meme goes. Everything is a phase. Our bodies go through phases. Our emotions go through phases. The day goes through phases. Seasons go through phases. Our desires go through phases. Honor your current phase by getting still, surrendering, and witnessing the moment.

Know that this, too, shall pass. Everything is temporary. The good, the bad, the ugly—it is all temporary. Just like we are. Let that light a fire under your booty to get you into the business of living. How can you honor your desires and honor the phase you are in?

Symbols: The triple moon, bow and arrow, and menstruation

Colors: Her colors are white and silver.

Auspicious times: Monthly full and crescent moons

Music: "Yeah I'm A Goddess" by afua danso and "Orange Moon" by Erykah Badu

Suggested offerings: Yams, adwira leaves, eggs, and dried okra fruit; anything moon related

Alternate names: N'game, The Shining One

Traditional Desire Ritual: Kunkuma Menstrual Broom

The broom is a spiritual tool, still used in rituals today, to sweep away bad energy and bad luck. When you sweep away what you don't want, there is room for your desires to manifest. To free yourself from a situation, maybe you need kunkuma.

In Ashanti culture, a suman is a magical charm created to protect you in difficult situations. They were traditionally blessed by a healer. The kunkuma (also called kankama) is a protective suman made from an old broom and menstrual blood.[5] Basically, it is a menstrual manifesting broom.

An old household broom is used because it has already made contact with dirt, representing the problems of the world. This makes it more potent. It should always be washed, and a menstrual pad or blood is hidden in between the bristles. It could also be brushed with eggs and sacrificial blood from a chicken. The owner then speaks words of power into the kunkuma, specifying exactly what they want to be protected from.[6]

Akom, the Akan religion, is the Twi word for "prophecy." The Ashanti are an Akan people. My Ashanti teacher was sharing the power of plantain leaves with me, as a sacred manifestation tool. I said, "I thought you said today we were going to talk about predicting the future." He was confused. He said, "We are. You predict the future by creating it."

Your Desire Ritual: Yoni Art Masterpiece

Ritual intention: To step out of your creative comfort zone and remember that you are art.

You can do this ritual in your Goddess Soulbook, as a piece for your wall, or cut it out as an amulet to add to your goddess altar. Or you may wish to do all three.

You are sacred geometry. This is your personal patipemba, firma, sigil, your vévé, Adinkra, pontos riscados, your homage to the goddess that is you.

Special note for this and all art rituals in this book: You are creating this work for your own personal power and healing. It is not about being an artist, even though you are, and it is not about being perfect, even though you are.

You will need:

- Your Goddess Soulbook

- Pencil

- Markers or crayons

- Feel free to include any creative items you can imagine, from flower petals to tiny crystals.

What to do:

Prepare your ritual space. You may wish to take a sacred bath and adorn yourself. Disrobe.

Sitting in front of a mirror, draw your beautiful yoni. Put your desires and that energy into this piece. Your drawing can be literal or abstract. It is up to you. Afterward feel free to adorn your artwork if you wish. Use your colorful art tools and have fun. There is no way to get this wrong. A woman I went to grad school with did yoni paintings with her menstrual blood. She was an artist, and so are you:

Answer in your Goddess Soulbook

- *What do you want to say to your yoni?*

- *What does your yoni want to say to you?*

- *What does your yoni desire?*

MODJADJI

Goddess of Manifestation
Balobedu/South Africa
Water Whisperer Ritual

"Divine blessings flow to me so easily."

MODJADJI'S MESSAGE

Dumela, daughter! I see you. You are a rainmaker, shape-shifter, an alchemist, a sorceress. May the Universe rain down blessings upon you forevermore. May we always make it rain upon you!

MODJADJI'S STORY

Great Goddess Modjadji, keeper of mysteries,
We see you. We say your name.

Meet Goddess Modjadji, alchemist extraordinaire, mother of the clouds and rain, she who can control the weather. Without the gift of rain there can be no life.

Rainmaking queen Modjadji is the living personification of a deity. Yes, this goddess is embodied by a human person who is considered to be immortal. All rain queens incarnate the spirit of Modjadji. Rain rituals are aimed toward the ancestors, who intercede on behalf of us mere mortals.

Modjadji is the hereditary rain queen of South Africa's Balobedu people, a matrilineal queendom for about 500 years. This monarchy is still active today. Only the firstborn daughter of the last rain queen can inherit the throne. This is the only royal lineage we are aware of that has had only women monarchs. Modjadji is considered to be the earthly representative of the rain goddess. If it rains the day she is born, she has extra powers.

Modjadji is considered both male and female, thus she needs no one else to reproduce.[7] The rain queen is not permitted to take a husband. This prevents any man's claim to her children or the throne. The man who is her shadow husband may visit her only under cover of night. The queen is, however, allowed to take wives from the royal family. These wives handle her personal chores, as she can only be seen by royal persons in nonceremonial times.[8]

Modjadji, the rain queen of this all-women dynasty, is a fertility goddess, linked to manifesting the richness of the land. She nourishes the parched. Rain helps make something—crops—out of nothing. This is natural magic, sorcery, alchemy. Rain cleanses us, purifies us, and feeds us by making the produce grow. Without rain, the land goes dry and we starve.

As we will see when we meet with the Yoruba goddess Oya, rain can create or destroy. Oya is the personification of the superhero Storm. But hold on to your umbrella! The rain queen is Storm's direct inspiration.

Modjadji queens are only recently able to appear in public, and they only speak publicly through a specially blessed intermediary. This queenship originated in the region of Zimbabwe.[9] It is said that Shaka Zulu asked for a blessing from the Modjadji of his time. Queen Modjadji V was friends with Nelson Mandela.

So how does the rain queen make rain? Modjadji lives in a lush valley of rare, sacred cycad trees called Modjadji's cycad or Modjadji's palm. Obviously, she has many secrets. But she manifests from reverence and gratitude, never despair. Specific rain queens have powers like clouds, streams, mists, and drizzles. Modjadji is seen as a part of the agricultural cycle. She may be assisted by a rain doctor. If rain does not come, the people approach her with gifts of cattle heads and dancers. During times of extreme drought, which is common in their region, they beat the graves of the ancestors.

Let's Talk Manifestation

The Law of Manifestation is the knowingness that you, like everything else on our planet, are magnetic—like attracts like—and you have the power to co-create worlds. Now notice the word *co-create*. Manifesting is a spiritual law, but it's only one spiritual law of many. So you are a part of co-creation with your Creator.

In Ngame's sanctuary (the last section), you activated a desire that we are calling your BMGV, Big Magical Goddess Vision. So it is time to make a high-vibe request. Yes, you have your desire; now you must ask for it!

Everything has energy. So what's the energetic frequency, the àse, of having your desire versus the frequency of not having your desire? What is the energy of seeing your BMGV? The energy of that juicy little movie you imagined didn't feel desperate, like "I've got to have it or I'm going to die," right? No, it felt natural. Close your eyes and see it again now.

It feels good, not desperate, right? We assume, *I've got to prove to God/dess how badly I want it through urgent, relentless begging.* But desperation is a manifestation repellent.

Create a high-vibrating asking ceremony to ask the Divine for what you want. It can be on a new moon, which is about inviting in the new. Or it can be on a full moon, which is about letting go of what doesn't serve you anymore. Make it solemn, fun, or high energy. It can be in a park, your home, or the ocean. Whatever works for you. This is your ask.

Say your version of *"Thank you,* Mother-Father-God, for giving me this thrilling desire. I am grateful for the gift of this day. I come to you as your daughter with my arms open wide to receive. I am asking for something that not only will make my life better but will also make the world better. I am here to ask you for this wonderful blessing. I thank you in advance for hearing me, seeing me, loving me. I see it. I receive it. I am so grateful."

That's what asking looks like for me, but asking for you may look different. It may look like watching a movie about your desire. It may look like lighting candles and praying at your altar. It may look like gluing intentions on a vision board. Just make it a beautiful ceremony for yourself.

Ask in a high-vibe manner, then celebrate the àse, life-force-energy feeling of having it. Find a manifestation song that celebrates what you are inviting in and dance to it. Moving your body is high vibe. That's why so many spiritual practices include dancing, swaying, swirling. See your highest self and then start showing up as her.

What are you manifesting right now? Wait—don't tell me yet! There is power in secrecy when it comes to your personal manifestation magic. Use the gift of discernment when deciding what to share with whom. When we are not grounded enough in our own beliefs, our manifestations can be dislodged by the beliefs of others. You don't need everyone's energy in your creations. Secrecy is powerful goddess juju. Protect your magic.

HOW TO HONOR GODDESS MODJADJI

When you honor Goddess Modjadji, you honor your manifesting power. You may choose to honor this energy inside yourself or invoke her energy according to your own tradition.

To honor the goddess in you: Allow your blessings to flow. Rainmakers make it rain. Modjadji is recognized as royalty by the South African government. If you could snap your fingers to shift something personal instantly, what would it be? Celebrate your power to create wondrous things by making a list of your biggest manifestations that you have already co-created.

Symbols: Modjadji's private gardens are lush with cycad trees. Other national symbols to celebrate her include the queen protea flower, the real yellowwood tree, the springbok antelope, the galjoen fish, and the blue crane bird.

Colors: Her colors are gold, orange, red, and white.

Auspicious times: Modjadji's annual ceremony is held every October or November, springtime in the region.

Music: "Modjadji" by Sello Chicco Twala and "Rain Child" by Neith Sankofa and Ascended Breath

Suggested offerings: A bowl of fresh rainwater on your goddess altar or dancing in the rain

Alternate names: Mujaji, Mudjadji, Modjaji, Modhadje, Transformer of Clouds

Traditional Manifestation Ritual: Raindancing

Rainmaking is a time-honored tradition in the motherland. With drought being a threat faced often, this is serious business. The intention is to celebrate the rain, giving it gratitude for being already present.

When there is a rain queen on the Balobedu throne, the annual rainmaking ceremony takes place in November. The rain queen is a sorceress. She leads the community rain-manifesting ritual, but everyone from the youngest to the oldest takes part. Modjadji leads rain prayers at five different shrines over five different weekends. She also has a dithugula (ancestral amulet), secret rain charms, and sacred beads.

There are sacred rainmaking songs and dances. Oh, the dances! One of the many mystical rituals is a rain dance of women elders with women drummers. These women wear colorful cloaks embossed with tiny mirrors. Mirrors represent water.

Raindancing is a key part of weather shifting throughout the continent. A rain dance can be performed by one or many. As making the skies fertile with water is a fertility rite, rain dancers are often women. In many traditions the dancers are women elders, who have already given birth many times.

Symbolism is powerful juju. They don't pray for rain; they pray as rain. Some rain dancers wear black to symbolize black clouds pregnant with water. Drums, rattle instruments, and leg rattles emulate the sound of falling rain and thunder. The dancers match the melodic rhythms of rain. "Making it rain" takes on a bigger meaning.

Your Manifestation Ritual: Water Whisperer

Ritual intention: To birth for what you want by harnessing the creation power of water.

Water whispering is an ancient art. Manifesting is your natural state. The purpose of this water-drinking and bath ritual is to clear negative energy and vibrations that may be blocking you.

Water is a conduit. We are made of water. We came here in water. Water is life. People don't remember why we throw coins in fountains for luck. It was a sacrifice to the water spirits.

I know the art of water whispering as Caribbean magic. But, sis! Last night, I dreamed for seven hours straight about water whisperers worldwide, knowing I would be writing this. This is ancient global granny wisdom, known and used by my Ashanti ancestors and healers known as "Whisperers" in Belarus.

The cleansing bath is a saltwater bath. Salt water, from our tears to the ocean, cleanses. Hammams in Morocco use salt to clear away jinni, malevolent spirits. Salt floors and walls are a part of the purification process. Salt is used for energetic and physical exfoliation.

You can use Dead Sea salt, table salt, black sea salt, Himalayan sea salt. There are some great South African and Kalahari Desert salts, but those may be hard to get.

Note: If you have health issues that require you to limit salt, leave the salt out of this ritual.

You will need:

- A glass
- Drinking water
- Salt of your choice
- Cleansing plant: seaweed or basil
- Protective plants: mint or hyssop
- Bathtub
- Oil of your choice

What to do:

Part 1: Prepare Water to Drink

Prepare your ritual space. Begin by whisper-charging your drinking water. Here's how: Pour three glasses of water, one after the other. Whisper your gratitude, fears, and desires into them as indicated below. Whisper these words:

First glass: (Past: Surrender your fears.)

My Creator, I am your daughter, the beloved.

Thank you for protecting me from _____.

Àse.

Dispose of the water. Do not drink it.

Second glass: (Present: Give thanks.)

My Creator, I am your daughter, the beloved.

Thank you for blessing me with _____.

Àse.

Dispose of the water. Do not drink it.

Third glass: (Future: Call in your desires.)

My Creator, I am your daughter, the beloved.

I am so grateful now for _____.

Àse.

Drink the water and enjoy it.

Part 2: Prepare Your "May I Be Cleansed" Bath

Note: Take a shower before for physical grime. This is a soaking bath for spiritual, mental, and emotional grime.

Mix and macerate the fresh herbs and salt in a basin or bucket of warm water. Fresh herbs will be easier to strain. Give thanks and speak to Spirit as you rip and prepare the herbs. Whisper-charge the ingredients with your intentions. Let the cleansing water sit for 90 minutes or overnight.

Fill your bathtub and add the salt of your choice. Add the basin or bucket of cleansing water. Whisper-charge the bath-water with your prayers.

Get in. Pray. Meditate. Give thanks. Thank the ingredients, the rain, the ocean, and even your bathwater, for abundance. Stay in it for 12 to 18 minutes. This is to cleanse your energy.

Dispose of the leaves at the crossroads of your understanding, and never look back.

MA'AT

Goddess of Giving and Receiving
Egypt
Goddess Intention Incense Ritual

"I give easily and freely. I receive freely and easily."

MA'AT'S MESSAGE

Dua Netjer en-etj, beloved! The scales say advance and retreat, ebb and flow, give and receive. Are you in the flow? Seek your own harmony. You can only create what you align with.

MA'AT'S STORY

Great Goddess Ma'at, keeper of mysteries,
We see you. We say your name.
Shhh . . . The winged goddess of justice hears all in the silence.

Goddess Ma'at is the embodiment of the Egyptian concept of truth, justice, and balance. Ma'at is a person and a principle. Her name means "order" as her father Ra, the sun god, rose out of chaos and put her in charge of it. She charts the course that the sun follows across the sky.

Everything was either of Ma'at or not, meaning "of order" or "of disorder." *Ma'at* also means "that which is straight,"[10] which in my New Yorkese I translate to mean "straight up." So if I tell you, "I am just keeping it Ma'at," that means I am keeping it 100, straight up.

Ma'at shows up as a winged woman wearing an ostrich's feather in her hair. An ostrich feather is identical on all sides. This unique symmetry represents balance and justice. In the afterlife, Anubis, wolf-headed god and Guardian of the Scales, uses Ma'at's feather of truth to weigh souls in the Weighing of the Heart ceremony.[11] Our souls are in our hearts. Ma'at's feather goes on one side of the scale, a person's heart on the other. Living an amoral and unethical life weighs down your heart and soul. So, is your heart as light as a feather?

To be deemed worthy of an afterlife in the heavenly Field of Reeds, the newly deceased affirm their morality by going through the Declaration of Innocence, the 42 Negative Confessions in the Hall of Two Truths or Hall of Ma'at.

The Assessors of Ma'at are the 42 deities that hear the Negative Confessions of the dead. Fail this test and be devoured by crocodile goddess Ammit. Pass and ascend to the Kingdom of Asar (Osiris). This is how the goddess of harmony and alignment regulates chaos.

The deceased and judged testify to reverse commandments including:

- *I have not committed sin.*

- *I have not committed robbery with violence.*

- *I have not slain men or women.*

- *I have not swindled offerings.*

- *I have not stolen from God/Goddess.*

- *I have not told lies.*

Ma'at also incarnates as the Eye of Ra. Remember, Ra is her dad. As the Eye of Ra, she is sent out to maintain order but does so by violent means. Her life-affirming aspect was celebrated, and her aggressive and potentially destructive aspect was used to protect and maintain control. Two halves of the same whole, harmony and balance, seemingly positive and seemingly negative.

Ma'at showed up with an ankh in each hand. An ankh is the ancient Egyptian symbol for life. You can also see ankhs in many temple drawings with other gods and goddesses, such as Iset (Isis) and Ma'at's mother, Hathor. Often the ankh is being held to the lips of royalty, living and dead. As the symbol of life, the ankh was giving the breath of regeneration for the new life after this one. Their frequency was being shifted for ascension.

Let's Talk Giving and Receiving

Giving and receiving is spiritual law. To be in harmony you must do both exuberantly. If you receive gleefully without giving, you are selfish and out of alignment. If you give gleefully without receiving, you are stuck in martyrdom and out of alignment. Neither is good for your well-being and manifesting your life.

How do you want to serve? Service should be a regular part of your earth assignment. You can give time, money, resources, or just good vibes. If you don't have anything physical to give, send people silent blessings when you meet them. My mother cultivated a culture of giving in our family. She gives freely to her siblings, family, friends, whomever. To this day, sometimes I don't compliment her earrings because she will tell me to take them! She sent barrels back home and also gives to charities. She taught me that even when it seems you don't have much, your life is richer when you give.

Giving and receiving is spellwork. The interesting thing about this spiritual law is that giving enriches your soul and your pockets. Whenever I notice that my finances are stagnant, I give even more. I know that's the opposite of what you may think you need to do. But tightening your purse strings signals to your subconscious mind (and the Universe) that you are in a state of lack. Give! Hide dollar bills at the bus stop with notes saying, "You are loved." Pay for the next person at the tollbooth or coffee shop. Go to a crowdfunding site and invest in someone's dream.

Receiving is a feminine-energy principle that makes many of us uncomfortable. You may be a generous giver and have trouble receiving. I bought some candles for a friend and she said, "Oh no! I don't have anything to give you." I wasn't expecting anything. I bought the candles because I knew she would enjoy them. That's it.

How can you actively receive? You must cultivate a practice of receiving. Receive compliments, joy, friendship, money, and love. It is all the same energetically to Spirit. When you receive something, even if it is a dollar you find on the ground, immerse yourself in the feeling of gratitude and abundance. Talk it up. Revel in it. Exclaim, "Yes, thank you!! More of this, please! I love receiving. This is natural to me." This is how we raise our vibration for receiving and make room for more energetically!

Sacrifices and offerings are an important part of our spirituality. Energy cannot be created or destroyed, only transferred. So if you need the energy for something, it must come from somewhere else. Tithing and blood are a part of almost every tradition. Sacrifices and offerings are, most importantly, an act of gratitude. Intention is everything.

Write in your Goddess Soulbook: *I give and receive easily and effortlessly.*

HOW TO HONOR GODDESS MA'AT

When you honor Goddess Ma'at, you honor your commitment to giving and receiving. You may choose to honor this energy inside yourself or invoke her energy according to your own tradition.

To honor the goddess in you: What would it feel like to give and receive freely? As above, so below, as within, so without, as the Universe, so the soul. If you are living with Ma'at, you are in alignment, harmony, and balance with your own truth. Breathe in what it feels like to be divinely in tune with your truth. Tell the truth. Truth enriches the giver and receiver.

Symbols: The ankh, ostrich feather, scales, the Eye of Ra, the heart, and the Was-scepter

Colors: Her colors are black and white.

Auspicious times: The equinoxes, when there are almost equal hours of day and night

Music: "Maat" by Sona Jobarteh and "Ma'at (Each Man)" by Jah9

Suggested offerings: Ma'at loves all feathers, but a white ostrich feather is her favorite.

Alternate names: Mayet, Eye of Ra

Traditional Giving and Receiving Ritual: Ethiopian Healing Scrolls

Traditional Ethiopian magic made it into their Abrahamic religious traditions. Ethiopian scrolls are used for spellcasting, prayer, healing, and manifesting. These scrolls are a devotional, magical, and often medical energy exchange of giving and receiving between the priest and the person seeking assistance. Healing is given and must be received.

From start to finish, ancient Ethiopian healing scrolls had a magical ritual creation process. First, goats were sacrificed in a sacred manner to create vellum, parchment, from goatskin. The colored inks, ornate borders, geometric designs, and other visual effects are part of the sacred magic too. The decorations are visual spellcasting. They included protective drawings of angels like a multi-armed archangel Michael.

These artistic scrolls were constructed by debteras, who are not ordained by the Ethiopian Orthodox Christian Church, but ordained Spirit. Many people still prefer visits with the highly trained clerics and their ancestral gifts. Debteras are wise healers who prepare amulets and also provide divination.

The original Ethiopian magic scrolls were enchanted handbooks written in Ge'ez, which was not an easily accessible language. Healing scrolls were long, often made to the height of the patient. The scrolls were stored rolled up, while the books took a form recognizable to us today. They could make the seeker stronger, be protective, or provide healing.

Touching the scrolls or pages ignites the power. The scroll itself is considered magic. They may be worn around the neck in an amulet as an ongoing prayer or carried in a leather pouch as a charm or talisman. Some spells were repurposed, but for people of means, they were/are custom created.

Remember back in Great Ancestress Marie Laveau's sanctuary (Chapter 2) when we discussed nkisi spirits and mojo bags? It is believed that images on these scrolls are also capable of direct action. In other words, the drawing of the angel doesn't represent the angel but is the angel. The eyes act as a magical portal to transfer energy. With this form of magic, incantations could be written on someone's body, and they could lick them off as a part of the ritual. The healing parchment could be soaked in water, and the practitioner could drink the liquid. There was also string magic, using knots to bind demons.

In addition to expected texts like a magic star book and *The Magical Book of Mary and the Angels*, there were love spell handbooks like the *Erotic Spell of Cyprian of Antioch*.

Your Giving and Receiving Ritual: Goddess Intention Incense

Ritual intention: To create a sacred incense to lift up your intentions, giving them to Spirit and preparing you to receive your joy.

Ready to make your own Goddess Incense? Incense has been used for millennia as a spiritual tool. In ancient cultures, incense was an offering for the gods. The rising smoke helps deliver your prayers to the Divine. In some traditions, the smoke is a wake-up alert for Spirit. Some people read the smoke as divination. The scent of the incense may also enhance its therapeutic properties.

Ancient Egyptians used cinnamon to make their temple incense, Kyphi, for both spiritual and medicinal purposes. Cinnamon was also an important ingredient in their perfumes. Considered holy, they even used it to prepare the dead for the afterlife. Cinnamon is a staple in Ethiopian foods and many other cultures.

You will create incense cones that are sealed with your intentions. Cinnamon opens us up for psychic connection and awareness, protects us from negative energy, and heats up cold situations. You will find cinnamon in many of our goddess rituals. It activates almost any intention, from love to money. When doing sacred work, cinnamon is an accelerant.

You will need:

- Cinnamon powder
- Water

What to do:

Prepare your ritual space. Put 13 teaspoons of cinnamon powder in a bowl, which should result in a yield of about 13 incense cones. Slowly add water to your mix. You can add it by the teaspoon to be safe. You are aiming for the consistency of wet, packed earth, not mud. If you add too much water, add in a little more cinnamon to counteract it. Thank the ingredients and speak words of positivity and love into them.

Knead and mold it together. As you do this, speak your intentions out loud in third person—for example, "Nia is so happy and successful. She is having fun and serving her community as a wonderful loctician, and customers always come back for her healing hair oils. Her loving family is healthy and thriving."

Scoop out each spoon and shape it into a small cone. Pack each one tightly.

Let it dry for 3 days, then turn each on its side so that the bottom can dry too. Let it dry for 2 more days and you did it!

Burning your incense for the first time: Note that it may take much longer to get burning than commercial incense. That's okay. Once it finally starts burning it will be fine. Now that you know how to do this, you can customize your personal Goddess Intention Incense with additional spices, herbs, and oils to your liking next time.

Sit and meditate or journal with your Goddess Intention Incense burning. See what comes up for you.

Record your process and experience in your Goddess Soulbook.

TANIT

Goddess of Pleasure
Tunisia
Sacred Erotic Magic Ritual

"It feels good to feel good."

TANIT'S MESSAGE

Nharek taieb, daughter! When the stars are bright and life is confusion, do you dream my story? I dream of you healed, happy, and whole. Peace be yours. Pleasure be yours. You are made of laughter and stardust. Allow yourself the pleasure that is your birthright.

TANIT'S STORY

Great Goddess Tanit, keeper of mysteries,
We see you. We say your name.
"If the full moon loves you, why worry about the stars?" they ask in Tunisia. And they would know. Tanit guides both the moon and the stars.

Tanit was the goddess of the stars in ancient Carthage, home of Hannibal, modern-day Tunisia, North Africa. She was often depicted with a crescent moon over her

104

head. All matters of the night sky fall into Tanit's domain: the moon, the stars, and dreams. Today, all the way over in Ibiza, they still have pleasure-filled, full-moon, midnight table-dancing parties to celebrate the African goddess Tanit.

As supreme goddess, Tanit represents protective motherhood, fertility, dance, and prosperity. In 300 B.C. her face was on the coins of Carthage. The night sky is her domain. Tanit has been associated with Akan triple-moon goddess Ngame, who we just met, Greek goddess Astarte, Egyptian goddess Neith, and Mesopotamian goddess Ishtar.

The hamsa hand is a protective symbol meaning "the hand of God." The hamsa was originally the Hand of Tanit. It often is designed with an all-seeing eye on it to ward off the evil eye and bad juju. Tanit's protection symbol has since been adopted by many different beliefs. It is also known as the Hand of Mary or Hand of Fatima in Abrahamic religions.

Tanit is the goddess of pleasure and making dreams come true. Her magic most likely also governed the ancient spellwork known as "curse tablets"—magical texts written with invocations and secret names to bring about an enemy's downfall or gain control of a situation. A clerk or a scribe would scratch a person's desires onto thin pieces of lead in tiny letters. The lead pieces were then nailed, rolled, or folded and buried underground. Some held love spells and were created with a doll that resembled that person's loved one.[12]

The Tuareg cross was called the Sign of Tanit. This cross is the symbol of prayer and surrender, with open arms like the ankh. Tanit's symbol was unearthed throughout the ruins of Carthage. Tanit's Oracle at Carthage rivaled the famous Oracle at Delphi, devoted to the Greek god Apollo. At these oracles, guidance is relayed from the deity to a priestess for interpretation.

Tanit finds pleasure in pomegranates, a mother goddess symbol. Tanit was also referred to as the Face of Baal. Baal Hammon was a deity of fruits and vegetables. This much-loved goddess was mistakenly associated with child sacrifice by archaeologists, as she is the guardian and protector of a children's cemetery and there was such a high rate of child mortality.[13] Thankfully that has been debunked. Tanit remains a goddess of many mysteries.

Let's Talk Pleasure

Pleasure is a creative force. We've been taught that the word itself is illicit and decadent. *Pleasure.* The dictionary says that pleasure is "a feeling of happy satisfaction and enjoyment." We'll take that! So why is that so forbidden?

Women's pleasure, like our desire, threatens patriarchal order. When we know true joy and pleasure, why would we accept anything less? A life without pleasure is not worth living. The capacity to laugh, feel orgasmic joy, and feel good is holy. Whether it is the simple pleasure of smelling your favorite flower essence or eating a meal that makes you squeal, pleasure is our gift from the Universe.

Our Goddess Temple Circle sister Antranette Doe channels the energy of pleasure in her healing work. If you happen to see a gorgeous, curvy queen posting erotic poetry and sensual self-portraits on social media, it's probably Goddess Antranette. Antranette is an Omo Oshun priestess and womb wellness practitioner. She helps her sister-clients find feminine wholeness through sensual energy, sacred sexuality, and womb alchemy. She also does yoni divination and earth-yoni Reiki. The energy of the pelvic bowl and the organs it holds guide the spiritual clearing. Our bodies are powerful!

Goddess Antranette says that being seen and expressing her erotica is an "ongoing offering to my yoni soul." The pleasure queen's self-care practices include "solo-sex magic, yoni breathing, and womb breathing." Do not underestimate the power of the guidance that can come from your own creation energy channel. This work helped Goddess Antranette through the unthinkable. She reveals, "The absolute most difficult challenge that I had to overcome was the birth and passing of my last child. I faced this through my sensual womb practice, welcoming support, the deep love and creative energy of my husband, and my ancestral traditions." Pleasure can be a healing force.

HOW TO HONOR GODDESS TANIT

When you honor Goddess Tanit, you honor the power of your pleasure. You may choose to honor this energy inside yourself or invoke her energy according to your own tradition.

To honor the goddess in you: Get your full-moon, midnight dance on to embrace this energy. If you can have a full-moon dance party with your goddess sisters, even better. How can you make more room for pleasure?

Symbols: Tanit has three famous totems: the hamsa, the Tuareg cross, and the Sign of Tanit, a triangular woman figure with arms open in prayer and the moon above her. Her symbols also include triangles, palm trees, and doves. Tanit coins are potent. She was sometimes depicted with wings or a lion's head.

Colors: Her colors are purple and midnight blue.

Auspicious times: Nighttime, full moons

Music: "Goddess Code" by Lizzy Jeff and "PYNK" by Janelle Monáe

Suggested offerings: Fish, grapes, or pomegranates

Alternate names: Tanat, Tanith, Tinith, Tinnit, Lady of the Moon and Stars, She Who Nourishes, the Heavenly Goddess, Dea Caelestis

Traditional Pleasure Ritual: Erotic Binding Spells

Ancient Egyptians were not above using their heka, magic, to cast love and sex spells. Several spells, which they considered magic recipes, have been uncovered on papyrus. In one spell dated from between the 1st and 2nd century A.D., a woman named Taromeway wants to bind a man named Kephalas. An Egyptologist called it a "sexual compulsion spell."

Taromeway also uses a bit of vision boarding in casting her spell. Either she or her priestess drew Anubis, the patron god of helpless people and lost souls, on the spell. In the drawing, the wolf-headed Anubis shoots an arrow of lust, similar to Cupid's, into a naked Kephalas with emphasized genitals.[14]

Clearly, she wants this man to be in a state of constant craving for her. Taromeway also summoned a spirit that may be an ancestor to help her capture Kephalas's heart. Taromeway is a pseudonym to protect her identity, just in case the spell got out. Well, okay, sis!

Here is a basic translation of the incantation:

Noble spirit of the man of the necropolis, find Kephalas

Give to him anxiety at midday, evening, and at all times

Until Kephalas seeks Taromeway in lustful desire

Until his male organs pursue her female organs

Taromeway may have then placed the spell in the tomb of the spirit she invoked.15

Another more intense love spell was found in Oxyrhynchus, Egypt. This one was engraved on copper, and the name of the target was left blank for the caster to fill in. The instructions state to burn a series of offerings in the bathhouse, so it may have been a spiritual bath. The writer calls on Gnostic gods, popular at the time.

The Gnostic tradition incorporated Christianity, so it mentioned demons, which I will omit, as that is definitely not a part of our practice. The spell says offerings should be made.[16]

Here is the incantation that the spell says to write on the bathhouse walls:
I adjure you, earth and waters,
by the [god] who dwells on you and
(I adjure) the fortune of this bath so that,
as you blaze and burn and flame,
so burn her (the person targeted)
whom (the mother of the person targeted) bore,
until they come to me . . .
Holy names, inflame in this way
and burn the heart of (the person targeted) . . .
until (the person targeted) falls in love with (the person casting the spell).

Your Pleasure Ritual: Sacred Erotic Magic

Ritual intention: To harness the power of sacred sexuality and self-pleasure to manifest your desires.

Sexual alchemy and transmutation are ancient heka. Sex is a creation practice. Sex magick is as old as time. How do you think we got here? This is energy alignment. This pleasure practice is making love to yourself.

Your erotic energy is powerful. If you have a clitoris, you have the only body part on human beings that exists solely for pleasure. There is a reason why most athletes are restricted from having sex before a game or match. They need their creative manifesting-energy force on the field.

Orgasm makes most people feel powerful and confident. This is creative energy. The rush from the feel-good hormones released, such as serotonin and dopamine, brings you to the frequency of creation. For many people, orgasm is the only way to reach altered states of ecstasy without artificial substances. This brings new meaning to high vibe, right?

Masturbation manifestation works in part because it removes the resistance.

Some scientists estimate that the subconscious mind is at least 90 percent of our brains.[17] This ritual bypasses our fear reflexes and speaks directly to the subconscious.

You will need:

- YOU!
- Your yoni art (from Ngame's sanctuary)
- Your BMGV
- Music that represents your BMGV

What to do:

Prepare your ritual space. This self-pleasure practice is potent to do on the new or waxing moon, but you can do it anytime. Play music that reflects the lyrics of your BMGV.

You can do this solo or with a partner, with a toy or without. When you are having sex you are merging energy fields with a partner. So you can absolutely do this manifesting process with someone. I advise you to do it solo first. It's just two different kinds of manifestation.

You are in the Temple of Conjurers. Conjurers get what they want, right? Manifestation requires us to match the vibration and frequency of the things we desire. Manifesting also requires us to be in a receptive state.

Pull out your yoni art. You created your yoni art to represent your vision, your Big Magical Goddess Vision. Look at it and see how the magic of your vision is embedded in it. Visualize it surrounded by the color gold. Remind yourself of your vision: What do you want to manifest and why? How do you want to feel?

Your orgasm is sexual spirit energy. Repeat mantras while you orgasm.

Ready, set, go for it!

Record your experience in your Goddess Soulbook.

THE SEVEN SISTERS

Goddesses of Creativity
New Orleans
BMGV Vision Doll Ritual

"I am a creative visionary."

SEVEN SISTERS' MESSAGE

Where y'at, baby girl?! Spirit has messages for you. You are a divine nation within one woman. Use the tools you have been gifted to access your creativity. You come from seers. Your blood remembers.

SEVEN SISTERS' STORY

Great Goddesses Seven Sisters, keeper of mysteries,
We see you. We say your name.
You're not seeing double, triple, or even quadruple.
The Seven Sisters were a famous family of identical master psychics and Hoodoo sisters who could help anyone get what they needed. . . but were they?

Local N'awlins lore tells a different story. Yes, you could absolutely go to the Seven Sisters for your spiritual needs, but that is all that is certain about the story. No one is quite sure whether the Seven Sisters were one woman or seven. If there were indeed seven women, were they actually related? If it was one woman, was she pretending to be the other women, or shape-shifting using her magical powers? NOLA is one of the best secret-keeping cities out there, so we may never know.

The Seven Sisters never aged. Ask around and folks will tell you that they seemed like they were in their 20s for decades. Legend has it that they owned seven identical homes on the 2300 block of Coliseum Street. The lineage of the Seven Sisters is all over New Orleans, with stores, businesses, and products named after them one hundred years after their reign.

Let's look closer. Some say the Seven Sisters were one Ms. Ida Carter of Alabama.[18] Ms. Ida says she received her calling to do rootwork when she was only seven years old. There are many misconceptions about what Hoodoo is. Hoodoo is the African-originated, spirit-centered, American-born art and magical science of healing, rootwork, conjure, and protection.

In all of her wisdom, Ms. Ida received clear guidance on how to do a Hoodoo self-initiation. She burned seven candles all night starting on the first of May. For seven years she repeated this process on May Day. She said that on her 14th year of life, 7th year of the initiation ritual, she was reborn as a conjure woman named Seven Sisters. Others say differently.

Blues singer John T. "Funny Paper" Smith must've been happy with her/them, whatever the case was. He sang their conjuring praises around 1930 in a song called "Seven Sisters Blues," asking them for their help in ruling the world.[19]

Let's Talk Creativity

How creative are you willing to allow yourself to be? Do you dare to step out of your comfort zone and into your creative fertility? I hear it often: "I'm not creative." "If only I were creative."

We already established that you have the power that creates worlds, so you are incredibly creative. So what might that mean for you? Maybe that means painting, baking, dancing, or something that you never did before. It may mean writing, singing, or reclaiming your voice with poetry.

Write in your Goddess Soulbook: *I honor my creativity.*

With so much grief energy in 2020, I needed to play and create to honor my creativity and heal my womb energy channel. I got back into my visual art practice, sketching with charcoals. Birthing this book is also an act of loving creativity and sacred fertility. I also delved deep into playing instruments for sound healing. Plus I'm making time for the divine sacred rebirthing sessions I do for others and having fun with cooking.

Sacred fertility is about creation, creativity, and birthing your magic. What is it that you love to do? Where can your creative expression shine? Hair braiding? Cooking? Sculpting? Jewelry making? Coding? Scrapbooking? Quilting?

Women's craft work throughout generations has been belittled and looked down upon. Maybe, like my mom, one of your artistic mediums is your green thumb and gorgeous garden. Make your creativity a part of your daily self-care practice.

One of the most healing things you can do to awaken your creativity is play. Do you have a sacred play practice? What makes you feel like a kid again? I'm talking about coloring books, crayons, Play-Doh, jump roping, knitting, skating, dancing—play!

If your creativity has just been dormant and stagnant, play will wake it up. Creating is birthing, is manifesting, is pleasure. It's all different faces of the same energy. Play is incredibly healing and opens up your pleasure receptors and your manifestation power. YES, play! One day we had a virtual unicorn queen party with my brilliant, bold, and beautiful six-year-old niece, Goddess Ava. We all—including my dad—dressed up in fun unicorn horns and ate unicorn ice cream.

You don't outgrow your need to play. Playing with the kids you love is awesome—but be sure to also indulge in play for you. Remember those toy dolls or cars you were into? Get them again. Get some grown-up toys too.

Allow yourself to imagine more. You have a right to play and pleasure. Fertile creativity means that you have the perfect conditions to create what you want.

HOW TO HONOR THE GODESSES SEVEN SISTERS

When you honor the Goddesses Seven Sisters, you honor your own creativity. You may choose to honor this energy inside yourself or invoke their energy according to your own tradition.

To honor these goddesses in you: The Seven Sisters' energy is open to connection. Their energy is light and fun but clear. Close your eyes and imagine that you are a creative force of nature. How can you express your creativity in a new way today?

Symbols: Their symbols are the symbols of New Orleans: colorful plastic beads, jambalaya, and gumbo. The African builders hid Ghanaian Adinkra symbols like

Hye Won Hye, which means "that which does not burn," in the ironwork of New Orleans. That's a great symbol to honor the Seven Sisters.

Colors: Their colors are jewel tones.

Auspicious times: Congo Square is said to be the oldest existing gathering place for African people in the United States. This was Marie Laveau's play space in the 19th century. We imagine that Vodou Sundays at Congo Square may have been the prime gathering day for the Seven Sisters as well, so Sunday is a great day to acknowledge them.

Music: "Seven Sisters Blues" by John T. Smith and "Dreams" by Solange

Suggested offerings: Gumbo, seven rainbow candles, powdered sugar, pralines

Additional name: Ida Carter

Traditional Creativity Ritual: Fertility Dolls

Fertility is the creative power to manifest what you desire. Making a baby is the ultimate act of creation/creativity. This may be a human baby, or it may mean something else. Fertility dolls are a powerful manifesting tool. Some prefer to call them fertility figures, as people trivialize the word *doll*. We call them dolls, but these are not playthings. Fertility dolls are a tangible prayer practice. They are often created by a priestess or priest, but some families do create their own.

The Akua'Ba fertility doll is the most known in the Western world. *Akwaaba* means "welcome" in Twi, but the name Akwaba, Akuba, or Akua'Ba for the ritual fertility doll comes from the name Akua and the word *ba*, meaning baby. According to Akan oral literature, a woman named Akua was distraught because she was unable to get pregnant.

Akua prayed for guidance. In tears, she consulted her holy man. He created a wooden carving of a baby for her. Akua found his actions strange, but she trusted the priest and was willing to try anything. The large round head on the carving represented a beautiful forehead and big brain. Rings on the neck reflected a healthy, chubby baby.

The priest told Akua to care for the "doll" as if it were a real living child. Wash her, clothe her, feed her, and love her. Akua put a string of beads on the wooden baby and loved her as instructed. She kissed her and carried her on her back, feeding her and taking great care of her. Akua became the village laughingstock, but she persisted in her vision, even after they took to mockingly calling the "baby" Akua'Ba.

Soon Akua was pregnant. It worked! She was grateful and gave birth to a healthy baby girl. Akua left the wooden baby at the shrine with the holy man in gratitude. Now no one was laughing. All those who needed help with fertility made their own Akua'Ba wooden babies. Akua'Ba dolls are an "act as if" ritual for manifesting a baby.

Akua'Bas are all regarded as female, as the society is matrilineal and Akua gave birth to a girl.[20]

In South Africa, the Bantwane include beaded fertility dolls as a part of the wedding to ensure the wife will have many children. In some other African countries and traditions, fertility dolls may be made from the roof of the marital home and burned with the placenta when the couple has conceived. Fertility dolls may also be charms on chains.

Your Creativity Ritual: BMGV Vision Doll

Ritual intention: To visualize your BMGV, Big Magical Goddess Vision, and create a vision doll.

You will need:

- Goddess Soulbook
- Writing utensil
- Creative materials of your choice

What to do:

Part 1: Clarify Your Vision with Creative Visualization

Prepare your ritual space. Pick one triumphant moment from your BMGV, Big Magical Goddess Vision, a future moment from when it has already happened. Close your beautiful eyes and take a breath. See this triumphant moment in your mind's eye. Create a mental snapshot from your POV in the scene.

For example, if your BMGV is you performing, see yourself on a stage looking out at the audience cheering. If your BMGV is having a baby, see a clear picture of you holding your newborn baby. If it is you launching a product, see your website with the banner that says, "For sale."

Now let's turn up the energy. Just as you did back in the "Let's Talk Desire" section in Ngame's sanctuary, turn that vision snapshot into a mini mental movie, a three-second clip in your imagination. You can use the same vision you had before. In fact, it would be extremely potent if you did.

What does that feel like to live in that three-second moment of your BMGV?

- *Sight: What do you see?*

- *Sound: What do you hear?*

- *Touch: What do you feel?*

- *Smell: What does it smell like?*

- *Taste: What do you taste in the air?*

See your mental movie clearly. Make it real in your mind and mentally experience it. Then take a deep breath, come back into the present moment, and open your eyes. You did it! Give thanks! You created and birthed your BMGV—and now you just need to just step into it.

Part 2: Create a Paper Vision Doll

Illustrate the BMGV scene you just visualized in your Goddess Soulbook or on displayable paper. Open to two blank pages facing each other so that you have plenty of room to create your successful scene. Think of this as a vision board that you are drawing. You may enhance your drawing with printed words and images from websites or cutouts from magazines.

It doesn't matter whether you think you can draw. This is not for a museum (although it could be). This art is for your creative fertile manifesting joy. You are a fertile and creative force. You can be fertile to make babies, have fertile land and soil, have a fertile imagination for creativity, and be fertile for success.

Create your vision doll, a paper "fertility doll" of yourself. Draw who you are when you are living your fully realized life. What are you wearing and why? Fill in the rest of the picture with the rest of the scene from your BMGV visualization. Who is there? What did you see, hear, smell, taste, feel? Add it to your vision.

Part 3: Activate Your Vision Doll

Here are some things you can do to awaken the energy of your vision: pray on it, pour ancestral libations and give thanks that it is already realized, activate it with sacred incense or crystals, blow on it, seal it with candle wax, or put coins or cowrie shells on it to symbolize abundance.

Leave your BMGV vision drawing on your goddess altar overnight to charge. Then go forward and act as if your vision is already real—because it is! Look at it daily with the joy of already having experienced it. Àse!

Congrats! You have completed the Temple of Conjurers.

Temple of Conjurers Creation Mantras

- *What I desire desires me.*
- *Divine blessings flow to me so easily.*
- *I give easily and freely. I receive freely and easily.*
- *It feels good to feel good.*
- *I am a creative visionary.*

Temple of Conjurers Journal Questions

- What is your BMGV, Big Magical Goddess Vision?
- What would a 30-second clip of your BMGV manifested look like?
- How can you act as if your BMGV is already fulfilled?
- How will you incorporate creativity and play into your life?
- What do you feel turned on about these days?

Temple of Conjurers Embodiment

- Add something to your altar that represents your creative goddess power.

Temple of Conjurers Integration

- Add the Temple of Conjurers goddesses and your experience with these rituals to your Goddess Soulbook.

4

THE TEMPLE OF WARRIORS: YOUR POWER ENERGY CHANNEL

Àṣẹ

BLESSING OF THE WARRIORS

God/dess of many names,

Thank you for this pathway to the Divine.

As you stand before the Goddess Warriors,

Ready to awaken your power,

May you one day be able to relinquish your sword and your shield;

You don't need them for true battles.

May you stand in your own truth.

May you know that you are worthy.

You deserve happiness, laughter, and pleasure.

You deserve to feel good in your skin.

May you have the power to protect those who need protecting.

May you exist on the side of justice.

May you be vulnerable enough to believe in you.

May you realize your own power.

This is the true victory.

May these blessings be with you always.

Let the circle be unbroken and infinite.

You are your pathway to the Divine;

May the Goddesses who summoned you protect you.

Deep bow, beloved!

You are now entering the Temple of Warriors in the power energy channel. The five goddesses, here just for you—Oya, Atete, Sekhmet, Asase Yaa, and Sitira—represent worthiness, courage, happiness, and resilience. They have been the keepers of this guidance from time immemorial. You now stand in an elevated circle of warriors who are here to guide you in elevating your power.

Sit in the center and take in their wisdom. They each have gifts for you. Should you choose to accept their gifts, you will integrate your warrior-goddess power. To finish this temple, complete their five rituals.

ABOUT THE TEMPLE OF WARRIORS

Warrior-goddess energy is all about standing confidently in your true power. To become a sacred goddess warrior in your own life is to remarkably stop being at war all the time. If you are truly powerful, you have no need to fight nonstop. You have nothing to prove.

Breathe on that. How does it feel in your body to decide that you no longer have anything to prove to anyone?

This channel is all about your àṣẹ, life-force energy. Life force powers us from within. We stand in that power regardless of external circumstances.

Write in your Goddess Soulbook: *I have nothing to prove.*

Owning our fierce feminine-warrior energy is necessary. If we can birth when called, we can also destroy when necessary. If you felt moved by the Dora Milaje, the all-women army in *Black Panther* movies and comics, allow me to introduce their real-life antecedents. The Mino, meaning "our mothers," were an all-woman army in the Kingdom of Dahomey beginning in the 17th century. They called themselves the king's celibate wives and were dubbed the "Dahomey Amazons" by Europeans. They were required to be celibate to focus on their duties, which included guarding the king's life at all costs.

This kind of physical brawn is not required of you. You are merely being called to be unfuckwithable.

Unfuckwithable (adj.): To be so aligned with your own divinity and so in love with yourself that you experience complete self-acceptance and are not affected by other people's opinions of you.

Example: They said what *about me? Who cares? I wish them love. I didn't notice. Guess they didn't realize that goddesses are unfuckwithable.*

Write in your Goddess Soulbook: *I am unfuckwithable.*

Our rallying cry and transformational chant for my Spiritualista Goddess Retreat in Belize in 2018 was "Queen. Warrior. Sorceress. Lover!" As we spoke each word, we invoked and embodied a goddess pose for each. We chanted at Altun Ha pyramids and then at the Lamanai Ruins.

A group of badass sacred ones, we hiked the rain forest in a thunderstorm to the Temple of the Jaguar Masks, built in the 6th century. Most of the other temples are buried, reclaimed by the jungle. Our guide shared the story of Ix Chel, the Mayan jaguar goddess of creation and destruction, war and love, fertility and weaving. I know her well as she is in my *Womanifesting* deck.

Much of the complex nature of Mayan spiritual philosophy mirrors the currents that run through African philosophies. They believed that there is sacredness in all things. This is what healthy warrior energy is all about. And despite ideas that Mayan people vanished, they are still here. Powerful Mayan Shaman Rosario Panti blessed us as a priestess at the retreat. Their numbers may have diminished, and their ancient civilization is gone, but Mayan people are still here.

Our riverboat ride to the Lamanai Ruins was a leisurely, picturesque, peaceful sightseeing adventure of birds, flora, fauna, and wildlife. On our return boat trip, all of the retreat sisters opted not to wear a life vest. Our vessel was a low-to-the-water, open-air boat. No cover, no seat belts, no nothing!

Everybody opting out of life vests really bothered me, as I am personally responsible for everyone who comes with me on retreat. I love these women, and my duty is to make sure they have an experience that is mentally, emotionally, spiritually, and physically safe. It was the end of the day, we had just safaried and hiked the rain forest, and we were all spent.

I didn't want to seem like the bad guy, so I didn't push it. Well, our return boat trip was anything but calm and peaceful. Having gone into overtime, the guide was pissed. He sped us through driving rain on rougher waters, bouncing past hungry-looking crocodiles. The tiny, open-air boat threatened to tip over at every turn. We all screamed, cried, and prayed the whole way back. Thankfully we arrived soaked but safe.

A few weeks after we returned, a Missouri duck boat accident killed 17 people, 9 from the same family. The tourists capsized during a rainstorm, not unlike the one we experienced. In fact, their boat was bigger and sturdier than ours. After the crash, fishermen raced to throw life jackets to the drowning people, but it was too late. Everyone's immediate question was: Why weren't they wearing their life jackets?

I was devastated by the survivor's stories and what they experienced. I also couldn't help feeling additional gratitude for making it through our jungle mishap. I was angry at myself for saying nothing. I mentioned it to a friend, and he responded, "You had insurance, and all of your guests had signed releases." He entirely missed the point.

As a leader, I should have stood firm and lovingly explained that not wearing life jackets was not an option. Being an empowered woman means being willing to make others—and yourself—uncomfortable. Life is not a popularity contest. Warrior-goddess energy is not about being liked or accepted. This fierce warrior energy lives in the gut, around where your umbilical cord was cut, your personal seat of trust. In the moment they said no and I said fine, I failed them. I was responsible for their lives as the mama of the retreat.

The act of spiritual bypassing is attempting to leap over things that don't feel so "love and light" filled. Life is not all ice cream and rainbows, although I love both. (When it comes to sacred duality: the ancient Mayans believed that rainbows are demon farts!) We fear the dark, but the dark kept us safe for nine months. The dark can be warm, protective, and nurturing.

A few years ago, I started asking people in my trainings for spiritual coaches, healers, and teachers: What is your activism practice? If your spirituality does not include being a voice for people who seem voiceless and standing for justice, then what is even the point? We cannot be aware of the energy of peace if we are not aware of the energy of war. Light cannot exist without the darkness. We will get more into that in the Temple of Shadows.

WHAT IS YOUR POWER ENERGY CHANNEL?

We all want to feel more power-full, right? The power energy channel is the seat of your inner light warrior. The energetic color of our personal power center is yellow. It also houses the abdomen, solar plexus, liver, pancreas, gallbladder, and small intestine.

Some folks see life as one great, big power struggle, but it doesn't have to be. When we are babies, we are fully in our power. We cry when our needs are not being met and laugh when we are content. We push the boobie or bottle away to say we have had enough. We explore and are open to new thoughts and ideas.

Then sometime between babyhood and adolescence, many of us feel like we lose our power. Other people's opinions of you eclipse your own. You pursue external means to regain your power. Some seek the approval of adults with achievement via grades, sports, performances, or other activities. We seek to feel powerful with the way we look—our clothes, style, hair, and physical bodies. Maybe you tried to steal power or compete for it by bullying, fighting, trying to change your social status, or making demonstrations of your might. You may have tried to control your world with substances or behaviors that gave you the illusion of feeling powerful, such as food, drugs, alcohol, sex, or popularity.

These things may give temporary hits of power. Hopefully you had a great young adult experience! But none of these temporary power blasts generate authentic power or àse, life-force energy. That is what the Temple of Warriors is about.

Real power is loving yourself, welcoming in your happiness, feeling worthy, speaking up against injustices, fighting for the underdog, and daring to live the life you would live if you knew that you would not fail. Authentic power doesn't say that bad times will never come or you will never face another obstacle. Instead, when your power comes from within, you have the capacity to weather inner and outer storms.

Write in your Goddess Soulbook: *I am a light warrior.*

This is a different idea of the warrior than you might have heard.

One morning I had the honor of being the keynote speaker at an annual wellness weekend created by Lisa Peyton-Caire's Foundation for Black Women's Wellness in Madison, Wisconsin. The theme was "Thriving in a New World," as the event was moved online because of the pandemic. The foundation's goal is to radically transform health by creating a world where we all live "long, happy, and thriving lives, defined by healthy minds, bodies, and spirits."

My topic was "From Wounded Healers to Goddess Warriors: How to Finally Heal Ourselves." I shared with the audience that being a goddess-warrior helped me realize that it is not about fighting and being strong all the time. Being vulnerable and open is a key warrior trait. When you have true power, you can lay your burdens down.

Now the goddesses in the audience had the "pleasure" of listening to me try to sing my own rendition of "Down by the Riverside." Let's just say, songbird Great Ancestress Mahalia Jackson, I ain't. So I sang my Harlem-girl, former-rapper version, "Down by the Bodega-side."

"I'm gonna lay down my burdens, down by the bodega-side. I'm gonna study war no more."

Don't judge! We all have to go with what we have access to. The key is to be powerful enough to know that you can lay your sword, your shield, and your burdens down. Because that stuff gets heavy!

Many of us were taught to be ride-or-die loyal to everyone but ourselves. When we roll, shields up, keeping out all the hurt and pain, impervious to our emotions, we also block the joy. That's a part of the grand design of this earth school. When you block the pain, you block the pleasure. Being a goddess warrior is about being strong enough to just be.

I remember sharing with my best friend that I was calling a program "Wild Goddess Woman." She said, "We're Black. You can't call it wild woman!" We were taught that it wasn't respectable to be wild women. We grew up pressed and curled, braided and beaded, and in control. Being regarded as wild would have been a source of shame for our families. Although she grew up in Houston and I grew up in New York, we were both taught to be nice, proper, and dignified young ladies. But every single one of us, pressed and repressed, needs to welcome our inner wild woman.

The wild feminine is the impolite, improper, not so respectable part of ourselves that we must own to step into true goddess-warrior power. There are an infinite number of ways that we are socialized to be seen and not heard, to be respectable and clean and to follow the rules.

Write in your Goddess Soulbook: *I embrace the wild feminine.*

We will go deep with shadow monster Medusa when we get to the Temple of Shadows. She is that bitch. And she is necessary. We welcome this aspect of ourselves into our warrior being. She has been so suppressed and disregarded for generations.

The wild feminine goddess warrior must be allowed, acknowledged, and celebrated. She is on the front lines of marches and protests. It is she who is starting movements on social media. It is she who is shouting down falsehoods on the nightly news. It is she who is saying you need to raise your rates. It is she who is twerking on tables and loving her life. It is she who is dancing in ecstasy as they throw tribute dollars.

Welcome and embrace your wild feminine self to stop being at war with your Self.

HOW TO KNOW IF YOUR POWER ENERGY CHANNEL IS BLOCKED

Do you feel powerless in your own life? Are you feeling stuck? Or invisible? Maybe you see everything through victim-colored glasses and see yourself as the loser in every situation. Is worry, overwhelm, and anxiety getting the best of you?

Perhaps you feel jealous because it looks like everyone else is moving ahead but you. Or you feel like an impostor or a fraud.

On the other hand, maybe you are self-centered, aggressive, egotistical, and braggadocious. Yes, the traits that the mainstream would usually assign to being a warrior mean that your sacred warrior is out of alignment.

Have no fear. Warrior goddesses Oya, Atete, Sekhmet, Asase Yaa, and Sitira are here to support you in moving from surviving to thriving through your power energy channel.

You may join each goddess in her sanctuary now.

OYA

Goddess of Storms
Yoruba/Nigeria
The Lightning Change Ritual

"I make shift happen."

OYA'S MESSAGE

Káàárọ̀, blessed daughter. The winds of change are in motion. Change is not always slow. Sometimes change is swift, and you are able to shift things in the blink of an eye. Allow momentum to carry you to where you are supposed to be.

OYA'S STORY

Great Goddess Oya, keeper of mysteries,
We see you. We say your name.
Great spirit of the wind, mother of nine . . .

Wielding her sword of truth, Oya is one of the most powerful of the orishas. Consider her the goddess of storms and lightning. Storms bring shift, rapid uncontrollable change, and at times, chaos. The name *Oya* means "She tore" in Yoruba. But Oya can also be as warm and soothing as a summer drizzle.

Didn't you hear? Oya was either originally an antelope with a secret ability to shape-shift into a person, or the reverse. When she removed her antelope skin, she would reveal a breathtaking woman.

One day Oya was in the marketplace, and Shango, god of thunder, became entranced by her beauty. He followed her and saw her turn back into an antelope. He was distraught. He couldn't marry an antelope. But Shango wanted Oya with him forever, so he hid her antelope skin in the sky when she became a woman again. Shango's wives, beautiful love goddess Oshun and lightning goddess Oba, weren't happy about these developments.

Oya became Shango's favorite and most loyal wife. She even out-thunders him. When Shango speaks he breathes fire, but Oya goes ahead of him in every fight. She is known as "the wife who is fiercer than the husband." When this warrior goddess waves her arms with her nine copper bracelets and the nine colors in her skirt representing her nine children, any fight is over. After all, Oya can walk through fire without getting burned.

How are storms? Powerful and confronting with nowhere to hide, right? Oya wields her power during winds, rainstorms, hurricanes, tornadoes, thunder, and lightning, nature's most ominous forces. She represents sweeping change, destroying the old to make room for the new. Word on the street is that she and Oshun don't get along.

Throughout the Caribbean and South America, Oya's energy shifts a bit from her Nigerian persona, and she also protects cemeteries, makes armies of the dead, and fights with machetes. Her death and rebirth persona was born in the diaspora. In Western culture, this daughter of Yemaya became the superhero Storm, a member of the X-Men, played on screen by Halle Berry, Alexandra Shipp, Jill Scott (voice-over), and others. Oya is eternal.

So is Mama Oya friend or foe? Put it this way: Do you want to be going with the storm or against it? Rain has the power to create and destroy. You want Oya on your side.

Maferefun Oya!

Let's Talk Personal Storms

What would you like to change in your personal life? So often goddess sisters in our community complain to me that they feel stagnant and stuck. I remind them that everything in nature changes. An object in motion tends to stay in motion. So we are not truly stuck, but we are changing life back consistently to the same ole energy instead of moving forward. We do this because our fears create patterns.

If you are not actively changing something, you are choosing it! When we are facing personal storms or want things to change, we spend lots of time obsessing about what is *not* working. We complain every chance we get. We ask for advice that we may not take. To make shift happen, we need to focus on what we want rather than what we do not want. Stop giving energy to what is not working.

Oya is the mother of chaos, and that is exactly what personal storms feel like. Most of us are at war with ourselves. But here is where we want to run into the storm, not away from it. We heal it by feeling it. But you must stop lying to yourself. Give yourself permission to feel your feelings.

We have all experienced times of personal heaviness, and most likely will again. Honor your path. Beating yourself up is self-harm. Tell yourself the truth and practice self-compassion.

Real talk. The biggest thing holding you back is you. If you attract betrayals, stress, and strife, the common denominator is you. If you want people and life to treat you better, you go first.

HOW TO HONOR GODDESS OYA

When you honor Goddess Oya, you honor the part of you that can weather any storm. You may choose to honor this energy inside yourself or invoke her energy according to your own tradition.

To honor the goddess in you: When it comes to inner storms, know that they will pass. You are protected, you are stronger than you think, and you are ready. Every time you feel the wind hit you, see it blowing out fear and blowing in love. Close your eyes and see your storm of challenges, then see them dissolve one by one into a healing breeze.

Symbols: Oya is associated with antelope horns. In Nigeria, these may be painted red and placed on her shrine.[1] Her other symbols include nine copper bracelets, lightning bolts, the wind, water buffalo, the black horsetail switch, and copper.

Colors: Her colors are deeper reds such as burgundy, the rainbow, and black.

Auspicious times: Oya's feast day is February 2. Her days are Wednesday and Friday.

Music: "Oya" by Ibeyii and "Oya" by Lazaro Ros

Suggested offerings: Oya loves red wine and shea butter. We salute a fully moisturized goddess! Toys that move in the wind, like kites and spinning wheels, also amuse her softer side. Nine copper pennies and a sword representative are a basic tribute.

Alternate names: Yansa, Iansa, Oiá, Mother of Nine, Mother of Changes, Goddess of the Weather

Traditional Storms Ritual: Protection, Binding, and Blocking

Disclaimer: You may find the following story a bit raw, but growing up in NYC wasn't always pretty.

When I was about 16, I got my ass beat by a bully. It was the only time that I have ever been in a physical altercation. This bully, a new girl to my block, decided that she didn't like my best friend and me. In her mind, we were bougie and "thought we were cute," so she wanted to fight us. She literally drew a line down the block that closed off access from our houses and told us to never cross it. My mother, who was not about that life, said, "Just stay away from her, or point her out and I'll talk to her mother." She didn't understand that talking to her mother would just make it worse.

Look, my bestie G and I could spit game we heard in any song, but we were soft, protected kids. We were Double-Dutching, box-braiding, roller-skating, bike-riding, block-party-cookout, shopping at the mall kids. We were not about throwing hands.

To make the fight story extremely short, this near-giant of a girl cut my face in three places with a soda-can tab. Every young person who lived on my block somehow magically appeared and witnessed me getting beat up. Then my nose, which always bled anyway, started bleeding. Now I was hysterical, humiliated, and even more terrified of this girl.

I screamed over and over again, "My face! She cut my face." My parents weren't home from work yet, and no one else, except my brother and my friend, seemed as upset about it as I was.

"That ain't nothing but a good old-fashioned ass whipping. It's just scratches. It happens! Wash your face and move on," my big brotherly neighbor declared. I called my older boy cousins over. But when they heard it was "beef between little girls," they left.

Then my high school sweetheart A and his mom rolled up. Unlike my soft-spoken mom, his mother was about that life. Later I learned that she had a machete hidden in her housedress. Miss L., my boyfriend's intimidating Jamaican mom, lovingly ordered me to write the bully's name nine times on a torn brown paper bag and cross it out nine times with red ink. My mom, still at work, had no idea any of this was happening, but I was willing to do anything. Miss L. hovered over me as she had me do this twice. She then said to put the two pieces of paper facedown under the soles in each of my shoes. Miss L. gave me a rainbow candle, took a daub of blood from the cuts on my face, rubbed it in, and told me to write the girl's name on it and hide it in the freezer. I wrapped it in a foil and told my parents it was a science project.

It sounds crazy to say now, but the girl never ever bothered us again. She was hospitalized to get help for her mental health challenges and apparent addiction issues. Her family moved away shortly thereafter.

Unbeknownst to me, we had done a Hoodoo-meets-Oya protection and blood binding to hold off the bully. We froze her intentions toward me and blocked her from doing further harm while not putting any harm toward her. The machete in Ms. L.'s housedress was Oya's sword of truth.

Your Storms Ritual: Calling in Rapid Lightning Change

Ritual intention: To make a shift fast by releasing what's not working.

You are probably super clear about the experiences that you do *not* want, right? Do you have a clear statement about what you *do* want?

At my Bali retreat in 2016, we did a full-moon fire-release ceremony on the black sand beach. There was such an emotional clearing that people are still telling me how it changed things for them years later. This type of ritual clears people, conditions, behaviors, and circumstances from your life. But Mama Nature hates a vacuum, so we want to replace the things we don't want with the energy of what we do want.

Stuckness is never something you have to worry about with Oya energy. In this ritual, you will accelerate your momentum and ride the wave of positive change.

You will need:

- Journal
- Paper
- Pen
- A safe way to burn paper

What to do:

Prepare your ritual space.

Ground yourself. Fold a piece of paper in your journal in half. Label the left column "I Release," and label the right column "I Welcome." In the left column, list nine things you wish to release from your life. In the right column, list nine positive alternatives you want to invite into your life instead. These are counter statements.

Now on a separate piece of paper, for nine days you will write down what you wish to release, then you will handwrite over that the counter statement of what you are inviting in. You can use a brown paper bag or any piece of paper. The paper can be in accordance with what you are releasing, e.g. birthday cards from an ex or an envelope from a bill.

On Day 1, begin with Item 1 from both lists. From the "I Release" list, write out what you do not want nine times. Make it a concise statement. For example, if you feel mistreated at the office, you could write: "People disrespecting me at work." Write that nine times in a row. Then turn the paper clockwise, a quarter turn. You will now write the counter statement from the "I Welcome" list of what you do want nine times over the initial statement. Maybe what you want is to be running things. You could write: "I am my own boss" nine times.

Close your eyes and see what it would look like when the "I Welcome" statement comes into fruition. Again, write the "I Welcome" statement nine times over the words of what you don't want. Do this twice more with quarter turns each time until the paper is back in the original direction.

Do you see? You are literally replacing what you don't want with what you do want.

Then safely burn it. As the flames rise, see Spirit taking hold of your situation, disposing of what you don't want and making space for what you do want. You can repeat your positive statement or gratitude as the release happens.

Dispose of the ashes with love. That is who you were, not who you are. Have compassion for yourself. You can allow the wind to blow the ashes away, bury them, or put them in the garbage.

Journal on how it felt to let go of whatever you released and how it feels to welcome in the new situation.

The next day, repeat the ritual for the second item on your list and so on.

ATETE

Goddess of Worthiness
Oromo/Ethiopia
Goddess Coffee Ritual

"I matter."

ATETE'S MESSAGE

Akkam oolte, my child. Please stop hiding. Your true power cannot be hidden or suppressed. Do not wait for conditions to be perfect to feel your own sense of perfection. Let it all be fine now.

ATETE'S STORY

Great Goddess Atete, keeper of mysteries,
We see you. We say your name.
"Only the man who is not hungry says the coconut has a hard shell," she answers.

Atete is a fierce protector of women and girls and the great goddess for the Oromo people, the largest ethnic group in Ethiopia. She is an earth mother who governs fertility, healing, and faith in the Zar religion. Nonviolent conflict resolution is an important warrior principle of Atete. She is known as the queen of the gods or the wife of God, so all conflicts come across her "desk."

The children of Arsa, the sun god, were fighting. As the story goes, Atete's brother Sete killed their younger brother, Ora. Devastated, Atete planted an odaa tree in Ora's memory. She asked her father to help her to make peace. The rains fell, the sun shone, and the tree grew, signifying peace and Ora's resurrection.[2] Irreechaa (thanksgiving) is still celebrated at the foot of the odaa tree whenever possible. The Irreechaa Thanksgiving Festival also marks the end of the rainy season, a time of darkness.

Atete's form of war is simply persistence. The more she is rejected by the dominant culture, the more she persists. She shows up in songs, in feasts, and even in coffee ceremonies. Atete's truth has been suppressed, but she still manages to come through for her daughters. Atete is venerated by both her Christian and Muslim followers as Mary. She has special cäle beads, colorful prayer beads, dedicated to her. Her cäle may also be disguised as rosary beads, as her worship is often hidden.

Women are Atete's intermediaries. There are many rituals, rites, and celebrations in Ethiopia that were originally to honor her. Coffee, the national drink of Ethiopia, is sacred to Atete as the coffee bean resembles a woman's vulva. Coffee is used for divination and is considered a fertility potion. The Oromo believe that coffee grew from the tears of their loving supreme god, Waaqa.

Ceremonial ritual staffs, like people-sized wands, are a part of Oromo culture. There is an ancestral power staff called the siiqqee given to women by their fathers when they marry. It is used to negotiate marital strife and issues with intimate partner violence. Debteras, healer-priests, also have prayer staffs.

The Ateetee is an Oromo ritual celebration to honor women ancestors. It is also a communication and conflict resolution space for community justice. In some practices, women sing their issues.[3] Atete teaches us that our voices matter.

Let's Talk Worthiness

You will read the words "You are worthy" over and over in this book. You will hear me chant these words when we meet in person. But no amount of affirmations can make you feel worthy. Like Goddess Atete, you may have your power suppressed by forces that seem beyond your control, but worthiness is an inside job.

Wishing you the daily Oromo blessing:

May not joy and laughter depart from you,
May the earth and the sky be with you.
May God protect you wherever you go.

May peace and blessings be abundant in your lives.
Pass the day in peace, and return in peace.
May the God of dawn awaken us,
May the God of sunrise make our day bright.
May the God of noon renew our strength.
May the God of sunset bring us home.
May the God of dusk soothe our soul.[4]

The only thing that will make you feel worthy is to completely accept yourself. The beautiful parts of you that everyone else likes are worthy. The parts of you that maybe you or others dislike and are trying to suppress are worthy too. So instead of aligning yourself with OPO, other people's opinions, align yourself with the highest part of you.

The part of you that formed the tectonic plates and birthed the rivers, the part of you that says you were created in the image of all that is inherently worthy. You are not less worthy on the days when you can't fit into your jeans. You are not less worthy when no one clicks "Buy" on your product site or "Like" on your post. You are still worthy when you are broken up with. You are inherently worthy. Worthiness is in your veins. You cannot get away from being worthy. How cool is that? Try as we might (and we do) to escape our own power, we just cannot.

Your birth certificate says that we need your magic, joy, vulnerability, and most importantly, we need you. You have only started to scratch the surface of all you were born to do. If you only do what you're good at because you're scared of messing up, you're missing your life. It's not about being perfect. It is about the joy of the experience.

HOW TO HONOR GODDESS ATETE

When you honor Goddess Atete, you honor the part of you that knows you are worthy. You may choose to honor this energy inside yourself or invoke her energy according to your own tradition.

To honor the goddess in you: Zar women-only celebrations include ecstatic dancing for days on end. They play hypnotic music with the tanbūra bowl lyre and the manjur rattle instrument you play by shaking your hips. Shake your hips in acknowledgment of how it feels to own your worth.

Symbols: Atete has a special rosary, colorful cäle beads.[5] Her symbols include coffee beans and the odaa (sycamore) tree. The birth of an Oromo person is traditionally celebrated by planting a seed.

Colors: She appreciates bright colors, but her element is black.

Auspicious time: The annual Oromo Irreechaa thanksgiving is held at the end of September.

Music: "Sanyii Koo" by Seenaa Solomoon featuring Keeyeron Darajjee and "Breaths" by Sweet Honey in the Rock

Suggested offerings: Coffee beans, figs, or seeds

Alternate names: Asis, Adbar, Ateti

Traditional Worthiness Ritual: Jebena Buna Coffee Ceremony

The jebena buna ritual is handed down from mothers to daughters. The buna can be a celebratory ceremony, casual with friends and family, or it can be used as a conflict resolution ritual. A transformation of spirit is believed to take place over the three rounds: Abol, Tona, and Baraka.

The buna generally lasts between one and three hours, depending on the circumstances. If you're a non-coffee drinker like me, politely decline and you will be given tea. The buna is also used to welcome visitors, and in traditional households in Ethiopia and Eritrea the three-course coffee ceremony takes place three times a day.

A friend from Addis Ababa told me that, "For Ethiopians, coffee is medicine, coffee is food, coffee is life." Coffee is originally from 9th century Ethiopia, so it makes sense that these beautiful people have perfected a way to combine coffee, love, and spiritual reverence. The story goes that Kaldi, a goat herder in Kafa, Abyssinia (Ethiopia), discovered coffee after he noticed how energetic his flock became from eating raw coffee berries. The jebena buna coffee ceremony is a part of the fiber of love and support in Ethiopia. The saying "Buna dabo naw," meaning "Coffee is our bread," says it all.

It is an honor to be the person, usually a woman, performing the ceremony and pouring the coffee. Of course, if it is your own ceremony, then you should be the host, sometimes called the "performer." The performer spreads loose grass and flowers on the floor as the stage for the ceremony. She also burns incense, brews the coffee, and serves it with a majestic pour.

Your Worthiness Ritual: Goddess Coffee Ceremony

Ritual intention: To allow yourself to be witnessed in a love army of your sisters.

You need and deserve a positive and supportive community. I have heard so many lightbringers say that it's difficult to make friends after you finish with school. One of the many reasons I love my in-person goddess retreats, circles, and temples is that we get to create physical community.

You don't have to live in the "Cradle of Coffee"[6] to create a buna. Support and community are essential. If you are good at supporting others, but don't get the support you need, your life is out of balance.

You can modify this ritual for your pre-existing friend group or use it to create new friends or form a goddess circle.

You will need:

- Shot glasses or mugs
- Coffee or coffee beans
- Fresh flowers and grass
- Incense and burner
- Appetizers

What to do:

Invite friends. Your intention can be to clear conflict or just to bond. This may be an opportunity to share your personal goddess story and intentions. A fun process could be having each person pull an oracle or affirmation card and chatting about what it means.

Prepare the ritual space. Spread fresh grass and flowers on the floor. Yellow flowers are often used. Burn the incense. Sandalwood, frankincense, or myrrh are great choices. Roasting, brewing, and cupping the coffee is all a part of the ceremony.

You may prepare your coffee in any way that works for you. Typically, the hostess washes and roasts the coffee beans in a long-handled pan over an open flame. Then she hand-grinds the roasted beans with a mortar and pestle. Guests are invited to observe and smell the infusion. The grinds and water are added to a jebena coffee pot in which you boil the coffee. (A friend told me that it is not a true jebena buna ceremony if you do not have a real jebena coffee pot.)

Coffee is typically high-poured from the jebena into shot glass–style porcelain coffee cups, filling them to the brim. This is an elegant art form and part of the performance. Please, please, please be safe and only pour in a way that is comfortable for you and your guests. I suggest that you tell them about the tradition while pouring it in your normal way.

Guests are served with the cup and a saucer, in order from oldest to youngest, and you may choose to sit on the floor at the same level if this is possible. Guests generally do not drink the coffee with milk. It is served with sugar, salt, or butter. Dried fruits, bread, peanuts, or kolo (roasted barley) are presented. Some people add cinnamon, cloves, cardamom, or honey, depending on the region.[7] Most often, popcorn sprinkled with sugar is served with the coffee. Using the same beans, water is added to each round, so that the cups go from bitter to mild.

The three rounds are:

1. Arbol, Abol, or Awel: This is the strongest round. If you have gathered for conflict resolution, present the issue and start to discuss. Allow each person to speak.

2. Tona or Kale'i: Add water to the brew. You must resolve the conflict in this round, or the final round will not be served.

3. Baraka: *Baraka* means "blessing." Celebrate. Share.

Record your event process and reaction in your Goddess Soulbook.

Modification: There is also a Senegalese tea ceremony you may opt for if your friends are not coffee drinkers. I will share it at womanifesting.com.

SEKHMET

Goddess of Wounded Healers
Egypt
The Sun Rises Disc Ritual

"It is safe to put myself first."

SEKHMET'S MESSAGE

Marhaban, my child! Are you afraid to awaken the warrior within because you may not be able to turn her off? If you have been drawn here, most likely you are a healer in your circle. Many healers, both known and secret healers, hold sadness, rage, and feelings of brokenness. Everyone gets your best—except you. The time has come for your own healing.

SEKHMET'S STORY

Great Goddess Sekhmet, keeper of mysteries,
We see you. We say your name.

Her messengers shoot seven arrows from their mouths. But we have chanted "The Book of The Last Day of the Year," so all is well. Lady of the Flame, the lion-headed one is well.

Sekhmet is the fierce ancient Egyptian goddess of war, but also of the sun and healing. Her name means "she who is powerful." Rather than wielding a sword, you often will see Sekhmet wearing a red dress and holding ankhs, which represent life-force energy. She has the head of a lioness and the power to grant destruction or be a stabilizing force. As a Leo, I have always identified with Sekhmet, Hathor, Bastet, and the other leonine goddesses.

Sekhmet's origin story says it all. The sun god Ra was furious with humankind and our shenanigans. He sent Wadjet, the Eye of Ra, to check out the situation. The Eye of Ra became his daughter Sekhmet, a ravenous and unforgiving warrior and hunter. She started to obliterate people—but this is not what Ra wanted. When Sekhmet refused to stop her destruction, Ra put beer and pomegranates in her path, making her drunk and sleepy.

Sekhmet has many faces. Nubian warrior lioness goddess Menhit was also merged with Sekhmet. Nubia was a kingdom that existed north of Sudan and south of Egypt. This lioness goddess was the mother of magic, Heka, and the protector of pharaohs. Ra's daughters Sekhmet and Bastet eventually became seen as two aspects of the same goddess. The warm motherly energy was attributed to Bastet, while Sekhmet ruled her fierce side. In Western culture, she became the superhero Catwoman, played by Eartha Kitt, Halle Berry, Zoë Kravitz, and others.

Sekhmet's hot breath created the desert. She can heal all ailments, except eye troubles. She also has dominion over issues of the blood, especially bringing her healing energy to menstrual challenges.

Our Goddess Temple Circle sister Ekua Ahima tapped into her fierce Sekhmet wounded-healer energy when she stopped fighting who she was. Goddess Ekua says that she was intimidated by her own strength and hiding behind a mask. She is now owning her sexuality and standing in her truth as a professional dominatrix and holistic healer. A professional dominatrix physically or psychologically dominates others as a business.

Goddess Ekua says that her spiritual and business practice is led and fortified by her ancestors. This path gave her the confidence to love her body again, experience pleasure in and out of the bedroom, and align with "wild femme" divine feminine energy. Publicly coming out of the dominatrix closet was terrifying, but finding the courage has been life changing.

Goddess Ekua grew up in a religious environment that does not support her sexuality or spiritual beliefs. She practices Hoodoo and divination through tarot and capnomancy to connect to her higher self and divine guidance. Womb dancing reminds her to put herself first.

Goddess Ekua says that we are taught "from damn near birth to be silent, submissive, and to take whatever life throws at us." She declares that she is "challenging that narrative and daring to do the opposite." She goes on to say, "Regardless of the shame, judgment, and lack of support I've received, I'm following my heart!" Goddess Ekua even created the #AfroDomme Academy to support others. She is dressing like a superhero and acting like one too! From wounded to healer. Go on, lioness.

Let's Talk Being a Wounded Healer

It's time to go from wounded healers to goddess warriors. Many of us inherited the message that we are strong and strong is a good thing to be. Being a warrior wasn't a choice for our foremothers. Being a warrior for them meant, "I never stop fighting. I bring home the bacon, fry it up in a pan, and never let him forget he's a man." At least that's what the commercials said. And we honor our foremothers. Our mothers and grandmothers and their grandmothers not only did the best they could, but they rocked it.

But what warrior means for us going into this new era is knowing that a true warrior has the choice *not* to fight all the time. A true warrior can lay the burden down along with the swords and weapons, take a breath, and stand in her innate power.

Zora Neale Hurston wrote that "Black women are the mules of the Earth." When I first read those words in *Their Eyes Were Watching God*, I was a teen, but I already knew exactly what she meant. I had seen the beautiful women in my huge family fight to keep things together, often in single-parent circumstances. I witnessed firsthand how these women worked nine to five, plus the second shift at home with sporadic support. It was expected that they deal with whatever. We were the ones leading the political movements at school while lamenting that our counterparts on campus were not attracted to us. Wounded healers, we were mulin' it at church, in our neighborhoods, and back at home.

Put your hand over your heart if you feel me. We have been holding society together for centuries with gum and rubber bands, and that is exhausting. When you are carrying the whole world, your back and feet get tired.

We hereby release martyr energy and victim-colored glasses. When you say, "I've got it" repeatedly instead of taking care of your own mind, body, spirit, and emotions, other people don't let up. They don't turn around and say, "Maybe she's overloaded." They say, "Great. She's got it. Pile more on her."

Originally, wounded healers referred to those who feel compelled to help others because of the reflection of their own open wounds. There is a greater definition for us in this global sister circle that is filled with natural healers, intuitives, empaths, highly sensitive people, and generous caregivers.

We in this circle feel a calling to connect and support others. Not because of our unhealed wounds, but because it is our sacred calling. We want to be who we needed but could not find. However, the pus from those unhealed wounds that leave us overworked and underpaid, co-dependent, drained, and sucked dry by emotional vampires is stinking up our lives. Even though you and I may not have physically connected yet, I know that you most likely put other people first. I know that you may have to beg, borrow, and steal this self-care and soulcare time for yourself.

There is a fighting sword in your right hand and a protective shield in your left. But contrary to what someone told us, there is no magnanimous dignity in being a wounded healer. Tend to yourself first. Put on your own oxygen mask. But I know you get that. That is why you're here, right?

But here's the real truth we must remember, even while we are healing. Any idea that we are flawed or broken is an illusion. We are perfect in our imperfections. The idea that we need to be something other than who we are is a lie. This lie is supported by the fact that most of us reading this live in a capitalist structure that requires us to think that we are broken and need to buy things to fix that brokenness. We saw it during the pandemic. The powers that be only cared that we could be cogs to keep the economy going.

Your entire being is sacred. We no longer cling to flimsy ideas of strength that strip away from our very being. Instead we claim our true power, which is the fact that we are connected and powered by Source energy. Wherever you are at this moment is where you are. We were given the exact family, the exact circumstances we needed in order to be who we were born to be.

Are you saving the world and losing yourself at the same time? You have nothing to prove. You were not designated to be anyone's mule. That's why I address you as "goddess." We are in this together. And we are our sisters' keepers.

You are just as powerful as you fear you might be.

HOW TO HONOR GODDESS SEKHMET

When you honor Goddess Sekhmet, you honor the part of you that is a healthy healer for yourself first. You may choose to honor this energy inside yourself or invoke her energy according to your own tradition.

To honor the goddess in you: Close your eyes and feel the sun's healing rays flowing through your body. Sekhmet's energy is what we call fiyahhh. What if you put the same love and care you spend trying to fix or control others into loving yourself? Where do you need to shift your loyalty from outward to inward? How can you stop betraying your own needs?

Symbols: Cats, lions, blood, and the sun disc

Color: Her color is red.

Auspicious times: You may celebrate her at the Festival of Drunkenness on the 20th day of Thoth if you catapult back in time. The month of Thoth was between September 11 and October 10.

Music: "Sekhmet" by Lavva and "Empress" by Ray BLK

Suggested offerings: Pomegranates or pomegranate juice and beer

Alternate names: Sekhet, Sakhmet, Scheme, Sakhet, Sakhmis

Traditional Wounded-Healer Ritual: Capoeira

Capoeira is a performative cultural art form that is also a martial art. Participants form a circle and two people engage in the middle. It was originally created by enslaved Africans in Brazil and is loosely connected to the religion Candomblé. Orixas (orishas) and saints are mentioned in capoeira music. First noted in the early 16th century, Capoeira's flowing movements include kicks, acrobatics, and traditional Kongo dance movements. It was declared illegal after slavery was abolished in Brazil.

Capoeira combines physical fighting, ritual, dance, performance, music, gameplay, spirituality, and philosophy. Old-school capoeira retains spirit possession and the greater purpose, which is to develop mandinga, meaning "magical wisdom."[8] There is a dispute over whether the enslaved Africans brought capoeira with them from the motherland or they created it in Brazil.

Referred to as playing capoeira (jogar capoeira), capoeira is less violent than it was two centuries ago. There is also an underlying philosophy that teaches the participants how to avoid physical fights. The intention is survival, no matter what. Capoeira demonstrates perfectly how something can be spiritual, artistic, beautiful, and simultaneously deadly.

Capoeira can be enjoyed as art or used to kick some ass! It is the same with all of your beautiful gifts. Are you using your gifts to bless or curse yourself?

Your Wounded-Healer Ritual: The Sun Rises Disc

Ritual intention: To raise your frequency and vibration.

Sekhmet is the daughter and the eye of the sun. The sun represents your life-force energy. If your goal is to reclaim your divinity, fall madly in love with yourself, and manifest your desires, this requires raising your frequency to the alignment of the sun. That means getting your energetic vibration as high as possible.

You will need:

- Your Goddess Soulbook, journal, or a large piece of displayable paper
- A writing utensil

What to do:

The Sun Wheel is a ritual we did as a group at the Goddess of Paris Miracles and Manifesting Retreat. You may have seen similar power circle rituals and activations in the Bakongo cosmogram, Lakota medicine wheel, art therapy's wheel of fortune, the manifestation wheel, or channeled energy Abraham-Hicks' focus wheel.

Draw a circle, like the sun, in the center of the paper. Then draw rays emanating from the sun. You want to have as many rays as possible with room in between each ray for you to write.

Write your sacred intention for the day in the sun center. What do you want to call into your life? Be specific. You can use your BMGV, Big Magical Goddess Vision, or it can be something else. This is your sun.

Now for the sun's rays, write out true positive belief statements and gratitude related to your sun intention. Each positive belief is one ray of the sun. Feel your energy around your desire rising as you move around the circle.

For example, if you wrote in the center, "My Dream Home," related true beliefs would be: "It's fun to live where I choose," "I like having good neighbors," "I love decorating new spaces," or "Owning where I live feels so good." These beliefs are already true. They raise your frequency and excitement about your intention.

Meditate on your completed circle. You can read it first thing in the morning or before bed. You can hang it somewhere it will inspire you. I have a former soul mate client who wrote hers on the bathroom tile in the shower so she could see it every morning!

ASASE YAA

Goddess of Joy
Ashanti/Ghana
Tolerations Ritual

"I feel like me when I'm happy."

ASASE YAA'S MESSAGE

Ete-sen, sweet child. The beauty of the earth is a reflection of your beauty. The wisdom of the seasons reflects your wisdom. The depth of the seas is your mirror. Happiness is your birthright.

ASASE YAA'S STORY

Great Goddess Asase Yaa, keeper of mysteries,
We see you. We say your name.

When pouring libations, the Akan mention the Supreme God Nyame, and immediately afterward they mention Asase Yaa, the mama of us all. She is also Nyame's wife. Like Yoruba goddess Oya, Asase Yaa owns a sword of truth. But when there is a need to fight, she need not lift a finger. Her sword fights on command, all by itself. It can also stop fighting on command, but her voice is the only one it hears.

Asase Yaa is the joyful crone goddess celebrated as Mother Earth by the Akan people. Her abosom (deity) energy is loving, fertile, and nurturing as she radiates from the womb of the earth. We owe her our gratitude for all the plants, herbs, flowers, fruits, and vegetables. Farmers sacrifice to her to insure a healthy harvest. Ask her permission and give thanks before picking flowers or tilling the soil.

We come to Asase Yaa in joy and gratitude, especially at the changing of seasons in our lives and on the planet. She and the sky god are also the parents of sacred clown Anansi, known in this book and American culture as Aunt Nancy. Anansi/Aunt Nancy is a trickster deity, showing that the earth has a sense of humor.

Asase Yaa rules life and death. As Mama Earth, she is also a fertility goddess. She needs no temples to show her love. Her name is invoked at major life transitions, like a baby's outdooring. You show her love through your respect for the earth and nature. She favors farmers, horticulturists, and those who work the land.

Don't assume that Asase Yaa is not desirable because of her big age. Twe, a water spirit, is madly in love with her. He's so obsessed with her magic that she need only touch the water and he gifts her with fish.

She is purposefully not reachable by divination. As the mother of all humanity, Asase Yaa wants her wisdom available and open to all. Love the earth to love her. In the sacred geometry of the people of Ghana, Asase Yaa's Adinkra symbol is Asase Ye Duru, meaning "The earth has weight." No matter what, she keeps spinning!

Let's Talk Joy

Is your happiness on a layaway plan? Have you decided, "I'll be happy when I get the job, car, partner, business, success, when I have kids, when the kids grow up, when I lose or gain weight"? If you believe in your heart "When I do/have X, I will be happy," your happiness is on a layaway plan, an account you get to cash out one day. No more. Let's take your joy off layaway.

Let's get fully present. Say out loud, "I am here." So often we don't allow ourselves to be present. We're always worried about what already happened or what's to come. But we are rarely in the moment.

Happiness begins with how satisfied you are with the moment. Joy is the thrill of enjoying the moment. Gladness is feeling pleased at the fullness of the moment.

Joy starts with being open to the idea that you can experience full happiness. If you can't imagine it, you won't be able to live it. Claim it now, because happiness is your birthright. Your Creator did not bring you here to suffer. You weren't born to be last on any list, especially not your own. I'm looking at you, my goddess sister. You were born to feel joy and pass that joy on. Your joy is a creative, evolutionary force.

Every morning, my mom would declare, "Rise and shine!" Goddess rising is you shining. So I say the same to you now: rise and shine. You are the sun. Your natural, default setting is to shine. All of this other stuff has just temporarily eclipsed that shine, that's all.

What makes you happy? Have you ever thought about this? Do you feel happy right now? How do you describe happiness?

Our Goddess Temple Circle sister Tynesha Keene had to figure out how to stop putting her happiness on the back burner. In addition to being a "wife to a loving sailor," she is a mom to two toddlers. Plus she has her own business. You see how prioritizing her own needs may be a bit difficult, right?

Everything shifted when Goddess Tynesha had to make her entire family vegan overnight for the health of her son. When he was 10 months old, he was rushed to the hospital with life-threatening food allergies. The drastic change was the best thing that could have happened to the young military family. They shifted to a plant-based lifestyle.

Now Goddess Tynesha says her spiritual practice involves "a connection with food, herbs, and all things metaphysical to create harmony and flow. By recognizing the synergy between mind, body, and spirit, life as a busy mother becomes less chaotic and more joyful." Yay for joy, and yay for reconnection to Mama Earth.

HOW TO HONOR GODDESS ASASE YAA

When you honor Goddess Asase Yaa, you honor your right to be unapologetically happy. You may choose to honor this energy inside yourself or invoke her energy according to your own tradition.

To honor the goddess in you: Mother Earth expresses her joy at every turn. Your laughter honors and celebrates Asase Yaa. The simplest earth goddess joy ritual? Walk by a fertile field of flowers. Asase Yaa wants you to know that this beautiful Earth is a gift to you. Look how much power you have. You have been gifted this beautiful planet as a home. How do you honor it in the time that remains before Asase Yaa guides your soul to the otherworld?

Symbols: Asase Yaa's Adinkra symbol is Asase Ye Duru. Other symbols include her sacred truth sword, soil, flowers, and vegetables.

Colors: Her colors are gold and green.

Auspicious times: Her day is Thursday. As no tilling or plowing is allowed that day, it is the perfect time to pour libations directly onto the soil.

Music: "Asaase Yaa (Great Mother)" by Sa-Roc and "Blessed" by Jill Scott

Suggested offerings: Libations must always be poured to Asase Yaa before you disturb the earth. That includes planting a new garden or burying a loved one. Ask her to protect your loved ones who lie wrapped within her soil. Honor her and all her creatures. To prove their truths, her children kiss their lips to the earth and recite her praise poem.

Alternate names: Aberewa, Old Woman, Asase Afua, Asase Yan

Traditional Joy Ritual: Renewal at Souvenance

Every year in Haiti, starting the Sunday before Easter, Vodou practitioners make a pilgrimage to Lakou Souvnans (Souvenance Mystique) in Gonaives. This is a week of renewal, new life, and resurrection to revere African ancestral spirits. This holy site was consecrated and founded by a group made up of people who escaped and others freed from slavery.

This is a week of celebration, dance, and drumming, along with deep prayer and meditation. Most women wear their hair wrapped. For some rituals, participants wear immaculate white. They don bright, happy colors for others. The drumming, singing, and dancing are acts of reverence. Trance dancing welcomes the lwas (deities). Goats, chickens, and cows are sacrificed. Practitioners daub with the fresh blood to celebrate life and call forth Spirit. People come to ask for healing and protection but also to express gratitude. Bathing together in the lake is a part of this celebration of joy and resilience.

The weeklong celebration represents the voyage back to Dahomey. The women carry and dance with machetes in honor of Ogou Feray, Ogun, god of war. He helped Haiti in her fight for independence. They honor the lwa Loko. Goddess Ayizan's husband, Loko, is considered to be the high priest of all of the lwa and the first houngan. Ayizan and Legba are also honored, although Loko controls the poto mitan. Ayizan is up in the trees gathering more herbal healing knowledge.

Poto mitan means "the pillar in the middle holding the sacred temple space up." All activities in the ritual celebration revolve around the poto mitan. Sometimes it is a living tree, like Souvenance's majestic sacred ceibo tree named Mapou Lisa. At other times it is a beautifully decorated piece of wood or palm tree trunk. This is the portal through which the spirits descend.

At Souvenance, they walk to the Mapou Lisa and circle the tree, representing the walk back home to Benin. They say that some of our old gods only still exist at

Souvenance. The seviteur, spiritual leader, holds a lit candle and the asou, sacred rattle. Participants are one with all elements, ancestors, spirit—and each other.

Your Joy Ritual: Tolerations and Happy List

Ritual intention: To get clear on the things, people, and circumstances that are blocking your joy.

A spiritual definition of tolerations is things that we have been putting off, ignoring, and not dealing with. Whenever I ask goddess sisters to examine their tolerations, the first thing that comes up is tolerating mess from other people. That matters, too, but the definition of *tolerations* is much bigger. Every person, place, or thing we encounter is either adding to your life-force energy or subtracting from you. We are in an energetic relationship with everything. Tolerations are the places we know we need to make a change but we have been merely tolerating.

So, what are you tolerating? Tolerations represent stagnant energy in our lives, things that need to be done, places where we are just surviving rather than thriving. Do you have buttons that need to be sewn on, light bulbs that need to be changed, or stacks of snail mail waiting to be recycled? All of these things are environmental tolerations. And when it comes to the people in your life, do you have conversations that need to be had? People you owe a phone call to? Unreplied-to texts and e-mail? RSVPs to make? All of these things are tolerations too.

Tolerations include bills, clutter, incomplete projects, unspoken breakups, things that need to be organized or fixed, health situations, and more.

You will need:

- Journal
- Writing utensil

What to do:

Part 1: Make Your Tolerations List

Make a list of at least 28 personal tolerations.
Be sure to include:

- *That bag of clothes you have been meaning to donate but never did*
- *That whole side of the closet of stuff that you will probably never wear again*
- *Those expired vitamins and medications*
- *Those gifts from deceased loved ones that you feel obligated to keep although they clutter your life*
- *That come-to-goddess convo you keep putting off*
- *The stack of notes from that project you've been procrastinating on*
- *Those unpaid bills that you've been dodging*

Awareness can be powerful magic. Do you want to spend your precious seconds, minutes, hours, days, months, years dealing with these things?

If you want to have healthy boundaries with other people, begin by having healthy boundaries with yourself. Raise the standard for what is unacceptable to you. Raise the ceiling for the kind of life you are willing to have, but also raise the floor for what is no longer acceptable.

Part 2: Make Your Happy List

Now you will make a Happy List. What makes you a glee-filled, giddy, laughing, orgasmic, joy-filled goddess? What brings you fun? List at least 28 joyful conditions—but the list can really be as long as you want. It can include the sound of your nephew's laughter, yoga, and shopping for crystals. There is no wrong answer. This is your list. And if you don't know what makes you happy, it's time you learn.

Start to eliminate things from the Tolerations List and incorporate things from the Happy List.

SITIRA

Goddess of Brazenness
Guyana
Liberation Dance Ritual

"I am bold, brave, shameless, and brazen."

SITIRA'S MESSAGE

W'happen, me daughter? Yes, gyal! May everything meant to diminish you elevate you. May all who mean you harm fall away. May you see now that hurdles are illusions because you are plugged into the Source. Step into your brazenness now.

SITIRA'S STORY

Great Goddess Sitira, keeper of mysteries,
We see you. We say your name.

Goddess Sitira is the energy and spirit of Buxton, Guyana, in South America. Sitira, also known as the Buxton Woman, is brave, bold, brazen, barefaced, and all of the so-called unfeminine things that we are not supposed to be. Buxton "Ooman," as we say, is warrior-goddess energy.

If you have heard about her, it was in the popular "Sitira Gal" folk song. According to the lyrics, someone greets Sitira and she hikes up her petticoat and starts "wining," dancing and rotating her hips like a "Buxton boor" or "Buxton whore," depending on who's singing the song.

Sitira's name is now used as a slur. A Sitira, like a Jezebel or a Sapphire, has become an insult even in the hallowed halls of parliament. Culture, like folk songs, is used for social control, to remind us of who's acceptable and who isn't. But these fun songs and minimizing slurs miss the magical truth.

You see, Sitira was casting a spell with her hips. There is a Buxton Spice mango that grows nowhere else. Sitira has Buxton Spice energy. She may be the spirit of Buxton, but she is powered by Aje.

Àse is life-force energy. Aje is the divine feminine. Aje is unfuckwithable. *Aje* is sometimes translated from Yoruba as "witch energy." That doesn't bother us, but our definition is slightly different. Aje is goddess energy. An Aje is a woman awake to her own power. Venerated by women, the Aje is also known as the Iya Nla, the Iyami Osoronga. The Iyami Aje are the daughters of Oshun.

Sitira's detractors saw a strumpet on the walk. They were too blind to see that Sitira was doing a juju dance, secret society ancestral conjure. This dance of realignment and reawakening is the forbidden dance of the WatraMumma. The wind of her hips represents the undulations of ocean waves, the rhythm of the Kaieteur waterfalls, the sweetness of sugarcane. There is ancient honey from the Osogbo Grove in every gyration, pure Guyana gold in every tilt, a calabash of black oil in every thrust.

If you half close your eyes and tune in to your own Aje, you can see it now. Throughout Guyana's history Sitira was there. When she wines her hips, the barn owl screeches and the Aje whispers the path. This lineage is our sacred inheritance. For all women are Aje. We are heiresses to the greatest power known. Oh, the things they have done to try to possess just a bit of our magic.

In the 1600s, the Dutch West India Company kidnapped and brought my ancestors to El Dorado, the Guianas. They dragged them across the Atlantic, but the umbilical cord was stronger than the chains. Sitira heard the call, and she was there. The barn owl screeched. She wine she hips. And the Aje whispered.

Some escaped right from the slave ships into the Iwokrama Forest. Eventually thousands would follow their siblings into the rain forest over the next couple hundred years, becoming the Maroons, the African Bush community. Down de road in Dutch Guiana, when Paanza, a young woman, escaped slavery with rice braided in her cornrows to feed the Saramaka Africans in the jungle, Sitira was there too.

Then in 1763 on the Canje River, Sitira heard the call again. The barn owl screeched. She wine she hips. And the Aje whispered. They torched the

Magdalenenberg Plantation house, kicking off the yearlong revolt known as the Berbice slave uprising. She was at the Demerara rebellion of 1823 too.

And if you ask anyone in Guyana about Buxton, Sitira's town, they will say, "Buxton people stop train!" and recount this true story from 1862. The newly emancipated villagers were getting bulldozed tax-wise in what was then British Guiana. The British governor denied their meeting requests and dismissed them as "barbarous." After all, why should he meet with ex-slaves?

Sitira heard the call and she was there. She wine she hips. And the Aje whispered.

Sitira's people, the people of Buxton, found out that the governor's train would be coming through their village. The men were off working the fields. So the women of Buxton stood on the train tracks, facing the oncoming train, and refused to move. Armed with sticks, cutlasses, and axes, Sitira's warrior women formed a human shield and stopped the train! My ancestors insisted that the governor disembark to address their issues. The phone hadn't been invented yet, so he had no choice. They could have been run over or shot and killed. But the badass, brazen Buxton women stayed there, and the men eventually followed.

Sitira was there. She wine she hips. And the Aje whispered.

Guyana's Black folks hail from West Africa originally. We are the Akan, the Yoruba, the Igbo, the Dahomey. We hid our goddesses in our folk songs, fables, and in their saints. Sitira's brazen energy is that of Mami Wata, Oya, Oshun, Yemaya. For too long, tales of the hunt have glorified the hunter. We elevate Sitira and are elevated by her. We reignite and deify Sitira, and today she moves from folk hero and local bad girl to deity. She is a goddess, our goddess, an Iyami Aje, a mother of the night.

She hears the call. She wines she hips. And the Aje in our lineage answers. She is the brazen song. Sing the songs of your brazen ancestors.

Let's Talk Being Brazen

Raise your hand if you have had enough of people telling you to be strong or saluting your strength. No, thank you. That is killing us. We are flesh and blood human beings with access to our full range of human emotions. Yes, we have been strong as a survival mechanism, but surviving is not living. That is no longer enough.

Focusing on strength means sacrificing your vulnerability, your humanity. Instead of trying to be strong, be brazen. God-force energy is brazen. Brazenness leaves the tyranny of needing to be respectable and people pleasing at the gate.

Our divine feminine definition of brazenness is a bit different than you might expect. There are all different kinds of ways to be brazen. It's up to you to find your own. It is brazen to raise your children differently than your parents. It is brazen to speak up for someone who is not in the room. Brazenness is choosing a path unbeaten. It is brazen to choose a different spiritual practice than your community. It is brazen to be unapologetically yourself. It is brazen and unfuckwithable to allow yourself to be vulnerable.

Brazenness is asking, "What would I dare to do if I knew I could not fail?" Brazenness is courage topped off with faith in your own divinity and power. There is a saying, "Don't tell God/dess how big your problems are; tell your problems how big your God is." Channel this energy when you want to leap over anything life throws in your path!

You can do it. To give us more context of the magic of brazen Sitira energy, let's take it further back. The Dutch started kidnapping and trafficking people from the West Coast of Africa to Guyana in 1620 to work on sugar plantations. Guyana was colonized by the Dutch, French, and eventually the British. Chattel slavery was abolished in Guyana in 1834.

After slavery, four years of "apprenticeship" as a transition period was instituted. During this apprenticeship period, the "free" men and women had to work for 40 hours for no pay on plantations. They were paid a pittance only for every hour they worked over the 40 hours of free labor. Plus, now they had to pay rent to live on the plantation on which they worked.

The British gave reparations—but not to the formerly enslaved. They gave reparations to the plantation owners for the loss of free labor. But somehow, Sitira's people were able to gather enough coins to do the unthinkable: the newly emancipated African-Guyanese people of Buxton pooled their money to proudly purchase their own plantations and establish villages. One hundred and twenty-eight formerly enslaved families purchased the village of Buxton where they had been enslaved in 1840 for $50,000. Then 168 formerly enslaved families purchased the neighboring town of Friendship, and they linked the two villages.

My family hails from Buxton. And I am so proud to say that my ancestors were a part of that magical group of original purchasers. This was only the second village purchased by Africans. They did that!

What even made them think that this was possible? If recently emancipated enslaved people could brazenly purchase their own village, what is possible for you?

Our Goddess Temple Circle sister Damali Abrams, aka the Glitter Priestess, is a brazen international visual and performance artist, healer, and professor. She is definitely a daughter of Sitira, and I'm not just saying that because she is my blood sister. Choosing to be an artist and healer in a world that is already uncertain for Black women alone is brazen.

The confrontational nature of Goddess Damali's work makes folks uncomfortable as she challenges them on race, gender, and sexuality. Dressed as a provocative golden mermaid, she instigates and awakens the audience with our folklore that "the Africans who threw themselves overboard during the Middle Passage to avoid slavery became mermaids and swam back home to freedom." She is Wata Mumma/Mami Wata, Yemaya, Oshun, La Sirène of Haiti, River Mumma of Jamaica, and Fairmaids, the water creatures that live in the black sea of Guyana.

After the devastating 2016 election, Damali led a public performance ritual called "Banishing | Binding | Incantation." She says, "My work casts spells and creates portals into spaces of radical fantasy." Goddess Damali's spellcasting art unleashes magic on the viewer, similar to the nkisi juju of mojo bags and Ethiopian healing scrolls where Spirit is manifested in sacred objects.

How can you be more brazen in the choices you make for your life? What makes you unfuckwithable?

HOW TO HONOR GODDESS SITIRA

When you honor Goddess Sitira, you honor the brazen part of you that is shameless. You may choose to honor this energy inside yourself or invoke her energy according to your own tradition.

To honor the goddess in you: The best way to honor the Sitira in you is to step into your personal boldness. Be willing to see things differently. Hurdles are an illusion. You are powerful. You easily leap over seeming obstacles and transmute challenges.

Symbols: Guyana is the "land of many waters." Sitira is resplendent in her "GT gold," the nickname for Guyana's famous gold jewelry. Her beverages include ginger beer or sorrel (roselle hibiscus).

Colors: The national Victoria Regia flower is white and pink, but the flag colors include red, black, gold, and green.

Auspicious times: In April, Sitira's home of Buxton celebrates its annual anniversary.

Music: "Sitira Gal" by British Guiana Police Force Band and "Watch Me Work" by Melanie Fiona

Suggested offerings: Buxton Spice mango, tamarind, and sapodilla are great fruit offerings. Have a meal of saltfish, curry anything, plantains, yams, or okra with Guyanese high wine, white rum, or coconut water.

Alternate names: Sataira, Satira

Traditional Brazen Ritual: Kwe Kwe Celebration

If a Guyanese person ever invites you to a Kwe Kwe, go! After prayers and libations of Guyanese high wine or Demerara rum open the ganda (sacred space), it's off to the races! The celebration can be indoors or outdoors, although it is outside whenever possible. If indoors, sprinkle the windows and doorways with liquor, too, to invite in the ancestors.

Kwe Kwe (Queh Queh) is our traditional Guyanese, African-derived, pre-wedding night celebration. In these modern times, though, it is often a week before. I had the honor of having an awesome Kwe Kwe; the marriage didn't make it, but the fun of the celebration did.

Traditionally, Kwe Kwe ceremonies started out with the acting out of the groom being rejected over and over by the bride's family. His family makes appeals on his behalf. Then the wrong bride is carried high on a chair with her face covered. The groom must know if it is his bride.

Most of the music is provided by live drummers, who also lead the crowd in Kwe Kwe songs. Oftentimes some of the drummers are the family members of the bride or groom. You can also get a Kwe Kwe caller to run things if you need one. The mostly satirical songs are supposed to lead the young couple through everything they need to know for a happy marriage, from love to family communication to sexual relations. The song "Show Me Yuh Science" is about making sure the couple can make babies.

I first learned about our goddess Sitira in the Afro-Guyanese folk song "Sitira Gal" that we sing at Kwe Kwe. In Sitira's song, someone sees her on the road and she lifts up her petticoat and starts wining. Wining (pronounced "wine-ing") is dancing by moving your hips and booty in circles. Her song warns against the perils of being promiscuous. In another song, "Lili Gal" is asked repeatedly, "What make you brazen so?" Then the women respond with, "This make me brazen, that make me brazen," with sexy hip movements.

The call and response songs have bawdy, politically incorrect lyrics like, "Woman in the bed, and the man can't function. What kind of man is that?" Each song is seemingly more scandalous than the last as the couple is commanded to "dirty dance" (by Western standards) together. Songs continue being sung by everyone until someone shouts, "Bato-bato!" and "raises" a new song.

The families bond so that by the time we get to the wedding, we are no longer strangers. The night is filled with food, drinks, love, and so much fun. As the Kwe Kwe song goes, "All of we is one family!"

Your Brazen Ritual: Liberation Dance

Ritual intention: To ignite your personal liberation and manifest your power with healing hip circles.

Ready to awaken the divine feminine in your body to reclaim your personal liberation? Let's do it! When I was in the UK, I learned that "dancehall queen" is a slur for first-generation folks of Caribbean heritage like me. Apparently our colorful style, loud hair, unique ways of speaking, and personalities are just too much for some folks.

Well, call me a dancehall queen and I say thank you. Dance has been a way of achieving spiritual states of ecstasy since time began. Moving your hips like only a dancehall queen can is a sacred empowerment practice. When you do the "dolla wine" dance, you clear generations of stagnant energy. When you twerk, every thrust is a love note to your own body.

You can cast a spell with your movements. There is spiritual magic in your hips! And if you are able-bodied enough to move them, it is time. Move your hips daily to cast a spell of fertility, creativity, and manifestation. And if you aren't physically able to, move what you can or move your hips in your mind's eye.

At my Goddess of Paris Miracles and Manifesting Retreat, one of the workshops I created was called "Josephine Baker Night School." I searched for months to find a priestess-teacher who understood the manifestation power of dance. The burlesque session was led by a Parisian cabaret dancer to awaken our creative, fertile energy.

Your hip circles are hypnotic. Whether in twerking, belly dancing, hula-hooping, or pole dancing, true personal liberation is owning the power of your body and the music it makes. There is a reason why all of these dances have been banned.

The San people use dancing to astral travel and shift realities.[9] That is manifesting power.[10] Twerking came up in New Orleans and places like the Jamaican dancehall scene, but its roots are in West Africa and Southern Africa. There are many similar dances on the continent, but mapouka, aka the Butt Dance, hailing from the Côte d'Ivoire, is advanced twerking. This is high-vibration, ancient feminine-energy body linguistics. Dances like the mapouka are traditionally a part of rites of passage.

You will need:

- Yourself and some music!

What to do:

Your affirmation for this practice is *"I am a divine goddess."* You are dancing to awaken the sensual mother energy that connects us all to Mother Earth.

Twirl your body, awaken your sacrum, wind your hips, and shake your booty. Learn the sacred language of your body. You can start with hip circles. Heal the energy by moving it. Twerk it up. Yoga of any kind that works your hip flexors is nurturing. Get that beautiful creative energy flowing. Move, move, move your hips. Again, if you aren't physically able to move, move what you can or move your hips in your imagination.

Affirm, *"I am a divine goddess."* Move your hips.

Write about your dance ritual in your Goddess Soulbook.

Congrats! You have completed the Temple of Warriors.

Temple of Warriors Power Mantras

- *I make shift happen.*
- *I matter.*
- *It is safe to put myself first.*
- *I feel like me when I'm happy.*
- *I am bold, brave, shameless, and brazen.*

Temple of Warriors Journal Questions

- What makes you feel powerful?
- What makes you feel powerless?
- When do you feel confident?
- What might your purpose be?
- What are you willing to release that isn't working?

Temple of Warriors Embodiment

- Add something to your altar that represents your purpose and goddess power.

Temple of Warriors Integration

- Add the Temple of Warriors goddesses and your experience with these rituals to your Goddess Soulbook.

THE TEMPLE OF SHADOWS: YOUR INNER MONSTERS
Jumbies

BLESSING OF THE SHADOWS

You've been hiding from the shadows,
Running from the dark,
Scared of what lurks inside you.

But you started in the dark,
You were planted in the dark,
You were formed in the dark,
You were soothed in the darkness,
You are perfectly made.

Your beauty is onyx,
Your soul is obsidian,
Your love is inky tourmaline.

You are wholly perfect.
The monster inside is not a monster.
Embrace her, accept her, honor her,
Love all of who you are.

Auspicious greetings, lightbringer!

You are now entering the Temple of Shadows, your Hall of Truth. The five shadows waiting for you—Long Bubby Suzi, Aunt Nancy, Soucouyant, Gang Gang Sara, and Medusa are the jumbies (monsters) who represent your own fears. They have been the keepers of this guidance from time immemorial. You now stand before a circle of those who are here to guide you to true self-acceptance.

Sit in the center and take in their wisdom. They each have a gift for you. Should you choose to accept their gifts, you will dive deep into your own psyche. To finish this temple, complete their five rituals and rites.

To enter this temple, we must step through a mirror . . .

ABOUT THE TEMPLE OF SHADOWS

To the ancient Egyptians, the khaibit, your shadow, was a critical part of human consciousness. In their philosophy, your shadow works together with your ba, your public personality. They believed that your khaibit could separate itself and that it had a life of its own. They were right.

Many of us are overwhelmed and unfulfilled, secretly being held hostage by the many faces of our own fears. Those faces of fear are our shadow beliefs that create our shadow selves. These shadow selves are the inner bullies, inner monsters, and inner demons that seem to test you at every turn. It's the voice telling you that you messed up, the child inside that is jealous, and the part stuck procrastinating again. It's the anger you don't know what to do with, the bad relationship choices, and the addictive behaviors. In this temple, you will begin to face the shadows inside.

Jumbies are the scary, otherworldly spirits and monsters of the Caribbean. "Don't let the jumbie hold you," is a Guyanese expression. A jumbie in Guyana is a spirit of the dead that could range from harmless and amusing to deadly. I grew up hearing jumbie stories, probably before I could walk. In Jamaica, jumbies are duppies. In Trinidad, the Virgin Islands, and other Carnival scenes, a moko jumbie is a stilts performer and dancer. *Moko* means "healer," from Moko, the giant healer god of the Kongo people. In East Africa, where these monsters are known as the invisible shetani, some even say that business folks use them to their benefit.[1]

A jumbie can block your blessings. They can take any form from beautiful to hideous and are terrifying. Some are considered evil and some aren't. Jumbies may have feminine energy, masculine energy, neither, or both. The shadows you will face in this temple are the jumbies of our goddess expedition.

The shadows you will meet are ominous spirits and creatures hidden in folklore of the African diaspora. They personify the dark goddess. The shadows represent the ugly, scary, and unloved parts of the spirit world—and ourselves. They reflect our greatest fears, but the secret of the shadow self is that our dark sides often hold our greatest gifts.

Yes, there are monsters among us, or shall I say, within us. The biggest, baddest, scariest monsters we will ever encounter are in our own subconscious minds. But the truth is they are not really monsters. We all have parts of ourselves that we think are unacceptable and unlovable. The parts of ourselves we think are not enough, stupid, bad, embarrassing, and unworthy. So we avoid, distract, numb, and deflect to hide these shadows—even from ourselves. There are parts of us that we do not acknowledge, see, or accept. But the unexamined parts of ourselves are running things. They are the patterns that show up repeatedly.

Your shadow is living a life you are unaware of. It affects your choices and behaviors. The shadow takes over when you are triggered, causes chaos, and wreaks havoc. Your shadow energy is manifesting and magnetizing people and experiences toward you that you do not desire! Still, your shadow self is not negative. Your shadows hold the keys to your disowned gifts and talents.

Here are some ways the shadow shows up: snapping at that person you love, eating ice cream in the middle of the night, procrastinating on getting that thing done, saying yes when you mean no and no when you mean yes, being caught up on social media or TV, lying, drugging, or drinking past your own comfort level.

In horror movies, the heroine slays the monster or scares it away with garlic and silver crosses. For the monsters inside, external weapons won't work. The more we stuff our shadows down, the louder they become. They become triggers, addictions, afflictions, and sore spots. These inner monsters wreak havoc on our relationships, finances, choices, and everything else.

What triggers you reveals you. The shadow teachings were brought to the forefront in the past century with analytical psychology. But the truth is that healers and shamans from the wisdom cultures have been doing this work from time immemorial.

The Bwiti healing and initiation ceremony with the plant medicine iboga is a shadow illumination and integration initiation in Gabon and Cameroon. Octogenarian Elder Bernadette Rebienot is a healer, master of the Iboga Bwiti Rite, and part of the International Council of Thirteen Indigenous Grandmothers. At the 2020 Summit of the Rose Retreat, she led a circle on the penumbral lunar eclipse called "Illumination and Shadow." She said, "The spirits of the forest of Gabon have said that we can't go backwards anymore. We don't have fear anymore. Time is short. Time is calling us. Spirit exists." She teaches that we have two bodies, the physical and the spiritual. Shadow afflictions are afflictions of the spirit.

Shadow work is not new, but it is necessary. Again, this is not a new thought movement. It's an ancient thought movement.

Global African folklore and mysticism is filled with tales of spirit monsters that terrorize from the shadows. These so-called monsters represent our fear and your personal dark side. I have harnessed them to illuminate the shadows we have within.

If you have had issues with self-esteem, relationships, manifesting, or traditional goal setting, the shadow is where we need to look. So often, I will meet an incredible person who shares that she has been chanting affirmations and making vision boards for years and is still stuck. You may be doing mindset work, meditating, and doing yoga and still feel like you're in quicksand. That is the work of the shadow. You run and the shadow runs with you. What you cannot be with will not let you be. But if you are in a dark room and you turn on the light, you can see everything.

Every single one of us has parts of ourselves that we suppressed as a child in order to be lovable and acceptable. We all just want to be loved. And a baby, if not loved, will die, right? The personality you present today is basically the person you created to get love from the folks around you and survive your childhood. So this shy but loud-talking chick, all that I am and all that I'm not, is the persona I subconsciously created at a developmental stage in order to be loved and accepted. None of this was conscious. It is all happening behind the scenes. And the same is true for every one of us.

Different behaviors, beliefs, and personalities got a thumbs-up or thumbs-down in different families. Some of us just wanted to be accepted, so we did the things that were acceptable in our households. Or maybe you went the rebellious route to get attention. In some households they said, "Go out there, kick ass, take no prisoners. Life is a fight." And in other homes they said, "Don't make waves. Just play nice." Different criteria for love. So we stuff down, silence, and hide the rejected parts, which become our shadows.

In much of the spiritual community, we often pretend those unacceptable parts of ourselves are not there. We abandon our full selves with toxic positivity. We don't want to be mean, bitchy, conceited, selfish, or angry. That would make you a monster, right? So love and frigging light, right? But you cannot love and accept yourself until you turn light on your shadow self—or this so-called monster becomes your inner bully. You must embrace and integrate the good, bad, and ugly shadow or dark side that you would normally try to suppress.

Metaphysically, everything that we experience is a mirror. So when you are at the store arguing with that lady who cut the line, she is a mirror of what you may be saying to yourself. When she says, "Screw you. You suck," it only triggers us when we agree somewhere within ourselves. It resonates with your shadow beliefs about you buried deep in your subconscious. Along those lines, like attracts like, so our shadow self is even manifesting for us. That's why your vision boards may appear not to be working.

Your shadow self has hidden desires, different desires than you think you want. Maybe your shadow self fears that you're not worth loving, so it's more important to impress others than to be happy. If you create your vision board from your shadow self rather than your empowered, self-loving, goddess self, then your vision board cannot help you birth a vision that will bring you joy.

Write in your Goddess Soulbook: *My life is a mirror.*

When we were kids, we made up stories about ourselves and the world around us to understand our experiences. Those stories become our adult beliefs. Maybe your story was "Nobody wants to play with me," or "I am the 'stupid' one." Or maybe the story was the opposite, that you are only lovable because you are smart. A parent scolds you for being too loud, and the story you believe is that the loud, unladylike, crass part of you is ugly and unlovable. You come to believe, *This part of me is not good enough. I've got to bury her. I've got to hide the part of myself that shows up and shines brightly because people might think that she's too much.* And so you also bury the part of yourself that has a voice.

Parents and caretakers projected their ideas and beliefs on you. You could have overheard adults talking about people with money. Then as an adult, you believe, *I've got to bury the part of me that loves money because that is selfish, unspiritual, unfeminine, or uncreative.* We usually don't know we believe this stuff! Like monsters in the dark, this kind of haunting is happening behind the scenes of our own minds.

You made up a belief, and a shadow was created. That shadow self rears its head at the most inopportune times. We think we're shoving that still-small voice down, but it continually shows up to terrorize us. The shadow says, "Ooh, you don't deserve to get paid that amount. Why would you charge that?" The shadow says, "Oh, why would somebody love you? You don't deserve to be loved in your current state." Then, instead of looking inward, we get upset with the folks and situations triggering these shadow beliefs.

Write in your Goddess Soulbook: *I deserve to be happy.*

If I give you a gift and you don't accept it, who does it belong to? It still belongs to me. So it's the same if somebody throws bad energy your way and you don't accept it. It still belongs to them. And it's the same with the trauma-inducing situations that we experienced during our formative years. This holds true whether we experienced horrific things or smaller things that we turned into trauma in our childhood minds. Those experiences and the stories you created to survive them have nothing to do with how beautiful and brilliant you are today.

Write in your Goddess Soulbook: *I am enough.*

When you chant the affirmation "I am enough" without shining light on your shadow parts, your brain says, "Yes, the light-filled part of me is enough." You believe the acceptable public part of you is enough. But the part of you that is jealous of your imagined nemesis, hates the neighbor's barking dog, or binges on bacon, that part of you is still not enough. You think, *She is a monster. I have to keep her hidden.*

Standing in your goddess power is realizing that all of you is enough. Then you bring your whole self to the party and truly know that every bit of you is worth loving. Even the parts that you are ashamed of or feel guilty about. Even the "ugly" part of you that slammed the door in that person's face. Every part of you deserves happiness.

Write in your Goddess Soulbook: *All of me is worth loving.*

Your shadow, your so-called dark side, the dark goddess, is not evil or bad. She's your battery.

WITNESSING YOUR SHADOW SELF

You will notice a section named "How to Witness" each shadow "monster." The monster you fear is not a monster at all. The best way to honor your shadow self is by witnessing first. Usually when we are triggered, we fight, flight, freeze, or people please to avoid our shadows. We must witness, honor, and face our shadows before integrating them with love. To witness sounds much easier than it is. When your shadow rears up, recognize it, witness your shadow monsters, and give these fearful energies grace. Then you can choose the healthiest reaction.

Still afraid of the dark? Have no fear. Long Bubby Suzi, Aunt Nancy, Soucouyant, Gang Gang Sara, and Medusa are here to help us integrate that which scares us the most. This house of horrors is deep within our own minds. But we will not be running from these shadows. Not anymore.

LONG BUBBY SUZI

Shadow of Shame
Garifuna/Central America
Body Map Ritual

"I am protected."

Shadow Fear: "I am broken and ugly."

LONG BUBBY SUZI'S MESSAGE

Buiti binafi, daughter! It is not your fault. Every part of you and every part of your personal odyssey is beautiful. Even the ugly moments. You have a body, a heart, a soul, and breath. That makes you beautiful. Breathe into your beauty. You are loved.

LONG BUBBY SUZI'S INNER TRUTH

We are terrified. We hate the skin we're in. We are scared that we are not good enough. This feeling is overwhelming. We hate feeling ugly, like something is wrong with us. What if we are unlovable? What if we are broken?

LONG BUBBY SUZI'S STORY

Long Bubby Suzi keeps the Garifuna and Creole children of Central America terrified. How? Long Bubby Suzi is known for with her long "shameful" and "scary" breasts. Parents use her to maintain order, as in, "Finish your homework or Long Bubby Suzi will get you." One of her breasts is filled with milk and the other with poison. She has the power to kill or to nurture. She and her bubbies (breasts) terrorize and chase people through the night.

Our folklore reveals our fears. The story of Long Bubby Suzi is about the horror of a poisonous and ugly woman's body. Long Bubby Suzi is considered abnormal and physically grotesque, and therefore dangerous. Consciously, we know that true beauty has nothing to do with our exterior. Still, many of us have deep-rooted shame related to how we look.

Long Bubby Suzi lives in the bush. The Garifuna, called the Black Caribs by Europeans, are Afro-Caribbean Indigenous people mixed with Amerindian cultures, including Arawak and Carib, based in Belize, Honduras, Guatemala, Nicaragua, and Panama in Central America.

In Jamaica, about 700 miles away, there is a cave in Woodside, St. Mary, with a petroglyph commonly called "One-Long Bubby Susan" or "One Bubby Susan." This prehistoric rock carving is of a woman with one of her breasts eroded. The powerful figure has been identified as Taino/Arawak goddess Atabey, mother of their supreme being. Atabey, she who gave birth to god, is the moon mother goddess of birth you met in Tituba's sanctuary (Chapter 2) and Ngame's sanctuary (Chapter 3).

What does it say that a powerful goddess with a perceived bodily imperfection becomes feared as a shameful monster? How does this reflect how you perceive yourself?

Uwala busiganu!

Let's Talk Shame

Undercover shame keeps you hiding and prevents you from fully expressing yourself. Shame puts your life on hold. It leaves you comparing yourself to others and jealous. You deserve better.

If you are looking at yourself with a critical eye and feeling that something is fundamentally wrong with you, that you are a bad person, ugly, or even broken, you are under the grip of shame. Shame is debilitating and permeates every part of your life. Shame, like any monster, thrives in the dark.

Shame was planted when we heard or interpreted messages that we were unworthy or bad, usually during our childhoods. Acknowledge the pain for your inner child, the tiny you within who experienced these things. Toxic shame also springs up in our adulthood when we make what we determine are unforgivable mistakes. Toxic shame permeates how you speak to and treat yourself and how you allow others to treat you. Plus, it affects your relationship choices and the kind of love you feel you deserve. When we address what we perceive to be ugly on the outside, we are often trying to fix what we perceive to be broken on the inside.

It is natural to feel ashamed, guilty, or embarrassed from time to time. But the deep-rooted shame that many of us have for things beyond our control is poisonous to our growth and well-being. Deep-rooted shame says that we are wrong and flawed by nature. This toxic kind of shame is isolating and can lead to unhealthy behaviors.

I have met so many incredible women with gifts to share who are afraid to be seen. You, my goddess sisters, have shared with me that you are afraid to be seen when you feel ugly or fat, when you're not as successful as you think you should be, when you feel ashamed of things not working as planned.

When our Goddess Temple Circle sister Jovhannah Tisdale became a single mom at a young age, her community said: "You're a whore. No one will love you. You ruined your life. You should have had an abortion. That's what you get for having sex."

The shame was overwhelming. Goddess Jovhannah says she was "broken, scarred, afraid, depressed, stressed, and living [her] worst life." She felt like she didn't have a right to leave her abusive relationship. Then when she shed the shame she shed the struggle. She had to face her shame and the shadows of the fear-filled beliefs keeping her stuck. She now helps other single moms find freedom as the Spiritual Love Healer.

Just because you believe something does not mean that it is true. Don't believe everything you think. Challenge your own beliefs, especially those about yourself. Pay attention to the chatter running in your mind. Is the voice inside cheering you on or beating you up? Does your inner voice tell you that you are not enough or that there is no hope for you? Are you willing to release these ideas about yourself?

Be curious about your shame. Ask it, "Where did you come from?" Instead of collecting evidence and making a case for how awful you are, make a case for how wonderful you are. Have compassion for yourself. You deserve it. Spend time on self-care and soulcare.

HOW TO WITNESS THE SHADOW LONG BUBBY SUZI

When you witness the Shadow Long Bubby Suzi, you hold space for the part of you that feels shame. You may choose to honor this energy according to your own tradition.

To honor this shadow in you: Take a breath. Close your eyes and put your hands over your heart. Tune in to the part of you that feels ashamed of yourself. Flood it with loving, healing light.

Auspicious times: This shadow may pop up when you feel inadequate, fear being judged, are around those who have judged you in the past, are meeting new people, or are in a situation where people learn your story. We all have unique shame triggers. Learn yours so that you can develop what author Dr. Brené Brown calls "shame resilience."

Music: "Song of the Jumbies" by Josephine Premice and "Zombie" by Fela Kuti

Answer these healing questions in your journal:

- What do I feel ashamed of?

- What do I do to avoid shame?

- Why am I judging myself?

- When is the first time I remember feeling ashamed of myself?

- What beliefs did I decide were true from the situation?

- What is the real truth?

- Feel free to sketch a picture of what shame looks like to you.

Suggested offerings: Every moon phase is a different ingredient for sacred healing rituals. Long Bubby Suzi may be a corrupted view of Atabey, the mama moon goddess who also represents fertility, earth, and fresh water. In June 2018, I hosted a goddess retreat in Long Bubby Suzi's magical jungle in Belize. We did lots of shadow work. For our temple priestesses, I included a Garifuna healer and a Mayan healer to honor the local culture.

Our Garifuna healer, Arzu Mountain Spirit, taught the goddess sisters how to release shame and pull in the light from the moon to feed our intentions. The solstice is an opening window. You feed your intentions into the moon and pull out your dreams. We bathed by candlelight in a garden hot tub and fed our intentions to the Universe.

Our goddess circle created beautiful magic, a combination of our divine feminine energy and the divine masculine energy of the summer solstice. We left a few generations of shame in the jungle and now lovingly send Long Bubby Suzi healing compassion and understanding. Compassion is necessary to heal toxic shame.

Shame causes us to constrict, withdraw, shrink, and hide. Show up and speak your truth.

You are not a burden or broken.

Alternate names: Lang Bobi Suzi, One Bubby Susan

Traditional Shame Healing Ritual: "Keeping Kumina" Ceremony

For some, Kumina is a healing ceremony of blessing, and for most who practice it is a way of life. Originating from St. Thomas in eastern Jamaica, Kumina groups are headed by a woman leader known as a Kumina queen and a male leader known as the king or captain. Imogene "Queenie" Kennedy was a famous and much-loved Kumina priestess and healer. She said that Spirit started her calling at a hollow cotton tree where she hung upside down for 21 days with no food or water. Kumina was wrongly dismissed by some for generations as evil witchcraft, but thankfully people are moving from shame to pride to reclaim and preserve it.

Kumina is primarily an ancestral veneration practice with singing, dancing, drumming, praying, and spirit possession. Slavery in Jamaica started in the early 17th century, bringing African peoples principally from West and Central Africa. Between 1838 and 1865, after the abolition of slavery, smaller additional groups were brought from the Kingdom of Kongo and other places to be indentured servants. Because of this, Kumina and its ancestral songs and dances have strong Kongo retention. In older forms, spirits are divided among ancestors, African gods, and earth gods. African gods may also be known as sky gods.

Kumina begins around 6 P.M. and usually ends around 12 hours later. Some people have annual Kumina ceremonies as an ancestral feast. Other reasons to keep Kumina include thanksgiving, wedding celebration, community intervention, personal healing, the nine-night mourning ceremony, court issues, and business prosperity. As with Komfa in Guyana, some people consider Kumina a religion and some don't.

To start, drummers take one shoe off and bless their drums with white rum. The Kumina king or queen sprays white rum libations from their mouth in the four directions. Participants dance counterclockwise in a rhythmic pattern around the drummers in the Kumina yard, expressing gratitude to the spirit guides. The drums invoke the spirit and people "get Myal," meaning that they are now dancing in a state of trance.

Call and response songs are in a mix of English and Kongo. Songs tell stories of the African experience, ask for guidance, and exalt at all that the people have been through. Household items like coconut graters, spoons, and pot covers become percussive instruments. More libations are poured and coffee is burned. A male goat sacrificed at midnight, in addition to white chickens, may be cremated or eaten.[2]

Bongos are people who perform and observe Kumina rituals. Some churches incorporate aspects of Kumina. Some Kumina groups incorporate Convince, another African-based spiritual practice. Although not common, some groups include smoking marijuana and tobacco as a sacrament.[3,4]

Your Shame Healing Ritual: Body Map

Ritual intention: To acknowledge shame held in the body.

Your pain has a story to tell. Today we stop betraying ourselves and start listening. I remember the teacher tracing us on paper and doing body mapping in kindergarten. But body mapping was popularized as a therapeutic practice by artist Jane Solomon to help South African women who were survivors of HIV/AIDS.

Heat mapping shows where different emotions live in our bodies. Regardless of country or culture, we all feel happiness, anger, shame, and guilt in the same places physically. Trauma and low-vibrating emotions like shame can get trapped in the body.

You will need:

- Blank paper
- Drawing paper
- Writing utensils
- Black eyeliner pencil

What to do:

Prepare your ritual space. You will draw two body maps. A body map is an outline of your body, as if you were outlining yourself lying flat. For this ritual, your body maps can be on separate pieces of paper or the front and back of one piece.

Body Map A: *What your body wants you to know*: Say to each part of your body, "Tell me about you or what happened to you." Write words or illustrate what you hear in reply. Fill in what each part of your body has to say to you or what you have to say to each part of your body.

Body Map B: *What you want your body to know*: Tell each part of your body, "I want you to know . . ." Fill your loving words, affirmations, and illustrations on your body.

Read these words to yourself in the mirror.

Body Map C: Get an eyeliner pencil or a washable body-ink pen. Using Body Map B as a guide, write loving words on your own body. YEAH! Take a picture for when you need to remind yourself.

Record your process and experience in your Goddess Soulbook.

Follow-up journal questions:

- What does your inner child have to say?

- What does your inner perfectionist have to say?

- What does your inner victim have to say?

- What does your inner warrior have to say?

AUNT NANCY

Shadow of Betrayal
Diaspora/Akan
Clearing Life Clutter Ritual

"I am willing to know the truth."

Shadow Fear: People always disappoint you.

AUNT NANCY'S MESSAGE

Maakye, my beloved! Everything is not as it seems. There will be chaos and trickery. It is a part of the natural order. Otherwise, how would you appreciate your joys? What is real and what is not? Am I real? Are you?

AUNT NANCY'S INNER TRUTH

We're scared. We don't trust anyone not to let us down. So we make jokes. We stay numb. We remain cynical. The truth is too heartbreaking. It hurts to feel so alone. It seems like everyone is a liar. Including us.

AUNT NANCY'S STORY

The Gullah Geechee are formerly enslaved people brought from Barbados and several African nations to the coast of South Carolina and Georgia because of their expertise in rice cultivation. Despite everything, they have been able to retain their African culture and folklore for hundreds of years. As a part of that tradition, while Gullah Geechee children were in their beds on the Sea Islands of South Carolina and Georgia, their elders regaled them with tales of Aunt Nancy, the tricky spider woman.

Almost 700 miles away, I heard the same folktales in my bed in New York City from my Guyana-born parents. Except my siblings and I heard "Nancy stories," and she was a witty teen spider. These stories were full of Nancy's tricks, shape-shifting, and deceptions where nothing was as it seemed.

The accents and the details differed, but we were all learning about Anansi or Kwaku Ananse, the Akan trickster abosom (deity) and sacred clown, who snuck into our folktales. Sometimes in the form of a wise woman and other times in the form of a man, this anthropomorphized, lying, cheating spider was a hoot! Anansi outsmarted all. Anansi can be an old sage or young and curious. Plus, "Nancy" has a regal divine pedigree. Her parents are Asase Yaa, Mother Earth, and Nyame, the sky god.

Anansi/Aunt Nancy laughs in silk webs. The magic of a trickster spirit is confusion and distraction. In Akan culture, this original spider superhero is the owner of all stories. There is power and magic in owning your narrative.

In all incarnations, Anansi/Aunt Nancy weaves, knits, braids, sews, and spins webs of discord and highlights betrayal. Ashanti storytellers introduce tall tales with the words: "We do not really mean that what we are about to say is true. A story, a story; let it come, let it go . . ." In fact, I feel Aunt Nancy spinning a story web of unexpected betrayal right now. . .

Aunt Nancy's best friend, Nanny Goat, was naively trusting, so she always made sure to look out for her. One day while Aunt Nancy was at the market, Nanny Goat came upon a huge well and heard crying inside.

"Help me," a thunderous voice boomed forth. Nanny Goat peered into the well and was surprised to see Lamar Lion, king of the jungle. He was trapped on the bottom. Nanny didn't know what to do. Lamar had been stalking her family for months. Lamar cried louder. "Please, Nanny Goat. Help me!"

"I can't," Nanny cried. "You'll eat me!"

"No, I won't, I promise!" said Lamar Lion. So Nanny pulled a thick vine over from the tree and strained to hold it while the huge lion lumbered up. By the time

Lamar made it to the top, she was weak, exhausted, and in pain. Finally, Lamar was out. Immediately he pounced on Nanny.

"What happened?" she shrieked. "You promised!"

"Yeah, but I am a lion," he said. "What did you expect?" Lamar was about to take a big bite of Nanny Goat's ear when Aunt Nancy came running.

"What is happening?" she yelled. Lamar explained that Nanny pulled him out of the well and now he was so hungry that he had to eat her. Aunt Nancy started laughing. "That's a lie," she said. "I wouldn't believe that unless I saw it for myself."

"You dare call the jungle king a liar?!" the lion asked.

"I tell you what," Aunt Nancy said. "I just passed a herd of water buffalo, your favorite meal. If you prove to me that li'l bitty Nanny Goat can pull you out of that hole, I will tell you where they are. Deal?" Lion licked his lips and jumped back into the hole. One betrayal to hurt and another betrayal to help.

There's a reason she is the owner of all the stories. The trickster gives us moral lessons. When you see spiders or webs, know that Aunt Nancy has a message for you.

Let's Talk Betrayal

Being played for a fool makes for great storytelling but is not good in our relationships with ourselves or others.

So many of us have abandonment wounds from our first relationship, the one with our parental figures. If you have experienced a betrayal or experience you interpreted as betrayal from your first relationship, this is a primal wound. Of course you might expect betrayal from the outside world.

Abandonment is the ultimate betrayal. If your parents separated or a parent died or just wasn't there enough, you may have processed this as abandonment. A parent can be physically present and emotionally absent. That, too, runs deep. As a child, no matter what the reason, you may feel betrayed by your caretakers. If the folks who were supposed to be there weren't, why would you expect anyone else to?

Betrayal is a mofo. If not addressed, every betrayal we experience leaves a tiny crack in our hearts. We have to heal those wounds so that we can love and trust. Whether you are betrayed by friends, lovers, co-workers, or—Goddess forbid—your family or life partner, betrayal cuts deep. The residue it leaves keeps us from feeling at peace. If you meet people and feel like they are too nice or you're waiting for the other shoe to drop or for them to show their "true colors," you have unhealed betrayal as a shadow.

I want to address self-betrayal, because life is a mirror. We treat ourselves like the lion treated Nanny Goat. We say, "I promise," but it means nothing because "that's just who I am." If there are people who seem to keep betraying you, you must first look at how you are betraying yourself. Self-betrayal can mean making promises to yourself you don't keep, eating poorly, rotating bad relationship choices, abusive self-talk, and not showing up for you. How do you betray you?

We are the trickster spirits in our own lives. You may start to see life through victim-colored glasses, thinking nothing ever goes your way and people always disappoint. Self-betrayal often tricks us by seeming to be one thing on the surface and turning out to be something else altogether. We are terrified of being betrayed by others, but we betray ourselves daily. Your relationship with yourself determines every other factor.

Your life is a series of choices. This is an exploration into your true self. You can't see your truth if you are distracted by emotional noise and physical clutter. Let's clear the noise, distraction, clutter, and bad juju so that you can begin to see your truth.

Like you, I have had my heart broken in love, by friends, and by family members. This is a part of life. It's important that we continue to love, trust, and open our hearts, allowing ourselves to be loved. The biggest lesson I have learned from heartbreak is that trust in relationships includes you trusting yourself enough to know that when you are betrayed, heartbreak won't break you. Don't close your heart. Keep on loving!

HOW TO WITNESS THE SHADOW AUNT NANCY

When you witness the Shadow Aunt Nancy, you hold space for the part of you that fears being betrayed. You may choose to honor this energy according to your own tradition.

To honor this shadow in you: Take a breath. Close your eyes and put your hands over your heart. Tune in to the part of you that is afraid to trust. Flood it with loving, healing light.

Auspicious times: This shadow may pop up when life is asking you to open your heart. Fears of being betrayed can come up in casual situations, like exchanges with neighbors or co-workers, or in deeper relationships with our partners, friends, or family of origin. Be aware of your relationship trust triggers. Trust yourself enough to know that you will not break.

Music: "Kwaku Ananse" by Apagya Show Band and "Anansewaa" by Kojo Antwi

Answer these healing questions in your journal:

- What currently triggers you into feeling betrayed or abandoned?

- When is the first time you remember feeling betrayed or abandoned?

- What did you decide that this betrayal or abandonment meant about you?

- What is another possible interpretation for why this betrayal/ abandonment took place?

- How have you betrayed or abandoned others?

- How have you betrayed or abandoned yourself?

Suggested offerings: Aunt Nancy/Anansi has a tremendous sense of humor and loves a good time. Anansi owns the stories. Bring your creative power to the table and share fun stories and even jokes about you being loved, appreciated, and respected.

Alternate names: Anansi, Ananse, Anancy, Nancy, Kwaku Ananse, Kompa Nanzi

Traditional Betrayal Healing Ritual: Energy-Clearing Incense

Clearing bad juju, meaning energetic decluttering, by burning sacred herbs, barks, and resins has always been a part of African spirituality across the continent and diaspora. This burning ritual, called smudging by some of our Native American siblings, repels bad spirits, cleanses the energy, raises the vibration, and creates a direct channel for communication with the Divine. There are also lots of nonsmoke ways to cleanse energy, from eggs to coconuts.

Here are just a few energy-clearing incense secrets from around the continent:

Prekese, a sacred plant in Ghana, is known as "soup perfume." Prekese, or Aidan fruit, is also known as the "fruit of God." It is used as an Ashanti cooking spice, but also to drive away bad spirits. Burning prekese drives away unwelcome energies and bad vibes. It is commonly believed that no harm can come to you when prekese is near.

Sacred Nigerian ka'aji incense is made with scented oils and aromatic wood. For centuries, ka'aji has been used in every special ceremony and rite for the Kanuri people, including burials, weddings, and baby namings. Ka'aji is used to scare away evil spirits. In fact, as soon as a baby is born, you get the ka'aji going.

Do you also know imphepho, the spirit herb? In South Africa, burning imphepho helps clear, cleanse and protect the home and body against evil.[5] Healers teach that imphepho can help you to relax, open your psychic channels, connect with ancestors and spirits, and become a clear channel for the truth. There are many different types of imphepho. Zulu sangomas use imphepho when throwing bones. It is a key part of all Zulu rituals and helps with spiritual protection and creating an energetic safe zone. Be sure that your intentions are clear, as imphepho will attract to you exactly what you are.

Juniper is known for clearing bad juju. The berries of the African juniper tree, native to Kenya, can be made into a cleansing floral water or a potent gin that can also be used for rituals. The bark, berries, and dried leaves may be burned as an aromatic energy-purifying incense that also can help with spiritual connection.

The spiritual properties of frankincense are well-known. Frankincense is used in Somalia, Egypt, and countless other cultures in religious rites as a deity offering, for energy clearing, for blessing, and for medicinal purposes. Science is now finding that frankincense can aid with mood regulation—aka bad vibes.[6] Somalian myrrh was used for sanitizing. It's not only helpful for psychic protection and banishing but was an offering to the goddess Iset (Isis). Frankincense and myrrh is a wise combination.

Making incense in many cultures is also an art.

Your Betrayal Healing Ritual: Clearing Life Clutter

Ritual intention: To clear the energy and release emotional, spiritual, energetic, and physical clutter.

Everything you own also owns you. You are in an energetic relationship with every object around you. When we have been living with personal confusion and self-betrayal for a long time, we tend to clutter. Clutter allows us to distract ourselves from facing our real issues.

You will need:

- A coconut
- Holy water or milk of your choice
- Cleaning tools and products

What to do:

There are all kinds of clutter. Physical clutter is the most obvious kind. But there is also emotional clutter in the form of unspoken issues, digital clutter, and body (health) clutter. Overcommitting is schedule clutter. Some of the self-declared minimalists I know have the most clutter in their lives. Their homes appear spotless, but the loudness of the secrets they are hiding, the emotions they are not expressing, and the conversations they are avoiding is deafening. That is energetic and emotional clutter. This is all spiritual clutter.

Part 1: Clear the Energy

Prepare your ritual space. Bathe a coconut in Kananga Water or Florida Water. You can also use moon water, sun water, or milk. Let it air-dry. Kick the coconut from the back of the house to the front of the house through every room and out the front door.

While you do this, pray according to your tradition and state the intentions of what you are releasing, preceded by the word *good-bye*.

For example: Good-bye to arguments, good-bye unpaid bills, good-bye feeling lonely, good-bye unreturned phone calls.

When you kick the coconut out the front door, don't pick it up with your hands. Kick it into a garbage bag or pick it up with gloves. Bury it or dispose of it at your crossroads. Say a good-bye prayer and don't look back.

Part 2: Clear Life Clutter

Allow yourself to do this clutter clearing throughout your goddess initiation quest. Doing this clearing while doing shadow work is especially powerful. Put a cup of water behind the front door to capture the unhealed energy, and refresh it daily while you are doing this clearing.

- Clear and release your physical clutter: donate or dispose of anything that no longer serves its purpose.

- Clear and release your digital clutter: delete files and apps that no longer have a purpose for you.

- Clear and release your emotional clutter: have conversations that you have been avoiding.

Record your energy-clearing process and experience in your Goddess Soulbook.

SOUCOUYANT

Shadow of Scarcity
Trinidad/Diaspora
Goddess Superhero You Ritual

"My blessings always overflow."

Shadow Fear: There's not enough to go around.

SOUCOUYANT'S MESSAGE

How allyuh doing, beauty? There are many who envy your riches. You have so much. You are an heiress to wealth. You are surrounded by an abundance of joy, love, good times, pleasures, and riches. Protect your energy. Protect your peace.

SOUCOUYANT'S INNER TRUTH

We are living in fear. We get our oxygen from attention. We get what we need from other people. We feel jealous and envious. We don't know if there's enough love to go around. We don't know if there's enough money to go around. Maybe there's not enough happiness to go around.

SOUCOUYANT'S STORY

If you see a ball of fire roll across a field at night, it just might be someone's granny. There's a story of an energy-sucking vampiress that has terrified folks throughout the Caribbean and the southern United States for generations. In Trinidad, she is known as the Soucouyant.

The Soucouyant is a shape-shifter who flies around at night. She's bright red because she takes off her skin and hides it in a huge mortar and pestle. When she gets to her victims' homes, she sneaks in through cracks in the walls or roof. She attacks while they are asleep, sucking the life out of them, but she leaves them very much alive. She feeds on a person's breath, and once she's got a good source, she wants to come back as much as possible.

Victims will have the best sleep ever until they wake up with unexplained bruises. If you've got nice skin, she might take it. She wears each skin until it runs out, but she's got to be home and wearing skin by dayclean (daybreak). The energy-sucking crone often appears as a beautiful young woman during the day. If sunrise catches her away from her house, she can sing for her skin to find her. If that's not bad enough, she shape-shifts into animals, and some of them do drink blood. She becomes a Soucouyant either through inheritance or by heading to a graveyard at midnight on the dark moon and mixing up a special oil.

"Don't let the hag ride ya!" If you hear that, you're in South Carolina, where the Soucouyant is known as the Boo Hag. The Gullah Geechee people say if you encounter her, throw broom straws. Here she flies without fire, and she will sit on your chest and steal your voice.

In Guyana, if you wake up tired, it just might be that you were visited by an energy vampire named the Ole Higue. Ole Higue (Old Hag) sucks you energetically, and she can take your breath or shadow until she fire-rolls out. Same Soucouyant, different location. Except whereas the Gullah Geechee say to throw straws to distract her, in Guyana, where Ole Higues can also be men, they say throw salt or rice. In Suriname where she is Asema and in the Bahamas where she is simply called Hag, the same rules of distraction apply.

The Soucouyant/Boo Hag/Ole Higue/Hag is extremely obsessive, and if you throw the rice or salt, she can't leave until she counts every single grain. If you can get to her house and put salt on her skin, she won't be able to get back into it.

This creature loves babies. My dad is the oldest of his siblings, because he had an older brother named Winston that he never got to meet. This brother died as a baby. My grandmother shared with us that when she was a young and inexperienced teen mother, her baby died suddenly, sucked to death by an Ole Higue.

Let's Talk Scarcity

Vampires take from others because they don't have enough life force for themselves. Blood, breath, love, joy, and money are all different kinds of energy. We treat our inner demons, fears, and challenges as if we are trying to outrun the Soucouyant tossing diversions in our own path.

That is scarcity consciousness. When you live like that, you are always hungry and always thirsty. You are jealous of the success of others. You can only truly rejoice in your own victories. This is the "I got mine" mentality or the "just enough to get by" mindset.

When I graduated from college, I briefly moved to L.A. My repeated prayer was, "Please, God, I need just enough space to lay my head." And guess where I ended up with this lack mindset? Renting a mattress on someone's dining room floor. But that is exactly what I asked for. I went to the ocean and asked for a thimbleful of water.

Prosperity consciousness is living with the belief that there is an overflow, more than enough to go around. With this window on the world, you realize that we are all in it together. Your sister's joy is yours too. You don't need to hoard anything or feel jealous.

It's the ole calabash half-full or half-empty metaphor. So which way do you see life? Energy is infinite and abundant, right? Both science and spirituality tell us that energy cannot be created or destroyed. Again, love is energy. Money is energy. Happiness is energy.

So why don't you see it that way? Well, it's not your fault. You are inundated with messages of scarcity and lack. You can have a scarcity consciousness whether you were raised wealthy, poor, or somewhere in between. Our current system is based on us believing in scarcity. We must believe that there is not enough, that we are not enough and competition is a way of life. If we believed that we were enough, we wouldn't buy more stuff.

How we do anything is how we do everything. So instead, we decide who gets healthy water and who doesn't, who gets medication and who doesn't. One winning means another losing. People who are emotionally healthy know that this is not right. You should have your basic needs met. No human should go hungry, and that is a failing of society to not take care of the basic needs of its people.

So how do you know if you have a shadow belief of scarcity consciousness? Well, are you stingy in how you give or receive love? Are you selfish in how you give or receive money? Are you restricted in how you give or receive happiness?

Close your eyes and see it: What is the feeling of scarcity and lack? Now, what does abundance and prosperity feel like? The feeling of scarcity and the feeling of abundance are energetic frequencies.

Expand your belief that there is more available, more good times, more love, more wellness, more happiness, and more money. You don't have to take from anyone else.

Expand your capacity to receive.

I remember sharing with someone that my mom's dad, the grandfather I knew, was extremely generous and sometimes fed his village. And my friend said, "Well, they must have been very privileged." And I had to think for a minute, even though I know the circumstances of my grandparents living in a two-room home with seven children. I know my mom grew up without electricity, running water, or an indoor bathroom. I am aware that she had to wash the same uniform every night for school the next day. So on paper, by U.S. standards, they were poor. But they didn't see it that way, so I never see it that way. They had family, the ability to farm, and each other. My grandfather was a village elder, although he only attended school until the sixth grade, because he loved his community and they loved him. He believed that as long as they could pick food, they could eat. So they *were* rich. "Yes, they were very privileged," I answered.

"Rain ah fall on roof, yuh put barrel fuh ketch am." If rain falls on your roof, put a barrel and catch it. That's a Guyanese proverb meaning there's always abundance for us. That's prosperity consciousness. Just like people can feel lonely in a room full of people, some are poor with a billion dollars in the bank. That is scarcity or lack consciousness.

You may believe that love comes at a price or you have to be perfect to deserve love. You may have an underlying belief that money is dirty or evil. You have to be willing to let those beliefs go because if you don't, then you won't allow yourself to receive.

The same Creator that created the stars, forests, and oceans created you. If you wonder whether Mother Nature is abundant and generous or stingy, greedy, sparing, and holding back, go to a garden or look up at the stars. The Creator that made you deals only in abundance. Aligning yourself with your prosperity is one of the most spiritual things that you can do. Open your arms and say, "My Creator, which I am created in the image of, only wants me to thrive!"

You are worthy. You are deserving.

HOW TO WITNESS THE SHADOW SOUCOUYANT

When you witness the Shadow Soucouyant, you hold space for the part of you that fears scarcity and lack. You may choose to honor this energy according to your own tradition.

To honor this shadow in you: Take a breath. Close your eyes and put your hands over your heart. Tune in to the part of you that feels that there's just not enough to go around. Flood it with loving, healing light.

Auspicious times: This shadow may pop up when your childhood fears around there being enough love, happiness, food, or money are triggered. Remind yourself that this is an abundant universe. There is enough to go around.

Music: "Suck Me Soucouyant" by Geoffrey Cordle and "Ma Soucouyant" by Slow Train Soul

Answer these healing questions in your journal:

- What triggers you to feel like there's not enough, whether it be love, money, or happiness?

- When is the first time you remember feeling like there was not enough?

- What did you decide the situation meant?

- What did adults, peers, or those in authority say about the situation?

- What are alternate interpretations you can see now for the situation?

- How does fear of not enough love play out for you?

- How does fear of not enough money affect you?

Suggested offerings: All stories of the Soucouyant talk about distracting her with grains of rice to count. Rice is the perfect symbol of abundance. Rice is nourishing, abundant, and the grains are virtually endless.

Alternate names: Soucriant, Ole Higue, Boo Hag, Fire Rass, Asema, Hag

Traditional Scarcity Healing Ritual: Sous Sous

My cousin just got a $10K payout from her sous sous. The sous sous has many names throughout the diaspora, but it is essentially collective economics. Sous sous (also sou sou or susu) helps people to achieve their savings goals. Clearly the practice has West African roots, as it is called osusu in Sierra Leone and esesu or ajo in Nigeria.

The way it works is super simple. The group or the leader agrees on what the amount contributed will be and how often each person must "put in." They also decide how long it will go for. So it could be, for example, a 12-week or 12-month sous sous with 20 people who put in $50 a week with a $1000 payout each time. Then each week one person in the group gets paid. You could have a small-ticket or big-ticket sous sous depending on the participants.

The sous sous master picks the order of the payouts. There are no paper contracts. Being the sous sous master is a huge responsibility because if someone squelches and can't make a payment, the organizer has to come out of pocket. Some people do sous sous for a year, and everyone gets a nice big payout on their birthday.

Many of my friends from other cultures don't get it. They say, "Why not use the bank?" Well, this is a bank. We didn't always have access to financial institutions. Sure there is no interest, but there are also no credit checks. You are there because you are friends or family, so no ID is required. Lots of folks in NYC where we have a huge immigrant population do a sous sous at work. Then you know everyone involved has an income.

In Haiti, the savings club is called a "sol" or "main." In Jamaica, it's "partner." In Guyana, we also say "throwing box" or a "box hand." In Somalia, it's known as "ayuuto." Folks in the Dominican Republic call it "sociedad." In Barbados, it's "meeting-turn." And it's "box money" in Antigua.

Your Scarcity Healing Ritual: Goddess Superhero You

Ritual intention: To turn your shadows into superpowers.

It's a bird, it's a plane, it's YOU as a supergoddess! Let's look at your desired and undesired traits and qualities and find the abundant gifts in them.

You will need:

- Goddess Soulbook
- Journal
- Writing utensil
- Two people you admire
- Two people you dislike or despise

What to do:

Note: When I refer to "mother" and "father" feel free to adjust the language to the structure of your family of origin.

Part 1: Journal Questions

Desired Traits: Caregivers

- What are your mother's three greatest qualities?

- What are your father's three greatest qualities?

- How do you share these traits? When do you exhibit or embody these traits?

- Are there times you hide, bury, or avoid these qualities? If so, why?

- What superpowers come from these traits?

Desired Traits: Heroes

- Who are two people you admire?

- For each of them, what are three things that you admire?

- How do you share these traits? When do you exhibit or embody these traits?

- Are there times you hide, bury, or avoid these qualities? If so, why?

- What superpowers come from these traits?

Undesired Traits: Caregivers

- What are your mother's three biggest flaws?

- What are your father's three biggest flaws?

- How do you share these traits? When do you exhibit or embody these traits?

- What do you do to overcompensate for them?

- What superpowers come from these traits? Let's find the positive. Turn those unwelcome traits into superpowers. For example, if your mother meddles in your marriage, the superpower version of that may be attention to detail.

Undesired Traits: Villains

- Who are two people you strongly dislike?

- For each of them, what are three things that you dislike?

- How do you share these traits? How do you exhibit or embody these traits?

- What do you do to overcompensate for them?

- What superpowers come from these traits?

Part 2: Super Powered You

In your Goddess Soulbook, draw "superhero you" with the superpowers you inherited from your folks.

Add to your Goddess Soulbook drawing:

- What is your supergoddess name?

- What is your supergoddess nemesis or kryptonite?

- What is your supergoddess fuel?

- What are your superpowers?

GANG GANG SARA

Shadow of Resistance
Tobago
The Mask That Grins and Lies Ritual

"This is me. I show up."

Shadow Fear: "I'm going to mess it all up."

GANG GANG SARA'S MESSAGE

Sistar! Don't worry. We got this. I know. You're just feeling a little haunted by past missteps. Things are beyond your control. But guess what? Today is a new day. You're going to rock it.

GANG GANG SARA'S INNER TRUTH

We all are a little scared. We've been ghosting our own dreams. We don't want to screw up, so we resist our magic. We were ripped apart. Abandoned. Made to feel small. So we hold back, worry, and pretend to seek perfection that will never come.

GANG GANG SARA'S STORY

Did you just see something float by? It may have been Gang Gang Sara, the famous witch of Golden Lane.

Gang Gang Sara was an enslaved woman who was said to have come from West Africa in the 1700s or 1800s. Her goal was to find her kidnapped family and emancipate her people. Old folks didn't recall where exactly in Africa she came from. Some say she blew across the Atlantic sea to the island of Tobago in a storm. Others say that she flew there. Or maybe she just levitated.

Gang Gang Sara landed in the mysterious and magical village of Les Coteaux at midnight on the eve of the pink moon. Les Coteaux is known as Tobago's home of obeah. Sara set off on her mission. She hid her things in a silk cottonwood, the ceiba, also known as the jumbie tree. Back home, these trees could move like people and often gathered together like old friends. Sara tuned in to the vibration of the island. She began the search for her stolen family members.

Then Gang Gang Sara's mass liberation goals were thrown off when she found Tom. Tom had been a childhood friend in their beautiful West African nation. He was captured and enslaved when they were kids. Seeing Tom again filled her heart and they fell madly in love. He called her his "Louisa," which means "famous warrior." Louisa was also close to her original name. Gang Gang Sara and Tom stole every moment they could to be together, sneaking into the hills just to lime.

One night during a visit, Sara was captured by an enslaver named Peter. He forced her to cook and clean, but her magic caused trouble in the plantation house. He sent her to work with Tom in the brutal sugarcane fields.

But Sara did not come to be a slave. So Emancipation came to Tobago. Everyone flew their Shango flags. Sara put her witchy powers to work as the village's midwife and bush doctor. In the tradition of Len' Han', all pitch in to make their community great. Sara partnered with the tall, majestic silk cottonwood tree for many a-healing. The townsfolk nicknamed her "Gang Gang" for her loving ability to deliver healthy babies.

When Tom died, our beautiful elder witch was heartbroken. She decided to fly back home. She climbed all the way up to the top of her friend, the jumbie tree, as it whispered her name. She couldn't hear what it said through her tears. Gang Gang Sara faced northeast, toward home, and leapt.

Some say she forgot how to fly, all of those years in Tobago. Others say the issue was the salt. Salt grounds witches. She had eaten the salt of Tobago and was now anchored to the land.

Gang Gang Sara and Tom were buried side by side in the African Cemetery at Golden Lane. Their headstones with their names carved on them are still on many tourist itineraries. One of their descendants, Alvin James, is the cemetery groundskeeper. His grandparents told him about Sara's magical powers.

On Christmas, men leave wine on her grave. A local Tobagonian recently confessed to trying to pry open Gang Gang Sara's crypt. He wanted to connect with her for a blessing. Just as he started to pry, a flash of light hit him, and he fell down. He says he "won't be so stupid again."[7]

Gang Gang Sara's silk cottonwood tree is still standing. The branches are filled with spirits. It is the gathering place for magical souls. You can find her there. Whispers can be heard in the vicinity by day. Strange noises come from the tree on starry full-moon nights.

Let's Talk Resistance

In the political arena, a resistance movement counters those in power. In fitness, resistance training workouts cause our muscles to contract. When it comes to you stepping into your greatness, resistance is the force that wants you to stay (safely) where you are now. In *The War of Art*, writer Steven Pressfield, who gave the force that holds us back a name, calling it *resistance*, says resistance recruits your loved ones to hold you back out of their resistance.

On the surface, resistance looks like laziness, disorganization, excuses, and being unmotivated. But there are deeper forces at play. The inner saboteur is clever. When we met Threshold Guardian Nana Buluku in Chapter 1, we talked about how self-sabotage is waiting to greet us at any new venture. This self-sabotage or resistance rears its ugly head and blocks our growth, creativity, and evolution. Why is it called resistance? Well, it is about us resisting our power, desires, and the force we truly are.

So you have a vision, purpose, or dream that you were born to share. It could be a book, political movement, a song, nonprofit service organization, or all of the above. But resistance greets you at the front door. Now you're doing everything except birthing your vision.

Resistance is fear in many masks, just like jumbies have many different faces. So what is your favorite brand of self-sabotage when you have a BMGV? Some people start with a big push and then burn out and never finish what they start. For others, getting started is the hardest part. Or you may be a shiny-new-thing kind of goddess who is easily distracted and off to the next big idea. Maybe procrastination is no problem, but your favorite flavor of resistance is perfectionism. Nothing is ever good enough to be complete.

Some other resistance shadow monsters that may have chased you include distraction, fear of rejection or criticism, jealousy, the need for another degree or certification to be considered good enough, not-ready-yet syndrome, undercharging, workaholism (yes!), fear of missing out, and, of course, good old perfectionism, procrastination, and worry.

If you are waiting for inspiration to strike, here's the big secret that nobody ever tells us. You will not feel like doing it at every step of the process. No one does. You're never going to feel like doing it consistently. If you sit around and you just wait until you feel like doing it, yes, you will have bursts of motivation, but then what happens tomorrow?

One of the members of our Goddess Temple Circle asked, "Why was this put in my heart if I'm not going to feel like doing it?" Well, our beautiful reptilian brain is programmed to keep you from doing it. Your brain wants to keep you alive. Your brain loves routine and safety. Your brain does not want you experimenting and risking; that means potentially harm. Your brain cannot read the difference between "I'm going to play guitar onstage" and "I'm going to jump off a cliff." Resistance is doing its job—stopping danger and evolution. The foundation under that resistance is fear.

You say, "I've got big plans!" Your brain says, "No, ma'am. I think not. There's a reality show on that needs your immediate attention. Our priority is to go to social media, eat some Cheetos, and stay safe."

You can't think yourself out of resistance. But what a relief to know that it's not you. You are not lazy, bad, or wrong.

Resistance is a part of the process. The same way that healthy earthly parents want to keep us safe, this resistance shadow says, "I don't want you to be out there and possibly get hurt." Whether it's French fries, a drink, or a sexy hookup, your brain says, "Yay, distraction!"

The size of the resistance matches the splendor of your vision. The bigger the dream, the bigger the resistance. Remind yourself, "Oh, I must be on to something good. Look how big the resistance is that I am feeling."

Discipline can be an intimidating concept. The goddess energy version of that is devotion. Instead of hitting yourself over the head asking why you can't be more disciplined, develop a practice of devotion. Why do you want to do whatever you are resisting? How can you deepen your devotion to your cause?

You can't control the outcome. All you can do is decide to show up for yourself every day. That is devotion.

HOW TO WITNESS THE SHADOW GANG GANG SARA

When you witness the Shadow Gang Gang Sara, you hold space for the part of you that is hiding, holding back, and resisting your own brilliance. You may choose to honor this energy according to your own tradition.

To honor this shadow in you: Take a breath. Close your eyes and put your hands over your heart. Tune in to the part of you that feels stuck. Flood it with loving, healing light.

Auspicious times: This shadow may pop up when exciting opportunities and possibilities come your way. The inner bully of resistance seeks to maintain the status quo and keep you safe. Forgive yourself for any missteps, and remember that you are beautifully human. Focus on your devotion to your mission and show up for yourself.

Music: "Ju Ju Warrior" by Calypso Rose and "Witch Doctor" by Mighty Sparrow

Answer these healing questions in your journal:

- What is resistance blocking you from doing right now?

- How do you feel about this?

- What is the first memory you have of sabotaging your own happiness?

- What story did you tell yourself at the time for why this happened?

- What are some possible alternate explanations?

- If you were visible and not resisting your own dreams, who might you be?

- How can you love and accept this part of you more?

Suggested offerings: Dance raises the vibration and awakens stagnant energy. In Mauritius the hip swaying Sega dance of the Maroons, escaped enslaved people, is about the soul transcending earthly issues. The reel dances of Tobago summon spirits and uplift with song and drumming accompaniment. On the Caribbean island of Monserrat where Jombee was considered to be a religion by some, there is a similar jumbie dance. The jumbie dance includes drumming and formalized dance steps, making energetic space for "turning," spirit possession, and speaking in tongues.[8] These trance ritual ceremonies bear many similarities to "catching Komfa" in Guyana, "keeping Kumina" in Jamaica, and "rele lwa" invocation dances in Haiti. In all cases connection with Spirit is celebrated and used for healing, therapy, problem-solving, changing luck, divination, and veneration.

Alternate name: Gang Gang Sarie

Traditional Resistance Healing Ritual:
Afro-Caribbean Masquerade

Have you ever "played mas"? Any of the carnivals and festivals celebrating African-diaspora culture worldwide are a place to raise your vibration, release your inhibitions, and just have fun. The most famous in the Caribbean diaspora are Trinidad and Tobago's Carnival, Toronto's Caribana, Crop Over in Barbados, the UK's Notting Hill Carnival, and for the grittier experience, NYC's Labor Day Parade. Others include Jamaica's Bacchanal, Kanaval in Haiti, Carriacou Carnival, and Mashramani and Carnival in Guyana. Jonkonnu/John Canoe dance parades for the Garifuna and Black folks from North Carolina, the Bahamas, Jamaica, and other parts of the Caribbean have mixed origins and cultures but the same root. Two of the world's biggest masquerade festivals, Rio Carnival in Brazil and Mardi Gras in New Orleans, also most certainly celebrate Black cultures.

There are many historians that speak of the European masquerade balls as the root of Carnival. In most cases, only the date was borrowed from European culture. Carnival season was originally the last hurrah before Lent, the time of sacrifice and restriction. Colonizers would have masquerade balls for the glut of beauty, food, and sexuality before 40 austere days of penance. The word *carnival* itself comes from the Latin *carne levare,* meaning "leave meat."

Masquerade, costuming, mask wearing, dance, pageantry, and musical and spiritual celebrations have always been a part of diverse African cultures. From the Egungun masquerades to the Dogon masks and Sigui Festival, the ancient Egyptian carnivals, headdresses of the Bamana people, Sande secret society, Mmanwu masquerades, and so much more, the African tradition of masquerade is ancient.

J'ouvert is the celebration the night before Carnival; then Carnival is the binge before the fast. Trinidad's two-day extravaganza is considered to be the mother of all carnivals. But the late Grenadian historian Joachim Mark controversially traced the famous Trini Carnival back to Grenada.[9]

Our diaspora carnivals thrive as a form of resistance against oppression and respectability politics, and most importantly, a way to have fun. Some Carnival histories discuss African people mocking and mimicking the Europeans, and others talk about the ties to celebration of Emancipation Day, which most of the English-speaking Caribbean celebrates on August 1. Some fests moved the date to line up with Lent.

Ritual mask work is powerful. Wearing a mask and costume in this format allows you to temporarily lose yourself. The issue becomes when we spend most of our lives wearing masks.

Your Resistance Healing Ritual: The Mask That Grins and Lies

Ritual intention: To uncover your social masks that block you.

Are you wearing a mask? In 1895, influential Black American poet Paul Laurence Dunbar wrote, "We wear the mask that grins and lies, It hides our cheeks and shades our eyes." Most of us have two faces, the face we show and the person we are inside. Sometimes we wear several different social masks all on the same day.

What is the face that grins and lies for you? You will create a two-sided mask to answer this question.

You will need:

- Paper or a blank plastic mask
- Writing utensil

What to do:

Prepare your ritual space. Use a blank premade mask or draw a mask with a basic oval face with two eyes, a nose, and a mouth. Draw one mask on the front of the page and one on the back of the page.

Part 1: How Do Other People See You?

First, decorate the face (front) of the mask with the face you publicly present. Who is the you that you show to the world? Use relevant colors and go for it. Is she serious, studious, funny, confident, self-deprecating, friendly, thoughtful, empathetic? When I've done this ritual in goddess workshops, some of the traits people revealed for the outer mask were confident, empathic, friendly, nice, successful, bitchy, and shy.

Part 2: How Do You See Yourself?

Turn the mask or page over. On the back or inside of the mask, illustrate who you are on your inside. Again, use relevant colors, symbols, and expressions. On the same side, write words that reveal who you really are. Who is the person no one or very few get to see?

Some of the traits on the inside our goddess sisters revealed were workaholic, pervert, dreamer, addict, softy, bold, angry, and terrified.

Now sit in front of a mirror and read the words to yourself. Read the face of the outside you aloud; then read the face of the inside you aloud. Put the mask on your goddess altar and treat it with love. Dispose of it when you are ready to move forward. Do something loving for yourself afterward.

Record your process in your Goddess Soulbook.

Follow-up journal questions:

- What are the differences between the face you present to society and your true self?

- Who do you allow to see the real you?

- If you stopped wearing the masks tomorrow, what might happen? Who would be angry about it? Who would be happy about it?

MEDUSA

Shadow of Rage
Libya
Rewrite Yourself Ritual

"I have a right to feel my feelings."

Shadow Fear: "I always get screwed over."

MEDUSA'S MESSAGE

Assalamu alaikum, child. Peace be upon you. Humans cannot judge you. Let your joys, hopes, beauty, and feelings rage on. No one knows your truth, and not everyone deserves it. They are not in control of your feelings. We are not even in control of control. Worry not about strength. Be your own beautiful.

MEDUSA'S INNER TRUTH

We are petrified and pissed off, angry and shaking. But under that we are hurt and heartbroken. Feeling undervalued is overwhelming. We can't stay silent anymore.

MEDUSA'S STORY

Medusa is a celebrity of magical creatures. We all know her. Maybe you read about her as a Greek Gorgon in school. Or you saw her on a TV show or movie. No matter where you first encountered her, chances are that she was labeled as an ugly, vicious monster with bloodthirsty snakes for hair.

Well, Medusa is actually African, by way of Libya. This Berber goddess of wisdom's rage is legendary. In many stories, Medusa was born a monster.

In the most famous tale, Medusa was a beautiful, loving priestess in the temple of Athena, the Greek goddess of war. Then Poseidon, Greek god of the sea, raped her on the floor of Athena's temple. When Medusa ran to Athena for help, Athena turned her into a monster.

In some interpretations, Athena was protecting Medusa from men. In others, Athena was punishing her for the desecration of her temple. Either way, any man who laid eyes on her would be instantly changed into stone. In this new form, according to Roman poet Ovid, her hair raged as venomous snakes.

Medusa represents righteous rage and judgment. Her name has come to mean an ugly monster. A woman's uncontrolled feelings are seen as wild, ugly, and unacceptable. In most versions of the tale, she was beheaded. Her dripping blood became her children. So Medusa, who was violated, was furious and heartbroken. Medusa, like many of us, was misunderstood.

One of the most powerful stories has Medusa making herself ugly and undesirable with a stone power gaze to keep herself safe. In this world of 10,000 things, everything is currency, especially beauty. Ugliness is the threat that looms for womenfolk. Disobey the rules and you are repulsive. Follow your own path and it may make you ugly. Don't buy the recommended products and ugliness may emerge. And of course, never ever age. But the only true ugliness is cheating us of your real beauty.

Medusa is a version of the goddess Neith. Neith is the Egyptian goddess who the Greeks modeled Athena after. In one depiction of Neith, she has the head of a serpent and is a triple goddess. Medusa was a triple goddess Gorgon with her immortal sisters, Stheno and Euryale. Medusa's people, the Berbers, worshipped Neith. Neith was the prime creator who wove the universe into existence on her loom. As a hunter and the goddess of war, her symbol was the bow and arrow. Neith also helped to settle major disputes. She could give birth without a partner, and there were images of her nursing a crocodile. She was wise, warlike, and just.

Medusa's anger is sacred rage. You have a right to your righteous rage, but don't let it eat you alive. Don't lose your humanity. You have a right to your love, vulnerability, and healing as well.

Let's Talk Rage

Growing up, I had so much repressed anger. Maybe like you, I didn't feel like I had permission to feel all of my feelings. My parents are both beautiful people who did the best they could. But they couldn't teach me healthy emotional expression because no one taught them. My parents are only three generations from slavery. Most of us on the planet today are the first generation that even had the privilege to consider healthy emotional expression.

My grandparents also did the best they could, but like most in their era, what they called discipline would qualify as abuse today. Many of the old common disciplinary practices from my parents' country, like kneeling on a grater to get whippings, are punishments inherited from enslavers. As a result, my dad is loving, generous, funny, kind, and brilliant but has extreme rage. My mom is also brilliant, loving, generous, and kind but a passive people pleaser, super empath, and highly sensitive person. So I never learned what healthy anger or conflict resolution looked like. I only learned that angry people are scary and everyone else must tiptoe around them and clean up or take the blame for the collateral damage left in their wake.

Many of the older women on my paternal side are angry, negative, and emotionally abusive. They take pride in "carrying on," cutting people down, and being rageaholics. If your feelings are hurt by their behavior, it's because "you're weak." In the cultures I come from, to even discuss this publicly is betrayal. But if we don't heal it, we pass it forward.

Our emotional and spiritual health also requires looking at the benefits of what we attempt to hide, suppress, and avoid. So here is the shadow benefit of "carrying on." Those same relatives whose mean behavior makes me want to avoid them are also geniuses at getting what they want. I remember traveling with them, and the hotel was running a bait and switch. They were able to get the issue resolved with a quickness. If I had beef and needed swift justice, they probably would be able to get it.

My mom and dad are my heroes, and I am so grateful that they are my parents. This is exactly the family I needed to learn the things I came to teach. My rage shadow is that when I am pissed off, I can carry on just like those family members I avoid. To paraphrase Great Ancestor James Baldwin, to be a Black person in the United States is to live enraged.

I love and accept all of me. I am proud of being the granddaughter of my dad's dad, the town "angry man" and the reason everyone in the village still knows the

Walla Baby Tribe. I wear that tribal name with pride. I also stand proudly on the side of the badass great-grandma that a judge called a "virago." That's who we had to be in order to survive. It doesn't mean that this is who we must continue to be to each other.

Although both of my amazing parents are becoming aware of the detriments of all of this now, my issues were already formulated. When I was on the outs with most acquaintances, I would just cut them out of my life because I didn't know how to have a healthy conflict. Or I would say nothing, and my built-up anger would suddenly explode over seemingly mundane things. I had to be drunk to tell my friends how I was really feeling. I also took out the anger at the men in my life that I felt I was not allowed to be angry at. Obviously, this is all hella unhealthy.

A group of goddess sisters and I were laughing the other day about how many men have no idea how much we tiptoe around their emotional needs. Last Thanksgiving at my house, I knew my mom wanted to have the turkey carved at the table, after we presented and blessed it. In trying to help, my brother went into the kitchen early and carved the bird within an inch of its li'l turkey life. Afterward my sister asked why I stood there and let him do that. I shrugged and said, "I dunno. Toxic masculinity. I didn't want to hurt his feelings." But that wasn't on him. That was my toxic (lack of) communication.

My brother is supersensitive, and I was just happy he was participating. I went back to my default settings where the only way to deal with an issue is be passive and smile or be angry and hurt the other person's feelings. But there is a whole range of other ways to communicate in between. My brother is probably the calmest person in my whole family. If we have an argument, I am more likely to be the one to yell or storm off. There would have been nothing wrong with saying, "Stop cutting the turkey up, dude! Mommy doesn't want it like that." It was my bad, not his. It was toxic "positivity," not toxic masculinity.

I am still learning healthy emotional expression. Healing your shadow fears means figuring out that you can love someone, have conflict, and they will still love you. You have a right to your full range of emotions—including anger. There is healthy anger. There is also unhealthy rage.

In the public sphere, our sacred rage inspires people to run for office, leads protests, gives voice to the voiceless, gets policies shifted, and demands justice. There is no right or privilege that we have that did not come from people being pissed off about something. Loving, embracing, and integrating our shadow selves starts with looking for the gifts in the shadow. You can't just turn a blind eye to the things you're angry about and bypass them with a "love and light." You have a right to your anger. You have a right to feel all your feelings.

HOW TO WITNESS THE SHADOW MEDUSA

When you witness the Shadow Medusa, you hold space for the part of you that feels rage. You may choose to honor this energy according to your own tradition.

To honor this shadow in you: Take a breath. Close your eyes and put your hands over your heart. Tune in to the part of you that feels out of control. Flood it with loving, healing light.

Auspicious times: This shadow may pop up when we feel that situations are beyond our control or when we feel powerless, disrespected, or attacked. Rage looks different on everyone. Loud, outward rage is obvious, but there is also quiet, inward rage. Be aware that just because you feel threatened, it does not mean that you are being threatened.

Music: "She's a Bitch" by Missy Elliott and "De Jumbie" by Scrunter

Answer these healing questions in your journal:

- What triggers your anger?

- Do you hold back on your anger?

- Who are you angry at right now?

- What is your first memory of being angry?

- How did the adults around you deal with your anger?

- What did you decide their reactions meant?

- How did they deal with their anger?

- Write a Dear Anger letter.

Suggested offerings: Libyan gold tektite was created from a meteor impact millions of years ago. This tektite has immensely powerful spiritual properties, including clearing negative energy and helping with mood regulation.

Alternate name: Gorgo

Traditional Rage Healing Ritual: Temple of Pythons

The Temple of Pythons in Ouidah, Benin, is not the place to go if you fear reptiles. The small Vodou temple is home to at least 40 snakes. We think of snakes as angry and ready to strike. These pythons may look scary, but they have no venom.

Snakes are sacred in Benin. A statue of a snake eating its tail represents the rainbow serpent goddess Ayida-Weddo. This is the town of Weddo/Hueda/Whydah, her home. Another goddess statue of a beautiful woman carrying a snake stands guard in the courtyard. She is Mami Wata, representing the cycle of unending life.

The temple is dedicated to the serpent deity Dangbé or Da. Initiates pay homage with scarification and tattoos that resemble fangs. There is also a statue of Shango and Legba/Esu-Elegbara with an erect penis. People also come here to honor different iterations of the snake deity from throughout the diaspora, including Dan, Dankoli, and Damballah Weddo.

This temple goes back to the 18th century. In the 1700s, the Kingdom of Whydah/Hueda was not a part of the Kingdom of Dahomey, which later became Benin. In 1717, Whydah, which was one of the most active slave-trading ports in Africa, was defeated in a war with Dahomey.

Their leader, King Kpassè, fled into the sacred forest to hide. While the notorious warriors searched for him, the pythons came out of the forest, protecting King Kpassè. The grateful king declared pythons to hereafter be known as royal pythons. He also dedicated three huts as shrines to the royal pythons.

The Kingdom of Whydah has become the city of Ouidah, and the Temple of Pythons is still maintained as tribute. It is a taboo for pythons to be killed, and those who do so unleash bad luck. The pythons at the temple are usually not fed. They are let out to forage and feed.

Temple visitors must also bring an offering for the 700-year-old iroko tree that houses the spirit of King Kpassè and other ancestors. After leaving the offering, you touch the tree and make a request. Every seven years, a ceremony is held to honor the pythons.

The Temple of Pythons is not about angry biting snakes at all; it's about joy and healing and celebration.

Your Rage Healing Ritual: Rewrite Yourself

Ritual intention: To rewrite the beliefs that hold you back.

Do you ever feel like you want to rewrite your programming? Our beliefs are our basic software for running the magical essence that we are. These beliefs either limit our view on the world or expand it. You are a whole human. Our rage encompasses many different feelings and beliefs. So let's broaden our window inward and look at all the shadow emotions and beliefs blocking you. Rewriting the beliefs that hold you back will help you in every area.

You will need:

- Journal
- Writing utensil

What to do:

Prepare your ritual space. You may want to sit in front of a mirror.

Part 1: Face Your Beliefs

You have done great work here in the Temple of Shadows. Some of the hidden shadow beliefs you explored include *I'm going to mess it all up, I am broken and ugly, People always disappoint you, There's not enough to go around,* and *I always get screwed over.*

We also examined the beliefs *I am not enough, I am not worthy, I am unlovable,* and *I am scared to betray my people.*

Choose one of these shadow beliefs or another one of yours to rewrite. You can go through this process as much as you wish for each belief, but you must only face one belief at a time.

Which belief would you like to face first?

Part 2: Dismantle Your Beliefs

Go through the following journal questions for the belief that you have chosen to face. Take as much time as you need.

Old Belief

- What is the shadow belief you want to clear?
- When is the first time you remember believing this?
- Was it true then?
- Is it true now?
- How do you know that it is not true?
- What has this shadow belief cost you?
- What are the secret payoffs and benefits of having this belief?

- What habits and behaviors do you have currently that support this belief?

- What triggers those habits and behaviors?

- What are the best reasons to release this belief?

Time-out alert: Take a self-care break. You may even continue this on the following day. If not, go for a walk, eat, get some water, and continue.

New Belief

- Who would you be if you didn't believe that old belief anymore?

- What would you like to believe instead?

- Who would you be with this new belief?

- What kind of habits and behaviors would this kind of person have?

- What is one action you can take today to support this new belief?

- What can you do when the triggers for the old belief come up?

- What is one action you can take every day for the next 7 days to support your new belief?

- What is your new mantra based on your new belief?

Part 3: Great Work!

Try your new belief on for size. Act as if you are already living it! Walk around today acting as if you believe your new belief. Dress, eat, interact, and behave as someone with the new belief would. Say the new mantra out loud.

Record your new beliefs in your Goddess Soulbook. You may want to use an integrative practice like tapping therapy or hypnotherapy to help you lock it in.

Congrats! You have completed the Temple of Shadows.

Temple of Shadows Illumination Mantras

- *This is me. I show up.*
- *I am protected.*
- *I am willing to know the truth.*
- *My blessings always overflow.*
- *I have a right to feel my feelings.*

Temple of Shadows Journal Assignments

- Write a letter of love, appreciation, and forgiveness to your resistance to your own dreams.
- Write a letter of love, appreciation, and forgiveness to your fears of betrayal.
- Write a letter of love, appreciation, and forgiveness to your shame.
- Write a letter of love, appreciation, and forgiveness to your fear of lack and scarcity.
- Write a letter of love, appreciation, and forgiveness to your emotions and rage.

Temple of Shadows Embodiment

- Prepare your ritual space. Read each letter out loud to your mirror. Safely burn each letter.

Temple of Shadows Integration

- Add the Temple of Shadows "monsters" and your experience with these rituals to your Goddess Soulbook.

6

THE TEMPLE OF LOVERS: YOUR LOVE ENERGY CHANNEL

Ubuntu

BLESSING OF THE LOVERS

Blessed be the lovers

Blessed be those who love

You have lived so much

And still you love

Heart ripped open

And still you love

Greeted by rejection

And still you love

Ate hate for breakfast

And still we love

Look, the butterflies in your hair are singing

We live to love another day

So love has been written

So lovers shall love

One love, enchanted one!

You have come from the Temple of Shadows.

You are much changed. You have dared to face your inner demons, stared the shadows in the face, and still you thrive. You are looking more fully like you than ever before.

The ancestors are well pleased.

You started at the Threshold with commitment. You faced and completed the Temple of Ancestors, the Temple of Conjurers, and the Temple of Warriors. The lower temples focused on how you interact with the physical world. Then you showed up for yourself and completed the Temple of Shadows. The rituals there helped you to start to integrate and welcome back the hidden and unloved parts of you. You have moved into the upper temples. These temples represent your spiritual channels.

You are entering the Temple of Lovers in the love energy channel. The five goddesses, here just for you, represent passion, compassion, gratitude, forgiveness, grief, and all matters of the heart. Oshun, Qetesh, Erzulie Dantor, Mbokomu, and Ala have been the keepers of this guidance from time immemorial. You now stand in an elevated circle of goddesses who are here to guide you in becoming a love goddess yourself.

Sit in the center and take in their wisdom. They each have gifts for you. Should you choose to accept their gifts, you will integrate your love goddess power. To finish this temple, complete their five rituals.

ABOUT THE TEMPLE OF LOVERS

Last night or the night before,
I met my boyfriend at the candy store.
He bought me ice cream, he bought me cake,
He brought me home with a bellyache.
I said, Mama, Mama, I feel sick.
Call the doctor, quick, quick, quick.
Doctor, doctor, will I die?
He said, Close your eyes and count to five.
Take a 1-2-3-4-5, I'm ALIVE!

That is a song from a hand-clapping game from my childhood. I'm holding a handful of rose quartz stones because we are in the Temple of Lovers. The pretend boyfriend in that hand-clapping song was my first love. Maybe yours too!

There are different kinds of love. There's the adoration we have for our heroes and celebrities. There is romantic love between you and your partner. There's filial love you have with your siblings and best friends. There's agape love between you and your Creator, the highest form of love. There is the love between you and those who created you on this earth plane, your parents or parental figures. And of course, there is self-love.

Ubuntu is the South African philosophy of love and compassion that says we are all in this together. It is translated as "I am because we are," or humanity toward others. Great Ancestor Nelson Mandela and Elder Bishop Desmond Tutu shared this ancient truth with the rest of the world. How often in our relationships do we feel like our basic humanity was not honored? Ubuntu is deep, full, wide, spiritual love.

Love is the highest vibrating energy there is. To give true, pure, unconditional love is to be one with God/dess. But that is only one half of the equation. Receiving love fully is just as important. This is a key conversation in the spiritual community because so often we think, *I don't need any other human relationship. I have my relationship with Spirit.* But you need human love and connection. Our relationships with other people are a key way we evolve. This whole universe was designed that way.

Write in your Goddess Soulbook: *It feels good to love and be loved.*

So how do we open our love energy channel to love and feel-good emotions? Many of us have never even seen a healthy, loving relationship up close. So how do we open ourselves to it? First, admit that making yourself vulnerable and open to love can be scary. This is true whether you are already in a soul mate or twin flame relationship or not. Just because you're in a relationship does not mean that you love freely and receive the love you deserve. Your imagination is not lying to you about how challenging it is. Loving is scary because it is a risk.

A couple of years ago, I was teaching about love goddess energy at the College of Psychic Studies in London. A gorgeous woman in the circle with her whole life ahead of her said, "Maybe love is just not in the cards for me. Maybe I just will ride this life out solo." Yet my beautiful, loving, and kind 80-year-old widowed auntie just found love again. She deserves it—and so do you. While you have breath, every moment is another opportunity for you to love and be loved. If you want to have the best life that you can, that includes you being loved.

You are worth loving now. You will not become magically worthy when you lose or gain 10 pounds, make 10 more dollars, move to the right neighborhood, get a shinier car, figure out your hair, accelerate your business or job, get some designer looks, or put on more makeup. You are worth loving in your worn-out pajamas with the crust in your eyes, when you haven't had your morning tea, with hair down to your ass or beautifully bald, with a job, unemployed, with or without a bank account, with or without debt. You are perfect in your imperfections.

Are you willing to receive the love? That's the game-changing question.

Write in your Goddess Soulbook: *I am worthy and deserving now. I am open for love. I now allow myself to be loved.*

As we discussed in other temples, many of us are wonderful givers but have challenges receiving. How we do anything is how we do everything. So if you have issues receiving, it can be difficult for you to receive compliments, help, money, and love. It is an energetic cycle.

You are love. Be the love you want to receive. If you want more love, be more love. How can you be more loving to the people that you already have rather than feeling a lack of love? Feeling the lack of love and the abundance of love cannot exist at the same time. Your love is not waiting in the future. Your love is already here. Who can you be more loving to?

When it comes to romantic love, seek it out to bask in it and appreciate it. When you see people in love walking down the street, feel their love vibration. Acknowledge your immediate reaction and feelings, then stop, take a moment, and start to just feel their love.

If you have an ex that found love, celebrate their love because you know that love is meant for you too. While we're having this conversation, somebody is praying for you. It could be the person you're in a relationship with, giving praise for you or saying, "I hope that I'm who she needs to be." Or it could be someone you've never met saying, "Please send me someone just like her."

Abundant love is the energy of, "I already have it. Who am I going to share it with? Am I going to share it with you? Maybe. Maybe not. I'm not desperate about it. Because I am love. And I love to share that love."

Write in your Goddess Soulbook: *I am love.*

If you are open to new love, have fun with it. Get out there. Be friendly and flirtatious with everybody. Let people know, "I am open to love." Flirting is enjoying your own beauty, joy, and light with others. Put yourself out there. Affirm the vibration of feeling lovable.

Write in your Goddess Soulbook: *I am lovable.*

WHAT IS YOUR LOVE ENERGY CHANNEL?

Are your current feelings and emotions grounded in love or fear? The love energy channel governs the vicinity of the heart, physically and figuratively. Your lungs, shoulders, upper back, and circulatory system are also housed in this energy channel. The main color of this center is green, although pink is also used to represent this energy.

Practice coming from the energy of love rather than fear. Treat yourself the way you want your loved ones to treat you. You cannot treat yourself like an enemy, bad talk yourself, eat unloving foods, allow unloving energy around you, and then expect someone else to be loving toward you.

Dare to surrender to the power of love. Be open and vulnerable. It is not easy, but we deserve to love and be loved in this way. Life is a mirror. We are ultimately only in relationship with ourselves. So treat yourself like the goddess you are. And let that be the reflection you put into the world.

You deserve big, juicy, glorious, unending love of every kind. You deserve to be loved like a goddess.

HOW TO KNOW IF YOUR LOVE ENERGY CHANNEL IS BLOCKED

Are you in disbelief that true love can exist? Do you feel closed off to love? Are you scared you'll get hurt? Do you find yourself settling for partners or behaviors that make you uncomfortable?

Here are some signs that your love energy channel may be closed: You feel unworthy of love and affection. You are skeptical of people who want to have a relationship with you. You think, *It feels too good to be true.* You have judgment when it comes to love and other people's relationships. Maybe you feel like you're unable to bond with others. You may make excuses like, "Maybe I'm too sensitive to have a relationship" or "I'm too spiritual to have a relationship" or "I'm too damaged for love."

If you live long enough, you're going to get hurt. You're going to feel rejection. You will feel disappointed. You're going to feel brokenhearted. The key is just to not stay in that energy.

Are you ready to deepen your love capacity? Love goddesses Oshun, Qetesh, Erzulie Dantor, Mbokomu, and Ala are here to support you in opening your heart in your love energy channel.

You may join each goddess in her sanctuary now.

OSHUN

Goddess of Revolutionary Love
Yoruba/Nigeria
Self-Love Sweetening Jar Ritual

"I give love. I receive love. I am love."

OSHUN'S MESSAGE

E kaasan o, sweet daughter! You feel everything so deeply. You are porous with a wall around your heart at the same time. This is the paradox of the highly sensitive, empaths, star people, and indigo children. We need your heart energy here. Dare to love. Begin with you.

OSHUN'S STORY

Great Goddess Oshun, keeper of mysteries,
We see you. We say your name.

Mirror, mirror, on the wall. Who's the honey-ist of them all? The Lady of Gold, that's who. The spirit of the river is love.

Are you a daughter of Oshun? So many of us are called by this Yoruba orisha (deity), goddess of the river and sweet waters. Oshun is the goddess of love and beauty, and a rock star in the Yoruba pantheon. Love is no trivial thing.

Oshun's love energy is magnetic. Did you hear about the time she lost the attention of her man, thunder god Shango? Oshun covered herself from head to toe with honey and sat by the river. Let's just say he never ignored her again.

There are many versions of the Yoruba creation story, and how important Oshun is as the keeper of the sacred feminine. My favorite version, told by New Orleans–born high priestess, storyteller Great Elder Luisah Teish, is as follows:

The Most High, Oladumare was busy creating universes. He discovered Earth and decided, "This is a great resting place." So he sent 17 orisha to create the world. The 17 he sends, including Obatala, lord of the clouds, Ogun, metal chief, and Shango, lord of the flame, head down to get the deed done. It's a boys' club, and Oshun is the only woman sent with them.

As they create mankind, oceans, valleys, and mountains, no one will listen to Oshun. The men are playing around, bragging, trying to outdo each other. They ignore Oshun's advice and find no value in her offerings. Finally, she has had enough.

"I'm leaving," Oshun declares.

"Who cares?" they respond.

So she goes to sit on the waxing moon. She stays there, meditating in her mirror and having a good time by her gorgeous self. Meanwhile, back on Earth, chaos ensues. The rivers, oceans, and streams dry up. The bees retreat, taking honey with them. Yams won't grow. Food disappears and the people go hungry. Nothing is working.

Love and the divine feminine have left the building. Life cannot be created or sustained. Oladumare notices that things are a mess, and he commands the gents to the heavens. They come running in and he asks why Oshun is missing.

"Who cares?" they tell Oladumare. "We don't need her."

"Of course you do," he booms. "Nothing works without the love, the laughter, the sweet waters, the honey."

Olodumare calls Oshun and makes them each apologize to her. Of course she eats it all up like a sweet potato meal.

After careful consideration, she accepts their apology. She only agrees because of her unconditional love for humanity. She is a natural protector and nurturer.

"Do not let it happen again," Oshun says, sunflowers in her hair. Beauty, fertility, love, and life soon returned.

When I was a recent college grad, I got to play with an incarnation of Oshun up close in *Cubamor*, a film by Joshua Bee Alafia. This indie film showcases the beauty and magic of diaspora spirituality and love in Cuba. I played a character named Fatima, and Bahamian model Shakara Ledard played Oshun. She was resplendent in her signature yellow gold and her favorite accoutrements: peacock feather fan, bells, mirrors, honey, and laughter.

In the film, the main character, Lazaro, promises Oshun that he will be faithful to his fiancée (my character), a daughter of Oshun, while he is in Cuba. While there, Lazaro is initiated into the La Regla Lucumi and Palo Monte Mayombe traditions. He also cheats on Fatima. This is a no-no after his pledge.

"Call me by my name and I will come. . . . Love isn't something that you take lightly. Love is heavy and buoyant at the same time," Oshun declares. She punishes Lazaro with blood.

Oshun's gripping energy possessed all of us working on the movie. Although I was already connected to her, seeing Oshun come to life in the sweet river and waterfalls in this magical realism film seemed like a direct message.

A few years later, I went to Cuba and the goddess summoned me directly. It was an awakening and a new beginning. Oshun is electric, and she will find you if she calls you and you do not come. Her mirror is not about vanity. The mirror is a lesson in unconditional self-love.

Ori Ye Ye O!

Let's Talk Revolutionary Love

This was originally a convo about unconditional love, but Oshun corrected me and said that her sanctuary was about "revolutionary love" instead.

Unconditional love is revolutionary love. Unconditional love sounds like a far-away notion, but it is all around us. In healthy parent-child relationships, parents love their children without conditions. And when we are emotionally and spiritually healthy, we love ourselves unconditionally. Unconditional self-love means loving every part of yourself and your experience. This is the stuff of ascended masters, and it begins with unconditional self-acceptance.

So can you truly love another person unconditionally? That is for you to decide. Love is a sacred contract, whether it is conditional or not. The healthy love contract says, "I am open, vulnerable, and committed. I am here for you. You are perfect in your imperfections. Now let's expand our consciousness together."

A sacred love contract does have conditions, though. Your partner acknowledging your full humanity is a condition. You and your love having the courage to seek open and honest communication is a condition and a contract. Each of you being responsible for your own emotional, mental, and spiritual health is a contract. To do our best and offer the sacred gift of soul forgiveness when we do not is a contract and condition. To offer the transparency of our soul, knowing that we can trust the other person to not wipe their feet on it, is a condition and a contract. Abuse of any kind is a condition that breaks that sacred contract.

You are worthy of a love that remembers your beauty at your ugliest behavior. You deserve to be loved in your language. As my friend Ginger's mom used to say, "You deserve someone who loves you down to your dirty drawers."

Our divine assignment is to remain open to revolutionary love, no matter what happens. Who is on your love résumé? Make a list of all those you have loved and those who loved you. What did you learn from each? Don't allow your past to block your future. Pave your love road with the lessons of loves past.

You are love. And you are worth loving.

HOW TO HONOR GODDESS OSHUN

When you honor Goddess Oshun, you honor the beautiful truth that you are worth loving. You may choose to honor this energy inside yourself or invoke her energy according to your own tradition.

To honor the goddess in you: Always ask yourself, *What is the most self-loving choice that I can make?* Legend has it that the first interaction between goddess Oshun and humans took place in Osogbo in Yorubaland. She allowed the people to build their city near the river in return for their love. She vowed to protect them as long as they remain devoted to her and keep Osogbo Grove as a sacred forest.

The annual Osun-Osogbo festival continues this devotion. People come from all over the world to make a pilgrimage to the sweet waters of the Osun River in Osogbo Grove. They ask for assistance and support with love, abundance, fertility, family, beauty, and health.

Guyanese-Brit Dr. Michelle Yaa Asantewa created a sister festival in London. Her voyage with Oshun started with a desire for fertility. She made ancestral offerings in her local river. Then she partnered with an Osun priestess to bring others for healing or opening. It has grown into a powerful community circle.

Symbols: Perfume, mirrors, amber, cowrie shells, brass, gold, river rocks, gold bangles, and dancing. Her number is 5.

Colors: Her colors are gold and yellow.

Auspicious time: Oshun's feast day is September 8.

Music: "Me" by New York sister-group Oshun and "Oxum" by Serena Assumpção

Suggested offerings: She loves beautiful and sweet things: honey, oranges, tangerines, corn, red palm oil, cinnamon, pumpkin, candies, and cake. She commands you to taste them first.

Alternate names: Osun, Ozun, Ochun, Oxum

Traditional Revolutionary Love Ritual: Ancestral Aphrodisiac Incense Parfum

In Mali, the art of making wusulan was handed down from mother to daughter. Wusulan is a perfume incense smoke created to scent the body and attract love. The wusulan secret recipe is made with flower petals, spices, aromatic vetiver grass, and wood chips that have been soaked in fragrant oils over a week. They then scented their skin and hair with the fragrant smoke.[1]

Wusulan's traditional elements may include jacaranda, frangipani, frankincense, and jasmine. Frangipani is a flower of devotion, mentioned in Swahili love poems. It smells sophisticated, sexy, and fruity. Flowers of the jacaranda tree clear bad spirits and represent rebirth and great luck. The sensual jasmine also represents beauty and love. The scent is floral and musky. Frankincense smells sweet, woody, and earthy. Its metaphysical properties are well-known.

Wusulan is notoriously difficult to find, but thiouraye from Senegal is equally as legendary as an aphrodisiac. Exact thiouraye recipes are also passed from mother to daughter and made with sacred ritual. Most versions contain some combination of sandalwood, musk, amber, and oud.[2] Sandalwood opens upper energies. Musk is sensual and magnetic. Amber resin was called nectar of the gods. The oud, they say, is the key. Oud has been used historically by monks for spiritual connection. While wusulan takes a week to make, thiouraye is kept in a glass jar to blend over months or years. Then it is burned in a terra-cotta incense container.

Word on the streets of both Mali and Senegal is wear only if you dare.

Your Revolutionary Love Ritual: Self-Love Sweetening Jar

Ritual intention: To honor your revolutionary and unconditional self-love.

We not only teach people how to treat us, but we show vibrationally how to love us by the way we love ourselves. Sweetening jars are used to sweeten the object of your affection and get their love to stick to you. In this ritual, you will be using the honey jar to fall more deeply in love with yourself.

Remember, life is a mirror. Love is a reflection. How do you treat yourself? How do you love yourself? If you are not in love with yourself, you will repel and reject any love you receive.

I love this Black American Hoodoo practice. In 1935, Great Ancestress Zora Neale Hurston shared her studies with Reverend Father Joe Watson, the "Frizzly Rooster," in *Mules and Men*. She wrote, "There was one jar in the kitchen filled with honey and sugar. All the 'sweet' works were set in this jar. That is, the names and the thing desired were written on paper and thrust into this jar to stay. Already four or five hundred slips of paper had accumulated in the jar."[3]

You will need:

- A jar with a lid (size does not matter)
- Writing utensil
- Paper
- Brown sugar
- Dark chocolate
- Local honey
- Pink or white votive or tea light candle
- Sacred stone of your choice
- Maple syrup (optional)
- Pink or red rose petals (optional)
- Bee pollen powder (optional)
- A personal effect (optional)

What to do:

Prepare your ritual space. Prepare and bless your sacred items and ingredients. As we are still in Oshun's sanctuary, you may wish to listen to "Oshun Prayer" Afro-Brazilian music by Café Da Silva[4] while you work.

Part 1: Write a Self-Love Petition

You may use brown paper or any paper connected to you, like an affirmation card, photo, or greeting card that makes you happy. Rip the edges so it gets your energy. If you are creating a honey jar for your relationship with another person, you can use the petition process you used in Ma'at's sanctuary (Chapter 3). That process can also be used for self-love, but I find writing a self-love letter to be more potent.

Write a proclamation of love to yourself. What do you promise yourself? How will you love you better? What do you wish a romantic partner would say to you? Here is a basic template; feel free to modify or create your own:

Hello, beloved one. You are a brilliant, beautiful, kind, and unstoppable goddess. I love you. You are more than enough, and you deserve the world. I see you loved, happy, healthy, wise, and wealthy.

Fold the paper toward you, rotate it clockwise, and fold again. Rotate once more and fold.

Part 2: Sweeten the Jar

Fill the bottom fourth of the jar with brown sugar. Place the paper in the jar. If you wish, you may add personal effects such as photos or DNA-related items. Add dark chocolate. You may add other sweeteners like maple syrup. Do not add any artificial sweeteners, as your self-love will be surface and fleeting. Bee pollen powder will give it an energy boost. Add rose petals for love and a stone connected to you for grounding. It can be rose quartz or a stone that means something to you.

Fill the jar with honey. I find that working with honey from specific geographical locations helps. It could be the geographical location you are from or where you live now.

Close your eyes and visualize what revolutionary self-love looks like. Blow on it and close the jar.

Part 3: Prepare the Candle

Now you will seal your self-love intention. Anoint the candle with oil. You can write a positive self-love affirmation on the candle. Put the pink or white votive or tea light candle on top of the jar. Burn the candle safely on top of the jar, letting the wax seal the lid. If you use a fixed-glass candle, just put it next to the jar.

Place your self-love sweetening jar on your goddess altar. Shake the jar weekly to wake up the àse.

Add your process and experience to your Goddess Soulbook.

QETESH

Goddess of Sacred Sensuality
Egypt
Cleopatra's Aphrodisiac Bath Ritual

"It feels good to feel good."

QETESH'S MESSAGE

Dewa-netjer en-etj, my love! You are an erotic creature. It is sacred to give and receive pleasure. You deserve to feel good. You have a right to experience all aspects of sensual ecstasy.

QETESH'S STORY

Great Goddess Qetesh, keeper of mysteries,
We see you. We say your name.
Find her naked, standing on top of a male lion. Qetesh wears the crescent moon on her head like a crown. Lions represent unbridled royal power and chaotic danger. She may hold snakes or arrows in one hand and carry a lotus flower as a symbol of lushness, prosperity, and fertility. What a badass!

Qetesh is the Egyptian goddess of sexual pleasure, sacred ecstasy, and fertility. Ancient Egypt was a sexually free society. They offered birth control and abortions. Qetesh was known as the "Mistress of All the Gods." She had two men. She was associated with the Egyptian fertility god Min, portrayed with an erect penis. At his harvest they played games naked in his honor. Her other man was Montu, god of war.

Qetesh was associated with the Qedesha, a sect of sacred temple prostitutes. The Qedesha were found throughout the Middle East. Temple prostitutes participated in sexual rites in connection with spiritual worship outside of Qetesh's Egyptian base. In the Book of Deuteronomy in the Bible's Old Testament, the word *kedeshah* is used to describe those taking part in the forbidden practice. For sacred prostitutes, sex was an act of worship. This was a devotional energy exchange where the women were extremely powerful. There was no shame in the connection.

Over in Morocco, the goddess of sacred sexuality, Qandisa, was also associated with the Qedesha. In her story, Qandisa's lust transforms her into a bloodthirsty monster. There are many tales throughout the diaspora of a beautiful woman creature who seduces men, maybe even turns them into sex slaves and then vampirizes them.

A big source of patriarchal anxiety has always been women's lust and sexual freedom. It's no surprise that they imagined sexually free Qandisa as a man-eating killer. Here in the goddess temple, we salute and welcome these free-love goddesses and their unbridled lust.

Let's Talk Sacred Sensuality

Raise your hand if you learned that sexuality and spirituality were at opposite ends of the spectrum. Yup. That's almost all of us.

Sacred sensuality and sexuality throughout history include sex as an act of worship. It is only our puritanical viewpoint that has a block in this area. Pleasure and sacredness are partners, not opposites. There is pleasure and ecstasy in loving the Divine and feeling loved in return. There is pleasure and ecstasy in marveling at the wonders of the Universe. There is magic in our bodies. And there is truth when we consider the fact that the clitoris, in all 8,000 of her glorious nerve endings, is the only body part made solely for pleasure.

Controlling women sexually is important for patriarchy to thrive. For Black women in the diaspora, most of our ancestors' bodies were up for grabs. If you have sexual traumas in your history, don't suffer alone. Address it as an act of self-care and self-love. Get help. We have to reckon with this history.

Honor your body temple. Your body is sacred—and erotic. You are gold, diamonds, and magic. What is the best way to honor your temple?

Practice self-pleasure to know what pleases you. Your first sensual relationship should be with yourself. If you don't know your body, how do you expect anyone else to? What pleases you? What displeases you?

Prepare your outer temple for sensuous love. What is your sensual environment? How does it appeal to the senses? What appeals to your sight? How do you want your sensual environment to smell? What does it taste like? What music is on your sexy-time playlist? Enhance the tactile nature of your space. Are you a leather or satin kind of goddess? What makes you happy?

Have sacred partnerships. Do you see your partner as divine? Does your partner see themselves as divine? What is the most self-loving choice you can make when it comes to your sensual life? Are you generous or selfish?

Mindfulness is being present in the current moment. Slowww everything down. Try leaving the lights on. And while you're at it, keep your eyes open. Spend time looking at each other, eye gazing. Explore breathing together with your partner. Smelling each other is primal. Take turns massaging each other.

Dare to experiment. Have an open mind and heart, and trust yourself.

Have clear boundaries. Are you clear on what you wish to explore? Do you know clearly what you are not interested in exploring? Have solid noes and yeses when it comes to your sexuality. Where are you interested in pushing your own boundaries? Declare your bedroom a fake-free zone. Be honest about what gives you pleasure.

Transmute your sexual energy together. Your orgasms can manifest magic. What do you want to create? Use the new moon to call it in. Use your imagination to have a joint visualization. Visualize yourselves together in a ball of pink or golden light, co-creating your dreams.

Sexuality is sacred, and our bodies are temples. What you choose to do with that truth is up to you.

HOW TO HONOR GODDESS QETESH

When you honor Goddess Qetesh, you honor the part of you that feels unbridled sacred lust. You may choose to honor this energy inside yourself or invoke her energy according to your own tradition.

To honor the goddess in you: How can you honor your own sexuality? Honor your body temple with self-pleasure. Have sacred partnerships. Slow everything down. Experiment. Have clear sexual boundaries. Transmute your sexual energy together for orgasmic manifestation.

Symbols: Tin, copper, bronze, lions, snakes, and lotus flowers

Color: Her color is blue, as it symbolizes fertility.

Auspicious times: The Egyptian Feast of the Sacred Marriage dedicated to Iset (Isis) and Asar (Osiris) was also a celebration day for Qetesh. Celebrate from sunset April 29 to sunset May 1.[5]

Music: "Qetesh" by Belle and the Beats and "Battle of Qadesh" by Sona Jobarteh

Suggested offerings: White or blue flowers

Alternate names: Qadesha, Qedeshet, Kedesh, Kadesh, Qedesh, Quetesh, Qudshu, Qadishtu

Traditional Sacred Sensuality Ritual: Sacred Sexuality

For the people of Rwanda, when it comes to sexual pleasure, women come first. The sexual practice known as kunyaza or kakyabali celebrates foreplay, female orgasm, and ejaculation. Kunyaza is the secret to multiorgasmic women. The goal of the couple is to bring down what they call "sacred water," women's ejaculation. Rwandan men call their partners who participate "shami ryiikivu." That means "Put a bucket under her." Wow!

This may seem shocking, but according to Nik Douglas, author of *Spiritual Sex*, there were many tantric practices in diverse African pre-Christian missionary intervention.[6] Many African societies viewed sexuality as a potent creative force. Warriors, such as the the Mino (Dahomey Amazons) and Shaka Zulu's army, traditionally abstained from sex so they would be stronger. Fang wood sculptors abstained from sex while making their artistic creations so that their creative power went into their work.

Sacred sexuality in Egypt brought together the energies of khat, the body, with ba, the soul, and ka, life-force energy. Ancient Egyptians didn't have a prudish view of sexuality. In their creation story, the sun god Ra masturbated the world into being! This is how they explain him "birthing" their Adam and Eve as recorded in the Egyptian Book of Knowing: "I had union with my closed hand, and I embraced my shadow as a wife, and I poured seed into my own mouth, and I sent forth from myself issue in the form of the gods Shu and Tefnut." Wow again.

Masturbation is viewed as a life-giving, manifestation process.[7] Ritualized sex practices and sex magic were a part of their belief system. Both the sistrum music rattle associated with goddess Hathor and the priests' scepter known as the sekhem have sexual connotations. Goddess Hathor was the goddess of physical love. Sex was a part of their heka, magic, as revealed by many sexual hieroglyphics on temple walls. Sex was even key to rebirth in the afterlife.

The Turin Erotic Papyrus with 12 sexual positions, including one in a chariot, reveals that they also had a bawdy sense of humor about sex. Couples who were having trouble conceiving could visit the Temple of Hathor at Dendera to spend the night in a Bes Chamber having sex in the presence of the fertility god. They had several means of contraception, meaning that sex for pleasure was a part of life. Ancient Egyptians also had no word for virgins or virginity, meaning that this was not an expectation in their culture.

Legend has it that Cleopatra invented the vibrator with a container of buzzing bees. You are sacred. Your sex is sacred!

Your Sacred Sensuality Ritual: Cleopatra's Aphrodisiac Bath

Ritual intention: To awaken your sacred sensuality.

The word *aphrodisiac* comes from Aphrodite, the Greek love goddess, and means something that enhances or increases sexual desire. Cleopatra, the last pharaoh of Egypt, was the most irresistible woman of her time. In this ritual, you will use her Cleo's bath as an aphrodisiac to turn up what we already know. You are irresistible.

You will need:

- Milk (of your choice)
- Red rose petals
- Honey
- Holy water of your choice (optional)
- Lavender (optional)
- Epsom salts (optional)
- Frankincense, myrrh, or Kyphi incense (optional)
- Bathtub

What to do:

Prepare your ritual space. How legendary was Cleopatra, that her bath is still revered today? Supposedly her recipe used the milk of 700 donkeys. Powdered cow's milk is easiest, but feel free to use the milk of your choice.

You may charge your ingredients in the moonlight or sunlight. If you are calling in a loving relationship with a masculine energy person, the sunlight is quite potent. You can also charge your ingredients by leaving them on your goddess altar.

Part 1: Prepare Your Bath

Set up your environment. Play music with lyrics in alignment with the love you wish to attract or solidify. You may wish to use the incense used by ancient Egyptian temple priests. They switched the incense depending on the time of day, burning frankincense at dawn, myrrh at midday, and Kyphi at dusk.[8]

Water is a conduit. As you did in Goddess Modjadji's sanctuary (Chapter 3), speak your sacred intentions into the water. How do you want to feel?

As you add each ingredient, thank it and tell it what it is for:

- As you add the tap water, say: Thank you, water, that we may share life essence.

- As you add the milk, say: Thank you, milk, that our love may be nurtured.

- As you add the honey, say: Thank you, honey, that my lover may find me sweet.

- As you add the roses, say: Thank you, roses, that I may be irresistible.

- As you add the salt, say: Thank you, salt, that our love will persevere.

- As you add the lavender, say: Thank you, lavender, that our relations may be peaceful.

- As you add the holy water, say: Thank you, water, that I am an irresistible love magnet.

Stir the water 7 times clockwise in a circle with your right hand. In ancient Egyptian numerology, seven was the number of perfection and completeness.

Part 2: Bathe in Your Beauty

Get in the bath. Close your eyes. Visualize returning here with your sweetheart. You may choose to write a love letter to yourself about how hot you are.

Afterward air-dry. Add your aphrodisiac bath recipe and ritual to your Goddess Soulbook. Plant or dispose of the ingredients at the crossroads (of your understanding).

ERZULIE DANTOR

Goddess of Energy Cords
Haiti
Cord Cutting and Clearing Wash Ritual

"I am worthy, compassionate, and whole."

ERZULIE DANTOR'S MESSAGE

Kòman ou ye, beautiful daughter? Remember your worth. Remember the love. You are the love.

ERZULIE DANTOR'S STORY

Great Goddess Erzulie Dantor, keeper of mysteries,
We see you. We say your name.

She fought elbow to elbow with her people during the Haitian Revolution to liberate and protect mothers and children. In fact, the strategy of the revolution in Ayiti started in 1791 at a feast where Erzulie Dantor was being honored. She is considered the national lwa (deity) of Haiti and the main lwa of the Petro family.

When I welcomed the goddesses into the Temple of Lovers, sanctuary of unbinding, I knew that Erzulie would show up. Erzulie is a family of passionate feminine-energy spirits in Haitian Vodou and other mysteries. However, I expected Erzulie Freda to come through. When we came together to birth this section for you, I was surprised to find Erzulie Freda's sister Erzulie Dantor at the throne instead. But it makes sense. Her name, "Erzulie D'en Tort," literally means "Erzulie of the Wrongs."

Although Erzulie Freda and Erzulie Dantor are both love focused, they are polarities. These two do not usually mix, but they appeared here in this sanctuary—not as rivals but wanting the best for you. They both hate broken promises.

Erzulie Freda is the lwa of love, connection, and romance, and Erzulie Dantor is the fierce lwa of passion and loyalty. But they both knew better than I did that cutting cords needed Erzulie Dantor's solid energy. Erzulie Freda is often invoked to find a lover. All who meet her are pulled by her charisma. In *Tell My Horse: Voodoo and Life in Haiti and Jamaica*, Zora Neale Hurston says that Erzulie has no children and her husband is all the men of Haiti.

Erzulie Dantor is usually invoked for harsher purposes. She has the energy of nurturing and strength, as she is a perfect mother. As the single mother of daughter Anaïs and son Ti Jean Petro, she is the patron of all minors. She represents the healing of the Dark Mother. She honors her promises. Her word is her bond. She is fully committed to all who love her.

As Erzulie Dantor is unvoiced, her daughter, Anaïs, speaks for her. People say she doesn't talk, which is not true. She shows you a map of the truth and leads by example. Erzulie Dantor is syncretized with Santa Barbara Africana or Our Lady of Czestochowa, the Polish Black Madonna. She cherishes loyalty and trust. She helps you to end bad relationships and reclaim your freedom. She is aggressive and works fast. Don't neglect her. Her passionate energy can be interpreted as jealousy, and she is associated with heavy, destructive rains.

In one story, Erzulie Dantor and her sister Erzulie Freda were both dating the iron god Ogun. Supposedly the sisters fought, and Mambo Erzulie Dantor stabbed her sister. Her sister removed the knife and cut her face with "twa mak," three marks, though only two are visible. Not everyone subscribes to this story, however. Some say this is just to explain her traditional scarification. Her vévé is a red heart with a knife.

Legend has it that Erzulie Dantor, in the form of the Virgin Mary, appeared on a palm tree twice in 1847 in the Palms Grove in Saut d'Eau. She began to heal and perform miracles. Ever since, Saut d'Eau has been revered by Vodouisants. During the Feast of Mount Carmel, many Catholics also make the pilgrimage to visit the area. Back in 1847, however, a Catholic priest, angry that people were seeing Erzulie rather than the Virgin Mother, cut down the palm tree. The priest died soon after.

Let's Talk Cord Cutting

A client asked me if she should forgive or cut emotional cords with an ex who she still felt connected to. Why not both?

We all have energetic connections between ourselves and other people. Truth be told, we have energetic connections between ourselves and everything in our environment. But the bonds between ourselves and other living beings are strongest because they are also creating their own energetic connections.

In metaphysics, we call these energy connections energetic or etheric cords. This means that you may be in energetic connection and relationship with people you have no desire to be attached to.

We all have a different bandwidth, energetic capacity, when it comes to these connections. For example, I am a highly sensitive person, and an introverted empath with social anxiety. If you are like me, you are porous to energy. We feel everything deeply. I have less energetic capacity to be corded to many different people at a large gathering than someone who is highly extroverted and impervious to the energy of others. This doesn't mean that I have to avoid these gatherings. It just means that I need to do a bit of spiritual maintenance before, during, and after attending so that I don't become completely drained. Part of my necessary spiritual maintenance or spiritual hygiene is cutting energy attachments with those I do not wish to be attached to.

What do these energy connections or cords look like? Close your eyes. Imagine that there are cords connecting you to each person you interact with. With the people you have the strongest bond with, maybe the cords are thick ropes. Sometimes, depending on the relationship, you may even see chains. The cords you share with your work buddies would obviously be much less strong. With the person you laugh with at the gym or your local barista, maybe you have threads. But say one of your casual acquaintances makes an offensive remark and you are now fuming and obsessing about it. Or you have a serious crush on one of these gym buddies. Perhaps a stranger bumps into you hard on the subway with no apology and you aggressively exchange looks. Your energetic cords will strengthen with each of these people.

At the end of the day, we come home with the normal grime of life attached to our clothes and our bodies. We also come home with spiritual grime in the form of these energy cords. Spiritual maintenance is required to clear this energy.

The client asking about her ex was unable to move on because she was still corded, attached, to him. She was in another relationship, but her ex was in her dreams every night. She hated this ex and spoke often about being mistreated by him. The strength and passion of those emotions kept her corded to him. We did an energetic cord cutting to release her from the etheric bonding to him. She never dreamed of him again. You can do this in visualization, and for some especially strong situations, you may have to do it more than once.

HOW TO HONOR GODDESS ERZULIE DANTOR

When you honor Goddess Erzulie Dantor, you honor the part of you that is protected from unhealthy connections. You may choose to honor this energy inside yourself or invoke her energy according to your own tradition.

Erzulie is from a closed practice. Don't ask her for anything if you are just getting to know her energy. She must choose you. You don't choose her. Her energy can be overwhelming—so tread lightly.

To honor the goddess in you: Are you ready to release the push-pull of simultaneously craving appreciation and pushing others away to avoid the pain of rejection? According to the HeartMath Institute®, our human hearts have a powerful heart brain that communicates with the brain in your head. A bitter heart is an unhealed heart. To activate healing and realign with love, they recommend you imagine breathing slowly in and out through your heart. Now recall a time you felt good. Close your eyes and try to reexperience the feeling.[9]

Symbols: Cacao cream, black coffee, black or red beans, strong tobacco, dark chocolate, red candles, and red wine. Seven is her number.

Colors: Her colors are blue, blood red, gold, and green.

Auspicious times: July 16 or August 15 are her feast days. Tuesday is her day.

Music: "Erzulie O" by RAM and "Black Girl Magic" by Chrisette Michele

Suggested offerings: Sing for her. She respects your offerings, whether you have a little or a lot. She loves dolls, knives, silver jewelry, and change. Griot, a Haitian dish made with wild pig or pork, is a fave.

Alternate Names: Ezilí Dantor, Erzulie Dantó, Erzulie D'en Tort

Traditional Energy Cords Ritual: The Okra Slip

The word *okra* or *kra* means "soul" to the Akan people of Ghana. This makes sense, as okra has been a life-force motherland connection to Africa's children throughout the diaspora. Okra is most likely of East or West African origin. It came to the Americas with the slave trade. In Afro-Latin cultures, it is called quimbombo.

In Guyana we call it okro; in the southern United States, it's made into gumbo. The great thing is it's not only delicious but also has spiritual properties.

Need to slip out of a situation? Feeling stuck where you don't want to be? Throughout the Caribbean diaspora and the American South, okra is used for spiritual hygiene.

People who hate okra usually dislike the gooey texture. The official name for this jelly is mucilage, but my late aunt Silvy and uncle Steve called that the "surwa." That surwa that so many find so gross is where the magic is. It helps you to clear hurdles, remove negativity, and slide out of sticky situations. It is also good for removing curses, hexes, or "bad eye."

Here's what the old folks would do to remove the death stare or evil eye. It wasn't pretty, but they swore by it. The old-school way was to get a bowl of warm water, squeeze the surwa into it, then rub the resulting water over yourself in a downward motion while saying your favorite prayer. Dress in white and keep it on you for 24 hours. Afterward, if there is a holy book you follow, read your favorite psalms or passages as you rub.

You can also add okra to an alternative energy-clearing bath I learned from Dr. Nana Guan Bay, my Ashanti herbalist in Ghana. You will also need several handfuls of cassava leaves, salt, and prekese/garbineau. Marinate for 3 days and remove the herbs. Then bathe with the mixture for 7 days between 9 A.M. and 11 P.M. Use your right hand 7 times to scoop up the bathwater and put it onto your body. Don't use a towel. Sit and wait for your skin to air-dry while you pray.

Your Energy Cords Ritual: Cord Cutting and Clearing Wash

Ritual intention: To slip away from obstacles and give yourself spiritual armor.

Okra came to the Americas with the slave trade, some say in the cornrows of my ancestors. You can use it in baths and workings to help you slip out of a bad situation or for uncrossing. One of my Yoruba friends told me that some Yoruba men are afraid to eat okra because they don't know what their wives or girlfriends are up to!

This ritual bath is perfect to repel and break unwanted energy and cut emotional cords. This is a tradition across Togo, Nigeria, and Benin, as well as throughout South America and the Caribbean. Do this if you need to slip out of a negative situation or you just want to clear your energy.

This positive energy wash protects against emotional vampires, psychic attacks, spiritual attachment, mental residue, and the evil eye. In other words, this bath is a cleaner for bad juju. This is not a social media–beautiful bath, but it is wonderful spiritual hygiene. Let your issues slide off.

You will need:

- 26 pods of okra
- 1 gallon of water
- 2 white candles
- Holy water (such as Florida Water, Kananga Water, moon water, or sun water)
- Coconut oil (optional)
- Strainer

What to do:

Part 1: Prepare the Drink

The night before the okra bath, marinate 5 okra pods in a glass of water overnight. Speak words of love and affirmation into the water. Put it in the fridge. You will drink this water before your bath. You can soak them whole or cut them up. If you cut them, the taste will be a bit more bitter.

Part 2: Prepare the Wash

Cut up 21 okra pods. You may cut them into a bowl with water or cut them on a cutting board and add them to the water. As you cut them, be clear on your prayers and intentions. After you add all of the okra to the water, squeeze out the mucilage. Massage the okra with your hands so that it gets your àse. Add your holy water. Call on your protection spirits to defend you and anyone who needs protecting.

Strain out the liquid. The liquid is the bath. Thank and plant or dispose of the okra at the crossroads of your understanding.

Part 3: Bathe and Visualize

Drink your okra water. Then put one of the white candles at either end of your tub, to create a passage of light. As you enter, see yourself entering into a cleansing temple.

This is not a bath you sit in. Pour the liquid over your head from a bowl or bucket. Note: Be extremely careful, as it is super slippery.

As you pour, close your eyes and visualize.

- See the cords attaching you to the person or the issue. Cords may be thin or thick.

- Choose which divine source energy you want to cut the cords. You can call on God/dess, the Universe, angels, ancestors, saints, deities, or whatever works for you.

- If you are seeking to cut the cords from a specific person or situation, visualize swords of love, protection, and truth. See swords of healing gold and white light cutting what binds you.

- See the cords being cut and dissolving away until you feel light and free.

Afterward shower and wash yourself clean. You do not need to air-dry. Seal your body with coconut oil. Put on white or brightly colored clothes.

Record your process and the results in your Goddess Soulbook.

MBOKOMU

Goddess of Soul Forgiveness
Bantu
Carry the Stone Ritual

"I forgive and free myself. I forgive and free others."

MBOKOMU'S MESSAGE

Wabukire, loving one. It is okay to release it, my child. You are free to let it go. Reclaim yourself now. Put this thing down.

MBOKOMU'S STORY

Great Goddess Mbokomu, keeper of mysteries,
We see you. We say your name.
"Carry me today, and I will carry you tomorrow."[10]

Goddess Mbokomu was loving life. For the Ngombe Bantu, she was the first woman on Earth. So she has seen some things! As the goddess of ancestry and community, Mbokomu was given the ability to speed up or slow down time.

Her father was Akongo, the one and only supreme god, almighty and the unending. They all lived in the sky with her children. The earth and the sky were pretty close together at that time, so she easily hopped back and forth to the earth and planted a luscious garden.

Mbokomu was an incredible cook. The kids were hooked on her seswaa with pap (cornmeal porridge), and morogo (greens) on the side. They wanted to eat it all the time. Of course, to get the recipe just right, she had to pound the meat day and night, tenderizing it with her mortar and pestle.

Bam-bam-bam! Bam-bam-bam!

Her father, Akongo, was cranky, old, and annoyed. It took much work to create the world. The noise of the constantly banging pestle bothered him, plus the kids ate all the food. Finally, Akongo couldn't take it anymore. He put Mbokomu and her kids in a huge basket and lowered them from the sky. As he did this, the basket pushed the sky and earth far apart. But Akongo made sure they were taken care of. The basket was overflowing with all of their faves, plus sugarcane, maize, grains, and cassava.

Then Akongo disappeared and left everything to Mbokomu, the ancestors, and the mediums to handle. Mbokomu urged her daughter to have a baby so there would be more people to enjoy her garden. Her daughter promised, and she was instantly pregnant.

Mbokomu warned her to be careful, as the evil Ebenga, the beginner, was always out there looking to cause trouble. Her daughter decided to go for a walk. She was singing in the forest when she came up on a friendly man. He looked kind of funny, with a super hairy body, but he definitely didn't look evil. They struck up a conversation.

The man asked for her help, so she shaved him and gave him a hug, and he revealed himself. It was the evil Ebenga! He waved his arms and cast a spell on her baby. The problems and sorrow of the world were unleashed.

The daughter went home crying. She begged her mother for forgiveness. Mbokomu loved her and her grandchild-to-be. She forgave her daughter and reminded her that *"A bitter heart eats its owner."* Mbokomu slowed time down, turning seconds into years so that despite the problems unleashed, her family could have a good life.

The Bantu speak in proverbs. *"A redeemer of people is a walker with people."* Proverbs tell the truth of the oldest people. Many of their proverbs are about the need for forgiveness. This is the gift of Mbokomu. Her energy is about healing and healthy ties that bind.

As the ancestor of all people and the first gardener, Mbokomu oversees community matters. Any community is only as strong as our ability to forgive each other and heal. The Bantu Nguni people have a saying: "Umuntu ngumuntu ngabantu." This means "A person is a person through other persons." This is the philosophy of Ubuntu.

Let's Talk Soul Forgiveness

"Adjoining houses always burn," the Bantu say. This is why your soul must forgive. I probably have less Bantu lineage than my DNA indicates, as I come from a family of professional grudge holders. Generations of folks who will stop speaking to each other at the drop of a dime.

When my first marriage fell apart many years ago due to repeated infidelity, I was deeply ashamed and didn't want the stigma of being a "jilted woman." So I declared, "I forgive him. We will be friends," almost immediately. I tried to stuff my agony down and move forward, but, of course, that didn't work. It was a conscious uncoupling without the conscious part. I felt sad, deeply hurt, and broken. Spraying perfume on the wounds didn't help them stink less. Healing took a long time. It was incredibly tough because I didn't allow myself to feel my feelings.

You can't rush forgiveness. The pain and resentment will simply wait for you if you do. This is not an argument for being unforgiving. Forgiveness must be an active practice. You can't spiritually bypass it. You have to feel it to heal it. Feel the pain, hurt, grief, and despair.

Know your own soul. Take your time with your heart. You have a right to feel what you feel. Burn the person you are in unforgiveness with in effigy if you need to. Feel your sorrows, pain, and rage. Ask your doctor if it is safe for you to use an African bloodstone yoni egg as a part of your healing. If not, just carry it close to your skin. It may help you ground your emotions.

So why do we want to forgive in the first place? When we are in a state of unforgiveness, it colors our entire world with lack, fear, and resentment. We lack access to love, fear getting hurt again, and are locked in resentment. As the aggrieved party, you start to see everything through victim-colored glasses. Forgiveness is a personal liberation practice, a gift of freedom for you from you.

You are still emotionally enmeshed with whoever you haven't forgiven. You are still energetically attached, even if you don't speak. This applies to former partners, friends, family members, co-workers, or the guy who bumped you on the train. Their energy is bound up with yours. Again, forgiving, for-giving, is about you, not them.

You will not have immediate access to forgiveness if your trust has just been violated. Forgiveness is a higher-vibrating frequency than the anger, hurt, and pain that you must allow yourself to feel. You can feel that vibrationally, hurt and resentment are a lower frequency. It's okay to inch up to forgiveness. Forgiveness frees you from your past—good, bad, ugly, or indifferent. If you have energetic connections with people you don't want to be connected to, it is unfair to you and those close to you.

A couple of years ago, I naively gave a business partner access to my bank account. The person squandered and misdirected thousands of dollars. When I confronted them about it, they were completely unremorseful and instead of apologizing, chided me for raising my voice. I had no written contract because I considered them to be my friend. I didn't feel like I could talk to anyone about what happened because I was super embarrassed. I felt like I could never forgive them, but my brain kept replaying the situation over and over again. I had to find forgiveness for my own freedom. I will never ever speak to them again, but I was able to forgive to set myself free.

On the other side of the coin, you need to forgive yourself and allow yourself to be forgiven. In the same situation, I was angry at myself for being so naive. I said mean things to myself about the situation. I had to forgive myself. The biggest resentments you have are toward yourself. You did the best you could. Stop blaming and shaming yourself. Release the obligation to feel guilty for things in your past. You deserve to be forgiven—by you.

If you can't find forgiveness in the human part of you, close your eyes and feel into the divine part of you. You must be what you came from, right? Tune in to the God/dess energy within. How does Spirit feel about you? Forgive yourself from that energy.

The road to forgiveness may be rocky, but that's okay. Take your time. Observe your thoughts. Feel your feelings. Don't rush it. But you don't want to live in the space of resentment either. Don't let your past eat up your future. You are love.

HOW TO HONOR GODDESS MBOKOMU

When you honor Goddess Mbokomu, you honor the part of you that can forgive and be forgiven. You may choose to honor this energy inside yourself or invoke her energy according to your own tradition.

To honor the goddess in you: Honor Mbokomu by choosing to forgive yourself and others. Her people believe that ancestors live only as long as someone remembers them. The same is true for grievances. Say this out loud: "I forgive myself with love."

Symbols: As the daughter of the first peoples, her number is one.

Color: Her color is blue.

Auspicious times: September 24 is Heritage Day.

Music: "Coming Home" by Shingai Shoniwa and "Strong as Glass" by Goapele

Suggested offerings: Offerings for Mbokomu include Bantu staples sugarcane, maize, yams, cassava, plantains, bananas, and beans. Rock your beautiful Bantu knots in Mbokomu's honor.

Alternate name: Mobokumu

Traditional Soul Forgiveness Ritual: Step on the Egg

The Ubuntu concept that we are all one works well during times of peace or as a reminder during light struggles. Many of us have a lifetime of grudges stored in our souls, built mostly on comparatively petty injustices. But how would Ubuntu apply to the aftermath of war atrocities when unspeakable, genocidal crimes have been committed?

In Northern Uganda, East Africa, many former child soldiers who have committed violent war crimes against their own communities are attempting to reintegrate. Acholi tribal elders in Uganda are calling on the power of ancient ritual to navigate this challenge to their collective well-being.

This symbolic healing ceremony is witnessed by the community as a first step. The former fighters are called "returnees" instead of soldiers to free them from the stigmas of war. After the reconciliation ceremony, they are considered cleansed of their former crimes.

The Nyono Tong Gweno (Step on the Egg) ceremony is simple but powerful.[11] The offender confesses their crimes and expresses sorrow, guilt, and remorse. They beg for forgiveness from their victims, if available, and from the community.

Elders place an egg on an opobo branch with a layebi, a forked stick. Opobo sap is a soap used for laundry and cleaning. Here, the opobo cleanses the returnee of bad influences, shameful experiences, and offensive behaviors. The returnee steps on the egg, breaking the shell. The egg represents a reintroduction to innocence and purity. If they have babies, their feet are also dipped in the raw egg.[12]

The now forgiven former offender hops over the opobo branch, symbolizing a jump into a new life. They are made whole and considered restored to who they were before the atrocity. The layebi represents breaking bread as a community. Food is put on the ground as a sign of unity, and everyone eats together.[13] As a final step, the returnee makes amends. They may compensate victims, survivors, and their families with sheep, goats, and cows. The community forgives.

Your Soul Forgiveness Ritual: Carry the Stone

Ritual intention: To forgive.

Ubuntu experts Bishop Tutu and his daughter Reverend Mpho Tutu created a four-step plan, called the Fourfold Path, for forgiving. Bishop Tutu was the chair of the Truth and Reconciliation Commission in South Africa. As Bishop and Reverend Tutu say in *The Book of Forgiving*, "Forgiveness is not a luxury."

Open with the forgiveness mantra "When I forgive you, you no longer define me."

You will need:

- A stone
- Something that you need to forgive someone else for
- Something you did that you need to forgive yourself for

What to do:

Part 1: Carry the Stone

Prepare your ritual space. To begin the Fourfold Path, get a stone. The stone represents a heavy burden that you have been carrying. Do you need to forgive someone else or yourself?

Look at the stone and think about the person, problem, or issue that it represents. Really see the issue transposed onto the stone. Then you need to hold the stone for 6 hours without putting it down. Set an alarm on your phone.

Go about your day and keep the stone in your hand until time is up. Then journal on what came up for you about the situation during the process of carrying the stone.

Part 2: The Fourfold Path

You can do this with an unrelated partner to witness you, with the person involved in the actual incident, or by yourself in front of your mirror.

The Tutus' Fourfold Path of Forgiveness is as follows:

- What happened? Tell the story of the incident. Allow yourself to be emotional and fully expressive.

- Name the hurt. Give voice to the pain of how the event affected you.

- Grant forgiveness. Complete this statement: "I forgive you today because . . . "

- Either renew or release the relationship.

Record your experience with this process in your Goddess Soulbook. You may journal about it for clearing as well.

ALA

Goddess of Grief
Igbo/Nigeria
Grief Release Circle Ritual

"I am supported by my loved ones, those who are seen and those who are unseen."

ALA'S MESSAGE

Ndewo, sweet one. Most humans are made of patches of grief sewn hastily together. Sob, shriek, bawl, shed tears. Grieve it out, wail it out, cry it out.

ALA'S STORY

Great Goddess Ala, keeper of mysteries,
We see you. We say your name.

Ancestors prayed to her first. The covenant your sages made with her still stands. Ala is the earth, the realm we live on. She is the ancient mother.

Ala is the foremost álúsí (deity) in Odinala, the religion of the Igbo people. Notice that *ala* is a part of the word *Odinala* itself. Goddess Ala oversees justice, death, mortality, and grief. Her name means "earth," and she represents the cycles of life. She handles all related to the afterlife, and deceased ancestors find safety in her womb. Her womb is the earth to which we will all return.

The Igbo are ruled by duality, so Ala also oversees motherhood and fertility. She safeguards women and children with her loving maternal energy. When babies are born, their umbilical cords are buried to anchor their connection to Ala, the earth.

Chukwu, the supreme being, created Ala and her husband, Amadioha, álúsí of justice, peace, and unity, first. They are considered to be two of the six aspects of the Most High. Amadioha is also the Igbo god of thunder and lightning.

There were 10 round pyramids built in the town of Nsude in Igboland to honor Ala. They said that she lived on top of them, near the moon. Ala's symbol is the crescent moon, and she is often pictured holding children. We see the crescent moon twice a month, waxing and waning. The waxing crescent after the new moon is the energy of expansion and growth. Then the waning crescent after the full moon represents the death of the old cycle.

Ilouwa, meaning "to come back to the world," is the Igbo philosophy of reincarnation. Energy cannot be created or destroyed, so life goes on. Reincarnation is a part of Ala's domain. When we die, we are replanted into the earth as seeds. We have eight chances to incarnate back to earth. Ala typically incarnates us within our same family groups with different roles. You may come back with the same scars or birthmarks.

We are currently in the dualistic state and realm in Igbo cosmology. Your family must have two funerals for you to return to the earth. If you lived a good life, your family will want you to return. They must atone for your sins. If you have not been a positive member of the community and they don't want you to return, they won't give you the second funeral. The first funeral is for your body, and the second is for your spirit. This explains why so many cultures in the diaspora have similar rituals. The Garifuna have the Dugu washing of the dead, and in Guyana, Trinidad, and Jamaica we have the Nine Night wake tradition and second memorials 40 days after someone has transitioned. During Nine Night, bereaved families are visited daily by loved ones with drumming and song.

Our Goddess Temple Circle sister Lady Shepsa Jones, author of *Nice for What?! How to Go from Being a Good Girl to a Badass Goddess*, unexpectedly lost her mother last year. She knew she needed to focus on healing and do the spiritual work to uplift her mother as an ancestor. Lady Shepsa is a practitioner of the orisha tradition, Haitian Vodou, and the ancient Kemetic (Egyptian) spiritual system. She knew that when someone in your family transitions, it is your job to make sure they make it peacefully to the other side and to connect with them through libations, offerings, and prayers.

A priestess of Yemaya told Lady Shepsa that the first 40 days are key in helping her mother transition. Every morning, at her ancestral shrine, she poured libation, tapped her ancestral staff (consecrated stick) on the ground, and called the names of her mother and ancestors.

Along with uplifting her mother and helping her transition into the Egun, the Yoruba realm of ancestors, she needed to heal herself. Her self-care practice included focused meditation, yoga, qigong, moxibustion, yoni egg work, sacred sex, dancing, resting, and reading.

Lady Shepsa shared this beautiful process daily with us as a community on social media. This allowed us to be a container for her grief and a witness for the beginning of her healing. It also allowed us as a virtual village to lift up her mother as well.

"Nyame nnwu na mawu." God never dies; therefore I cannot die.

Let's Talk Grief

When a person dies, they return to the womb of Ala and are replanted in the soul to reincarnate. Give her your grief. Surrender it.

For Igbo people, death is not the end of life but a transfer to a new plane. A procession of dancing and singing as the family and community accompany a coffin and hearse is a key part of the funeral. After a loved one is buried, the lavish ikwa ozu celebration ensures that they will have a safe transition to their new station among the ancestors. Ceremonies may even include a mock trial to suss out if any enemies are responsible for the death. During the ino uno akwa, the ada, meaning the oldest daughter, eats the favorite meals of the loved one who has just transitioned.

The finality of death and loss can be brutal. Even if we believe there is no death, the belief can be of little consolation. We want to hold, kiss, and smell the people we love. Loss is still loss, no matter.

There are all kinds of grief that feel like we severed a part of ourselves. There is the grief of losing someone we love. There is the grief after breakups and betrayal, which some feel is worse than death because the person is still here. There is the grief no one should ever feel from losing a child. There is grief after loss of a job or opportunity. There is grief after the loss of a dearly loved pet friend. There is grief for the state of things after political elections. We grieve for who we were before a traumatic event. When the #MeToo truth telling began, we realized that we feel grief when a celebrity, public figure, or teacher we admired or considered a mentor turns out not to be who we imagined. We also have communal grief, being forced to publicly grieve over each video of unarmed Black human beings being killed by those who are supposed to protect.

Rumi, my favorite Sufi poet said, "Don't grieve. Anything you lose comes round in another form." He is absolutely right that anything you lose comes around in a new form. But grieve we must. The human heart that does not grieve is too constipated to love.

You may be holding unprocessed grief in your body and your heart. Grief is usually hidden and silent in Western culture, as if it is shameful to be sad or shameful to not be over it yet. I remember when my aunt Silvy died on December 4, 2004. That February, not three months later, my ex wondered why my cousin was still having a hard time over the loss of his mother. Grief is not linear. When we avoid grief, it waits. Grief is a part of the condition of being a human.

Let your grief cleanse your soul. We grieve at the loss of relationships, jobs, opportunities, and of course lives. A year ago, I had a miscarriage. Only the people closest to me knew that I had been undergoing in vitro fertilization. Afterward I grieved, and so did they. I felt overwhelming sadness for a long time, as my friends didn't know what to say. When one of my friends realized months later that I was still grieving, she said, "I didn't realize it was that serious." Another friend said, "Maybe if you would have done XYZ instead, the baby might be here." Neither of these were helpful. People don't know what to say. So we grieve alone.

Doing my own ritual baths with clove, rosemary, and basil and ancestral healing helped. The modern ritual of tapping therapy or Emotional Freedom Technique (EFT)—which I share on my blog—was also incredibly helpful. In addition, I invited our Goddess Temple Circle community to join me in a grief healing circle. I learned that two other goddesses in our group had also recently experienced pregnancy loss.

The Adinkra symbol for grief, Owuo Atwedee, is a ladder. It represents the Akan proverb for grief: "Owuo atwedeɛ baakofoɔ mforo" means "Death's ladder is not climbed by just one person." We all will die and we all will grieve.

As I type this, there is the feeling of grief in the air. My childhood best friend's husband was buried today. My cousin's father died. And two family members in Guyana died of COVID-19.

Nyame nnwu na mawu.

But grieve we must.

Write in your Goddess Soulbook: *I am choosing to take good care of myself and hold space for my own healing.*

HOW TO HONOR GODDESS ALA

When you honor Goddess Ala, you honor the part of you that is grieving. You may choose to honor this energy inside yourself or invoke her energy according to your own tradition. Allow yourself the gift of grief.

To honor the goddess in you: Ala's energy is open, loving, and welcoming. Close your eyes, put your hands over your heart, and tune in to your grief. Allow yourself to feel what or who you feel you have lost. Send loving, healing energy to your own heart.

Put the grief back in Ala's womb; put your tears in the womb of the earth. Honor Ala with the cycles of the crescent moon. The waxing crescent moon takes place after the birthing energy of the new moon. This is the energy of expansion and growth of seedlings planted on the new moon. Then the waning crescent moon is after the "let it go" energy of the full moon. The waning crescent represents the ending of, or death of, the old cycle, and preparation again for the new moon.

Symbols: Her symbols include the crescent moon, yams, and the earth. Ala's messengers are pythons, snails, and monkeys. Treat them with respect.

Color: Her color is white.

Auspicious times: Igbo people pay tribute to Ala during the annual Iwa-Ji, New Yam Festival, in early August. The newly harvested yams must not be eaten before the festival. Before the festival, children in traditional families do a ritual bath called imacha ahu iri ji mmiri.[14] Taking a spiritual bath may be a great way to celebrate Ala.

Music: "Eternal Bliss" by The Igbo Goddess and "African Queen" by 2Baba

Suggested offerings: Yams or natural ephemera. Earthing, bringing your bare skin in contact with soil, is a beautiful way to honor her. Give her your tears.

Alternate names: Ani, Ana, Ale, Ali

Traditional Grief Ritual: Mbari Temples

Mbari houses are temple shrines created primarily for Goddess Ala as Mother Earth and the fertility goddess or occasionally local deities. But these shrines are like no shrine you have ever experienced. Mbari are also works of art. Outsiders may view them as an art installation or museum. They are built when the diviner receives a message from the goddess that she feels neglected in this location.

These two-story houses take months or sometimes years to build, and it is a devotional practice for everyone involved. The artists and artisans are initiated as spirit workers. Huge, life-sized or larger sacred statues of the goddess Ala are a central part of the design. She is flanked by accompanying statues of one or two children.

Artists create an entire world that may include animals, other deities, and signs of an abundant life.

As Great Ancestor Chinua Achebe, the Nigerian novelist, said, "Mbari was a celebration through art of the world and of life lived in it. It was performed by the community on command by its presiding deity, usually the earth goddess, Ala, who combined two formidable roles in the Igbo pantheon as fountain of creativity in the world and custodian of the moral order in human society."[15]

At the end of the creation of an Mbari, there is a huge festival of life. Elders and the community come in joy, gratitude, reverence, and humility. The entire festival is a love letter to the goddess. The spirit workers may focus on other things again.

Here's the most incredible part of it: After the celebration, the Mbari is complete. No one must ever visit it again. It is never maintained. There is no upkeep. The creators and the town must allow it to decay. It is taboo to ever look at it or go near it again.

This is the cycle of life and death. The Mbari has completed its purpose. Built from clay that is symbolically called yam, the Mbari will decay and return to the earth. The energy will be transferred to the next Mbari house and to all of the new life celebrated here. It will die, but it is not dead.

Your Grief Ritual: Grief Release Circle

Ritual intention: To hold space for unprocessed grief.

We are living in a time of grief. As Sobonfu Somé, the late renowned Dagara (Burkina Faso) grief ritualist, often said, we are not meant to grieve alone. In many African cultures, we grieve together for Nine Nights. This is a ceremony to honor your unspoken griefs with your community in that tradition.

You will need:

- A circle of 9 people
- A means to meet either in person or virtually

What to do:

Prepare the ritual space. If you need help deciding who to invite, consult the "How to Create a Goddess Group" section in the Introduction's "How to Use this Book."

Ask everyone to bring one to three items representing grief to share with the group. If you are meeting in person, create a joint grief altar in the space. If this is a virtual gathering, ask each person to create their own grief altar or shrine that they can share on camera with the group. It can have the items they wish to share, an earth item, water, and a candle. The air represents the spirit of the people who passed on. You should have a set amount of time, such as 90 minutes to 2 hours for this circle.

Each day you hold space for one person in the group, the griever. Each day's griever will share the story of each of their three items. Begin the story of each item with the words "I am grieving the loss of . . ." The listeners should listen actively and respectfully. Do not interrupt. You're not there as a counselor but as a witness and friend.

Types of grief a griever may share include the death of a loved one, a betrayal, a breakup, the loss of a pet, the loss of a job, or a big change. It doesn't matter how old or small the grief is.

Icebreaker: Each person has 4 minutes in the first session to introduce themselves and describe how rice is prepared in their culture. Then begin the circle.

Suggested active listening questions:

- What loss are you still grieving?

- Can you tell us about your loved one?

- How are you feeling about that?

- What brings you comfort?

- Please share more about that.

Document your grief release circle in your Goddess Soulbook.

Congrats! You have completed the Temple of Lovers.

Temple of Lovers Emotion Mantras

- *I enjoy giving and receiving pleasure. I deserve to feel good.*
- *It feels good to feel good.*
- *I am worthy, compassionate, and whole.*
- *I forgive and free myself. I forgive and free others.*
- *I am supported by my loved ones, those who are seen and those who are unseen.*

Temple of Lovers Journal Questions

- Describe your revolutionary love in detail.
- What gives you pleasure?
- Which attachment(s) do you need to break?
- What do you still need to forgive?
- What loss are you still grieving?

Temple of Lovers Embodiment

- Add something to your altar that represents your love goddess power.

Temple of Lovers Integration

- Add the Temple of Lovers goddesses and your experience with these rituals to your Goddess Soulbook.

7

THE TEMPLE OF GRIOTS: YOUR VOICE ENERGY CHANNEL

Akoben

BLESSING OF THE GRIOTS

Speak, speak

In the presence of ancients.

Speak, speak

In the presence of mortals.

Speak, speak.

Tell your story, tell your truth.

Speak, speak.

Speak your life into being.

Speak, speak.

Let your words ring forth.

Speak, speak.

May your voice be a bell.

Speak, speak.

Let your voice be a bell.

Rise and shine, sacred one!

You are entering the Temple of Griots in the voice energy channel. The five goddesses here just for you represent telling your story, speaking your truth, manifesting with your voice, and clear communication. Mami Wata, Yasigi, Mama Djombo,

Mame Coumba Bang, and Nunde have been the keepers of this guidance from time immemorial. You now stand in an elevated circle of goddesses who are here to guide you in activating your empowered voice.

Sit in the center and take in their wisdom. They each have gifts for you. Should you choose to accept their gifts, you will integrate your griot goddess power. To finish this temple, complete their five rituals.

ABOUT THE TEMPLE OF GRIOTS

In many African societies, a griot is a storyteller, a bard, an historian, a librarian, and a philosopher entrusted with cultural continuity. It used to be that each tribe or clan had a griot who was the keeper and interpreter of the chronicles, narratives, and histories for thousands of years going back. These literary scholars, poets, authors, and musicians spent a lifetime passing those stories down to the next generation's griots. Griots often only married each other as a caste unto themselves, ensuring their power of memory and archival continuation.

In some African cultures, praise singers tell their stories in song. As a daughter of hip-hop, it is clear to me that our griots are to be found among our hip-hop artists and spoken-word poets as well as our playwrights, filmmakers, and other artists. Telling your story breaks generational curses.

We have already lost so much of our history, and it is easy for our heritage to disintegrate. My extended family is now spread out in several countries. We started a virtual lineage group specifically aimed at preserving our family histories, stories, and culture, in addition to attempting to reclaim what was lost in the Middle Passage. It has been incredible.

We have recovered so much history through family members, documents, and narratives previously lost to the winds. We even learned that one line of my maternal lineage still has their original Akan surname because we were brought to be healers/doctors to our fellow enslaved people. My healing heritage deepened! I've seen soccer players, beauty queens, authors, and newscasters pop up with my family names, only to realize that we are close relations. This online group is our modern-day griot vehicle, the campfire we gather around to share the story of us.

Write in your Goddess Soulbook: *My story matters.*

My mom said that when she was growing up, they would announce all of the births and deaths in the region on the radio. Television didn't become common in Guyana until the '80s. They would even announce, "Guyanese born overseas," every time someone like me was born in another country to Guyanese parents. The radio functioned as the griot or town crier.

Akoben! The Akan (Ghana) proverb "If you take your tongue to the pawnshop, you can't redeem it later" means that you have to own your voice. On your goddess path, your griot energy is about awakening the energy of your voice, telling your story, and owning your truth. The Akan principal of Akoben is that of the call to action. An Akoben, represented by a swirly Adinkra symbol, was an ancient war horn. The Akoben would be used to sound the alarm in an emergency. But you could also blow the horn to make music or announce a birth. The horn could be blown as a warning to be vigilant or as a means of expression.

WHAT IS YOUR VOICE ENERGY CHANNEL?

In the '90s, there were all of these great "girl power" anthems about self-expression. There was En Vogue's "Free Your Mind," Queen Latifah's "Ladies First," Salt-N-Pepa's "Expression," TLC's "My Life," Janet Jackson's "If," Mary J. Blige's "Be Happy," and Madonna's "Express Yourself," just for starters! This makes sense because women were claiming our voices more.

So, what is your story? The voice energy channel governs the throat, thyroid, ears, teeth, and neck. The main color for this energy channel is blue.

Many of us are striving to reclaim our stories and voices. Sometimes, under the guise of teaching you manners, the well-meaning folks who raised you taught you that your voice was not welcome. Maybe you heard, "Be seen and not heard," "Shut up," or "Stay out of grown folks' business." Now here you are, grown folk yourself, and you're still staying out of grown folks' business because you were taught as a good little girl to be unheard.

Generations of us were taught to prioritize other people and their needs, thoughts, wishes, dreams, and voices over our own. Some of us learned that being loud was rude or unladylike. I was inadvertently taught that to be likable, I shouldn't make waves or make other people uncomfortable.

Well, we are not having that anymore. As Great Ancestress Audre Lorde once said, "Your silence will not protect you." Reclaiming your voice is not only powerful but necessary.

Write in your Goddess Soulbook: *I reclaim my voice.*

Even as we talk about this now, I feel my throat closing up. We still have the fear in our sense memories of being whipped, burned, hung, sold, or ostracized for saying the wrong thing. Our bones remember the history of us as women gathering in corners to whisper our truth and being silenced, scolded, or killed. It is still happening today.

Start to heal your voice energy channel by speaking your truth, mindfully and with compassion. You may have been on mute so long or telling lies to yourself so long that you need to begin with telling you your truth.

Healing means prioritizing your self-expression and your creativity. This also means allowing yourself to cry with your full voice, loud and proud. We cry silently to feel our pain in a way that does not disturb or inconvenience others. Are you whisper-gasming? We whisper our tears and our orgasms. No more. Bawl, let your voice out. Orgasm your voice out. Let yourself feel life. If you can't be vulnerable with yourself, then who can you be vulnerable with?

Is your inner voice coming from you, your family who raised you, society, or your current community? Any voice that says it wants to keep you quietly safe, even if it is well-meaning, ultimately may keep you small. Speak up and out. Growth and expansion happen when we are courageous enough to step beyond what makes us feel safe. If you want to go somewhere different, you can't get there by doing the same thing.

This means speaking up for injustice and being a voice for the voiceless. This means speaking up for others who are not in the room. Say what you must say.

Write in your Goddess Soulbook: *I share my truth.*

A degree of openness in sharing our stories is important. Our traditions have been buried, hidden, and suppressed so much that in some of our cultures they are in danger of disappearing. I see it in my own family. We need to reclaim and pass down our hidden wisdom. We have to share our secret knowledge with each other so we all rise.

As someone who was born around much of this work and the secrecy surrounding it, the openness of the present moment is new for me. Putting your initiations in your social media bio, sharing pics of every altar, or telling folks which orisha is on your head feels foreign. Not that it is wrong or bad; it is just interesting.

One of my most powerful teachers, Baba Credo Mutwa, was persecuted for sharing secret sacred knowledge. But the knowledge is disappearing as people move to other traditions and dismiss their own as "backward" and "antiquated." His shift from oral tradition knowledge inheritance to written tradition knowledge inheritance was controversial. But his courageous decision allows me and others to bring his teachings to his new-world kin who have had this knowledge severed from our ancestors.

Write in your Goddess Soulbook: *My voice matters.*

When it comes to the voice, don't confuse volume with value. So many of the most vocal religious folks I know are not in alignment with what they claim. We see the same thing in the world of spirituality. The loudest people proclaim to be the most righteous gatekeeping enforcers of faith. No matter what your belief, you can't be sanctified and sanctimonious at the same time. These people are seductive because we think they know something we don't. But the wading you'll have to do through their personal baggage to find any gems is not worth it. Detach, disengage, learn the lessons, and move forward. Spiritual teachers, mentors, and godparents who take your soul (and voice) are abusive and not worth it. Love is always the most powerful divine feminine spiritual force.

I hear from many women who feel like they're hiding or invisible in their own lives. A healthy voice energy channel is about being able to be seen and heard as you want to. Perhaps you want to be heard around the dining table. Or maybe you want to be heard on global stages. Both are equally vital. It's up to you.

HOW TO KNOW IF YOUR VOICE ENERGY CHANNEL IS BLOCKED

There is a reason public speaking is almost as terrifying for some as death. Speaking your truth is a primal fear. Hundreds of years ago, if you said the wrong thing and were kicked out of a tribe, it was hard for you to survive by yourself. If your tribe canceled you, you were pretty much screwed on the savannah, desert, or prairie. So fearing that your friends or family won't love you if you believe something different from the tribal group makes sense. It's a logical fear to have, but it does not serve you.

Three of the most common voice blocks, which are just stories we tell ourselves, are:

- *What if I make a fool of myself?*
- *What if I betray my circle or shine too brightly?*
- *What if speaking my truth gets me in trouble?*

Are you afraid of what "they" will think? "People say, 'Be yourself,' but what if I am being myself and I make a fool of myself?" This is a major block that also shows up as the impostor phenomenon. "What if they find out that I'm not as good as they think? I'm going to fall on my face. People will laugh at me. Then I will be embarrassed and ashamed."

Another common block is fear of shining brighter than your circle allows. Your circle can be your family of origin, ethnicity or culture, socio-economic group, or friends who you socialize with or work with. You may fear that if you use your voice or speak your truth, you may betray or outshine the circle and then be unloved.

In Black American culture, we talk about the crab mentality as social punishment for daring to shine too brightly. When one crab tries to shine by climbing out of the barrel, the rest of the crabs pull her back down. In Australia and New Zealand, they have tall poppy syndrome. They say when a poppy (person) grows taller (shines brighter) than the rest of the poppies (circle), you need to cut it back down to size. Germans have schadenfreude, joy at witnessing the misfortune of those who dared to rise.

No wonder we are scared to speak up, express ourselves, and shine! These voice energy channel blocks are sneaky. What you choose to do for a living is a part of your self-expression. If your circle are all lawyers and accountants, you may be scared to express yourself as an artist or performer. You may subconsciously be perceiving yourself as somehow betraying the circle. Or it could be the opposite, where you're from a community of artists and outsiders and you want to be a banker. We will do anything to preserve our identity, who we perceive ourselves to be.

Do you feel comfortable sharing good news and expressing yourself positively with your circle? When you decide that you are going to speak words of love, affirmation, and positivity into your life, it can shift the way you socialize. It is customary in many circles for us to relate to each other by being self-deprecating. We say, "I'm such a pig. My hair is a mess. I gained so much weight. These jeans are the worst." We bond over dogging ourselves (and others) out. When you decide not to participate in that and don't want to be around that energy, that is a tribal shift that may feel like a betrayal of your social pact.

You also have a scared child inside who fears, "If I speak my truth, I might get in trouble." Getting in trouble as an adult is different than getting in trouble as a child. Getting in trouble as an adult could mean getting fired, canceled, ostracized, divorced, or rejected.

Will owning your voice make you feel uncomfortable? Of course. But that's okay. Just come back to your breath. We naturally hold our breath when we're afraid of expressing ourselves. Start with a nice, big, deep breath and let it out with a big sound.

Some of us feel like, "I don't have a problem speaking out; I just spew whatever, wherever, however, to whomever." That is a sign of unhealed voice channel vibrational energy. Just because you're cussing people out right and left doesn't mean you don't have a self-expression issue. Speak your truth mindfully, responsible for the energy you bring, and with compassion.

Meet Mami Wata, Yasigi, Mama Djombo, Mame Coumba Bang, and Nunde. The outspoken circle of griot goddesses is ready to hold space for you to speak your truth.

MAMI WATA

Goddess of Nakedness
Diaspora
Water Gazing in the Hidden Lake Ritual

"I have the courage to be vulnerable."

MAMI WATA'S MESSAGE

Maakyé! Look who it is! My girl! What a grand day to be unapologetically you. The water only drinks your reflection. The water only sees your true face. Hide no more. Be naked. Emotionally naked.

MAMI WATA'S STORY

Great Goddess Mami Wata, keeper of mysteries,
We see you. We say your name.

The mermaid goddess is ancient. The oldest art in the world is the rock paintings created thousands of years ago by the Khoisan people in South Africa and Botswana. These drawings show sangomas (healers) with magical half-human creatures—including mermaids. Mami Wata has been here.

Mami Wata is known as the mother of the water throughout West Africa, Southern Africa, Central Africa, and beyond. Mami Wata and her sisters are said to live in the Ikpoba River in Benin City, Nigeria. Her origins are also claimed by Benin, Togo, and Ghana. Folks mistakenly honor her as an orisha, which is fine, but she is not an orisha. She is, in fact, her own pantheon and venerated throughout many traditions. Mami Wata has one of the most devoted, active followings worldwide. She exudes griot energy as her story is told through diverse cultures.

Warning: the energy of a water spirit or deity is never passive. As a water queen, Mami Wata has great influence over the emotions of her devotees. We spent the first nine months of our lives safely floating in water. To be a Mami Wata initiate is no light commitment. Pledging to Mami Wata requires you to be honest about who you are and how you show up. Being Mami Wata's devotee requires you to live and speak your truth. She gifts her followers with clairvoyance and healing powers.

My parents didn't talk about Mami Wata, but they told us about the Wata Mumma and Fairmaid. Her name shifted when she reached the shores of South America. I was taught that the siren call of Wata Mumma was to be feared. She had the power to abduct anyone she wanted. In West Africa, everyone knows someone whose cousin heard of a water spirit abduction. I wonder if the fear stories of water abduction came before or after the Maafa, Middle Passage?

In my parents' country, Mami Wata worship was illegal. The Minje Mama or Water Mama veneration dance was persecuted when the country was named British Guiana. There is even a case in 1819 of them blaming the death of a woman on having unwillingly participated in the Water Mama dance.[1] The ancestors worshipped Mami Wata by dancing. So the enslavers believed that if they stopped the dancing, they would stop her worship. It was seen as a part of obeah, which the colonizers feared could lead to uprisings by the enslaved people. They had good reason to fear. Uprisings and revolutions in Haiti, Jamaica, St. Vincent, South Carolina, the Guianas, and many other places had our priests and priestesses at the forefront.

In the 1740s, one of the colonizers just over the border in Dutch Guiana (now Suriname) wrote: "It sometimes happens that one or the other of the black slaves either imagines truthfully, or out of rascality pretends to have seen and heard an apparition or ghost which they call Water Mama, which [the] ghost would have ordered them not to work on such or such a day, but to spend it as a holy day for offering with the blood of a white hen, to sprinkle this or that at the waterside and more of that monkey-business."[2]

Yes, Mami! So in the 1770s, the colonial authorities in Dutch Guiana passed laws banning Mami Wata. They cited that "the Watermama and similar slave dances" had "dangerous effects." They also noted that enslaved people "who are brought here under the name of [Ouidah] slaves, have introduced certain devilish practices in their dancing, which they have transposed to all other slaves."[3] Remember back in Medusa's sanctuary (Chapter 5) how we learned about the Mami Wata statue in Ouidah at the Temple of Pythons? Now some African evangelicals spread fear that Mami Wata adoration will lead women down the wrong path.[4]

In the Guianas, Europeans outlawed Mami Wata in part because she was telling the enslaved people not to work for the enslavers. Mami Wata was protecting her children. Today their descendants in the Afro-Surinamese group Black Harmony proudly sing her praise in their song "Watra Mama." Band member Orlando Ceder translates the lyrics into English as: "Watra Mama, we are calling you/We are standing by the sea and want your permission to cross it/Aye Watra, hear us and show your beautiful self/Nana Barinya, come and show your powers." Nana Barinya is another name for Watra Mama in the Surinamese African-derived religion Winti.

Mami Wata is so powerful that as her energy spreads globally, people tend to merge or collapse the water spirit stories of their locale into her story. Mami Wata spirits can be any gender, as with Suriname's Watra Papa, although they are most often women. Mami Wata's reputation is multifaceted because when you hear about her, you are hearing about many different energies. Currently there are so many stories of mermaid Water Mumma sightings and even capture in Guyana that the country was featured on the show *River Monsters* on Animal Planet.

Let's Talk Emotional Nakedness

What does being naked emotionally mean? We are talking about being vulnerable enough for people to experience the real you. I looked up *vulnerability* in the dictionary, and no wonder we are scared to open up. It said, "capable of being physically or emotionally wounded, open to attack or damage, vulnerable to criticism." No, thanks! Opening yourself up to be judged, criticized, or rejected is not at the top of anyone's wish list.

In many of our families, being vulnerable is equated with being weak. We despise vulnerability not only in ourselves but in others as well. Learning to cultivate an appreciation for vulnerability in others is healing for our own vulnerability.

So what does being vulnerable have to do with empowering your voice energy channel? Everything! Broadcasting your thoughts and opinions without vulnerability is flat, hollow, and rings false. Think about some politicians. The ability to be vulnerable, to be naked emotionally, is our humanity.

In addition to being vulnerable, being emotionally expressive personally also matters. Otherwise your relationships stay shallow and at the surface level. True intimacy is being able to go deep and be vulnerable with people. You can't have friendship or romance without vulnerability.

"All you need to do is be yourself" is easier said than done. But we all want to hear, "I love you just as you are." We all want to be loved and accepted for our true selves. To truly own your voice and your story, you must have the courage to be emotionally naked. Spiritual nakedness is also goddess energy. Surrendering is being vulnerable to Spirit.

Write in your Goddess Soulbook: *It is safe for me to be vulnerable.*

To be vulnerable, practice being transparent. Start by being transparent with the people closest to you. Say, "I just realized that I haven't been showing the whole me. I am starting today." Have the courage not only to feel your feelings but to express your feelings as well.

Being a vulnerable, emotionally naked, fully expressed person is scary. What will people think? What if they reject you? What if they judge you? Or hurt you? Some will, and that is okay. Take small steps and small risks first if you need to.

Speak your truth. Share your story. Become comfortable with feeling uncomfortable. Also become comfortable with making others feel uncomfortable. You daring to be vulnerable is not about anyone else. It is first about your own emotional health and well-being. The fact that it will make all of your relationships truer and richer is a bonus.

HOW TO HONOR GODDESS MAMI WATA

When you honor Goddess Mami Wata, you honor the part of you that is authentic, naked, and raw. You may choose to honor this energy inside yourself or invoke her energy according to your own tradition.

To honor the goddess in you: We come into this world naked. After the age of maturity, it is up to us how we live. Surrender the need to be in control. Release your attachment to outcome. Open your heart and allow yourself to be you.

Are you one of Mami Wata's children? Priestesses of Mami Wata are known as Mamisii. In Djimon Hounsou's 2018 documentary, *In Search of Voodoo: Roots to Heaven*, you can see the beauty of Mami Wata's followers at the ocean in worship.

Symbols: Like Oshun and Erzulie Freda, Mami Wata carries a mirror. She also carries other expensive toys and baubles, as she brings the wealth. Her sacred toys include jewelry like pearls, gold, and diamonds.

Colors: Her colors are red and white, symbolizing her duality.

Auspicious times: All Mami Wata rituals are performed on Fridays. Her feast day is June 25.

Music: "I Am Mami Wata" by Casey Malone and "Watra Mama" by Black Harmony

Suggested offerings: Coconuts, shells, cola, and alcohol in addition to grooming products such as pomade and soap. She loves pythons.

Alternate names: Mommy Water, Mamba Munti, Wata Mumma, Mami Wota, WatraMumma, Mammy Wata, La Sirène, Maman Dlo, Ribba Mooma, Fairmaid, Madre de Agua, Nana Barinya

Traditional Emotionally Naked Ritual: Hydromancy

When we connect to Spirit, we should come in a state of being emotionally naked, vulnerable, and surrendered. In most places in West Africa where people practice water gazing, they do it in natural sources, like streams or lakes. Water has been on Earth for 3.8 billion years. It knows and has seen some things! Water gazing, or hydromancy, is a form of divination that we all potentially have access to.

Elder Malidoma Patrice Somé said that his father's form of divination was also water gazing. They are Dagara people from Burkina Faso. Elder Somé's father could stand in the kitchen, gaze into a bowl, and see clear pictures of what was happening at his farm miles away.

Great Zulu shaman and sanusi Vusamazulu Credo Mutwa shares: "My grandfather told me that a sangoma must be able to draw knowledge from what he called the hidden lake. There is, he said, a huge unseen lake somewhere in the spirit world where all the knowledge of the Universe—past, present, and future—is to be found.

"You must never say again that you do not know something. You must just ask the lake, the unseen lake, to provide you with the knowledge that you seek."[5] What Baba was talking about is the field of knowledge that the West refers to as the Akashic Records.

Water divination, like all kinds of divination, trusts in the intelligence of nature and the Universe. Hydromancy, popular in Egypt, was mentioned in the Bible and is the form of divination that the famous Nostradamus used.

Your Emotionally Naked Ritual:
Water Gazing in the Hidden Lake

Ritual intention: To learn what lessons the hidden lake holds for us.

All African rituals begin with some form of cleansing, from libation to baptism. There is a reason why so many meditations use the sound of water. Water is soothing, and it can help us get present. Water holds all of our memories and secrets.

If you are reading this, chances are that you are a natural healer. Being able to own your voice, speak your truth, have the courage to be seen, communicate with your loved ones, and speak out for what you believe in all requires you being emotionally as well as spiritually naked. Being spiritually naked means without pretenses or ego.

You will need:

- A bowl (preferably blue or a dark color)
- Water (can be charged by the moon)
- White candle
- Journal

What to do:

Prepare your ritual space. Fill a bowl, preferably a dark-colored one, with water. A blue or dark-colored bowl more closely mimics a natural water source. Alternatively, you can use a lake, ocean, or bathtub. Feel free to use any kind of water that you feel connected to.

Light a white candle, and turn off the lights. Place the candle between you and the bowl. Sit and meditate with your eyes open, looking into the bowl of water, for at least 5 minutes. Set a timer so you can focus.

Imagine that you are looking into the hidden lake of the Universe that Great Zulu Ancestor Credo Mutwa said has all of the answers. If it helps, add a concentration point to the center of the water, such as a crystal or a coin.

You can say, "Ancestors, I come to you humbly and openly. Please show me what I need to know."

Follow-up journal questions:

- What do you want to say that you haven't said?
- Where are you invisible?
- When was the last time you felt vulnerable?
- What seems easy for everybody but you?
- When was the last time you felt jealous?
- What is holding you back?
- Who can you share this with?

Record the experience in your Goddess Soulbook.

YASIGI

Goddess of Self-Expression
Dogon/Mali
Vision Mask Ritual

"I am free to express myself fully."

YASIGI'S MESSAGE

Aga po, daughter. Hey now! We want to hear you. We wish to listen to your words. Express yourself now. You have something to say. Wait not another minute.

YASIGI'S STORY

Great Goddess Yasigi, keeper of mysteries,
We see you. We say your name.

Pay all attention to the goddess behind the mask. Yasigi has the reputation of being a free-spirited party goddess who, like many of her magical sibs, began as a legendary mythic ancestor. For the Dogon people of the cliffs of Mali, this goddess has the energy of "I am fully expressed."

Yasigi could be easily dismissed because her tribute statues depict her with beer and a beer ladle. Women were the beer brewers in most of sub-Saharan Africa. Many sites also reference her big breasts. Yes, her statues have glorious breasts *and* Yasigi is a significant spiritual figure. As an elder, Yasigi was the first Yasigne. The Yasignes are the only women empowered to participate in the masked dances of the Dogon.

Yasigi's mother/father is the supreme being sky god/dess Amma, after all. Dogons pray to the Most High, Amma, with their arms stretched out toward the mighty heavens. To speak Amma's name is to ensure that s/he keeps holding up the earth. Rhythm is considered to be a language. The first rhythm to appear was played by the ancestor of the griots. The Dogon distinguish between what they call "front speech," for children and strangers, and "clear speech," when you go deeply and honestly.[6]

Amma used the power of the spoken word to turn a seed into an egg that contained all of the knowledge and elements of the Universe. Yasigi and her divine siblings, including her twin brother Omo/Ogo and the Nommo, four pairs of twin, fishlike water spirits, all came from this magical egg. Things were off to a rocky start, as Omo/Ogo tried to steal the egg's placenta to create his own world. During his siege, the Nommo hid and protected Yasigi. Omo/Ogo lost his ability to speak and was turned into a fox for his disobedience.

Still, nothing could damper Yasigi's energy. Every 60 years, the Dogon people have a Sigi ceremony. At the first Sigi, the first dignitary Yasigi brought the calabash of beer made by the women. Her beer celebrated the gift of speech being transmitted from the Nommo. Then, for some reason, Yasigi decided to use her clitoris as a garden hoe (ouch!), causing her to cut herself and impregnate the earth with her blood. The earth was now covered with her seeds. Red fibers remain a key part of Dogon costumes.

The satimbe mask commemorates Yasigi's role in the first Sigi during the Dama ancestral ceremony. The word *mask* includes the entire sacred ritual vestment from the elaborate wigs to sandals. The colorful masks reflect the kize nay (the four elements) and all aspects of life. Mask wearers shout mantras but are mostly silent, letting the mask speak for them.

Yasigi's people are otherworldly. The Dogon have long had advanced astronomical and celestial knowledge acquired in modern times only with the advancements of telescopes. Ethnographers who studied the Dogon from 1931 to 1956 revealed that the Dogon had "their own systems of astronomy and calendrical measurements [and] methods of calculation."[7] They knew about the rings of Saturn, the four moons orbiting Jupiter, and the presence of the stellar companions of the star Sirius, all unable to be seen with the naked eye.

Dogon oral history says that they learned from visitors from the celestial system of Sirius, the Dog Star. Ogotemmêli, a blind Dogon spiritual chief and elder, was able to draw the orbit of one of the stars of the Sirius cluster. He said he learned it from Yasigi's protectors, the Nommo spirits.

Let's Talk Self-Expression

In Mali they say, "A rooster is not expected to crow for the whole world." Yes! The way you express yourself won't make everyone happy. That's okay. You are not meant to.

Self-expression looks different to all of us. For outgoing extroverts, self-expression may mean dancing on tables, being the queen of karaoke, and loudly sharing their points of view. Introverts may speak out in other ways and save the louder parts of their personalities for the people they love.

It doesn't matter how you express yourself; the important thing is that you do! Express YOU. Give voice, color, and magic to the force that is you. As a generation, all of us who are currently living have more access to personal freedom than ever before. This does not mean that we are all individually free. This also doesn't mean that we don't face systemic oppression. It simply means we most likely have more access than our grandmothers' grandmothers.

So what are you doing with it? And what are you doing to claim your personal liberation? I had a mentor who used to say we have to earn the right to complain. I think we have an obligation to pursue personal liberation and self-expression, as so many people sacrificed for us to have the freedoms we have now. We are far from where we need to be, but I will not invalidate their sacrifices by not acknowledging forward movement. So ask yourself, *What does personal liberation mean for me? What would make me feel free in my bones?*

How can you empower your voice? Remember when we were talking about play? Let your expressive voice be linked with your creativity. Some say that our vocal cords, housed in the voice energy channel, and vulva and vagina, housed in the creative energy channel, physiologically parallel each other.

Open up your self-expression energy with messy finger painting and sculpting with clay. Get yourself some coloring books and color outside the lines. Express yourself with cooking and baking.

Develop your voice and ear. Expose yourself to other opinions and ways of seeing the world. Pop culture has already been curated for you. It tells you which designers are chic, which music is banging, and the shows and movies to watch. But who cares what the tastemakers think? The way you dress and move in the world is part of your self-expression. How can you open up? Check out some foreign movies and music you wouldn't usually be into. Go see a show off the beaten path. Express yourself!

HOW TO HONOR GODDESS YASIGI

When you honor Goddess Yasigi, you honor the part of you that is ready to speak up and speak out. You may choose to honor this energy inside yourself or invoke her energy according to your own tradition.

To honor the goddess in you: Yasigi energy is open and expressive, like the night sky and the stars. There is knowledge that you alone have that we will miss if you choose not to express yourself. How can you be more expressive in your voice, clothing, artwork, and other choices? The Dogon believe in the generative power of the spoken word. Each word creates. Speak more joy, beauty, abundance, and truth over your own life.

Symbols: Sirius the Dog Star, stars, hills, masks, eggs, hornbill birds, sacred fly whisk

Color: Yasigi is bright and colorful but especially appreciates the color red.

Auspicious times: The mask society of the Sigi/Sigui festival is celebrated every 60 years.

Music: "Iyo Djeli" by Oumou Sangaré and "This Is for My Girls" by Michelle Obama and other artists

Suggested offerings: Poems and songs, red hibiscus, beer, dancing, masks, fly whisks, seeds, and eggs

Alternate names: Yasigui, Yasigne, Sister of the Mask

Traditional Self-Expression Ritual: Sisters of the Mask

The Yasigne are sisters of the mask in Dogon society. Mask performance is traditionally a male rite. But the Yasigne break gender norms.

According to the Dogon, around when time began, a woman named Yasigi came across a group of supernatural beings. They were startled by her sudden appearance and ran off. But they left behind gorgeous masks and costumes, which she brought home to her village. Now she had all these beautiful, colorful, and extravagant masks. The men in the village were jealous, and Yasigi's husband stole the masks. The jealous men decreed that masks would be only a male rite going forward.

She was decreed Yasigne, the sister of the mask. She was not bitter, and she cultivated red hibiscus to make the skirts that the men wore to perform. She also carried a sacred fly whisk to show a position of prestige.

In her honor, a select group of young women initiates still bear the designation Yasigne, sisters of the mask. They dance and wear imina, masks, including heavy elaborate headpieces and costumes. Other women may not approach but watch from high boulders and rooftops.

Mask ceremonies celebrate big events and openings. The dances are a part of the post-burial rituals and battle cries for war. A mask is also performed before the rainy season. The sanuguroy mask runs through the village scaring and threatening to whip children who are not initiated. If a young man opts not to join the mask society and pay dues, he is mocked for being woman-like.

For the Dogon, masks are considered to have their own nyamam, life-force energy, and pangan, power. The Sigi festival is held once every 60 years to honor the fact that life is now temporary. The Sigi lasts seven years and is in the Guinness World Records for the longest religious ceremony. Girl children who are born during a Sigi festival year will be initiated into the Yasigne, sisters of the mask. The satimbe mask represents Yasigi, now elevated to goddess.[8,9]

Your Self-Expression Ritual: Vision Mask

Ritual intention: To create a mask reclaiming your voice and celebrating your own evolution.

You will make a mask to represent your future self and future life. This is who you already are. You are just now evolving into her. In most African cultures that work with masks, the mask has an essence and life force of its own. Consider that as you create your own.

You will need:

- Piece of paper or Goddess Soulbook
- Writing utensil
- Art supplies (optional)
- Magazines or image printouts (optional)

What to do:

Part 1: Design Your Vision Mask

Prepare your ritual space. Either use a piece of paper or a page in your Goddess Soulbook. I recommend using a separate piece of paper if you want to display this mask. You can then make a copy of it and add it to your Goddess Soulbook.

There is a you that you are in a state of becoming. It is the real you. The goddess you. We honor her and witness her voice. Feel free to use your BMGV from the Temple of Conjurers (Chapter 3) if you wish.

Let's bring the "Vision Board you" into the present moment. Draw a simple oval face with eyes. Add a nose and mouth if you wish. Then go for it!

Draw, design, birth, and create the face of your future self, your vision. You may write words like *loving, outspoken, confident,* or *funny* or use images. It is up to you. What do you want to say? Add those words to your mask.

Write, "I am so grateful. This or something better for the good of all involved," on the bottom.

Part 2: Activate It

Close your eyes and see yourself as the person you portrayed on the mask. See yourself speaking, living, loving, and moving forward in life as her. Blow the breath of your life-force energy onto the mask. You may choose to leave it on your goddess altar overnight to turn up the energy.

MAMA DJOMBO

Goddess of Shine
Guinea-Bissau
Goddess Self-Praise Poem Ritual

"I am ready to be seen and heard."

MAMA DJOMBO'S MESSAGE

Esama, child! You were born to shine. We need to know your name. We want to learn your dance. You will not be silenced. Be seen. Be heard. Be a movement.

MAMA DJOMBO'S STORY

Great Goddess Mama Djombo, keeper of mysteries,
We see you. We say your name.
Speak her name.
Mama Djombo is revered as the goddess who shines and expresses herself through lush, green forests. She also protects her devotees through new cycles and transitions in Guinea-Bissau.

Mama Djombo's daughters rock. The women in her culture don't just own their homes, they often built them from scratch. They are also in charge of the relationships with spirits. In this culture, women choose their husbands and decide when they want a divorce. If they think a man would be a great husband, they leave a plate of food by his door to indicate their interest.[10]

If the name Mama Djombo sounds familiar, it may be because we all know the phrase "mumbo jumbo." If someone is speaking "mumbo jumbo" in American vernacular, it means that they are speaking gibberish.[11,12]

The colonizers most likely bastardized "Mama Djombo" into "mumbo jumbo." Check out this incredibly disrespectful entry that was in the *Oxford English Dictionary* well into the 1960s for "mumbo jumbo": "Name of a grotesque idol said to have been worshipped by some tribes. In its figurative sense, mumbo jumbo is an object of senseless veneration or a meaningless ritual." Wow.

Nonetheless, still she shines. Mama Djombo continues to be celebrated. During their War of Independence, freedom fighters in her country petitioned her for their safe homecoming. The Guinea-Bissau band Super Mama Djombo, founded in the '60s, chose their name to honor the goddess.[13] Maamajomboo is also used as the name of Mandinka masked dancers who took part in religious ceremonies. The Mandinka live mostly in the Gambia, Senegal, Guinea, and Guinea-Bissau.

Now Mama Djombo's energy is about using shine to protect and be in service to nature. The traditional priestesses of Guinea-Bissau's Orango Island have had to rise up. As people convert from the traditional spiritual beliefs, the environment is in danger. The reverence for the plants and trees is being forgotten. The baloberas, sacred priestesses, are using their power to protect the trees from "progress." Sacred baobab trees are being cut down.

In Sierra Leone, it is tradition to ask someone, "How's the body?" when greeting them. The response is "I tell God thank you." Your body and the forest are gifts.

Let's Talk Shine

What does it mean to you to dare to rise and shine? It starts with the courage to be seen and heard.

This section was originally called "Fame," but I didn't want you to get the wrong idea. Being comfortable with shining, getting attention as a result of claiming your voice, is not being famous for the sake of being famous. When I talk about getting comfortable with your shine, people think I am talking about Beyoncé shine or fame. That's cool, too, but that's not what I mean. We are talking about feeling at home enough in your skin to be seen. So many of you have told me you believe you need to stay in the background or be invisible so others can shine. We are talking about daring to shine as brightly as you can at home, at work, in your community. Again, it starts with daring to be seen and heard.

When you speak your truth, eventually at least one person will bear witness to your splendor. Your message will shine brightly for that person. They may tell a couple of other people. Then your message will shine brightly for those people. The community that witnesses your shine may be in your own household, center of worship or friend group, or maybe you are on global stages. This calling mandates you to raise the ceiling on how much criticism and applause you can stand and how worthy and deserving you think you are of the spotlight. Know that your voice matters.

As we have been talking about repeatedly throughout the voice energy channel, this will require you becoming comfortable with making yourself and others uncomfortable. Shine also means becoming comfortable with praise while no longer seeking external validation. If you believe them when they say you're the best, you will also have to believe them when they say you're the worst.

It is this fear of shining brightly that keeps so many of us in the shadows, hiding and shrinking. You feel uncomfortable with praise and recognition while simultaneously craving it. We are love-starved for our own voices.

Your story matters, and there is someone who needs to hear it. As someone with anxiety, it was not easy for me initially to become comfortable being seen and heard. But the conundrum is I have important things that I felt called to share, sacred medicine I was born to put into the world. There is no way to claim your voice and avoid rejection, criticism, and judgment. If everyone likes you, you are not being authentically you.

I am not for everyone. I had to let my message and my love for you, my goddess sisters I am being called to share with, be greater than my fears. So I issue the same challenge to you. If you have something to say, everything starts with the courage to shine, the courage to be seen. This means daring to let your walls down.

Imagine showing up for this life every day as you. What would people see? What would we hear? How would you express yourself? What would it feel like to be so vulnerable and be you anyway? Tell your story. Speak your truth. Be seen and heard.

Write in your Goddess Soulbook: *The sky is my limit. I am willing to embrace change with open arms. I am limitless.*

Our Goddess Temple Circle sister Nyla (not her real name) is recovering from being in an abusive marriage. She recently had the courage to write a victim impact statement. The court system invited her to make the statement if she wanted to share what happened to her on record. At first she said no. She was raised to believe that vulnerability is weakness. In her family, the rule was to just suck it up and get on with it. Then she decided that her experience and voice were too important not to share.

Nyla wrote her statement to reclaim her voice, and it is part of public record. Although she is not ready to talk about it publicly, she is working her way up to it. Nyla asked me to share her story here as a first step. She said that for her young daughter and son, she feels she must. We applaud her for having the courage to take these steps. Be where you are. This is shine, the power of being seen and heard, even if you never know Nyla's real name. She is making an impact.

HOW TO HONOR GODDESS MAMA DJOMBO

When you honor Goddess Mama Djombo, you honor the part of you that is ready to shine. You may choose to honor this energy inside yourself or invoke her energy according to your own tradition.

To honor the goddess in you: What do you really think about yourself? Thoughts become beliefs and experiences. You are magnificent, and no one can hide your shine but you. As they say in Guinea-Bissau, "No fist is big enough to hide the sky." Although Mama Djombo was dismissed as "mumbo jumbo" in the United States, thankfully, through oral tradition, we are able to continue to learn about her. Lies could not hide her shine—or yours.

Symbols: Trees

Colors: Her colors are green and brown.

Auspicious time: Celebrate her on September 24, her country's Independence Day.

Music: Super Mama Djombo is the name of a politically conscious music group formed in the 1960s in Guinea-Bissau. They chose their name because their soldiers sought Mama Djombo's protection during their War of Independence for freedom from Portuguese rule. With singer Goddess Dulce Neves at the helm, they were the voice of the uprising. Rock out to any of their high-vibe, melodic harmonies such as their song "Faibe Guiné" or "Casabe África" by Dulce Neves.

Suggested offerings: Leaves, plants, earth, rocks, and anything you'd find in a forest

Traditional Shine Ritual: Oríkì Praise Poetry

Oríkì is traditional Yoruba praise poetry that can easily be viewed as a precursor for dancehall and reggae toasting, spoken-word poetry, and hip-hop. Praise poems are called izibongo by the Zulu, dithoko in Lesotho, lithoko by the Basuto, maboko in Setswana, and buraanbur by the Senegalese. Deities and VIPs have praise poems made about them, and because the traditions revere nature, so do animals and plants.

These fluid poems are handed down, invented and added to as the need arises. For families that follow the tradition, each person in Yoruba culture also has a set of praise names. Your name blesses you with your spiritual essence. As it says in *A Poet's Glossary* under the entry for the term *oriki*, "Call people by their oríkìs and you inspire them."[14]

Praise poets themselves traditionally held positions of high esteem. They had political sway and community influence. I see this handed down with the importance of recitation in so many of our cultures. My mom can still recite extended sonnets, monologues, and poems she learned in grade school.

Here is a well-known oríkì for Oshun:

(You can find it in Yoruba at womanifesting.com.)

Exist, exist always, mother . . .

Exist, exist always in our tradition.

The spirit of the river, turtle drummer

Open the path of attraction, mother of salutations.

Cleansing spirit, clean the inside and out.

The maker of brass who does not pollute the water.

We are entitled to wear the crown that awakens all pleasure.

We are entitled to wear the crown that awakens all pleasure.

The spirit of the earth that wanders freely.

Àse-o.

Praise to the goddess of mystery,

Spirit that cleans me inside out.

Praise to the goddess of the river,

Spirit that cleans me inside out.

Praise to the goddess of seduction,

Spirit that cleans me inside out.

Mother of the mirror,

Mother of dance,

Mother of abundance,

We sing your praise,

Àse-o.

Oríkìs are used as prayers, incantations, songs, theatrical performance pieces, meditations, invocations, and, of course, just as poems. The longer version even includes the line, "One who has large robust breasts!" Yes! Come through, bodacious and divine feminine!

Your Shine Ritual: Goddess Self-Praise Poem

Ritual intention: To write a praise poem for yourself and salute your inner goddess.

I loved learning that Nigerians are considered the premiere praise poets in West Africa.[15] This means that when I was a teenage rapper, I was fully in alignment with my Yoruba roots! (With all due love and respect to all of the other African nations, and all of my other ancestors, of course.)

You will need:

- Writing utensil
- Journal
- Goddess Soulbook

What to do:

Prepare your ritual space. You can either do this assignment directly in your Goddess Soulbook or copy your finished praise poem into your Soulbook.

Answer these questions to complete your goddess praise poem:

- What are the 10 most wonderful things about you?

- Compare yourself to something in nature. How would you describe it?

- What do you and your ancestors have in common?

- How do you identify yourself?

- Compare yourself to a food (e.g., solid as a biscuit).

- Compare yourself to an animal (e.g., intense as an owl).

- What is your favorite part of your body?

- What are you most proud of?

- Brag about your goddess superpowers.

- Describe yourself as an element (e.g., fiery).

- What do you and your favorite goddesses have in common?

- End with, *"I have something important to say. My voice matters. My story matters."*

YES! This is your goddess praise poem. Record it on audio or video. Share it if you dare!

Bedtime ritual: Read your oríkì to yourself in the mirror nightly before you go to bed.

MAME COUMBA BANG

Goddess of Speaking Up
Senegal
Goddess Mission Statement Ritual

"I reclaim my voice. I speak out and speak up."

COUMBA'S MESSAGE

Jaam nga fanane, beauty! We are listening. Speak on it. You have a right to say it. Speak on it.

COUMBA'S STORY

Great Goddess Coumba, keeper of mysteries,
We see you. We say your name.
The river speaks.
Folks have reported seeing her in the flesh, Mame Coumba Bang, if they were early or late enough. Rubbing red powder around your eyes may help. She sits on the

water's edge to get some air, especially at the end of the rainy season. Coumba and her family like to roam the streets at night. But when the sun rises, splish-splash, she's gone. If you see a large calabash of veggies floating in the water in the morning, Mame Coumba Bang was hungry.

The river is loud.

Sing for her, chant for her, call to her, give Mame Coumba Bang your voice and she'll be happy.

The river protects.

Goddess Coumba protects the mouth of the Senegal River in St. Louis and angers if you cross the wrong boundaries. (Yes—there's a St. Louis in Senegal!) The area near the bridge is called her armoire, and her living room is the dip in the island. You don't just go into her residence. Everyone knows that you can drown if you just show up disrespectfully. She has a large family of spirits, gods, goddesses, and her own children in the river with her. Her sister Mame Cantaye is the goddess guardian of Langue de Barbarie.

Mame Coumba Bang offers safety for the fishermen and surrounding communities and asks for her sarax, special offerings of white foods, such as curdled milk, kola nuts, or couscous in return.[16] When making an offering to Mame Coumba, you must not speak to anyone else, coming or going. Save your voice and attention for her. To be a Coumba specialist who can see the goddess at will, it must be in your lineage. Coumba pundits protect the city by making sure she is happy with regular offerings, although anyone may give. The more, the better. Her fast currents, rising waters, and flooding are a serious issue.

For the offering before the rainy season, a chosen girl must take a pirogue to the center of the river while the older women sing. Doing this correctly will ensure a safe season.

The river has boundaries.

Don't worry, riverside dwellers. She protects you too. Coumba is known to be a helpful goddess, but not one who heals or cures. She will support you to be self-empowered and give you the gift to cure. Coumba also helps babies be born safely when the mothers and grandmothers do a good job giving the offering.

She loves when her followers sing to her, especially with dancing and drumming tams-tams. This is called the Ndiaguabar. The voice is important. Exaltations in song manifest her power. Traditional families of "griots of pure origin that do the Ndiaguabar dance" calm Coumba down. [17]

Mame Coumba Bang is temperamental, and her clear emotional and physical boundaries must be respected. Her wants and needs are clear. We have much to learn from this river goddess, don't we?

Let's Talk Speaking Up

What did Queen Mother Nanny of Jamaica, Mbuya Nehanda of Zimbabwe, Dutty Boukman of Haiti, Cuffy of Guyana, Gullah Jack of South Carolina, and so many others have in common? They were spiritual and revolutionary leaders who fought against the colonizers and would also be considered sorcerers, witches, or magicians. It's no mistake that so many revolutionaries of the diaspora were also spiritual leaders and healers.

For the Baka people of Cameroon and Gabon, the girls' initiation into adulthood includes learning to own your voice. They are a society of hunters, and hunting requires having full access to your voice. Each girl is given medicinal leaves, water, and honey as a sacred tonic to be able to access guidance. They ask their god Komba and spirit Jengi, chief of the forest, to give each girl new power and the ability to sing. Their unique yodel-style singing, yéli (or yelli), hypnotizes the animals and blesses the hunt.[18]

Do you own your voice? What do you stand for? As the old adage goes, stand up for something or you will fall for anything. So again, What do you stand for? If you are reclaiming your goddess power, neutrality is not an option.

If you are claiming to be neutral on anything, you are lying to yourself. When you stand firmly in your truth you have thoughts, opinions, beliefs, and convictions. You may not have the courage to always voice them, but you have them. I'm not saying that you need to share your opinions on the evening news or even social media. I am saying that you are betraying yourself by not speaking up for your own beliefs.

We live in a polarized world as the patriarchy makes its last gasp at gripping power. Your goddess energy is needed. There is an us versus them mentality where people are willing to see others starve and suffer. We see who is allowed to have a voice and who isn't.

Your words have power. So I ask again, What do you stand for? Who do you speak up for?

Write in your Goddess Soulbook: *My words have power.*

In high school, I hung fliers that had the inflammatory words "Battle for the Brooklyn Bridge." They were to invite people to a protest against repeated racist incidents happening in New York City. My rap group, FBC, Females Beyond Control, with my girl Goddess Debbie, rapped on the school stage about the injustices that were happening. So did the school mobilize into action? No, the headmistress called in my parents because the flier also had the "scary" words "Black activist Abiola Abrams." My headmistress didn't say, "What is happening? How can we be involved? Is there a safer way to do this?" She basically said the flowery version of "We feel threatened. This is scary, and this kind of free speech is not allowed."

Do you speak up for others when they are not in the room? A couple of years ago, one of my uncles was over for a holiday. He's a fun person, and I enjoy his company. However, in sharing his "funny" stories, he used a slur against a group that was not represented in the room.

To be clear, I have taboos against "talking back" to my elders embedded in my veins. No matter how old I am, it is ingrained in me to respect those who are older. But I want people who don't know me speaking up for me when I am not in the room. When you are with your family and they say something derogatory about dark-skinned, kinky-haired Black women or "those damned immigrants," I need you to say something. That is a social contract for those of us who want a better world. So I had to interrupt my uncle and let him know that terminology was unwelcome and we don't speak like that. Was it awkward? Heck yeah! But thankfully, we moved forward.

So how and where can you speak up? Signing petitions is an accessible way to speak up. Having a conversation with your family members may not be as easy—but it is speaking up. Starting a hashtag about a cause that matters to you is speaking up. Protesting in person or online is speaking up. Saying something at work to protect others is speaking up.

Speak up. Speak out.

HOW TO HONOR GODDESS COUMBA

When you honor Goddess Coumba, you honor the part of you that speaks up for what is right. You may choose to honor this energy inside yourself or invoke her energy according to your own tradition.

To honor the goddess in you: This is a moment to challenge yourself. What do you care about? Your voice is needed now more than ever. How can you dare to speak up and speak out about what matters to you? Take action today by speaking up for yourself or someone who is not in the room.

Symbols: River water, silver coins, milk

Colors: Her colors are blue, black, and white.

Auspicious times: Coumba's days are Wednesdays and Fridays.

Music: "Coumba" by Orchestra Baobab and "Don't Play with Your Own Life" by Coumba Gawlo

Suggested offerings: Mame Coumba Bang prefers her sarax to be white foods. She respects where you are. Just pour curdled milk into the river (or a water source) if that's all that you have. She also loves sugar, couscous, baobab juice, and kola nuts. Her favorite is laax porridge served with yogurt. An offering of white ox, sheep, or goat meat is sure to bring you favor.

When giving food to this goddess, you must give half to the impoverished to eat. If you can, divide the remaining half equally between the sea and the river. Be sure to sing and dance for her.

Alternate name: Maam Kumba Bang

Traditional Speaking Up Ritual: Inkulisela Voice Power

Inkulisela was a traditional Zulu corn-growers' ceremony. Elders, accompanied by young women and men, would go to the cornfields. The young people would sing songs of praise to each growing corn plant. They would give the plants names and touch each one with love. Corn was gifted from sky goddess iNkosazana, who we'll meet in the Temple of High Priestesses (Chapter 9). Inkulisela's purpose was to ensure an illustrious crop and help the corn grow. Honoring all living things is a key part of Zulu consciousness.

The European missionaries dismissed and discouraged the ceremony as superstitious nonsense. The Inkulisela died out and only the eldest elders remember it. Maize, corn, has been a staple food of the Zulu since the 1600s. From Zulu rainbow maize, large multicolored heirloom corn, to Umqombothi, beer made from corn and corn malt, most Zulu eat some form of maize daily.

Now science has shown that the processes of the Inkulisela work. Studies as far back as 1962 show that plants that are played music have a 72 percent increase in biomass and up to 62 percent more growth.[19] Experts advise plant growers to speak to their plants. The Royal Horticultural Society in the UK found that communicating with plants, especially women's voices, helps them to grow faster.[20] In another study of two plants in the UAE, one was played complimentary statements in a loop while the other was played bullying statements. You know what happened next, right? The bullied plant withered while the praised plant flourished.

Recently there was a maize crisis in South Africa. Poor conditions, including drought resulted in a shortage. I wonder if they considered reintroducing singing to the fields and the powerful Inkulisela ceremony.

Your Speaking Up Ritual: Goddess Mission Statement

Ritual intention: To create a personal goddess mission statement declaring what you stand for.

A goddess personal mission statement defines and clarifies who you are as a person, your values and purpose, what matters to you, and what you stand for.

You will need:

- Goddess Soulbook or piece of paper
- Writing utensil

What to do:

Answer the following questions to create a personal goddess mission statement:

- What matters to you?
- How do you want to feel every day?
- Who do you want to impact?
- How do you want to make them feel?
- What are your favorite qualities about yourself?
- What makes you smile?
- What do you want to create, and why?
- What class could you teach right now?
- If you had one-minute in an elevator to share your best advice, what would it be?
- What legacy do you want to leave?

Read it out loud to yourself in the mirror.
Add your personal mission statement to your Goddess Soulbook and/or frame it.

NUNDE

Goddess of Truth
Benin
Awkward Conversation Challenge

"The truth is my friend."

NUNDE'S MESSAGE

Vbèè óye hé? It is she! All will be revealed. What is your truth? Remember who you are. Release the fear of your power.

NUNDE'S STORY

Great Goddess Nunde, keeper of mysteries,
We see you. We say your name.

Nunde is the bold, outspoken wife of Legba. Legba is the trickster lwa (deity) of Benin Vodun who was reborn as Papa Legba of the crossroads in Haitian Vodou and Louisiana Voodoo. Nunde was feeling neglected by Legba, the bratty son of Mawu-Lisa. In Haiti, Legba is a serious old man, but he is a virile youngster in Benin. He bored quickly, and even with several wives his head easily turned. Plus he was busy opening up spiritual communication, a job he did very well when he was not wreaking havoc for his own amusement.

So Nunde stepped out on her non-attentive husband. Fa, the god of divination caught her eye, and she decided to take on a lover. KoniKoni, one of Legba's other wives, told Legba immediately, although she didn't care for him lately either. KoniKoni had always disliked Nunde and often made trouble for her. Legba was furious. He demanded to know why she would cheat on a husband as amazing as he thought himself to be.

"You have a small penis," Nunde blurted out. This was the truth.

Legba was distraught. He conjured up a magical concoction to make his penis grow and drank it day and night. It worked! He was victorious. Everyone in the village started to sing about his penis. To celebrate, he started sleeping with every woman who approached him.

As the people drummed, Legba sang:

Gudufu
The path of my destiny
Is large
Large, large
Like a large penis
Oh, Gudufu
You are large[21]

Girl! His intention was to shame Nunde. Nunde, however, didn't care about any of that drama because she had a more pressing issue. She wanted to know why KoniKoni disliked her. Legba's other wife, Ayizan, was much older and indifferent toward her, but she wanted to be friends with KoniKoni.

Nunde sent Brer Rabbit to the diviner to find out what was up. She was advised to fill a calabash with water and create a sacred offering of a chicken, goat, pepper, and palm oil. It worked like a charm—and the two women became best friends. With the magic of the gods, it was revealed that KoniKoni and Nunde were actually the same person. She was her own worst enemy, but when she told the truth, she became her own best friend.

In Benin there is a saying, "We can only speak the truth when we turn off the light." That sounds like Legba wrote it. Nunde's choice was to tell the truth in the light and the darkness. It was her destiny. And she ended up madly in love—with herself.

Let's Talk Truth

Telling our truth is not always easy in the public sphere. Historically, saying something unwelcome could get you labeled as angry, crazy, or difficult. All potentially the kiss of death, both personally and professionally. Thankfully things are shifting. Everyone deserves to be able to be honest about their experiences.

In our personal relationships, truth telling matters. Being able to hear the truth matters just as much. We have been indoctrinated with the values of "go-go-go, broadcast, take the stage," but the goddess energy of receiving means being able to receive what other people have to say. Learning to speak and listen with compassion is important.

Think before you speak. You don't ever want to say something you will regret and cannot take back. Words have impact. Some people replay hurtful words in their minds for decades. Feel free to say, "I really want to talk to you about this, but I need a minute/day/couple of days first." This way you honor yourself and others.

Be gentle and stay calm in truth-telling conversations. We all have triggers. You may come from a background where you can yell something out and move forward, no big deal. For someone else, that yelling may be a trigger that echoes abuse patterns they have witnessed or experienced.

Write in your Goddess Soulbook: *I easily tell and receive the truth.*

Disagreements are a part of life. Each person has their own version of the truth. How you fight in every interpersonal relationship dictates the health and longevity of the relationship. If either you or the person you are communicating with feels like the other monopolizes the conversation, set a timer. For 7 to 10 minutes, each party speaks while the other listens uninterrupted. This prevents waiting for your turn and inspires listening.

Validate the other person's experience. Even if you disagree, be clear that you understand what they are saying. If you are unclear, ask, "Are you saying XYZ?" This will give them the chance to clarify. You may be hearing something totally different than what they are trying to say.

Use more "I feel that" statements that speak to your experience instead of "Why do you" statements, which sound like blaming. Watch how you use the word *but*. If you say, "You are an incredible friend, but . . . " everything after "but" might as well be invalid. Don't let a "but" cut you off where an "and" may be able to open a path.

We have all heard that there are three versions of the truth, right? Yours, mine, and the actual truth. If you need a mediator or third party present, invite one. Seek professional help if needed.

Write in your Goddess Soulbook: *I am loyal and devoted to the people in my life.*

HOW TO HONOR GODDESS NUNDE

When you honor Goddess Nunde, you honor the part of you that walks in truth. You may choose to honor this energy inside yourself or invoke her energy according to your own tradition.

To honor the goddess in you: What is true for you? Challenge yourself for the next seven days to only speak truth. Tell no so-called little white lies or people-pleasing alternative facts. When you choose to speak, be gracious, understanding, and compassionate, but be true to yourself. See how things shift.

Symbols: Kola nuts, palm leaves, yam

Color: Her color is green.

Auspicious times: January 10 is Fête du Vodoun, a public holiday in Benin and the perfect time to celebrate Nunde.

Music: "Koni Koni Love" by Klever Jay and "Nan Dòmi" by Riva Nyri Prècil

Suggested offerings: As Nunde was attracted to Fa, god of divinity, she loves palm nuts, 16 to be exact. Benin is called the "land of songs" because singing is always welcome. Sing to her.

Alternate name: KoniKoni

Traditional Truth Ritual: Ash Circle

For the Dagara of Burkina Faso, if you need to have a conversation with someone, loving or difficult, the ash circle is the sacred space. This can be one-on-one or with a group. The goal of the ash circle is to resolve conflict while clearing anger and fear. Everyone in the circle commits to listening without judgment.

The ash is created from burning sacred herbs and plants. The herbs provide protection from negative energy and spiritual powers of discernment and communication for all who are invited to enter. The person initiating the conversation draws the ash circle and sits in the center with an earthen pot full of water in the center. Spirit invites the other person to show up. When they arrive, you both pray for your intention and ask for guidance in this safe intimate space.

Each person takes a sip of water. Water represents peace. Facing away from each other, they spit the water out. Then they face each other and scream at each other freely until catharsis is reached. If they are a couple at odds, they may sit back to back. Then they have difficult, awkward, ugly conversations. Each party is allowed to speak without interruption. Listening to the other person's truth is key.

For community issues, the ash circle may be in front of the group for truth telling. For those kinds of groups, elders may be present to be the ears, along with Spirit and the ancestors. At the end, they may throw the remaining water at each other to represent tears and release.[22, 23, 24]

Your Truth Ritual: Awkward Conversation Challenge

Ritual intention: To speak your truth in your relationships.

Are there conversations that you have been avoiding?

You will need:

- Yourself

What to do:

Prepare your ritual space. Choose 5 from the list of 10 potential conversations. Have 5 truth-telling and truth-hearing conversations with love, empathy, and compassion.

Pick 5:

- Tell someone something you've never told anyone.

- Share something that makes you uncomfortable.

- Tell someone you have a crush on them.

- Tell someone you love them.

- Ask someone for a raise or tell them you raised your rates.

- Thank someone.

- Tell someone they hurt you.

- Ask someone close to you to tell you something that you can improve on.
- Confront someone about something.
- Contact someone about a professional opportunity. Record your experience in your Goddess Soulbook.

Congrats! You have completed the Temple of Griots.

Temple of Griots Voice Mantras

- *I have the courage to be vulnerable.*
- *I am free to express myself fully.*
- *I am ready to be seen and heard.*
- *I reclaim my voice. I speak out and speak up.*
- *The truth is my friend.*

Temple of Griots Journal Questions

- How can you be more vulnerable?
- What's a new form of self-expression you are willing to try?
- Are you ready to be seen and heard?
- If there was one message you were born to share, what is it?
- What do you need to tell the truth about?

Temple of Griots Embodiment

- Add something to your altar that represents your voice goddess power.

Temple of Griots Integration

- Add the Temple of Griots goddesses and your experience with these rituals to your Goddess Soulbook.

8

THE TEMPLE OF QUEENS: YOUR INSIGHT ENERGY CHANNEL

Chi

BLESSING OF THE QUEENS

You see beyond

Higher knowledge

Inner vision

Super consciousness

Limitless

We see you

Third eye grounded

Head held high

You float

You levitate

You see beyond

We see beyond

A majestic hello to you, empress!

You are entering the Temple of Queens in the insight energy channel. The five great queens here just for you, Queen Nandi, Queen of Sheba, Queen Mother Nanny, Queen Nefertiti, and Queen Yaa Asantewaa, are here to guide you in elevating your intuition, alchemy, dreams, alignment, and imagination. They have been the keepers of this guidance from time immemorial. You now stand in an elevated circle of royalty who are here to hold space for you in tuning into the magic of your third eye.

Sit in the center and take in their wisdom. They each have gifts for you. Should you choose to accept their gifts, you will integrate your regal goddess power. To finish this temple, complete their five rituals.

After you ascend from the Temple of Queens, only the Temple of High Priestesses remains. You have come so far.

ABOUT THE TEMPLE OF QUEENS

Look at you, my goddess sister! In this sacred temple, we move from I to eye. You are in a co-creative drumming circle with the Universe to evolve all consciousness. Yes!

We have up-leveled to the Temple of Queens in your insight energy channel.

Mother Africa has many incredible queens, like Queen Amina, the warrior queen that the TV series *Xena: Warrior Princess* was allegedly based on. Queen Amina, also known as Queen Aminatu, was a 16th-century Hausa warrior queen in what was known as the Zazzau region of Nigeria. From the Kandakes of Nubia to Empress Marie-Claire Heureuse Félicité of Hayti, queens and queen mothers are community leaders and exalted rulers. Perhaps you grew up in a queen-led environment.

The Temple of Queens continues the energy of the Temple of Ancestors, as these goddesses were all living queens of the diaspora. These queens are goddess energy on Earth. In the patriarchal cultures that most of us live in, the thought of an ancient queen who is actively fighting for your power is healing. What if just one of these queens could guide you daily? It's even better than that.

There is guidance available for us, insight if we know how to tap into it. The word *insight* means "inner sight, eyes of the mind, mental vision, and understanding from within." The ancients understood that there was another eye or set of eyes committed to understanding our lives.

Anyanwu is the Nigerian Igbo goddess or álúsí of the sun. Her name, a combination of the words ányá and ánwụ́, means the eye of the sun. She is the reason Igboland was known as "the land of the rising sun." Anyanwu helps with your chi, meaning your personal spirit.

The Eye, the Eye of Ra, and the Eye of Horus (Heru) were all feminine-energy Egyptian deities, or different aspects of the same. They were able to see farther and assist the sun or sun gods Ra, Re, and Aten. This is the third eye in Hindu philosophy. You also see ancient Egyptians depicted with pine cones. Pine cones represent the pineal gland, a small pine-shaped endocrine gland in the brain. The pineal gland governs being awake and asleep in the physical world and being spiritually awake as the third eye.

Among the Dagara, masters of observation and intuition are called "nimwie-dem," which means "those that have eyes." The Zulu say, "The eye crosses the full river," meaning all things are possible. As the great Credo Mutwa said, the Zulu believe that when women tap into the divine feminine, aka "mother mind," we will change the world because we think "sideways, sideways and upward and downward" instead of just linear. This is insight.

We have all heard of women's intuition, but it's much deeper than you think. Each of us has a chi. In Igbo spiritual science, your chi is your personal guardian spirit that you were assigned before birth. Chi is internal divinity. Some say that our chi determines our destiny. This is a simplification of a philosophical concept that people study for a lifetime to understand.

You may know this concept as guardian angels. Everything has chi. Ancestors intercede if needed to help the chi, your personal guardian angel. In Yoruba culture, the ori, or head, is the site of àse, life-force energy, and your personal guardian spirit. This is why people in traditional Yoruba art have bigger heads. Your chi is not to be confused with qi in Chinese medicine. There is some overlap with qi but also major differences.

You should have a great relationship with your chi. Your chi is your partner. Talk to your chi before you start something new. Dreams are a great way to speak to your chi. Thank them at your altar. An obi chi is a sacred space altar just for your chi. You also must feed your chi. Alom chi is a feast in honor of your chi.

Dibias, Igbo healers, teach that your chi provides guidance, letting you know if you are on the right path. What you do to others, you are doing to your chi. There is an Igbo proverb, "Your chi is greater than a wise woman." When you feel blissful, creative, and in good health, you are in alignment with your chi. Is your manifesting power strong? That means your chi is in alignment and you are on the right path.

WHAT IS YOUR INSIGHT ENERGY CHANNEL?

Imagine how powerful you would be if at every step you had access to divine intelligence. What if the Creator, your ancestors, angels, spirits, deities, and ascended masters were whispering guidance to you? Well, they are. Your insight energy channel governs your brain, eyes, face, and lymphatic and endocrine systems. The main colors of this energy channel are indigo, dark blue, and purple.

Right this minute, you are being guided toward some people, experiences, and behaviors and away from others. Usually, we ignore that guidance, although most of the time not on purpose. Mostly, we are missing it altogether. Divine guidance is always there for us. It's up to us whether we choose to tune in to it or tune it out.

Although at times it can seem like it, none of us are walking alone. As the Great Ancestress Maya Angelou declared in her poem "Our Grandmothers," "No one, no, nor no one million ones dare deny me God, I go forth alone, and stand as ten thousand." What did she mean? She meant that not only do we have each other, but each and every one of us has an army of ascended masters, all different aspects of the Divine, with us.

As we discussed in the Temple of Ancestors, you have hundreds (at least) of ancestors. Written in the codes of your DNA is that millennia of ancestral memory, wisdom, and knowledge. The ultimate conjuration is to access it and use it. This energy channel is our command post and temple of wisdom. Ways to access and use your insight include intuition, mindfulness, channeling, trance states, astral projecting, and divination, just for starters.

You are as infinite as the force that made you. That means that there is infinite guidance for you. The Divine is infinite and expansive. And when we align with that energy, the energy of miracles, we are infinite as well.

A friend told me she lost her keys, and I said, "Ask your angels to help you." She said, "I just lost my keys. I don't want to bother the angels. They're doing their thing." No, their "thing" is you. The thing that the Universe is doing is you. How amazing is that? You may feel like, "I don't want to pray or ask for that small thing because they are busy." Yes. They're busy "doing" us, co-creating this world for us, with us.

Our requests are only too small with our puny earthly understanding that if you're helping this kid over here, you can't be helping that lady over there that needs something greater. But I want you to expand the possibilities of the Divine having abundant energy to help. So they could be helping you find your keys in Brooklyn, helping Kwame in Seattle, and helping Stacey in Australia. Spirit is infinite.

Write in your Goddess Soulbook: *My chi is taking care of me.*

My mom and sister attended my Goddess of Paris Retreat in 2019. After the incredible weeklong experience, we packed up to fly back across the pond to New York. I had arranged a pickup for three adults carrying six suitcases to the airport. Imagine our surprise to see a mini sedan pull up. They sent a tiny car that couldn't even fit just our luggage to take three adults to the airport. They needed to send another car and had no idea how long it would take.

I started freaking out. What if we missed our flight? I wouldn't mind missing the plane if it were just me, but my mom has knee pain, and it would be difficult for her to stand around in an airport. I couldn't believe this was happening.

But then I remembered the lessons of my own retreat. We are always being guided—and life is happening for us, not to us. How many stories are there where people say, "Oh my gosh, I was going to be on that plane that crashed?" We don't know how life is being orchestrated for us. If I'm missing a plane, it's because I'm meant to miss that plane. I can't miss the plane that is for me. Spirit has my back.

I shifted from anger and frustration to gratitude. *Thank you for sending the wrong car so that I wouldn't be on that plane. I don't know what the reason is, but I'm going to trust it. I come as one, but I stand as 10,000 and my spirit family is just as infinite.*

Let's talk about your spirit family. What's the difference between your ancestors, angels, and spirit guides, and how do we connect? There are as many answers as there are traditions.

We are spiritual beings having a human experience, and we tend to think of it the other way around, right? We think, *I'm a human being with glimpses of magic, glimpses of spirit.* But it's the other way around. You are divine, magical, spiritual, and perfect, and all of us chose to incarnate together at this moment for a purpose that you may or may not know.

The wondrous thing is that although you walk solo, you are not walking alone. You are here with your guides, and those guides can be God/dess, your chi or ori, ancestors, saints, angels, or other deities, depending on your tradition. But there's no tradition that says that you are here by yourself. And so when people say your great-grandmother's prayers are still protecting you, it's not only the prayers they may have had for you before they knew who you were. The prayers and intentions that they have for you right now are protecting you. They are interacting with your life daily. Now you may look at certain situations and think, *But Abiola, if I'm being protected by angels and ancestors, then why did all of this happen?* Well, do we know what could have happened without them? You have breath. You have free will. We are earthlings doing earth things.

Write in your Goddess Soulbook: *My instincts are strong.*

My brother O (he's shy) had a car accident that was so horrible that it was on the news. A Mack truck hit him and crushed his car. We all rushed to the hospital. My dad sat on the subway, crying the whole way there. O had to be lifted out of the mangled car with the Jaws of Life. But physically he was perfectly fine. This was shortly after my maternal grandpa had died, and everyone at the hospital kept saying, "That boy has some angels around him." And in my family, we knew exactly who his angel was. It wasn't a question that my grandfather had my brother's back in that moment.

Somebody prayed for you. And we have no idea what their prayers have done for us. And so we should be sending out prayers—or if the word *prayer* makes you uncomfortable—send requests, gratitude, and intentions. We should be intending for the generations that come after us. Those who will know you and those who may never know your name. Right now, in another dimension and time, our energy, our prayers, our intentions are protecting and keeping and guiding and watching over them.

Our Goddess Temple Circle sister Allison Rozzel had an experience that left her clear that she is being guided. A few weeks before Thanksgiving 2019, she started thinking about her dad's mother, Big Mama. Big Mama passed away over 20 years ago, and Goddess Allison never really knew her. But she suddenly found herself longing to connect with her.

Her mother shared that when she was ill, Big Mama created a home remedy that helped. Goddess Allison was intrigued and wondered if her grandma was into holistic healing. Then Arzu Mountain Spirit, the Garifuna healer you met in Long Bubby Suzi's sanctuary (Chapter 5), told Goddess Allison that Big Mama wanted her to visit her grave. Goddess Allison was already heading to Knoxville for the holiday, the same town where her grandma was buried. The cemetery said no one would be there that day but they would e-mail a map.

When Goddess Allison got to the deserted cemetery with her son, she couldn't find Big Mama's headstone. They walked around frustrated in circles and were ready to give up. They couldn't miss Thanksgiving. Allison was about to cry when she suddenly smelled fresh flowers. But there were no flowers around. Then there was a breeze and the smell got more intense.

Goddess Allison's son yelled, "Mom, is her name Hazel Cook Rozzel?" She ran to find him at her grandmother's grave. Allison sat and explained to her grandmother, "I want you to understand what I'm doing as a spiritual liberation coach, since I'm no longer a Christian." Allison is a certified Reiki master healer and intuitive oracle card reader. She told her grandma about her spiritual practice and asked if she was okay with it. The wind blew again, and Goddess Allison's heart felt full.

After dinner Goddess Allison was eating dessert with her aunt and aunt's her in-laws. Her aunt introduced her, trying to explain what Allison does for a living. She asked Allison to explain it. Suddenly her aunt looked different. She was intensely interested, and Allison had a feeling that this wasn't her aunt anymore. It was her Big Mama! So Allison looked into her eyes and shared. Big Mama said,

"Oh, that sounds like something really good." Then as quickly as she came, Big Mama was gone. Goddess Allison knew she had her support and approval.

So who are your spirit guides? Who do you want them to be? Feel into the Divine with your insight and you can feel your spirit guides. Try it now and feel into your ancestors, those who choose to connect and those who don't, those related to you and those who are not blood kin. Like I said earlier, you can have claimed ancestors, people who are not blood relations. Great Ancestresses Josephine Baker and Zora Neale Hurston are two of my claimed ancestors and spirit guides. I feel soul close to them. They are my soul family. They are my spirit family.

There are people who can channel spirits, and at first glance that may sound creepy, but many of us have seen Baptist or Pentecostal tradition churches where people speak in tongues. What do you think they're doing? If you've seen people speaking in tongues, you have seen people channeling spirits. There are some people who can channel and then interpret that transmission or download it into words and guidance.

There are different gifts that we all have to interpret our spiritual transmissions. If you are not attuned to being clairvoyant, clairaudient, or clairsentient, you still have access to channel and download.

I am one of those people who finds it easier to connect and dance between realms. As I am writing this book, I am also creating a sister deck of *African Goddess Rising* oracle cards. For the past six months as I have been working on this project, the spirit world has been super active with me. When we started, I was on overload because the goddesses and ancestors would not leave me alone. I thought I knew what this book and card deck should be, but they had completely different ideas. They were dreaming me nonstop! That's the way we say it in Guyanese spiritual philosophy. I wasn't dreaming about them; they were "dreaming me."

Start to be in clear conversation with your guides through prayer, meditation, and ritual. Feel into their energy, set a place for them at the table on their birthdays, acknowledge them. Pour libations. Play their favorite music. Honor them at the altar. Be willing to connect.

Write in your Goddess Soulbook: *I am willing.*

Willingness is a superpower. If you're coming to your chi, angels, ancestors, and spirit guides with closed, skeptical, prove-it-to-me energy, that won't work. Ask and invite them to guide and help you. You can simply say, "Angels, please help." Or go to your altar and make a goddess request. Just ask, "Ancestors, please help me." Invite their guidance and assistance. And take good care of them in return.

You are so loved that not only have you incarnated here at this moment and been given breath by the Creator of the whole universe, but you also have a spirit gang with you that has your back. You want ride or die? You got it. Open your heart.

Just start with asking questions. The questions that you ask help create the answers you need. If you ask, "Why does everything suck? How come nothing works out for me? Why would this happen to me?" Those are the answers you're going to get. Guidance will say, "Well, let me tell you why nothing works out for you." If the questions you ask are along the lines of, "What is my purpose? How can I make my life greater and more exciting? What is the next path that I should take? I'm feeling joyful. How can I expand that?" Now, those are questions that will change things. The questions that you ask are going to expand or shrink your possibilities.

There's a vision that's been put into your heart and no one else's. Follow your vision. The more in tune you are with your own BMGV, Big Magical Goddess Vision, the more the right people and situations start to come into alignment. Don't live in the world of woulda, coulda, shoulda. Move into the world of, "Yes, I can."

Write in your Goddess Soulbook: *I am now connected to my inner vision.*

HOW TO KNOW IF YOUR INSIGHT ENERGY CHANNEL IS BLOCKED

The most magical thing is that you're already connecting with your chi, angels, ancestors, and spirit guides. Now you just want to do it purposefully.

First, get your energy channels clear. Ground yourself, raise your vibration, and clear things that are holding you back. The fastest way to ground yourself is to walk barefoot in nature.

We are in energetic communication with everything in our environment physically and emotionally. Unspoken conversations, debt, and unexpressed feelings are all in energetic communion with us. If you are attuned to, "I forgot I have to have this conversation and pay the water bill and I didn't like the way they spoke to me yesterday," your channel is not clear.

Whenever we talk intuition in a goddess circle, someone asks, "How can I tell my intuition voice from my fear voice or inner demons?" We all have that inner fear voice that says, *Ooh, don't do that. That's scary. That might mess up your life. Don't listen to her. Let's stay stuck. Let's stay small. That sounds crazy.* That inner fear voice wants to keep you safe. And any attempt at safety is keeping you, at the same time, small because growth and expansion include risk.

So the way to know whether the energy is from divine guidance/God-dence or the energy of fear is your intuition and inner guides will never make you feel small. They won't beat you up. They won't say you're a fraud or asshole. Divine guidance will never attempt to belittle you. Instead, it will guide you to the next choice or option, the next open door. The fear voice will attempt to diminish you. Your God/dess voice is guiding you and opening you up to the possibilities.

Take a breath.

Queen Nandi, the Queen of Sheba, Queen Mother Nanny, Queen Nefertiti, and Queen Yaa Asantewaa will be your guides in this temple. They want you to know that you are regal solely by your birth. You are connected to them and their wisdom through your insight energy channel. They are here to help you surrender, tune in, and trust.

QUEEN NANDI

Goddess of Intuition
Zulu/South Africa
Mirror Gazing Meditation Ritual

"I am knowing."

QUEEN NANDI'S MESSAGE

My daughter, Unjani? You already know. Take a deep breath and surrender to what you know to be true. Trust your inner wisdom. Trust your ancestors. Trust your guidance.

QUEEN NANDI'S STORY

Great Queen Nandi, keeper of mysteries,
We see you. We say your name.
Nandi Zulu!

Queen Nandi was the mother of the famous warrior king Shaka Zulu. Before Shaka was born, Sithayi, a seer, prophesied that "a child will be born who will bring about a new order and a new nation."[1] Nandi's son certainly made his mark, but what is less known is that she was a powerful ambassador in her own right. Nandi had an incredibly difficult time, but her story is one of love and perseverance.

Nandi was born around 1766, the daughter of a chief. She fell in love with the king's son, Senzangakhona kaJama. They started sneaking around. At the time ukuhlobonga, sexual contact without penetration, was accepted. But unmarried Nandi got pregnant, so everyone assumed that she had forbidden premarital sex and did not stick to just ukuhlobonga.

Her family contacted the king, but the royal court rejected them and denied that Nandi was pregnant. They said that she perhaps had a stomach bug from the iShaka beetle. Obviously as time went on, her truth panned out.

Nandi's people, the Mhlongo, demanded that the royal family compensate them for their son getting her pregnant. Usually, the girl at the center of such a controversy would shut up and let the families negotiate. Not Nandi. She requested 55 herds of cattle as payment. The payment was made, but the price was steep. The royal family initially denied paternity. Finally, Nandi was brought to the Zulu capital but without the usual festivities because she was already pregnant.

She gave birth to her young prince and named him Shaka after the iShaka beetle. Take that, royal court. Soon after, her relationship with Senzangakhona deteriorated and he kicked her out of his personal kraal. Nandi returned to her people to be ridiculed, scorned, and humiliated. Shaka was dismissed as illegitimate. At the time, this was taboo and an issue of great strife and shame.

Nandi trusted her intuition. She believed in the insight and guidance of the healer and did the best she could. The Zulu unity concept "We are all the same" was an important part of her household, even though she was treated poorly by the community.

Nonetheless, Queen Nandi went on to become a shining leader for both her family and her country. Nandi's son Shaka eventually became king. She served her country as the clan queen and official legal advisor. Her son was one of the most enigmatic rulers in history, loved and hated by many. It is said that many of the negative stories about him were created by the region's European invaders.[2]

Queen Nandi's lesson is trust guidance: we are all fertile at any time with the dreams for ourselves and the dreams for our people.

Let's Talk Intuition

So how do we pay "tuition in"? Trusting your own inner voice, your chi, is the easiest way to begin.

Divine guidance connects with us through our intuition. Do you trust your internal GPS? Do you believe you have access to divine guidance? Intuition is a muscle we all have access to.

Are some people perhaps more gifted in some areas than others? Of course. For example, I am clairsentient and clairaudient, but I have no clairvoyant gifts at all—at least not yet! But messages from your soul don't have to look like a big=screen TV.

When I was a kid, both of my parents worked. Back then, we were called "latch-key kids." My parents felt guilty about this, so they would tag team, calling us non-stop as soon as we got home from school. One afternoon, my mom was supposed to go Christmas shopping with her office friends. There was a big sale, and maybe in a group they could locate the elusive Cabbage Patch Kids.

It was the end of the day. The office was buzzing, excited about the shopping trip. Then my mom heard, "Go home, Norma." It was not a loud voice, but it was clear. Abandoning the shopping trip would disrupt the group because they would have to take her home and then make it back to the stores before they closed. My mom is not one to make waves or ever want to disturb the status quo. So she called to check on us and we said we were fine, but she heard the nudge in her soul again. "Go home, Norma." This time she listened and asked her work friends to drop her home. They were annoyed and angry. They'd had to coordinate many schedules to plan this day.

My mom got home and ran into the house to find my brother, sister, and me upstairs watching TV, doing homework, and playing. She was relieved and went to make dinner. Then something told her to check in the basement. Thank God/dess she listened.

Quietly, in the basement, two floors down from where we were all camped out, a fire had started in the oil burner. It was small but growing. She called 911 and got us outside. When the fire trucks came and the fire was raging, they said that it was a miracle that she got us all out.

Yes, it was. Your intuition gives you access to your miracles. Trust the still, small voice. Spirit speaks to us in the nudges, whispers, and winks. It's the thought of, "Hmmmm, maybe I shouldn't go in today" that is the gift of intuition. We can all trust our guidance when we agree with it. Can you trust your intuition when it makes no sense?

Write in your Goddess Soulbook: *I trust my inner guidance.*

We have to practice trusting and hearing our intuition because we are so practiced out of trusting ourselves. We're practiced into betraying ourselves instead.

How magnificent must you be that God/dess loves you so much? How enchanted you are that ascended masters, goddess, angels, ancestors, and saints show up to love up on you and have your back. Feel that and stand taller. Practice tuning in to your guidance and intuition.

When my brother's wife was pregnant with my niece Ava, I dreamed it way before they announced it. I called him up and said, "You're having a baby." He was like, "I'm not talking about that." I said, "I know y'all may not be ready to announce it, but I know, and you know I know." Having an intuitive family is cool in some ways, aggravating in others. Growing up, it was annoying with my mom seeing things, aunties dreaming things, or my dad saying he knew that a relationship was not going to work.

Everyone can strengthen their intuition. We are all intuitive beings. We just have different access. Start by simply being present and being mindful. We're in a pro-hustle world. Being present is a spiritual practice that allows you to feel, hear, see, and sense your guidance. We are transmitting, receiving, and sharing messages all the time, but we're in too much of a hurry to hear them. Slow down. Breathe. Create or deepen your meditation practice. Go for a walking meditation. Just be present with nature and pay attention.

With social media, we spend lots of time in broadcast mode. "Here's what I have to say." Intuition is you turning the tuner from broadcasting to receiving. You have to choose to allow yourself to be a transmitter and a transmuter, transmuting energy, to hear divine guidance.

Here are a few goddess intuition tips:

- You are a pendulum. Ask your body, "Is this right for me?" Then feel whether the energy is moving you forward or backward. If you're feeling pushed forward, then it's right for you. If you feel pushed backward, the answer is no.

- Ask, "If I knew what the answer is, what would it be?" Then follow your first instinct.

- Remember when the doctor hit you on the knee? Your muscles have an involuntary response. You can use muscle testing as a spiritual intuition tool. Connect your pointer finger and thumb, making an "okay" symbol with your right hand. Ask a yes or no question, then try to pull the circle apart with your other hand. If the link is easily broken, the answer is no. A strong connection means yes.

- You have a brain in your heart and a brain in your gut. As we discussed in the Temple of Conjurers, you also have spiritual intelligence in your yoni. Ask, "What is the most self-loving choice I can make?" And feel into your guidance from your yoni.

- Tune in to the seeming coincidences. Pay attention to the people who happen to call you when you say, "I need a new direction." What is that person you just met here to teach you? It may not be immediately apparent, but trust that there is a divine order.

- Notice the synchronicities. You may even want to keep a daily synchronicity list. When I was first starting to become more in tune with my own guidance, I would list one to five coincidences every day. And as you start to notice them, like anything you pay attention to, they accelerate.

HOW TO HONOR QUEEN NANDI

When you honor Queen Nandi, you honor the intuitive part of you. You may choose to honor this energy inside yourself or invoke her energy according to your own tradition.

To honor the goddess in you: Your guidance led you to this book and this pathway. Think about how you found this work and how you first found me. How many "coincidences" needed to happen? Where did you have to take a leap of faith? How did you have to trust your gut? Trusting your inner guidance is a process of learning and unlearning. As singer Alicia Keys said, "I've needed a lot of practice at putting my own ideas and intuition at the forefront."[3]

Symbols: Nandi's symbols are the beetle, colorful beads, milk, maize, and sorghum.

Color: Her color is green, meaning joy and contentment in traditional Zulu beadwork.

Auspicious time: Celebrate Queen Nandi on August 9, National Women's Day in South Africa.

Music: "KwaZulu (In the Land of the Zulus)" by Miriam Makeba and "Nandi's Suite" by Ndabo Zulu and Umgidi Ensemble

Suggested offerings: Beautiful beads of every color
Alternate name: Queen Nandi Bhebhe

Traditional Intuition Ritual: Momone Community Cleansing

The Sefwi women in Western Ghana use their intuition and the power of ritual to transmute any impending crisis, danger, or an outside threat. Whenever inner guidance tells them that something dangerous is on the horizon, the women come together for the Momone energy cleansing. The practice clears bad juju and banishes negative spirits.

Like the Ashanti, the Sefwi are an Akan people. This ritual appeals to the abosom (deities) and the ancestors. It became an all-women's rite when performed during wartimes, as men were on the battlefield. This ritual, which includes singing, dancing, and drumming in a parade-like procession, also lets women express their concerns. Momone is used for natural disasters, witch detecting, deaths, pandemics, and more.

The goal is to cleanse the community and block evil. Early on the morning of the ceremony, the women bathe and smear their bodies with kaolin. Kaolin is white clay. They wear red underwear, white clothes, and white dukus (headwraps). They then gather at a major crossroad. Mediums and priestesses take the forefront to connect with the abosom through spirit possession. Unlike most Ghanaian rituals, the Momone starts with song instead of libations.

The opening song goes:
Yie! Yie! Yie!
Glory Yes! Yes! Yes!
Nana the Great o! We rely on you!
We, the least privileged, rely on you!
We rely on you, we rely on you, Lord!
We shall not disturb you!
We shall disturb you!"

Fresh garbage created from food is thrown along the street to signify evil spirits or bad vibes. Then the Momone women clean it up with brooms. As they sweep, they sing and dance in a procession, repeating: "Sweeping ourselves! Yɛpraee! Yɛpraee yɛwon oo! We are sweeping! We are sweeping ourselves!"

The dust, dirt, and garbage is bathed in kaolin and cleansed away with the ginger lily herb. The ginger lily keeps evil spirits away. Ginger lily, also known as costus afer and anyain, is a key part of cleansing rituals as it is said to have healing physical and spiritual properties.

The group faces in the direction of the bad energy. They sing, scream, wave sticks, and yell curses, depending on the situation. They also pound empty mortars and pestles as a weapon for spiritual warfare. If they wish to curse someone, they sing: "When I reach a river I shall call your name, and the river will handle it!"[4]

Your Intuition Ritual: Mirror Gazing Meditation

Ritual intention: To awaken or deepen your intuition with captromancy, mirror gazing.

What's your relationship with the mirror? Do you avoid your reflection? Do you give a glance and a "Hey, cutie"? Do you peer at yourself and look for flaws?

Like water, mirrors can be a portal and a meditative tool. Mirrors represent our connection with the spirit world and our inner worlds. Some secret initiation ceremonies in Sierra Leone compel new initiates to gaze into mirrors. Goddesses Oshun, Erzulie Freda, and Mami Wata all carry mirrors. Powerful Okuyi masks in Guinea are designed with mirrors. Some Zulu rain dance ritual performance clothing also features mirrors. Zora Neale Hurston shares that a Hoodoo mirror ceremony is used to allow ghosts to cross water.[5]

Can you read your soul using a mirror? I love this pataki (story) by Luisah Teish, priestess of Oshun, in her book *Jambalaya: The Natural Woman's Book of Personal Charms and Practical Rituals:*

The human screamed and cried, "Please, Twirling Woman, Help me. Help me!" Oya flashed her dark mirror and said, "If you wish release, human, simply look into my mirror and change. You who need courage, look into my mirror and change. If you desire wisdom, simply look into my mirror and change. Power can be yours if you will look into my mirror and change."

You will need:

- Mirror
- Candle
- Writing utensil

What to do:

Prepare your ritual space. Light a candle and turn off the lights. Set an alarm for 10 minutes to start. See protective white light surrounding you while you shield yourself with white light, as mirrors can be a powerful portal.

Ask your chi, or personal spirit, "What do I need to know right now?" If you have a specific question, you may ask that instead.

Close your eyes and be aware of your breath. This is easiest when you are sitting in front of a mirror you don't have to hold.

Open your eyes and continue to be aware of your breath. Gaze into the mirror and see what guidance comes. Your inner bully may come up and start to criticize you or the practice. Just observe those thoughts and let them pass. Pay attention to your breath. Gaze into your own eyes with love and compassion. Be silent and present.

Afterward drink water. You may feel parched from extending so much energy. Write down any guidance that came up.

Record your process in your Goddess Soulbook.

QUEEN OF SHEBA

Goddess of Divination
Ethiopia
You Are the Oracle Cards Ritual

"I am connected to the Divine."

THE QUEEN OF SHEBA'S MESSAGE

Tena-ysitilign, daughter! It is safe for you to see the truth. Your spiritual vision is now crystal clear. You are connected. You see all connections.

THE QUEEN OF SHEBA'S STORY

Great Queen of Sheba, keeper of mysteries,
We see you. We say your name.

Most likely you have heard of the Queen of Sheba. In the Old Testament, she learns of the splendor of King Solomon's kingdom and takes off on a bold, creative adventure with a camel-led caravan to experience it herself. She meets King Solomon with her majestic delegation in Jerusalem. They welcome her warmly, regent to regent, as she brings a wealth of valuable resources and gifts including precious stones, gold, and spices like turmeric, ginger, korarima (Ethiopian cardamom), and saffron. Some say that she could have been on a trade mission from the Horn of Africa. Talk about an adventure!

One legend has it that upon meeting Solomon, Sheba reached into her braid and pulled out a golden ring. She gave it to Solomon, and he gasped. It resembled the Urim and Thummim divination breastplate of 12 gems worn by his priests. Answers to questions asked would be answered by the way lights reflected from the 12 gemstones on the vest.

According to the Ethiopian holy book, the Kebra Nagast (Glory of the Kings), the Queen of Sheba was their Queen Makeda from the Kingdom of Axum. The Ethiopian orthodox church teaches that their King Menelik I was the child of Solomon and Makeda.[6] When the Bible says that the Queen of Sheba and King Solomon exchanged gifts, the seed of the baby prince Menelik was the gift.

The queen was enamored with King Solomon but had taken a vow to remain celibate. Solomon reportedly had 700 wives and 300 concubines, but he was obsessed with our queen. The night before she packed up her camels to return home, they made a deal that neither would give the other anything. But King Solomon was enchanted by our Ethiopian majesty. He served her highly peppered food and water laced with vinegar to make her thirsty. When they went to bed, he put a bowl of water between their suites.

The queen awoke thirsty in the middle of the night. When she went for the bowl of water, Solomon reminded her of their promise to not give each other anything. She agreed to break the promise, drank the water, and also consented to have sex with Solomon. Before she returned to Ethiopia, he gave her a special ring to take home for their child-to-be.

Black and comely, the Queen of Sheba appears in Christian, Muslim, and Jewish religious texts. In the Bible, she is bold enough to test the king. After all, she is a queen. During the Middle Ages, some Christians said that the Queen of Sheba was a sibyl—a prophet and oracle—named Sabba. Other claims to the Queen of Sheba come from the people of Yemen, but historians say she could have ruled over Saba and the Ethiopian region. The Yoruba Ijebu clan identify her as a wealthy noblewoman known as Oloye Bilikisu Sungbo, said to be Queen Bilqis.[7]

Let's Talk Divination

Flipping a coin is basic divination, a simple reading without consecrated or sanctified tools.

Divination is a key component of African spiritual philosophies. In the Western world we think of divination as fortune-telling, trying to predict the future. Yes, there is some of that. But to be more accurate, divination is about going deeper into the present. It is like x-raying your soul.

It is magical to learn how many beautifully different divination paths the daughters and sons of Africa have been given. Obi divination with coconuts, reading bones, cards, and shells are just the beginning. The Mambila people of Cameroon and Nigeria have a form of divination called Nggàm, where they read spiders and crabs!

Dogon diviners draw a sacred grid in the dirt or sand and leave it overnight. During the night, the sand fox is attracted to the grid. The next morning, the markings left on the grid by the sand fox are read by the diviner. The fox is the intermediary between the priest and the Most High.

There are an infinite number of types of divination. Our Goddess Temple Circle sister Antranette does yoni divination, and our goddess sister Ekua does smoke divination. In addition to oracle cards, some of my personal divination favorites are cowries, tarot, Lenormand tarot, and runes.

Divination is part of most traditional African spiritual practices because divination is about knowing yourself. You don't always have access to your subconscious. The key to self-actualization is to know thyself, right? That is the gift of true divination. We are usually aware only of our surface level of fears. The word *divination* itself comes from *divine*, meaning "inspired by the Most High."

Divination is a strong branch in my spiritual lineage. I am the daughter of parents with psychic gifts and come from a family where people alternate between clairvoyance, clairaudience, claircognizance, and clairsentience, although they never use any that language. I have some of these gifts. Still, I grew up terrified of tarot and other forms of divination. When I was scared of divination, I would say, "If God has something to tell me, I will hear it directly." Well, Spirit has all kinds of ways to communicate with us. Why limit the hand of the Most High?

I love oracles and divination as extra tools to hear the voice and the guidance of God/dess. When I am creating, or should I say downloading, a new oracle card deck, I am simply creating a new communication system between the reader and the Divine. Divination can help you to know if you are on the right track and in alignment with your path.

HOW TO HONOR THE QUEEN OF SHEBA

When you honor the Queen of Sheba, you honor the part of you that is ready to unleash your creativity. You may choose to honor this energy inside yourself or invoke her energy according to your own tradition.

To honor the goddess in you: You have the power to shift your future. Divination, being inspired by the Divine, allows you to know yourself on a deeper level. There are things you will not consciously allow yourself to see. You don't know what you don't know. Allow yourself to be guided by the invisible hands of the Divine.

Symbols: Camels, luxurious textiles, precious stones, gold, and spices

Colors: Her colors are gold and black.

Auspicious times: The Timket Festival takes place on January 19 every year. The Epiphany festival celebrates Christianity in Ethiopia and Queen Makeda's role.

Music: "Rainha Makeda" by Batuk and "Makeda" by Les Nubians

Suggested offerings: Honor her with abundant and luxurious gifts such as gold and copper, and spices like turmeric, ginger, cardamom, and saffron. Coffee, maize, and grains are abundant in her queendom.

Alternate names: Queen Makeda, Queen Bilqis, Sibyl Sabba

Traditional Divination Ritual: Throwing Bones

You have heard about throwing bones, right? Maybe somebody you know had a grandma that cast chicken or possum bones. Bones are a potent spiritual tool because they come from a living animal.

For the Zulu, the bones that are read by diviners are called dingaka. They cast four bones to communicate with the spirits of the ancestors. Each set of dingaka bones is personal to the reader. As a sangoma and sansui progress, they may feel called to add shells, ivory, stones, stalks, man-made items, and other bones to their set.

Traditionally healers acquire their bones during initiation. A goat or calf is sacrificed at a feast. The initiate (ithwasa) wears the animal's inflated bladder in their hair as a sign that they are ready for the next phase. After the animal is cremated, the initiate must search through the ashes for four perfect bones.

This will be their dingaka set. The four oracle bones are cleaned and blessed. Sacred symbols are carved on one side only. Some will pass these bones on or add to inherited sets. They are typically stored in a bag, basket, or bowl on or near an altar. Imphepho incense is burned to call in the spirits. Imphepho also opens the healer's energy and psyche to receive the querent's ancestors.

The Zulu have a saying, "Bones must be thrown in three different places before the message must be accepted." Sometimes the sangoma feels the need to confirm guidance. In those cases, they do readings in several locations to see if the answers change. Whether we are reading inside or outside, on a rainy day or on the sand is important, as all of nature communicates with Spirit. The most common surfaces for readings are an animal hide, mat, right on the earth, or more recently, a table-top. Many readers cast in a circle.

You can get a simple yes or no reading, but a practiced sangoma will have access to much more info. Most will not need you to tell them what is wrong. They will tell you! The position of the bones individually and the patterns of the bones all come together to communicate the message.

Flute music and drumming deepen the sangoma's divination voyage. They are able to see mental, emotional, and spiritual blockages. They see the querent's lineage, growth experiences, and historical traumas clearly. They also make recommendations for healing.

Your Divination Ritual: You Are the Oracle Cards

Ritual intention: To create your own oracle cards for personal empowerment use.

La Madama is an Afro-Caribbean spirit gifted in intuition, oracles, and spiritual alchemy. She actually represents a group of spirits. La Madama is controversial because she was an enslaved woman who worked in the plantation houses in the Spanish-speaking Caribbean. She wields a broom as a magical tool and usually carries a basket on her head. Because La Madama is depicted as similar to a stereotypical "mammy," some mix her up with American fortune-teller images and call her the creation of a white American artist. This is untrue. I trust our Afro-Caribbean oral history that remembers her for hundreds of years. She is my family. Spiritual alchemy is our birthright.

Oracle cards are a powerful tool that can be used for divination, psychological healing, inner knowledge, clarity of purpose, and so much more. As I write this, I am in the process of lovingly birthing my fourth oracle card deck for you, the *African Goddess Rising* oracle cards. I love this deck and feel its full power, although, at this stage, it is printed art by talented Goddess Destiney Powell attached to standard white index cards. These cards are potent because Destiney didn't just interpret the guidance I received from Spirit to bring our goddesses to life. She connected with her own guidance. The result is BOOM—ancestral love runs through the veins of this deck. It already has its own àṣẹ, life-force energy.

Oracles are a sacred communication tool between us and the Divine. The first oracle deck I created was a set of runes I drew on tiny slips of paper for personal use. I am excited to see what you birth.

You will need:

- 28 blank 4 x 6 index cards
- Artistic tools of your choice

What to do:

Prepare your ritual space. Divination means connection to the Divine.

Part 1: Download Your Oracle Language

1. Choose four words that inspire you (e.g., love, freedom, travel, adventure)

2. Choose four words that scare you (e.g., scarcity, loneliness, fear, desperation)

3. Choose four words that remind you of a person that you love (e.g., fun, generous, sexy, wild)

4. Choose four words that remind you of a person that you despise (e.g., selfish, delusional, annoying, greedy)

5. Choose four words that describe your spiritual journey (e.g., evolving, rocky, exciting, beautiful)

6. Choose four words that describe your favorite location (e.g., glamorous, natural, muddy, peaceful)

7. Choose four words that describe how you feel today (e.g., hopeful, doubtful, giddy, relieved)

You now have 28 electric words that are connected to your àṣẹ, life-force energy.

Part 2: Create Your Oracle Design

Find or create images to match each word on each index card. What is the theme? You can use any kind of art that inspires you. Use your own photography or copies of personal pictures. Paint, draw, or color with crayons. You can print the pictures out or go old-school and get some magazines and cut them out.

Here are some additional ideas:

- Create your own sacred geometry with symbols and meanings.

- Paint the backs all one color for uniformity.

- At this point in your process, your Goddess Soulbook is rich with affirmations and declarations. Maybe you wish to use some of those.

- Cards don't have to be rectangular. My deck of *Sacred Bombshell Self-Love Journaling Cards*, for example, are hexagon shaped, and I plan to do a round moon deck.

Part 3: Awaken Your Cards

Get to know your deck. Charge it on your goddess altar and light of the new moon. Sleep with it so it connects even more to your energy.

Simple spreads (layouts) for reading your oracle cards:

- Choose one card for immediate inspiration or guidance.

- Choose three cards to delve into a situation representing PROBLEM (Card 1)/ADVICE (Card 2)/OUTCOME (Card 3). Note that the OUTCOME card only means a probable path if you follow the ADVICE card.

- Upside-down or reversed cards may represent either the opposite aspect of the card or an emphasized message. Decide in advance whether opposite aspects or reversed messages for upside-down cards works with your oracle deck. For example, if you pull a card meaning joy upside down, the card's opposite aspect is sadness. But the emphasized meaning is that you really need to focus on joy right now.

- Any spread that works with any other oracle or tarot deck will work with yours.

Woo-hoo! Record your process in your Goddess Soulbook.

QUEEN MOTHER NANNY

Goddess of Dreams
Maroons/Jamaica
Dream Traveling Ritual

"My dreams empower me."

QUEEN MOTHER NANNY'S MESSAGE

Yes, my daughter! Break free. Your dreams hold the power and keys to your liberation. In fact, you are freedom herself. Rise up.

QUEEN MOTHER NANNY'S STORY

Great Queen Mother Nanny, keeper of mysteries,
We see you. We say your name.

Would you like to bear witness to a healer who freed over 800 enslaved people? Queen Mother Nanny of the Maroons was a renowned spiritual leader, obeah woman, military strategist, and revolutionary in Jamaica. Mother Nanny was a badass from the jump. This Ashanti queen was born in Ghana. Although she was brought to Jamaica in chains to the sugar plantations, oral tradition has it that she never worked a day as a slave. She and her five brothers escaped to form communities and lead rebellions.

The British were terrified of Mother Nanny. By 1720, she had her own settlement of liberated people called Nanny Town. They raised animals and grew crops. They raided plantations for additional food and weapons as the community grew. They also burned those plantations to the ground and freed the folks enslaved there.

The Jamaican Maroons established free communities in the partially hidden, mountainous interior. The First Maroon War started in about 1728 and went to 1740. Along eastern Jamaica, the British reportedly were getting their behinds beat by the Windward Maroons, Queen Nanny's community.

Maroons are African people throughout the Caribbean and the Americas who were able to escape slavery and survive. In some countries, they mixed with the native peoples. In other countries, they hid and formed new communities in what we call "the bush."

The African dream root plant helped the Jamaican Maroons to victory. This native South African flower found its way to the Americas the same way the Maroons did, through the Middle Passage. The wild growing dream root, or cocoon vine, provided cover for the Maroons, as they camouflaged in it after escaping.

Nanny's reign lasted about 50 years. Within that time, she freed about 800 people. Jamaican oral history attributes the victory in large part to Queen Mother Nanny's supernatural powers. Legend says that she was able to redirect bullets aimed her way. This is called redirection magic.

As propaganda to divide and conquer, the British spread a story that Nanny had been killed by a loyal slave. But oral literature has it that she got to live out the fruits of her labor.[8] She looks proudly on from the Jamaican $500 bill, which is called a "Nanny."

Let's Talk Dreams

Music and poetry are the conscious voices of our dreams. "We tend to the whispers/Under the night skies/Allowing our voices to be instruments/As divinity speaks into the hearts of our sisters." Those are the dreamed words of our Goddess Temple Circle sister Queen Keisha Diamond, an artist who paints pictures with words and inspires through her music. Born in Jamaica and living in England, she is inspired by messages in her dreams to create. She says, "My Jamaican culture is all about vibrancy and full expression." Queen Keisha explains, "Queen Nanny of the Maroons used music and songs from Africa to instill confidence and pride, inspiring our people to maintain the spirit of freedom, our natural inheritance."

Your dreams are not random. Dreams are powerful. There is dream symbolism that is common to most people, but when you start to study your dreams, you learn your own dream language. If you do this with family members, you find that every family has its own dream symbolism. In most African cultures, we believe that we are our reincarnated ancestors. So we have been dreaming these dreams for a long time.

Here's how to begin to tap into your sacred dream power: start to write down your dreams when you wake up. We all have access to dream guidance. Some may just be more in tune. If you have to make a decision, ask for guidance to dream on it before bed. If you are deciding between Door A or Door B, say Door A is represented by the color red and Door B is represented by the color green. When you wake up, write down your dream and the colors you saw right away. The answer will come to you.

For those of you who want to know the names of your guides, invite them to introduce themselves in your dreams. Do this if that matters to you. It doesn't have to. Some people like me feel, *I'm good, I'm guided, I trust in that and know the names of many of my ancestral guides who are protecting me*. And that for me is enough. But there's nothing wrong with wanting to know the names of other guides you may have.

You can use various crystals, totems, things that mean something to you, to help you connect with your energy. I have a piece of wood from my mom's ancestral home in Guyana that Cousin Arlington gave me. We cannot count how many generations of us lived in that home. That wood is charged with generations of me. It is like a cell phone connector to my ancestors.

In Guyanese culture, instead of saying, "I dreamed about Aunt Silvy last night," we would say, "Aunt Silvy dreamed me." Aunt Silvy was one of my family matriarchs and she is legendary. She is still looking out for all of us.

A few years ago, after my uncle Steve died, he dreamed me. He was in an agitated state. He told me he needed me to get in the car and drive to his home in Brooklyn ASAP. Uncle Steve was one of our great patriarchs. In the dream I reminded him that I don't drive. He was frustrated and told me to just be sure to look over the paperwork. I asked, "What paperwork?" and then I woke up. I told my mom to find out what was going on. It turned out that at that moment, our family was selling his home. We didn't know anything about it. It was perfectly fine, but I guess he wanted to make sure.

You have your dreams of how you want your life to be, and your dreams that are gifted to you every night. It's no coincidence that we use the same word for both.

Pay attention to your dreams.

HOW TO HONOR QUEEN MOTHER NANNY

When you honor Queen Mother Nanny, you honor the part of you that dares to harness the power of your dreams. You may choose to honor this energy inside yourself or invoke her energy according to your own tradition.

To honor the goddess in you: What do you dream for yourself? Daring to manifest your dreams is a part of personal liberation. Enjoy your freedom to honor Nanny. Find your own liberation codes. Life is too short to live within the confines designated for you by someone else. Rise up. The Creator's magic is on your side. Trust in your power to set yourself free and turn your dreams to reality.

Symbols: The abeng, the Akan side-blown horn, is used to call Maroon ancestors. Nanny and the Maroons are also associated with African dream root, the Kindah Tree, and camouflage.

Colors: Her colors are black, gold, and green.

Auspicious times: In Jamaica, Nanny is celebrated on the third Monday of October on National Heroes' Day. January 6 is also Maroon Day.

Music: "Queen of the Mountain" by Burning Spear and "Grandy Nanny" by Group of Maroons of Scott's Hall

Suggested offerings: Rum libations are a must. Boiled, unsalted pork is offered to ancestors and eaten by Maroon people to bring luck for a year. Ackee and saltfish and callaloo and bammy are meals Nanny would enjoy.

Alternate names: Nanni, Granny Nanny, Grandy Nanny, Queen Nanny, the Mother of Us All

Traditional Dreams Ritual: African Dream Root

African dream root, used as a sacred plant by the Xhosa, inspires out-of-body experiences. Also known as Ubulawu, Undela Ziimhlophe, or *Silene undulata*, this plant creates channels for astral projection, lucid dreaming that reveals prophecies, and quantum jumping. These are all forms of reality shifting.

Astral projection is traveling during a trancelike state without your body. Quantum jumping is taking your body briefly with you to experience another realm. In lucid dreams, you are aware that you are dreaming and can choose how to proceed.

The unassuming white flower sleeps during the day, only opening under the stars at night. The perfume it emotes is an intoxicating part of its magic. Xhosa diviners may chew or drink the roots for access to sacred knowledge. They also use this plant as a part of their initiation process.

This is spirit medicine. Xhosa dream root ceremonies and rituals generally take place under the full moon. First, focus on the questions you want answered before you begin dream traveling. Then ritual participants drink the alchemically created preparation on an empty stomach, which reportedly feels like going under water, until they throw up. The purification process includes cleansing the body with the foam part of the potion. The vividness of the dream root experience depends on the trip you are meant to have.

The dream root also could be made into a potion that was used to communicate with ancestral spirits. How incredible is it that the Maroons were able to hide in this plant? Mama Africa was looking out for her children in the diaspora.

Your Dreams Ritual: Dream Traveling

Ritual intention: To ask a question and dream on the answer with lucid dreaming.

You will need:

- A question you need answered
- Goddess Soulbook or journal

What to do:

Prepare your ritual space. Please do not light candles and go to sleep.

Thank your bed and pillow in advance. You may wish to drink a relaxing tea like chamomile or peppermint tea before bed. My sister Goddess Damali recommends mugwort, which is readily available, for dream traveling. But you can also just use your mind.

What is your question you want answered? Think about it before bed, and as you fall asleep, tell yourself, "The next time I am dreaming, I want to know that I am dreaming."

Sleep and dream, gorgeous! While you are sleeping, in your dream, practice asking, "Am I dreaming?" Also be prepared to test to see if you are in a dream or in reality. Look at the floor to see if it looks normal. You can also check your reflection in mirrors or water sources in the dream to see if you look normal. If you see anyone in the dream, ask them what they think of your issue.

When you wake up, immediately start freewriting in your journal. Write for 20 minutes or three pages, whichever comes first. As you freewrite, focus on the dream. Other unrelated things, like remember to call XYZ or grocery lists, may pop up. Just write them in the freewriting process to get them out of your head, and keep going back to the dream.

Interpret your writings. Pay attention to colors, sounds, and symbols. People may represent themselves or others. It should feel as if you are going back into the dream as you delve into the notes. Sometimes, if there are other people involved in your question, they may contact you with an answer.

Record your experience in your Goddess Soulbook.

QUEEN NEFERTITI

Goddess of Alchemy
Egypt
Choose Your Goddess Name Ritual

"Everything I touch turns to gold."

QUEEN NEFERTITI'S MESSAGE

Ahlan wa sahlan, daughter. You have turned everything thrown your way into gold. Your beauty is eternal, and so is your life force. Live life fully. Your joy and pleasure expand consciousness.

QUEEN NEFERTITI'S STORY

Great Queen Nefertiti, keeper of mysteries,
We see you. We say your name.
Great of praises! "The beautiful one has arrived." This is the meaning of her name. Nefertiti was a legendary queen, who may have ruled as pharaoh after her husband's death. Her iconic bust has people centuries later proclaiming her beauty. She was a keeper of power who was considered a creator and deified as a sensual goddess.

In ancient Egypt, royalty were regarded as gods and goddesses. Nefertiti led a spiritual revolution by convincing her husband, Pharaoh Amenhotep IV, to worship Aten, the sun god. Together they changed Egypt to the monotheistic religion of Atenism. They even changed their names to Neferneferuaten and Akhenaten to honor Aten. Roofs were opened so Aten was worshipped in the sunlight instead of in closed, dark temples.[9] Whereas Ra, the old sun god, was the personification of the sun, Aten was the actual sun disk. *Aten* meant "the visible sun itself."

Nefertiti's holy temple choir most likely sang the Great Hymn to the Aten:

Your rays are in the midst of the sea.
Who makes seed grow in women,
Who creates people from sperm;
Who feeds the son in his mother's womb,
Who soothes him to still his tears.
Nurse in the womb,
Giver of breath,
To nourish all that he made.
When he comes from the womb to breathe,
On the day of his birth,
You open wide his mouth,
You supply his needs.

Like the sun, Queen Nefertiti represents divine power, sacred beauty, and the capacity for joy. As she lived during Egypt's wealthiest period, opulence and pleasure were her domain. On her famous bust, her right eye is filled with a quartz crystal painted black and covered with beeswax. Her left eye remains a mystery. Nefertiti and her husband promoted Egyptian art and were very much in love. They were illustrated kissing and riding in the same chariot. This was unusual, especially that she was always shown as equal to the king.

Nefertiti had six daughters, two who also became queens. During her reign, she and her daughters took on the role of the fertility, sexuality, and rebirth goddesses.[10] The energy of rebirth is connected to the sun.

Since 1924, Egypt has been waiting for the repatriation of Nefertiti's famous bust by Germany. It was plundered and removed from Egypt without their knowledge.

Let's Talk Alchemy

Alchemy is most known as the ancient magical practice of turning lead into gold. Magic was so much a part of Egyptian consciousness that heka was personified as a god. In fact, the word *alchemy* itself may come from *Kemet* or *Khemia*, the ancient name of Egypt, meaning "land of black earth."

Alchemy is bending universal energy, the same way that a rainbow is bending light. You may have no use for turning lead into gold, but we certainly want to turn crappy circumstances into happiness and ashes into beauty, right? We want to manifest the things that we desire. This is transmutation and we see it all the time. Water can be a solid as ice, a liquid, or a vapor as steam. You can transmute fear into love.

Spirituality and science say the same thing. Energy cannot be created or destroyed. We are ancient machinery. Sometimes the thoughts we have are not our own. We're just tapping into the zeitgeist, the universal current of thoughts. If you can get quiet and listen to your own thoughts, who is the you that is the listener?

Alchemy is creating something out of nothing. Our folks have been doing that since the beginning of time. Look how much you have manifested already. Imagine for a moment that everything already exists. Then we just need to invite the things we want into our lives.

So how do you do it? See it first. You are a happy person. See it. What does that look like for you? You are a person who is loved. What does it look, taste, and smell like to be loved unconditionally? You have a wonderful, healthy, and vibrant body. It feels good to be in your skin. How does that look for you? You are a magnet for money and great opportunities. What does it feel like to be a money magnet?

This is why vision boards are an exciting tool. They help us to visualize, but some people are not visual people. So what does your vision sound like? What does it taste like? How does it feel in your body?

Write in your Goddess Soulbook: *I am an alchemist. Everything I touch turns to gold.*

This is your one wild and magical life, and it deserves your full attention. So let's start off with be, do, have. Who do you have to *be* to *do* and *have* what you desire?

I am so proud of you. Look how far you've come and how your vibration is rising. Oh, it feels so good to bask in your energy.

HOW TO HONOR QUEEN NEFERTITI

When you honor Queen Nefertiti, you honor your inner alchemist. You may choose to honor this energy inside yourself or invoke her energy according to your own tradition.

To honor the goddess in you: Bask in the sun and embrace your light-filled connection to honor Nefertiti. Close your eyes and feel the natural alchemist in you reignited. You have always defied odds. People expected one thing from you, and you became another. You are an alchemist. Believe in your own magic to transmute fear-based beliefs into love.

Symbols: The ankh, scarab beetle, quartz crystal, blue flat-topped cap crown, her bust, and the sun

Colors: Her colors are gold, blue, and violet.

Auspicious times: Celebrate Nefertiti during the annual Sun Festival in Abu Simbel, Egypt. The temple there was designed so that on February 22 and October 22, the sun illuminates the statues within the temple of Ra, the sun god, and Amun, king of the gods. The temple was dedicated to Queen Nefertari, who came after Nefertiti.

Music: "Nefertiti" by Miss Amutha Nature and "I Am Light" by India.Arie

Suggested offerings: Nefertiti most likely ate lentils, figs, dates, onions, fish, and eggs.

Alternate names: Neferneferuaten, Nofretete, Lady of All Women, Hereditary Princess

Traditional Alchemy Ritual: Baby Naming

Your name is a code. In almost every African nation, religion, and people, baby names are traditionally significant. We believe that a child's name is a link to who they were before they came here and who they will be. A seemingly simple custom like naming babies for the day of the week that they were born connects us to everyone else who shares the meaning of being born on that day. Our names can give those in the know insight about us.

The Dagara perform a hearing ritual to get to know a baby before birth. They have a conversation with the baby, who speaks through the voice of their pregnant parent. The baby shares her likes and dislikes. Her name is chosen based on this info and is given to her when she is four weeks old. The name has its own life-force energy. Children own their name until age five; then it owns them.[11]

As Somali-British poet Warsan Shire said, "Give your daughters difficult names. Names that command the full use of the tongue. My name makes you want to tell me the truth. My name does not allow me to trust anyone who cannot pronounce it right." This makes my soul sing!

One of the most beautiful baby naming ceremonies I have ever been a part of were the namings of my little cousins Tehuti and Ptah. They are two of the smartest, kindest, most handsome teens you ever want to meet now, but not that long ago, we ventured outside at dawn when each was an infant. At the most auspicious time, they were held in the air and their names were called in from the ancestors in morning dew. Their baby brother, born just the week before the time of this writing, is named Prince Hannibal. My cousin Goddess Adana gets it! Those names are alchemical codes.

Among the Xhosa of South Africa, the Sifudu blessing ritual purifies and protects new babies. The ceremony takes place three days after the baby is born. Family members gather to pray as leaves are burned from the Sifudu tree. The newborn baby is passed through the smoke several times and then under the leg of her mother. The purpose of the ritual is to make the child stronger and more courageous.[12]

Then on the 10th day, an Imbeleko ceremony to introduce the child to the ancestors takes place. A goat is sacrificed, and the mother eats the meat. The umbilical cord is removed, and the baby is named. They bury the umbilical cord in the soil on the family's property to protect the child from any evil spirits. Names include clan and family names. Clan names are the names of the first ancestors.[13]

Your Alchemy Ritual: Choose Your Goddess Name

Ritual intention: Your rebirth and your goddess name.

What is in a name? Everything. Our names tie us to our ancestors and descendants. They tell a story about us to the world and to ourselves. Your name is a spell that unlocks and frames your purpose. Imagine that every time someone speaks your name they are casting a spell to reinforce how powerful you are.

In cultures with rites of passage, you receive a new name after you are initiated. In some traditions, your priestess or godparent who initiates you will choose your new name. My mother was given a confirmation name. If I was initiating you at a retreat, for this ritual I might receive a transmission of your name. In other traditions, this is called your ritual name or your craft name. When I pledged the sorority Alpha Kappa Alpha, we were given line names by our big sisters.

Naming was also weaponized as a tool of ownership and control. Colonizers renamed us and our countries. Naming signifies possession. Name yourself to own yourself.

You will need:

- A candle
- Your goddess altar

What to do:

1. Prepare your ritual space. Sit at your goddess altar. Light a candle for divine light.

2. Meditate and consider the questions the Dagara ask a baby before birth: Who are you? Why have you come here at this time? What is your purpose?

3. You may choose to access guidance and choose to name yourself after one of the goddesses here in this book, or you can use divination or the traditional naming system of your choice.

4. As an alternate method, go outside before dawn and pick a name out of the dew.

5. This is your secret name. Whisper it to the Universe. You decide whether you want to share your goddess name. You may decide to make your goddess name your permanent public name. It is up to you.

Record your goddess name in your Goddess Soulbook with an image of yourself.

QUEEN YAA ASANTEWAA

Goddess of Quantum Leaps
Ashanti/Ghana
Burn-and-Release Visualization Ritual

"Divine timing is on my side."

QUEEN YAA ASANTEWAA'S MESSAGE

My daughter, my daughter, Agoo! A leap forward for one is a leap forward for all. You raise the frequency of the planet. You are starting to believe that we are truly one.

QUEEN YAA ASANTEWAA'S STORY

Great Queen Yaa Asantewaa, keeper of mysteries,
We see you. We say your name.
All hail, she who fights before canons.

Queen Yaa Asantewaa was a mother, farmer, and legendary warrior queen of the Ashanti empire. In 1900, she led the famous War of the Golden Stool, aka the Yaa Asantewaa War, against British colonizers. What's the Golden Stool? If you look up the Ashanti flag, you will see a Golden Stool at its center. The Golden Stool, the throne of the Ashanti people, is the sacred symbol of power. Legend has it that

Okomfo Anokye, the first Ashanti high priest (and nation's co-founder) called this throne down from the sky. It magically landed on the lap of their first king.

Each Golden Stool is the seat of the owner's kra, soul-force energy, so it must never touch the ground. It is placed on a special blanket and only belongs to the current regent. When not being used by royalty, this throne is braced against the wall for ancestral souls to rest on. During state events, the Golden Stool is carried to the king or queen on a pillow and sits upon a throne of its own.

So it was no small thing in 1900 when the British colonial governor exiled Ashanti king Asantehene Prempeh I and demanded to sit on his Golden Stool. This governor even mounted a secret expedition to locate it so that he could capture it. This dude had the nerve to gather the Ashanti chiefs to say, "I am the representative of the paramount power in this country; why have you relegated me to this ordinary chair?" Well, sis, they listened to him silently then left to prepare for war.

As the sister of the king, and then the grandmother of the appointed king, Queen Yaa Asantewaa became regent when the king was exiled. The purpose of the War of the Golden Stool is often trivialized, but it was not about wood and gold. It was about the soul of a nation and the respect of a people.

Yaa Asantewaa definitely saw it that way. The chiefs were not moving strategically enough for the queen. She gave them a verbal lashing, inspiring the men to take back their power by commanding, "If you, the chiefs of Asante (Ashanti), are going to behave like cowards and not fight, you should exchange your loincloths for my undergarments." She fired a gun to make her point.

The queen then brought it on home with, "If you, the men of Asante, will not go forward, then we will. We, the women, will. I shall call upon my fellow women. We will fight! We will fight till the last of us falls in the battlefields."[14]

Yaa Asantewaa was a queen, a badass, and is considered the spiritual mother of her nation and matrilineal culture.

Let's Talk Quantum Leaps

The dictionary defines *quantum leap* as an abrupt transition from one discrete energy state to another. That's the physics definition, but it works for you and me too. A quantum leap is a multiplier. It feels drastic and huge. But the big secret is that quantum leaps happen pacito pacito, little by little.

Soon you will conclude this part of your goddess initiation experience. You will have completed 42 transformational rituals. There is already an alchemical shift in your molecules. Some will say you have changed. Perhaps they are saying this already. But they will not see how you showed up for yourself to meet 42 goddesses in nine sacred temples. Quantum leap.

I told a civilian friend that I was having a growth spurt. She could not understand what that meant. (I call those who are not yet open to their magic "civilians.") After all, growth spurts are for kids, right? Wrong, we never stop growing and evolving. And there are experiences that can help us to have a quantum leap, exponential growth spurt. We all have growth spurts. Folks who are not introspective do too; they just don't notice. With growth spurts come growth pains.

So how do you actively create a quantum leap? You are doing it! Rituals, movement, meditation, and visualization are great places to start. Hypnotherapy was so transformational for me in dissolving limiting beliefs that I started studying it. Spiritual and scientific magic are healing and welcome.

Our Goddess Temple Circle sister Amanda Elise is a life coach and Reiki healer, passionate about helping heal generational trauma. When she experienced her own dark night of the soul, she turned to plant medicine to help her to make a quantum leap. She says that plant medicine helps her heal on a cellular level.

Goddess Amanda's deep shame over a gut-wrenching breakup had her wanting to move for fear of running into her ex. She was filled with anxiety. A co-worker told her about an upcoming ayahuasca ceremony. Ayahuasca is a psychoactive plant medicine from South America that some say opens the portal to the spirit world. If you ask the Indigenous healers how the ancients figured out the recipe to the brew, they simply say, "The plants told them so." These medicines are legal in many places across the United States, from Oakland to Washington, D.C.

The ceremony was magical. Goddess Amanda saw past lives, met with ancestors, and healed a situation she thought had no effect on her. She was able to see ancestral trauma that was passed down through her DNA. It was painful, filled with tears and vomit, but magical. She made a quantum leap.

In the Guyanese spiritual philosophy and the Spiritual Baptist tradition we believe that our spirits travel to other places while we are asleep and dreaming. There is more than one dimension. Linear time, as we have been taught it, is an illusion. Quantum leaping may sound crazy, as crazy as telephones and fax machines once did.

Reality shifting with conscious quantum leap meditation allows us to call on our own knowledge from other energy fields. Maybe in another field you are a singer, a surgeon, a better mother, or whatever gifts you are looking to acquire. Dare to level up to the quantum reality where you are in alignment with your goddess frequency.

HOW TO HONOR QUEEN YAA ASANTEWAA

When you honor Queen Yaa Asantewaa, you honor the courage to stand firmly in your choices and leap forward. You may choose to honor this energy inside yourself or invoke her energy according to your own tradition.

To honor the goddess in you: Whether you believe that quantum leaps are possible in you or not, you are correct. So do you think you can make a quantum leap in your personal evolution this day, week, month, or year? As a speck of the Universe, you are the Universe. Whatever you wish to be, go there first in your mind.

Symbols: The Golden Stool, brass, kente cloth, the Akrafokonmu (soul washer's emblem), and gold. Gold is considered to be an earthly representative of the sun for the Asante/Ashanti people.

Colors: Her colors are gold, black, and green.

Auspicious times: Traditionally, Queen Yaa Asantewaa's festival is the first week in August.

Music: The queen is celebrated in the Ghanaian folk song "Koo Koo Hin Koo." The lyrics translate as: "Yaa Asantewaa/The woman who fights before cannons/You have accomplished great things/You have done well."[15] Also, check out "Yaa Asantewaa" by Star Gal and "Nana Yaa Asantewaa" by Melz Owusu.

Suggested offerings: Cocoa, yams, cassava, and gold fit for a queen

Traditional Quantum Leap Ritual: Iboga Ceremony

You enter an iboga temple on the right side and leave on the left. The right side symbolizes the divine masculine world that we live in, representing the sun, life, and man. The left symbolizes death of the old, the moon, and woman. This is a trip into the sacred feminine.

Iboga ceremonies are used to expand the energy field. The psychedelic iboga is ancient plant medicine that has been used throughout the ages in West and Southern Africa. Traditionally, the spirit of iboga is summoned through ritual practice to empower initiates to make a quantum leap through altered states. The Bwiti have accompanying rituals and dances when iboga is used as a rite of passage for adolescents, and it is also used to heal adults.

The bark and the root induce visions—and vomiting. Vomiting is viewed as a negative energy purge.

In ceremony, the heart-opening experience of iboga helps participants go on an altered state journey beyond what can be seen with basic consciousness. The visions enabled by the iboga help strip away fears and break the illusions of this world.

Some healers use it to recreate the feeling of a life-altering near-death experience. As with ayahuasca in the jungles of South America and the Caribbean, initiates report feeling extreme clarity afterward.

You can find the same psycho-spiritual healing effects and altered states with extended meditation and spirit possession trances.

At my Spiritualista! Goddess Pray Love Retreat in the jungles of Belize, we had a cacao ceremony. I was inspired by my mother's stories of her grandmother pounding cacao. My sister pounded the cacao for us, and I led the ceremony in our beautiful Maskall Village treehouse. The cacao spirit entered with gentle power. The cacao helped us to open our hearts and deepen our connection with ourselves, each other, and the land. Cacao as sacred medicine is a much gentler voyage, as you don't hallucinate, but it was a divine one.

Your Quantum Leap Ritual: Burn-and-Release Visualization

Ritual intention: To release what you no longer need.

Our mantra for this sanctuary is "Divine timing is on my side." Let's clear energy you no longer need to make way for all of the new blessings coming your way.

You will need:

- Paper
- Writing utensil
- Lighter
- Fire-safe bowl or receptacle to burn paper

What to do:

Part 1: Get Clear

Prepare your ritual space. What do you wish to release? Write it down. Be detailed. Begin with the phrase, "I am saying good-bye to . . ." and then describe the situation. You may wish to write on the bottom, "Divine timing is on my side."

Part 2: Do a Quantum Leap Visualization

Close your eyes and get centered. See the situation you wrote about. Imagine a parallel twin world where this issue no longer exists for you. All is well and you are happy in this world. Your loved ones are safe. There are no negative effects or ramifications from releasing the situation. See yourself in your mind's eye leap from this world into that one. Walk around and feel how good life is. Everyone there is happy to see you. The feeling is one of overwhelming love.

Open your eyes and say out loud, "Divine timing is on my side. This or something better for the good of all involved."

Part 3: Release It

Safely burn the piece of paper. Divine timing is on your side. Release it. You don't need it anymore.

Record your process in your Goddess Soulbook.

Congrats! You have completed the Temple of Queens.

Temple of Queens Insight Mantras

- *I am knowing.*
- *I am connected to the Divine.*
- *My dreams empower me.*
- *Everything I touch turns to gold.*
- *Divine timing is on my side.*

Temple of Queens Journal Questions

- How do you plan to tune in to your intuition more?
- What is your favorite form of divination?
- How can you align with your dreams for greater insight?
- Where in your life do you need to transmute fear into love?
- Describe the quantum leaps you have already taken.

Temple of Queens Embodiment

- Add something to your altar that represents your insight goddess power.

Temple of Queens Integration

- Add the Temple of Queens goddesses and your experience with these rituals to your Goddess Soulbook.

9

THE TEMPLE OF HIGH PRIESTESSES: YOUR ECSTASY ENERGY CHANNEL

Umbilini

BLESSING OF THE HIGH PRIESTESSES

Be, daughter, be.

Beings of Land

Spirits of the Air

Creatures of Fire

Beasts of Water

Souls of Nature

Be, daughter, be.

Great awakening, O.G., you Original Goddess!

You are entering the Temple of High Priestesses in the ecstasy energy channel. The five goddesses, here just for you, are here to guide you in accessing secret knowledge, miracles, and awakening. Yemaya, iNkosazana, Ayizan, a-Bol-Nimba, and Iset have been the keepers of this guidance from time immemorial. You now stand in an elevated circle of goddesses who are here to hold space for you in ascension, awakening, and transcendence.

Sit in the center and take in their wisdom. They each have gifts for you. Should you choose to accept their gifts, you will integrate your high priestess goddess power. To complete this temple, complete their five rituals.

After you ascend from the Temple of High Priestesses, you will have completed this blessed phase of your initiation adventure. Instructions will find you for the next one.

ABOUT THE TEMPLE OF THE HIGH PRIESTESSES

You are created in the image and likeness of God/dess.

You are God.

The Temple of High Priestesses is about communion with higher consciousness. These wise-woman goddesses hold the mysteries of the Universe. This is the final temple in this journey. This is the energy channel of spiritual enlightenment, transcendence, and nirvana.

You have been on quite the adventure: walking rocky paths, hiking through secrets, swimming in hidden dimensions, sprinting up energy fields, and dancing across consciousness. This is how we make shift happen. Flying with fear. Life is not a spectator sport. Divine guidance requires interaction from us. You rearrange the molecules with your interaction. You shift the tectonic plates with your choices.

If you have fulfilled your goddess rituals and opened, healed, and balanced all previous energy channels, all energies are flowing together. Some of you may feel like you are levitating. Others may feel like you need to start over. It is all good.

WHAT IS YOUR ECSTASY ENERGY CHANNEL?

Ready to have an ecstatic moment with the Universe? We are all craving ecstasy. Not the drug. The feeling. This energy channel is located at the crown of your head and vibrates with the colors violet, white, and iridescent gold.

Mini ritual: Put down this book for a second. Stand up with your arms in the air, smile as big as you can to the goddess within, and twirl 18 times counterclockwise, then twirl 18 times clockwise. Imagine that there is a huge wheel above you and your job is to spin it toward happiness. Turn your body as you spin the wheel. With each twirl, know that you are cranking up the healing energy of the Universe. Come back after you're finished.

Are you a bit giddy? Laughing, even? Feel that euphoria, that elation, that excitement, that high? The dictionary defines *ecstasy* as "an emotional or religious frenzy or trancelike state, originally one involving an experience of mystic self-transcendence."

You just raised your frequency and turned up your vibration. And if you didn't do the ritual, come on! You know better by now. This is not a game for spectators. Do it! (If you don't have the physical ability to do this, visualize it.)

We get temporary glimpses of that bliss feeling, laughing, meditating, orgasming, dancing, praying. We chase the feeling of fulfillment and exuberance if we don't get it. It is the feeling that all is right, the knowingness that we are right in the world. This is oneness with the Divine, the feeling that you are the Divine. Because you are. Little pieces of the mountain have every element of the mountain.

Write in your Goddess Soulbook: *It feels good to feel good.*

Ecstasy heals and elevates us when we allow it. Unfortunately, many of us are living with repressed ecstasy. Repressing your natural ecstasy can lead to acting out. If we don't feel this glee naturally, we pursue it by artificial, potentially harmful means, like drugs, alcohol, co-dependent relationships, gambling, and other compulsive false highs. In a society where there is no place for the glee or bliss that is natural, we are yearning for it, hungry and starved for it.

Ecstasy is the feeling of inspiration, being in spirit. You feel oneness, boundless and eternal, like you are making love with the Universe. Because you are.

Write in your Goddess Soulbook: *My life is a love letter to the Universe.*

So why would we suppress this feeling? Society is designed so that we need permission to let loose and lose control. The bliss, pleasure, glee of ecstasy feels forbidden. It's the "messy" and "disorderly" spirals and coils of the divine feminine instead of the linear thoughts that are accepted. People are too afraid to explore ecstasy in the way they truly wish.

There is also another reason for the repression. You are protecting your identity.

Are you willing to release your identity? I asked you this at the beginning of this expedition.

The ecstasy energy channel is about our connection to the Divine. This requires seeing past the matrix, seeing through the simulation. What does that mean? Seeing through the illusion of the stuff that doesn't matter.

What we are talking about here is umbilini access to higher consciousness. In ancient South African spiritual philosophy, umbilini is primal-source energy that lives inside of us. You may have noticed that there have been many serpents accompanying the goddesses here. Umbilini energy sits at the base of your spine, coiled up like a snake. Snake dreams are a spiritual beacon in Zulu culture. (If you are familiar with kundalini energy, yes, the words and definitions are similar. Isn't that incredible? I believe that it's because the ancients were pulling from the same stream of consciousness to acquire this wisdom.)

Umbilini entered when we were in the womb. Its job is to give us our consciousness. Umbilini energy is then blocked and repressed by the resistance to our true selves that we build up during life. When we remove the resistance and allow our umbilini to flow, it feels like an awakening. You have been on a quest to release that resistance through goddess rising rituals in every temple of consciousness. Although we may describe umbilini energy as primal-source energy, the authentic you is umbilini energy. Activating our intuition helps to awaken our umbilini energy and vice versa.

This energy connects the lower temples or energy channels that address our basic human needs and the upper temples or energy channels that address our spiritual needs. In other words, it connects your lower and higher selves/energies. We get glimpses of it throughout life, but that's different from turning it on consciously.

Write in your Goddess Soulbook: *I am one with Spirit.*

Ancient Egyptians were aware of umbilini energy too. If you look at the pharaohs on statues and temple walls, you often see a snake extended at the brow. This Uraeus, upright asp, represented the serpent goddess Wadjet and umbilini power. In Haitian and Louisiana Voodoo, Damballah the snake god holds the world together. We met his associates in the Benin Temple of Pythons. Folks being possessed by lwas is umbilini energy. Through spirit possession, "horses" become one with the Divine. People catching the spirit and speaking in tongues in church is umbilini energy. This requires releasing resistance to the Divine and your own divinity.

Umbilini awakening is described as subtle energy up your spine. It feels like you're losing control because we are not used to living resistance free. Great responsibilities come with awakening this energy, as you will come face to face with your ego. You are not used to suddenly seeing through the matrix and feeling your complete oneness with the Divine. This can be immensely pleasurable or terrifying and jarring.

So how do you awaken your doorway to this potent energy? Sunlight recharges and heals. Begin with breathing mantras, dancing, and drumming. Heal this energy center with meditation; be still and know.

Ask your Self how you can be more selfless. This is the seat of your personal values and ethics.

Write in your Goddess Soulbook: *I am grateful for my life.*

HOW TO KNOW IF YOUR ECSTASY ENERGY CHANNEL IS BLOCKED

Are you unable to surrender to the power of Spirit? Do you feel overwhelmed by injustice and abandoned by God/dess? Do you believe that life is every person for themselves? Are you attached to material things? Are your anxiety and worry on overdrive? Do you have trouble seeing life's beauty? Do you lack spiritual involvement?

Our relationship with the Most High is not measured by how vocal or visible our praise is to others. Growing up, we sometimes had private family prayer services in my house. As a kid, much of it seemed annoying. But there were many occasions when the bishop, my dad, would teach us something that I felt in my bones.

I remember him giving us a homily about the scripture of praying in the closet. And then oddly enough on a random visit to his church in Brooklyn years later, he gave the same sermon, so I know it was a key for me. The scripture he taught said, "Go into your closet, shut the door, and pray in secret, and the Divine will reward you openly." That resonated with me so much.

When this center is blocked, ego is usually at the source. If this channel is closed, you may have challenges with belief, faith, hope, and your connection to the Divine. If this channel is too open, you may disassociate from your body, have a solitary life, experience challenges with sound and light, and find everyday human life mundane.

It's time to bring it all together.

Have no fear . . .

Yemaya, iNkosazana, Ayizan, a-Bol-Nimba, and Iset (Isis) will be your guides on this part of your trip. They want you to know that you are regal solely by your birth. You are connected to them and their wisdom through your ecstasy energy channel. They are here to help you surrender, tune in, and trust.

YEMAYA

Goddess of Awakening
Yoruba/Nigeria
Coconut Head Wash Ritual

"I am receiving and radiating love."

YEMAYA'S MESSAGE

Ẹ n lẹ, daughter! We meet again. Let me take in who you have become. Yes! You and I have met many times through many lives. I know you. You know me well. Awaken now to yourself. Awaken to your true power.

YEMAYA'S STORY

Great Goddess Yemaya, keeper of mysteries,
We see you. We say your name.
Are those tears of joy? Or tears of sorrow? If you have to cry, let it out. Wail, scream, thump the wall, laugh it out, bawl. Yemaya swallows your tears. Her tears form the Niger River.

Whether you first meet her as Yemoja, Yemanja, Iemanjá, or Yemaya, the healing, loving energy of this Yoruba mother goddess never leaves you. Yemaya, as she was called by her enslaved children in Cuba, controls the ocean, the amniotic fluid that nurtures us before we know ourselves. She is the protector of women and the creative endeavors that we birth.

With the movement of the ocean waves, her body gave birth to the other orishas (deities). Yemaya was there at the beginning when God (Oladumare) asked her to assist with the formation of humans. She is primordial divine feminine energy. Like the ocean, Yemaya can be calm, warm, and soothing or angry, violent, and overcoming.

She was there when her enslaved children in the United States sang the spiritual as a code, while hoping for freedom warriors like Great Ancestress Harriet "Moses" Tubman:

Wade in the water, wade in the water, children
Wade in the water,
My God's gonna trouble the water
See that young girl dressed in blue?
My God's gonna trouble the water
Looks like my people, they're coming through . . .

Dogs could not track our scent into the water.

We dream of fish when someone is pregnant because Yemaya is the mother of the gods. Her original name translates to "yey omo eja," meaning "mother whose children are the fish." The regal queen of the ocean walks or swims where she wishes, as sometimes she chooses to be a mermaid.

In some stories, the orishas Yemaya and Oshun are sisters. In others, they are mother and daughter. Either way, you rarely find them in the same place at the same time. This nurturing goddess does not like drama! As Yemaya rules the ocean, she is also associated with the power of the moon.

In one story, Yemaya knew of Oshun's love of mirrors, jewels, and the beauty of her coily, curly hair. These things may have seemed superficial to others, but Yemaya knew her heart and loved her for who she was. When things were good, they were splendid. But when the wars invaded their realm, everything changed.

Oshun was forced to flee with the white dress on her back. Yemaya heard of her anguish but could not get to her. Oshun sold her jewels to eat and lost her pride. She washed her one white dress in the river until it turned yellow. From the agony of the situation, her beautiful hair fell out in clumps.

When mother Yemaya finally found her, Oshun was distraught. Her vibrancy was gone. She felt poor and ugly. Yemaya took her in her arms and hugged her tight. "I will return," Yemaya promised.

In 28 minutes Yemaya floated back in with jewels, which she showered on Oshun. "You are a queen always," she said. She gave Oshun a peacock. "This beautiful creature is now yours, and will forever reflect your beauty, inside and out," Yemaya said. And she pulled back her gele crown, revealing that she had cut off half her big, curly afro. The other half, she had made into a beautiful wig. "And here is your hair, my daughter, until yours grows back. You will never ever lose what makes you you." Since then, daughters of Oshun have always defended Yemaya, and vice versa.

Yemaya's human daughters are also emotionally expressive and magnetic. This certainly describes the late Great Ancestress Celia Cruz, known as the Queen of Salsa. She left her country, Cuba, after the Cuban Revolution of the 1950s, but she never lost her strong Afro-Cuban pride.

During Goddess Celia's life there were "is she/isn't she" questions surrounding her connection to Santeria. Even though she sang songs about Yoruba orishas like Obatala and Babalú-Ayé, Celia grew up in a time where African religious practices were illegal. And when they were legal they were highly stigmatized. Word on the street was that she shouted, "Azucar!" on stage in tribute to her ancestors enslaved in the sugar fields of Cuba. When asked about it, she shrugged it off. She was already banned from her home country; we can only imagine her fear of losing her livelihood in another.

After she transitioned from this life, Celia Cruz's early recordings of sacred Afro-Cuban Lucumi chants were finally publicized. This project, "Toques de Santo," was never advertised when it was originally recorded. Slavery was abolished in Cuba in 1886 and Celia was born in 1925, so young Celia and her fellow liturgical musicians were only about the second generation from slavery. These studio mixes of ceremonial santero recordings from the 1940s include titles like "Yemaya," "Ochun," "Changó," "Obatala," "Eleggua," "Babalú Ayé," and more. According to music historian Rosa Marquetti Torres, "This was the first time ever that Afro-Cuban liturgical music was recorded." The recording studio had to be sanctified before the musicians could perform this playlist of salutes to the orishas.

In the song "Yemaya," Celia refers to the goddess as her mother and queen. Celia told her biographer, Ana Cristina Reymundo, "That music soon became much more than a religion—it became a beautiful way to express my African roots."[1]

I have felt Yemaya's loving embrace in the waters of Cuba, Barbados, the Cayman Islands, Dominican Republic, the Bahamas, and Coney Island in New York. And each time she had something new to offer.

Omio Yemaya!

Let's Talk Awakening

You may have heard many things about a spiritual awakening. I have news for you. You are in it. The fact that you were called to this sacred initiation circle means you see beyond the matrix. This has been a journey of opening your energy channels. Keep it up.

The path of awakening is not a straight one or an easy one. You have chosen to lift the veil and have a real relationship with the Divine rather than be a passive observer.

People talk about transcendence. You didn't come here to transcend this world while you're living in it. You came here to dig your fingers in the soil, plant yourself in it, and evolve. This ascension is your divine purpose.

You are vibrating at higher and higher frequencies. You dared to answer this calling, and you are now fulfilling your purpose.

This is goddess rising!

HOW TO HONOR GODDESS YEMAYA

When you honor Goddess Yemaya, you honor being a compassionate mother to your own awakening. You may choose to honor this energy inside yourself or invoke her energy according to your own tradition.

To honor the goddess in you: You have been asleep. In your dream state, you were confused. You thought you were less than someone else. You believed that your worth could be quantified. You misheard that you had something to prove. Be still and know that you are a goddess, an earth child of the Divine. Awakening to this fact is why you came.

Symbols: Yemaya's number is seven. Cowries and parsley represent wealth. Watercress represents health.

Colors: Her colors are ocean blue and white.

Auspicious times: In Brazil, Festa de Iemanjá is celebrated on January 1. Devotees wear white and gather on the beaches starting New Year's Eve, to jump over seven waves and leave offerings for the goddess. You can do the same at your closest water source, even if it is your bathtub.

The annual 17-day Yemoja Festival in Ibadan, Nigeria, begins in October. The exact date is selected by the diviners. All-women ritual dances are performed during her fete. Her day is September 7 in Cuba, February 2 in Uruguay, and December 8 in other places. Her day of the week is Saturday.

Yemaya is associated with the moon. Most harvest festivals in West Africa, like Nigeria's New Yam Festival, are planned around the moon. The Yoruba year begins on the first moon of June. It is celebrated with the Ifá Festival. Ifá is the religion, spiritual system, and guiding light for the Yoruba people. Ifá Festivals are now held worldwide from Grenada to South Carolina.

Music: "Yemaya" by Celia Cruz and "Iemanjá" by Serena Assumpção

Suggested offerings: Bring Yemaya river stones, seashells, white flowers, perfume, anchors, indigo, seaweed, fish, and fishnets. She also loves watermelon and pork rinds.

Alternate names: La Sirène, Yemonja, Yemoja, Yemanja, Iemanjá, Iyemanja

Traditional Awakening Ritual: Lave Tet Head Washing

Need a clean slate? In Haitian Vodou, a Lave Tet is a spiritual cleansing ritual and consecration of the head that should only be performed by a priest/ess, houngan, or mambo. They will let you know if this treatment is in alignment for you. *Lave Tet* translates as "washing the head." In this holy service, the herbs are prepared specifically for the prescription of the bath. Although water and herbs are used, Spirit is doing the cleansing.

The purpose of the cleansing is to strengthen your head, your ori, the seat of your soul. The Lave Tet clears negative energies and replaces them with positive, desired energies. You also become closer in your relationship with the lwas (deities), as you are now cleansed to receive them. You may be told to have a period of celibacy beforehand and afterward.

The Lave Tet begins with prayer, and I cannot share most of the rite with you here. The participant's head is typically washed seven times. Ideally, the process lasts for three nights. Each batch of herbs may have a different preparation. Each round will also honor different lwa. Your Met Tet, the spirit who has been with you since birth, is also revealed in the process.

Afterward you are dressed in white with a white headwrap. You lie down on a white mat. A white chicken may be sacrificed. Your energy is open, so be aware of who you allow around you and have physical contact with. It's easier now for you to have spiritual connection in your dreams and possession.

Some lineages view this as an entry to a house and family. Others view it as general spiritual maintenance. It can be used as a proactive or reactive treatment. Lave Tet may be performed toward the end of a Kanzo, a devotee's rite of passage initiation and commitment.

Ibori and Lave Tet are two spiritual head-washing traditions. There are many others. Some you must be initiated for and others are open. Your ori is sacred. Be particular about who you allow to touch your head.

Your Awakening Ritual: Coconut Head Wash

Ritual intention: To clear blocked energy and cleanse your spirit.

This coconut head cleansing is a Caribbean spiritualist practice based on several West African, specifically Nigerian, philosophies. This is spiritual hygiene. You can go to a healer or priest/ess for a higher-level work, but this head wash is just something you can do for yourself to bless your ori, love up on your chi. Think of this cleansing as a personal baptism or head cooling. It helps you restore balance during the regular chaos of life.

In Yoruba culture, your ori (head) has to be nourished and fed. The same for your chi in Igbo culture. Think of this energy as your soul or guardian angel, the guardian of your destiny, who lives at your head. Think about the saying "Well, it's on your head then." This saying means that something is your responsibility. The spirit of your ori or chi is connected to the Most High. The Creator has your back. *Orí Hùú!*

Don't let everyone touch your head or your hair. They are doing an energy exchange with you. Wash and pray over anything—headwraps, extensions, wigs, hats—that covers your head. I stopped going to hair salons because they were touching my head while gossiping or arguing. I didn't want that energy on my head.

You will need:

- 3 coconuts or pure coconut water

What to do:

Part 1: Prepare Your Head Wash

Prepare your ritual space. Bless and prepare the coconut water. Speak love over it at every step.

If using a fresh coconut: Pierce 3 holes in the coconut. Pour out the water. A little goes a long way. You can mix it with distilled water or just use more coconuts if you want more coconut water.

If using prepackaged coconut water: Buy the coconut water as pure and organic as is available. Get as close as possible to 100 percent pure with no other ingredients. Please note, coconut water is different from coconut milk and coconut cream, although every part of the coconut is spiritually potent.

Part 2: Bless Your Inner Guardian

As you wash your head and face, pray words of gratitude, blessings, and appreciation. See all negative energies being cleansed from you as you exhale. Wash the nape of your neck, your crown, forehead, and face. Do this 3 days in a row.

Part 3: Aftercare

Pat your face dry and allow your head to air-dry as best you can. Afterward wrap your head in white and dress in white.

Feel free to drink some coconut water as well. If using fresh coconuts, you can eat the coconut meat too.

Coconut water is used to break spells, curses, and protect new babies. A simple mixture of coconut water and pure, raw, undiluted honey can be mixed together for a daily blessings hand and face wash. You can use the mix once daily in the morning to get into alignment with your highest and best good. Botanicas also sell coconut soap.

Record your process in your Goddess Soulbook.

INKOSAZANA

Goddess of Alignment
Zulu/South Africa
Umbilini Mantra Meditation Ritual

"I am always being guided in the right direction."

INKOSAZANA'S MESSAGE

Unjani, daughter? Your natural path is alignment. No one can take from you what they didn't give you. Let your passion inspire you to stand in your truth. We're rooting for you!

INKOSAZANA'S STORY

Great Goddess iNkosazana, keeper of mysteries,
We see you. We say your name.

"Iso liwela umfula ugcwele," iNkosazana's children declare. "The eye crosses the full river." This means that you are as limitless as your imagination. Your desires go beyond this realm. Nothing can stop you. The eye has perceived it already.

This is the perfect declaration as iNkosazana, the sky goddess, scares many with her blunt and direct commands. When the Universe whispers a message, we only see a step, not the whole staircase. The idea that your desires can align with divine power may be scary if you don't feel ready.

iNkosazana is the healer of healers and the teacher of teachers. When she appears on the mist clouds, approach her with song and prayer. Although she dwells in foamy waters, she is known as the Heavenly Princess. As above, so below is sacred alignment. As the bringer of soft-soaking rain, she can manifest as raindrops, a mermaid, a rainbow, or a snake. To meet this goddess you must either be called to the craft of healing or have a pure heart.

If you find yourself being called to heal, you may find yourself on a tumultuous underwater voyage with iNkosazana. That python you see may be more than just a snake. Don't worry—she will not hurt or drop you. She will merely coil around your body while she is in serpent form and dive into the water to bestow you with its liquid knowledge.

Surrender. iNkosazana calls sangomas, divination healers, in their dreams.[2] When you awake in an altered state, soaked in your own sweat, you know things are just beginning. You were on a deep dive with iNkosazana. You are fertile and dripping with ancient knowledge. You have been given the sacred gifts of healing and divination. A leap forward for one is a leap forward for all. The ancestors are well pleased.

A person who dreams about snakes in Zulu culture is considered spiritually gifted. The snakes mean that your ancestors are trying to contact you. If the snake bites you, fear not. It just means that they have been trying to get your attention for a long time. It is time to transmute whatever has been holding you back. This is a time of transformation. You are protected. Pay attention.

iNkosazana makes the corn grow and also presides over the cabbage fields. If you need plants within her domain, approach with reverence, but do approach. She is about your healing and growth. Take the plant and leave white beads in gratitude. To ensure a good harvest, the Venda people pour libations of beer into Lake Fundudzi and young women enact the sacred Domba, or python dance. You may also offer silver coins. The messengers of the water, crabs, frogs, snakes, and related creatures are not to be eaten. Every spring, young women appeal to the goddess to help them find life partners. Only those who are loving in spirit may approach her sacred water bodies.

Several Zulu societies combine agricultural goddesses iNkosazana, Mbaba Mwana Waresa (Lady of the Rainbow), and Nomkhubulwane into one deity, although they are still honored separately.

Let's Talk Alignment

How do you want to feel?

Divine alignment is the spiritual principle of being in sync with the frequency of the sacred. Everything we desire is in that frequency.

We think often about what we want, but goddess energy speaks to us in feelings. Divine alignment is the feeling and frequency of fullness, not of perfection. You want to be filled with you-ness. This means something different for each of us. As Elder Nikki Giovanni once said, "Show me someone not full of herself and I'll show you a hungry person."

Get clear on two things:

- How do you feel now?

- How do you want to feel?

Why am I asking you how you want to feel? This may take a moment to consider, as you may not even know how you feel now. But how you want to feel will define what the sacred feels like to you.

You must know how you want to feel so you know what energetic frequency you want to align with. Do you want to feel blissful? Bold? Loved? Sexy? Safe? Carefree? More open? Turned on? Free? Juicy? Rich? Full? Gleeful? Unstoppable? Unfuckwithable?

How you want to feel is the energy and frequency you want to match. That feeling is what goddessness is for you. That is the energy of God/dess.

HOW TO HONOR GODDESS INKOSAZANA

When you honor Goddess iNkosazana, you honor your alignment with the Divine. You may choose to honor this energy inside yourself or invoke her energy according to your own tradition.

To honor the goddess in you: In agriculture as in life, alignment is important. The sun, soil, rain, and seeds must all be aligned for growth. Comfortable in the heavens or underwater, iNkosazana is responsible for growth. As such, she is a mediator and helps with decision-making. Our decisions and choices put us into or out of alignment. What decision or choice can you make today to align you with God/dess energy?

Alignment is pretty simple. If you feel good about yourself and your life, you are in alignment with the Divine. If you don't, you are out of alignment. However, you are never broken. There is nothing wrong with you. Point yourself back in the right direction by honoring the force of Spirit within you. Tune in to faith, trust, and belief. If that's too far off for you at the moment, begin with hope.

Symbols: Corn beer, crabs, frogs, snakes, the harvest, the thunder drum, soft-soaking rain, and white goats

Colors: iNkosazana's colors are the rainbow.

Auspicious times: You may not work the fields or rivers on Saturdays and Mondays. Those are her days.

iNkosazana's spring planting ceremony begins with a gated patch of land dedicated to her. It must be fenced off by the men. The women fast for the day, as this is their ceremony. Then the chief's mother, his wife, and elder women in the community plant a bit of grain from each household. All ascend the mountain, where a white goat is sacrificed and bile from its bladder is sprinkled in the river. No men are allowed for the final part of the ritual. Women dress in flowers and leaves from the Msenge cabbage tree, sacred to iNkosazana. They take a sacred bath together, naked in the river, leaving the cabbage leaves behind.[3] No woman may leave until she is cleansed by the spiritual bath. Those who weep are pitied by the goddess.

Music: "Nomkhubulwane" by Nduduzo Makhathini and "Mermaid" by Sade

Suggested offerings: Rainwater, cabbage, and especially corn. You can also honor her with a spiritual bath.

Alternate names: Nomkhubulwane, Nomkhubulwana, Mbaba Mwana Waresa

Traditional Alignment Ritual: Rocks, Stones, and Crystals

Stones, crystals, minerals, and related natural materials have always been a key part of our alignment with the Divine in African traditional spiritual and healing practices. If they don't seem ancestral to you, they are. Just note that this is the first period in history where mined crystals are readily available in large quantities.

For the Dagara people of Burkina Faso, sacred rocks and crystals are so important that they are a separate element all their own. Their five elements are earth, fire, water, nature, and mineral or stone. Like the bones that hold us together, they see stones as the bones of the earth. Stones are energy conduits, and they hold our history in every pebble. Bless and clear any natural item before use.

Quartz crystals had special spiritual significance for the Nubians, located in what we now call Sudan. Excavated crystals are found alongside gold because they were considered to have divine properties. Quartz crystals were worn around the neck and waist. Nubians prized jewelry not only for its beauty but for its magical and healing properties. They used the rare silvery-blue chalcedony to honor the moon god. Malachite was used in creating Ma'at amulets. They found the stone's properties to be protective and magical. Lapis lazuli was used on pendants praising supreme god Amun. Carnelian was paired with glazed crystal and silver for amulet necklaces.

This all came to the fore a few years ago with the "Gold and the Gods: Jewels of Ancient Nubia" exhibit at the Museum of Fine Arts in Boston.[4] Nubia was long ignored and dismissed by the history and archaeology worlds. The exhibit featured valuable jewelry, amulets, and spiritual talismans of ancient Nubia. The pieces not only revealed much about the religious significance but also showcased masterful glassmaking and other technologies that wouldn't be reinvented in Europe for another thousand years.

South African healer Credo Mutwa taught about sacred healing stones. The women of different groups like the !Kung of the Kalahari Desert vigorously polished sacred stones to charge them up. Women then danced around the stones clockwise and then counterclockwise. They did this until they "aroused the energies of the earth." The stones were then considered electrically charged and used on the sick people. Healers felt the energy from the stones rise up out of the earth and up their spines.

This energy is similar to umbilini, but the !Kung call it num. With the crystals, the medicine person was then able to heal through the power of touch. Baba Credo said that the healing power of the earth is directed through crystals. They also used the crystals to attempt to send spiritual messages. South Africa's wealth of natural crystals include topaz, tourmaline, titanite, aquamarine, and amethyst and precious stones such as diamonds, rubies, opals, emeralds, and sapphires.

In ancient Egypt, obelisks were embedded with quartz crystals. Tyets, known as the "knot of Isis," were made with red jasper. Red gemstones were believed to represent menstrual blood, fertility, or contraception.[5] Green stones, including green jasper, emeralds, and green beryl, were used to symbolize life in Egypt. Fifth Dynasty pharaoh Sahure ordered the earliest expedition to modern-day Somalia for malachite and electrum, a gold and silver alloy. Carnelian and blue Egyptian faience were used on pieces such as trinity amulets featuring Iset, Heru, and Nephthys.[6]

Steatite and amethysts were used on scarab necklace pendants back in 300 B.C. Sacred scarabs were most often made with faience, amethyst, green jasper, and carnelian. The most used crystals in ancient Egypt include garnet, lapis lazuli, microcline feldspar, jasper, and carnelian. Fluorspar, malachite, hematite, jade, obsidian, peridot, and agate were also used to a lesser degree. Libyan desert glass, also known as Libyan gold tektite, was formed from a meteorite impact and decorated the breast-plate of King Tut and has been a tool of healing.

Followers of the Yoruba god Shango collect his thunderstones, Edun Ara, in sacred Arugba Shango bowls and feed them with palm oil for his shrines and altars. Obsidian flakes were found in the moon god Almaqah Temple of Meqaber Ga'ewa in Ethiopia,[7] along with a sacred arrangement of stones, a libation altar, and limestone incense burners. Gemstones found in Nigeria include garnets, topazes, diamonds, sapphires, tourmalines, amethysts, aquamarines, and emeralds.

Natural materials such as coral, cowrie shells, bitter kola, and amber have great spiritual and healing significance for us. Don't ever let anyone tell you that stones and crystals are not part of African spirituality again!

Your Alignment Ritual: Umbilini Mantra Meditation

Ritual intention: To come into alignment with your divine consciousness and summon umbilini energy.

Meditation was a practice in many African cultures before colonialism. Using breath to focus the mind, find stillness, and surrender in the silence is a part of initiation rites throughout the continent. Zulu sangoma (healer) Baba Credo Mutwa learned what he called the African form of meditation to summon umbilini from his grandfather, who was born in the 1800s. He noted that the purpose is to access the divine feminine, which he calls the mother mind. Sangomas can summon this energy at will, at the beat of a drum, or through deep meditation.

For the Zulu, you can reach umbilini through fasting and pain, depriving yourself of food and drink, or through joy, happiness, and ecstasy. Follow the joy route by thinking beautiful thoughts, eating pure food that loves you back, and drinking pure water sparingly.

The fastest way to find alignment and harmony is to surrender, to release the attempt to control everything around us. Like those ancient drawings of an ankh being held to a pharaoh's lips or Ma'at's outstretched arms holding the ankhs, we want to regenerate our life force. We also want to shift our frequencies for our ascension, right here on Earth. Meditation, mindfulness, and surrender are the fastest ways to do this.

You will need:

- A quiet environment
- A timer
- Comfortable pillows or seating area

What to do:

Part 1: Prepare

Prepare your ritual space. You may want to sit at your altar and/or do this without music. Sit on pillows on the floor if possible. Support your back if needed.

You will be doing a mantra meditation based on the Zulu umbilini meditation. A mantra is a word, phrase, or syllable that you repeat during meditation. Mantras help us to connect the heart, spirit, and mind. "Sawubona" will be our mantra. Practice saying it now: Sawubona. Sa-wu-bo-na.

When you started this quest, I greeted you with, "Sawubona." That is the Zulu greeting meaning "We see you." It is plural because, as you know by now, we don't walk alone. I witness you and hold space for your humanity, and so do my ancestors. For this meditation, we will use "Sawubona" as a mantra and chant to honor holding space for ourselves, for those who came before, and for those to come. We see you.

Here are five tips for Zulu meditation in Baba Credo's own words:[8]

1. "Sit very, very still."

2. This is the "secret art of joining [your] mind to that of the great gods in the unseen world."

3. Start with the "art of breathing properly."

4. "Eliminate all thoughts from [your] mind and call upon the hidden powers of [your] soul."

5. "Breathe softly and gently like a whisper until you feel something like a hot, coiled snake ascending up your spine and bursting through the top of your head."

Part 2: Meditate

Your body is a temple, and your voice is the instrument for mantra meditation. The first time may feel a bit awkward as you learn the logistics. It will become much easier. You will most likely feel benefits after the first time. Set an alarm for 9 minutes. We begin with box breathing for calm and focus. Box breathing is inhaling for four counts, holding for four counts, and exhaling for four counts.

Close your eyes. Begin with a cycle of box breathing to get centered:

- Inhale for four counts.

- Hold your breath for four counts.

- Exhale for four counts.

Then chant each of the four syllables of our mantra, Sa-wu-bo-na, holding each syllable for four counts. Do the 4/4/4 box breath after each full word.

Feel each syllable nourishing every area of your body. Observe your breath and any thoughts. Consider what *Sawubona* means. As you chant, feel the energy enter at your tailbone and spin up your body and exit from the crown of your head.

Here are the 8 steps of one cycle of mantra meditation:

1. Inhale for four counts.

2. Hold your breath for four counts.

3. Exhale for four counts.

4. Chant: "SA" for four counts.

5. Chant: "WU" for four counts.

6. Chant: "BO" for four counts.

7. Chant: "NA" for four counts.

8. Repeat from the beginning.

Repeat the cycle for 9 minutes at first. Work your way up to 18 minutes. Extend the time as your practice deepens.

Record your process in your Goddess Soulbook.

AYIZAN

Goddess of Miracles
Haiti
Manifesting Miracles Rice Ritual

"My life is full of miracles."

AYIZAN'S MESSAGE

Sak pase, daughter! Miracles abound. Bountiful gifts are yours. You are a miracle, so if you haven't witnessed your miracle yet today, ask for it and allow it in.

AYIZAN'S STORY

Great Goddess Ayizan, keeper of mysteries,
We see you. We say your name.

The royal palms are waving. The protector, Gran Mambo Ayizan Velekete, must be walking. Great queen of the marketplace.

Gran Mambo Ayizan is the first priestess of Vodun, both in Haiti and Louisiana. Vodun is based on the natural elements and has no beginning and no end. Vodun

343

traveled from Benin and Togo with Ayizan's kidnapped children, bringing miracles into dark spaces. You have been taught to fear that which empowers you.

This wise healer of the earth was an ancestor before becoming a lwa (deity), God-force manifestation. Her energy brings order and peace, clear channels for abundant surprises. Her magical presence is so strong that when she enters, an immediate cleansing and purification takes place.

What? You didn't know about the magic of the mambo? In 1791, Mambo Cécile Fatiman sacrificed a black pig at Bois Caïman, igniting the Haitian Revolution. Mambo, a Vodou priestess, is a term of respect. Mambos are community and spiritual leaders who can speak to the spirit world. Mambos or manbos are channels for miracles.

If it happens with commerce in the marketplace, Ayizan knows all about it. She wants you to succeed and cares deeply for the weak and struggling. Her husband, Loko, the first houngan (priest), is guardian of the sanctuaries and magic. He knows all secrets. Together they make a formidable pair.

Gran Mambo Ayizan's ancient energy is prosperous and protective. The mother of initiation into the sacred, you will only meet her if you are called. The Fa (Ifá) must be consulted. The Kanzo initiation venerates her. It used to be that she would never mount (possess) anyone during ritual. Times are changing, though. The lwa evolve as we need them to. They are not prayed to. They are served.

Ayizan makes way for miracles. Our Goddess Temple Circle sister Guerda Victor is known as the Money Mystic. Growing up in Haiti, she lived next door to a mambo. Guerda was intrigued, but her religious family warned her that their neighbor was an evil witch. The priestess had a daughter Guerda's age, but she wasn't allowed to play with her. Guerda tried to peek into their house, but her family said she'd go blind if the woman caught her.

Guerda grew up hearing about people being cursed, hexed, or killed by Vodou. She couldn't even lend or borrow books or pens in school because her classmates might use her stuff to curse her. Her soul could be taken away, and she could be turned into a zombie to do the bidding of evil spirits. She was terrified even though her maternal grandfather and other members of his generation were Vodou practitioners.

Years later, she started studying metaphysics and saw glitches in her family's stories. Guerda no longer wanted to be afraid, so she did the forbidden thing. She went back home to Haiti to attend Fèt Gede (Feast of the Ancestors), one of the most important Vodou celebrations. She also attended ceremonies with the priest as her teacher and the great spiritual waterfall called Saut d'Eau.

Guerda clearly remembered being at Sodo (Creole for "Saut d'Eau") with her mom as a child. Saut d'Eau is a place of miracles for Vodou practitioners. Thousands pilgrimage there every year to bathe in the waterfall and ask for miracles. Her soul sang and she was expanded by the experience. Her mother insists that they never went. Guerda realized that despite what she had been taught growing up, her spirit had been there before.

All things are possible. Let's meet under the baobab tree to talk about the times Gran Mambo Ayizan has made a way out of no way. She governs all outdoor spaces and keeps watch over gateways, doorways, and windows. Ayizan's vévé, sacred geometry based on her initials, helps her find her children's exact location. Her magical essence extends into the fields with her intimate knowledge of healing roots and herbs. She knows what you need for your healing.

Her cleansing energy leaves us open to receive blessings. Miracles abound.

Ayizan eh, Ayizan eh
Ayizan eh, Ayizan eh
Ayizan, I'm going to Guinea to see if I can free myself
Ayizan, we are all tangled.[9]
Ayibobo!

Let's Talk Miracles

When you choose to see them, miracles are all around us. When you have blinders on to the mysteries, signs, and phenomena that move matter, your world is flat. Choose to exist in the sphere of miracles.

When you expect miracles, you can see the hands of the spirits around us, the heart of God/dess just beneath the surface and behind the scenes. Your life is being rearranged in your favor. It is a minor miracle that with over seven billion people on the planet, you and I are here in dialogue. Our connection may not have been possible at any other time in history.

Miracles abound. My ancestors came to the Americas chained to the hull of a ship, with rice and okra seeds braided into their cornrows. And now their daughter is here in a global healing circle with you. Not because of any American dream but because they believed that miracles would save their grandchildren's grandchildren from their nightmares.

I called you here to this sacred pilgrimage. Or perhaps they called you here. Or did you call me here? I believe in possibilities. Decide now that you will live in the realm of possibilities.

Write in your Goddess Soulbook: *I live in the realm of possibilities.*

You are alive, so you have felt pain. That pain is not you. Your heart has been broken and you have been betrayed. Your past is not your present. You may have suffered unspeakable horrors. But you are not those horrors. You are magic. You are a magical fleck of stardust. You are not the worst of what has happened to you. You are the best reflection of the Creator's magic.

You are a miracle. Of course you would attract other miracles to you. Miracles are a realistic part of your life when you start to believe they are. Pay attention to the coincidences. Seek out the miracles.

HOW TO HONOR GODDESS AYIZAN

When you honor Goddess Ayizan, you honor your ability to embrace and welcome miracles. You may choose to honor this energy inside yourself or invoke her energy according to your own tradition. Ayizan is from a closed practice, so to go deeper you should seek a reading and guidance from a priest or priestess.

To honor the goddess in you: Ayizan comes down as an old woman. Anyone may touch their hands to their heart and then touch the ground three times to honor her when her name is mentioned. As she was the first priestess, you also may ask Ayizan with love and great reverence if the priestesshood is in your path.

Do you believe in miracles? Look around you right now. How many miracles are in your view? Miracles are merely the hand of God/dess. If you want to increase the frequency of miracles you experience, then you must notice and appreciate the ones you already have.

Symbols: One of Ayizan's main symbols is royal palm leaf fronds. Palm fronds are named azan. Ayizan's vévé is a spiritual symbol used by initiates as a beacon and doorway for her to enter their consciousness.

Other symbols include straw hats, roosters and chickens, leafy greens, and the asson, a sacred priesthood rattle made from a calabash gourd strung with glass beads and sometimes snake vertebrae.

Colors: Ayizan's favorite color is white, followed by silver, yellow, and gold.

Auspicious time: Her feast day is August 11.

Music: "Ayizan" by Mizik Mizik and "When You Believe" by Whitney Houston and Mariah Carey

Suggested offerings: Honor her at your altar with palm leaves, palm oil, money, yams, or earth from a crossroads or marketplace. She loves white offerings: white chickens, white eggs, rice, and milk. She drinks no alcohol. The bell on her altar should not be copper or brass.

Alternate names: Ai-Zan, Aïzan, Ayizan Velekete, Ayezan

Traditional Miracles Ritual: Spraying Money

The Nigerian celebratory practice of spraying money is a beautiful and fun ritual that represents showers of abundant blessings and raining down miracles. Spraying money is primarily a wedding ritual. As the couple dances, wedding guests "spray" cash on them. Using new, fresh, crisp bills is preferred. Money is placed on the forehead with love and falls to the ground. The longer you dance, the longer you get sprayed with riches.

Spraying money is also used to celebrate birthdays, graduations, performers, concerts, and almost any happy occasion. Big bills can be exchanged for singles for a more extravagant display. Friends and family help to collect the cash for the guest of honor afterward. Sometimes family members get sprayed separately while dancing too.

Spraying money is fun, knowing that you are sharing abundance and prosperity in celebration. The traditional practice is to honor the celebrant by putting the money on their heads. But now for some it has become just throwing cash.

The interesting thing is that spraying money is officially illegal in Nigeria, although families of many leaders all continue to participate. The central banking system considers it to be disrespectful to the Naira (the currency of Nigeria). I have also seen people request that there be no money sprayed at their event. Some people fear that it becomes a show of ego and extravagance for the money sprayers and not the celebrant.

Yes, even "making it rain" is connected to our roots!

Your Miracles Ritual: Manifesting Miracles Rice

Ritual intention: To call in your miracles, magic, and abundance.

What you seek is seeking you. Brought west by enslaved people, rice is used throughout the motherland for ritual purposes. Rice is a symbol of prosperity and good luck. Although we have focused our practice on liquid libations, grains such as corn flour and rice are also poured as libations. Today we will be making Manifesting

Miracles Rice, made in many of our cultures globally but known primarily in the African American Hoodoo tradition. This is a wonderful ritual for the new moon.

Important: This rice is not for human or animal consumption.

You will need:

- 1 cup of uncooked rice
- Dollar bill (shredded)
- Glass jar
- 1 teaspoon green food coloring
- Herbs: basil, bay leaves, mint of any kind, parsley, thyme, cinnamon powder, cloves

What to do:

Part 1: Bless and Mix the Ingredients

Rice is an important spiritual tool. You may use any rice for this ritual, but if you can get an ancestral rice like glaberrima, go for it! Glaberrima is an African rice used primarily for rituals.

I purposely included ingredients that are easy to find, but you may also wish to use a small sprinkle of holy water or oil of your choice, hyssop, five-finger grass, coins, green stones, green sugar, green or gold candy, or green or gold glitter. Your inner wise woman will tell you how much to add.

Prepare your ritual space. Cleanse and bless your bowl. Visualize wonderful things happening as you add each ingredient.

- As you add your rice, repeat your version of, "Thank you, God/dess for multiplying my blessings."
- As you shred the dollar bill, repeat your version of, "Thank you, God/dess for multiplying my blessings."
- Affirm: *"This or something even greater for the good of all involved."*

As you add each ingredient to the mix, tell it what it is here for. For the herbs, you may use fresh ingredients, but the moisture in them makes them harder to separate. If using fresh herbs, chop them up finely. Blow on them and get your àse in them.

- Basil, thank you for your energy of abundance.

- Bay leaves, thank you for the good juju.

- Mint, thank you for energy of prosperity.

- Parsley, thank you for your fertile energy.

- Thyme, thank you for your energy of boldness.

- Cinnamon, thank you for accelerating my riches.

- Cloves, thank you for the energy of protection.

Put all the ingredients in a jar (or storage container of your choice) and shake well to mix. Pray over it and consecrate it on your altar. When it is dry, mix in the cinnamon powder.

Affirm your abundance and miracles as you mix. Give gratitude to the Most High and your ancestors and positive spirit energies as you mix it.

Here are some abundance affirmations to speak into your rice as you mix:

- *My Creator blesses me with miracles daily.*

- *Abundant love, money, and happiness are mine.*

- *I live abundantly in the overflow.*

- *Everyone around me prospers with me.*

- *I am a magnet for miracles and money.*

- *Great opportunities find me everywhere I go.*

- *I am so grateful and so prosperous.*

- *Every day in every way life is working out for me.*

- *I am always so well taken care of.*

- *Money flows to me with ease.*

Part 2: Ways to Use Your Manifesting Miracles Rice

- Sprinkle the rice in the four corners of your home or business.

- Put it in your wallet with fresh, crisp bills.

- Use it in a mojo bag.

- Just as they throw rice for luck at weddings, you can throw it in your own home.

- Sprinkle it on the floor, then sweep it from the back to the front of your house and out the front door.

- Use the rice as glitter or decoration on a prosperity vision board or in your Goddess Soulbook.

- Carry the rice in your bra, pockets, or bag.

- Put a jar of the rice behind your front door.

- Keep some in your everyday bag.

- Use it to create an abundance altar.

Alternative: If you don't have access to all of these ingredients, just use plain rice for now. Intention is the most powerful ingredient of all.

A-BOL-NIMBA

Goddess of Harvest
Baga/Guinea
Womanifesting Womb Awakening Ritual

"We are always prospering."

A-BOL-NIMBA'S MESSAGE

I nu wali, my child! Great Harvest time! Pray attention. A season of great harvest is a season of great epiphanies.

A-BOL-NIMBA'S STORY

Great Goddesses a-Bol and Nimba, keeper of mysteries,
We see you. We say your name.
Boom. Thump. Boom. Boom. Thump. Pum. Pumparumpum. That is the sacred drum.
When a-Bol and Nimba showed up to this sacred circle, it was mandatory that I introduce them to you. For as they say in Guinea, "Knowledge is like a garden: if it is not cultivated, it cannot be harvested."
Boom. Thump. Boom. Thump. Pum. That is the sacred drum.

a-Bol and Nimba are actually two spirit entities. a-Bol is the fertility goddess and women's lineage spirit. Nimba is her beautiful mask headdress, a living spiritual energy force. a-Bol and Nimba represent abundance and miracles for the Baga people of Guinea and Sierra Leone. Together they are a living testament to the energy of thriving and harvest.

Boom. Thump. Boom. Pum. That is the sacred drum.

a-Bol's alternate name is The Matriarch. To preserve her power, no outsider is allowed to see her face. Her husband, the great a-Mantsho-ño-Pön who led the Baga from mountain to mountain, visits every seven years.

a-Bol's daughters sing:

O! Nimba! Goddess of fertility

O! Nimba! Thou who brings forth fruit from the dust

Here are my breasts, may they be as big as yours

Here is my womb, may it bring forth the children of the Bagatai![10]

Nimba's mask is worn at harvest celebrations and weddings. She is depicted with long, flat breasts that represent milking children and scarification that represents grains. Harvest and motherhood are miracles that we are blessed to witness often. When looking to manifest, we must begin with gratitude for the manifestations already at hand.

In the early 19th century, the Indigenous culture of the Baga people was dismissed, denigrated, and practically wiped out. At that time, their masks, drums, and pottery ended up in the hands of European museums and institutions. After Europe vilified their sacred art, Nimba's masks and imagery inspired the work of European artists, including Picasso and Giacometti.

Then from 1958 to 1984, the Republic of Guinea government initiative called the Demystification Program purposely destroyed any ties to traditional spiritual practices, rituals, customs, and art.[11] This included any talk of Goddess a-Bol, Nimba masks, or any related Indigenous spirits and deities. Now most of their creative artisans have died out. Those who practice their traditional faith, dismissed as animism, are still being persecuted for their beliefs today. There is little information available about their gods, goddesses, and rituals. If you have not heard of a-Bol or Nimba, it is for a reason. This is by design. The scant knowledge that has survived is miraculous evidence of their ability to harvest survival power.

a-Bol-Nimba's daughters have the power of the drum. Yes, Baga women have their own drum called a-Ndèf. Their society is unique as their drums typically represent women, and some of their best drummers were women. a-Bol and Nimba have universal mother energy. Nimba's mask masquerade is danced at harvest festivals, as well as at the start and close of life—in other words, any time we as humans interact with the Divine. Women and children all participate in the masquerade dance.

Nimba's mask is a woman mixed with the hornbill bird, a symbol of faith and better times to come, as the beak always points upward. Nimba represents beauty, social duty, and dignity. The voluptuous feminine figure of her mask is usually worn by a strong man, as it is quite heavy.[12] At over seven feet tall, the Baga masks are among the largest in all of Africa.

Boom. Thump. Boom. Boom. Thump. Pum.

Pumparumpum.

That is the sacred drum.

For a-Bol, for Nimba. For you.

Let's Talk Harvest

One day I heard a voice clearly say, "Get up, it's reaping season." I'm a city goddess, so I wasn't even fully sure what that would mean to me. My grandparents were farmers, but unfortunately I am not. I knew the saying "You reap what you sow," usually said ominously where I'm from, and that's it. One of the ways you can be sure that it's Spirit talking to you and not your imagination is when it's not your usual language.

"Get up, it's reaping season" means it's harvest season.

What does harvest mean to you? For most of us, if I said, "Celebrate your harvest," we would translate that to mean accomplishments. That's cool too. You should celebrate what you accomplish. But that's still surface-level patriarchal-energy values. Capitalism celebrates you as a dollar amount.

So how do you celebrate your harvest?

In my 20s, I co-hosted an annual Kwanzaa celebration in a Harlem community center. On this internal pilgrimage where we are sharing African-diaspora rituals, Kwanzaa is one of my faves. I love that as a seven-day celebration of heritage, values, and history, Kwanzaa celebrates the harvest, not just of the season but of the people. Yes!

This is the true harvest. The harvest is not just the fulfillment of your dreams but the creation of them. Your thoughts, your imagination, the blessing on you being here another day on this earth. That is all harvest.

We are not here to step on other people. We are not here to be proud that we are fully out of fucks. We are here to evolve with love and compassion and build good character. In the Yoruba Ifá corpus, it states, "Owo ara eni, La afi I tunwa ara enii se," meaning "Each individual must use their own hands to improve on their own character."

Iwa pele is a Yoruba principle that means being of gentle and good character. That is the harvest. The literal translation of the words is "I come to greet the earth." It's about being a good citizen of the planet and doing that what is right because it is right. That sounds corny in a world that is all about winning prizes, but that is the harvest.

The Luba proverb "Vidye wa kuha buya nobe wa mukwasbako" means "God gave you beauty and goodness, but you must help Her/Him." Every woman for herself is a lie. No one reaps by themselves and goes home. That's the old, tired, third-dimension world.

How's your character? What is your relationship with the people you love? How's your relationship with the people you can't stand? What is your relationship with Spirit? What is your relationship with nature?

As my grandparents, all farmers, would agree, we celebrate the harvest by sharing it.

HOW TO HONOR GODDESSES A-BOL AND NIMBA

When you honor Goddesses a-Bol and Nimba, you honor your connection to reaping a bountiful harvest. You may choose to honor this energy inside yourself or invoke their energy according to your own tradition.

To honor the goddesses in you: a-Bol and Nimba represent the sacred feminine and the community concept of ideal womanhood for Baga people. For us, this means ideal personhood and humanity. What seeds of generosity, love, support, and goodwill can you sow in your community to create a bountiful harvest for all?

Symbols: In addition to traditional masks and headdresses, they are honored by serpentine water spirits called Niniganne. Toads and snakes or the gold and diamonds of Guinea are the way to honor this energy.

Color: Their color is rich chocolate brown.

Auspicious times: Kini Afrika or Festival des Arts de Conte, held on the second week in April, is an important reclamation of Indigenous Guinean arts and culture after the forced demystification movement.

Music: "Yingi yo su" by Baga Guiné and "Harvest Moon" by Cassandra Wilson

Suggested offerings: Cassava, yams, and plantains will honor the energy of the harvest.

Alternate names: D'mba, Yamban, u-Thembra

Traditional Harvest Ritual: The Yam Festival

Yam festivals abound throughout the continent of Africa and the diaspora. These celebrations of thanksgiving celebrate the bounty of harvest and abundance. Yams symbolize healing, nourishment, wealth, and sustenance. These festivals are a time of reconciliation and renewal. During harvest, you give thanks for the bountiful crops that you manifested through the last season. You asked, you planted your seeds, you believed, and now you are receiving and planning for the next bounty.

Even though yams are an everyday staple through much of Western and Central Africa, they are a sacred food. There are many yam deities like Igbo goddess Aha Njoku and maternal Hausa Bori goddess Inna. Many of the goddesses you met here, like Gran Mambo Ayizan and Ala, are also associated with the nourishing aspects of yams. Yams are presented at fertility and marriage ceremonies. The northern Kikuyu mothers in Kenya gather yams a week after giving birth.[13]

The Igbo Iwa-Ji festival is in early August. There are also New Yam Festivals in June. The Asogli Te Za Yam Festival in Ghana is in September. Dates vary based on the most auspicious spiritual timing. At the Iwa-Ji, the newly harvested yams must not be eaten before the festival. This is a huge taboo. Don't eat before the festival or you ruin the crop! Before the festival, children in traditional families also must do a ritual cleansing bath called "imacha ahu iri ji mmiri."[14]

Early on festival day, a priest sacrifices a goat. The goat is later made into soup. Yam is pounded to make fufu. The priest prays for the last season and the harvest to come, then tastes the soup and fufu. They pour libations, and the festival is open! New yams can be eaten. There is dressing up, music, dancing, singing, drumming, praise, and of course, eating.

There are about 600 species of yams. The yams with white "meat" my family eats in Guyana in the starchy, unsweet dishes of provisions and fufu differ in color and taste from the orange flesh sweet potatoes considered yams in North America. When one of my beautiful West African clients was launching a product with a color named "Yams," I expected it to be the golden color of sweet potatoes I grew up eating in New York. It was chocolate brown. On our harvest celebration days in the U.S., sweet potato pie and my mom's candied yams are mandatory staples. This is our sweet potato inheritance.

In Haiti, the Manger-Yam Harvest Celebration is on November 25. As with the continental African yam festivals, you never eat the new yams before the festival. First yams are offered to the ancestors.

Your Harvest Ritual: Womanifesting Womb Awakening

Ritual intention: To activate, awaken, and bless your womb energy.

You are a force of creation. Harvest is when we reap the blessings that we have sewn. Womb energy is simultaneously the most powerful and most neglected force in the Universe. In this harvest ritual, you will bless your womb or the energy of your womb if you do not have a physical one.

Do this womb awakening preferably twice a month, once on the full moon and once on the new moon.

You will need:

- Yourself
- Yams (optional)

What to do:

Part 1: Full Moon Blessing

Prepare your ritual space. This blessing can also be done at the crescent waning moon, which signifies restoration, or any time that works best for you.

Close your eyes. See your womb connecting back to the wombs of generations. See this energy anchored in the womb at the center of the earth. If lying down, you may choose to use flowers or healing stones to cover your womb area for this blessing.

Rub your hands together vigorously while feeling healing light fill your body.

Put your hands over your womb space. Pray according to your practice.

Mother-Father-God/dess,

You who have made me sacred;

You who have made me healed;

You who have made me whole.

Thank you for the blessing of my womb;

Thank you for the fruit of my womb;

Thank you for gifting me with inner wisdom;

Thank you for gifting me with my inner temple;

Thank you for the harvest of love and blessings.

I come to you with open arms and an open heart.

Please help me to heal my inner sanctum;

Please help me to love, honor, and accept myself;

Please help me to forgive myself;

Please help me to forgive them;

Please help me to release now anything that is not of you.

My body is whole and healed.

I release all pains, deception, violations, and transgressions from my womb space.

May I feel loved;

May I feel wanted;

May I feel whole;

May I feel safe;

May I feel you and stand in the truth of my soul.

We now lovingly release all fear, blockages, hindrances, and obstructions.

Thank you for my healthy, whole, and loved body.

Thank you for my healthy, whole, and loved mind.

Thank you for my healthy, whole, and loved spirit.

Àse! Àse! Àse!

Ancestors, thank you for my womb wisdom.

Thank you for your guidance;

Please guide me to my next steps.

Àse! Àse! Àse!

Take notes on whatever guidance comes up for you. Record your process in your Goddess Soulbook.

Afterward, you may desire to eat yams to celebrate. Yams are sacred in many cultures and represent the divine feminine. This is no surprise as yams can have healthy estrogen-related hormonal effects. Our ancient cultures were so wise.

Part 2: New Moon Blessing

Prepare your ritual space. This blessing can also be done at the crescent waxing moon, which signifies intention, or any time that works best for you.

You will now bless your womb or the energy of your womb if you do not have a physical one.

Close your eyes. See your womb connecting back to the wombs of generations. See this energy anchored in the womb at the center of the earth. If lying down, you may choose to use flowers or healing stones to cover your womb area for this blessing.

Rub your hands together vigorously while feeling healing light fill your body. Direct your energies to your womb.

Put your hands over your womb area. Pray according to your practice.

Speak your goddess name three times.

Thank you, my beautiful womb, I bless you and I thank you for being.

You are whole, you are healed, you are loved.

Blessings to the wombs that carried me in your body.

You are whole, you are healed, you are loved.

Blessings to the wombs that carried me in your soul.

You are whole, you are healed, you are loved.

Blessings to the fruit I carried in my body.

You are whole, you are healed, you are loved.

Blessings to the fruit I carried in my soul.

You are whole, you are healed, you are loved.

Blessings to the wombs of the earth.

You are whole, you are healed, you are loved.

Please forgive me for neglecting you.

Please forgive me for undervaluing you.

Please forgive me for not seeing you.

Thank you for where I am in my cycle.

Thank you for where I am in my life.

I love you. I love you. I love you.

Please tell me what I need to know.

Please guide me where I need to go.

Àse! Àse! Àse!

Take notes on whatever guidance comes up for you. Record your process in your Goddess Soulbook.

Afterward you may desire to eat yams to celebrate. Yams are sacred in many cultures and represent the divine feminine. This is no surprise as yams can have healthy estrogen-related hormonal effects. Our ancient cultures were so wise.

ISET

Goddess of Spiritual Surrender
Nubia/Egypt
Anoint Thyself Ritual

"Everything I need to know finds me at the perfect time."

ISET'S MESSAGE

SabāH al-xeir, daughter. Lean in to me. Surrender. These words will cast a spell. Breathe them in. Bite them. Chew them. Swallow them whole. We began in the bush as energy. Secret names unlock truths. Secret spells cast life. Everything does not need to be known. Let go.

ISET'S STORY

Great Goddess Iset, Isis, Aset, keeper of mysteries,
We see you. We say your name.

Iset, she speaks: "I am all that has been and is and shall be, and no mortal has ever lifted my veil." This is the inscription on her statue in the ancient Egyptian city of Sais. Her name means "throne," and her secret knowledge has never been revealed.

You may know her as Isis, her Greek name. She was called the "Great Lady of Nubia" by the Kushites.[15] Or maybe you met her as Auset, Aset, Wuset, or one of the many other translations. After all, in the Egyptian Book of the Dead, she is called "Iset Nudjerit em Renus Nebu," meaning "Goddess in All Names."[16] Iset was worshipped in ancient Nubia (the Sudan region), Egypt, and beyond.

Iset is a legendary goddess, renowned for her magical gifts, healing powers, and beauty. When it came time to distribute gifts to humans, Iset made a point of giving equally to women and men. She is a generous and loyal mother and leader. As the need arises, she has been a bird, a scorpion, or a cow.

Iset's mother, sky goddess Nut, was the vault of the heavens. Nut swallowed the sun at dusk and gave birth to it daily. Iset's father was earth god Geb, whose laughter created earthquakes.

Iset married Asar (Osiris), first king of Egypt, ruler of the underworld and master of agriculture. They were happy. But Asar's brother Set was jealous and vengeful. Set drowned his brother and scattered his body. Iset was devastated. The sun god Ra promised to give her the powers to save her man only if she could guess his secret name. No time for games, Iset fooled him into revealing the name, making her power equal to his.

Iset then transformed herself into a bird and went to the ends of the earth over 12 days to recover and assemble her Asar. She found every part of him except his phallus. That's love! Iset used her enhanced magic to reconstitute her husband's penis and impregnate herself with his seed. In one story she flew his semen in on a kite; in another she used his severed phallus. She anointed Asar with oils, gave him new breath, and resurrected him.

Thus, Iset became the virgin mother of her son Heru (Horus), a sun god and sky god. Images of Iset and her infant son are echoed with the Virgin Mary and Jesus. Iset and Heru were protected by seven charmed scorpion deities.

When she surrendered to her own sacred power, her potent spellcasting was the strongest of all the gods. After she released life's drama, Iset used her magic spells to help everyday folks. She uses red jasper, representing her life-giving blood, to heal. Her symbol, the tyet, known as the "knot of Isis," was a precursor and inspiration for the ankh. In some depictions she is Nature herself.

The Thunder, Perfect Mind is an ancient poem discovered in the ruins of the Nag Hammadi Library in Egypt. It is dated to the 4th century AD. No one is certain about the author, but it has been called the "Hymn of Isis."

For I am the first and the last

I am the venerated and the despised

I am the prostitute and the saint

I am the wife and the virgin

I am the mother and the daughter

I am the arms of my mother

I am barren and my children are many

I am the married woman and the unmarried

I am the woman who gives birth and she who never procreated

I am the consolation for the pain of birth

I am the wife and the husband

And it was my man who created me

I am the mother of my father

I am the sister of my husband

And he is my rejected son

Always respect me

For I am the shameful and the magnificent one[17]

As always, Iset surrenders to her magic. The "Mysteries of Isis" were esoteric initiation rites that spread into the Roman and Greek worlds. An Iset temple was found all the way in Pompeii, where she was regarded as protector of the downtrodden, indigent, and outcast.

Let's Talk Spiritual Surrender

Iset went to the ends of the earth for her love. Spiritual surrender is realizing that we don't have to stay in that energy of struggle and control. Living like that all the time is exhausting and out of divine alignment with our sacred goddess energy. Surrender is releasing the reins and allowing God/dess to carry us and fill in the gaps.

A sister in our Goddess Temple Circle said, "Abiola, I am confused. You say surrender. Let go, let God/dess, but you also tell us to take responsibility. You say start with intention and take inspired action. And you say mindset and mentality matter. Which is it?"

Well, suppose you were in Brooklyn and wanted to drive to California. Is it most important to have a car, GPS, gas, the road, or money for refills and tolls? Yes! You need all of it. Your mentality is the belief that empowers you to set off on your trip. Taking responsibility is saying, "I was gifted with free will. How magnificent! I take responsibility for how I show up and focus on faith over fear." And we need to take inspired action because in this earth form, it may be challenging to levitate to your dream job. Inspired action can be buying a ticket or pulling out your crystals, tuning into your goal's frequency and relaxing. If you're growing a garden, you need seeds *and* soil *and* sunshine *and* water.

Life is co-creative; we are creating with Spirit. That's beautiful because surrendering means that we don't have to figure it all out. We make it complicated, but you are already doing this. You already know—I've got to get in the car, get the gas, and know where I'm going. And then I surrender to the belief that I'm going to get there. You do it effortlessly. You surrender to the fact that California will be there when you arrive.

Raise your hand if you like being in control. (Hand raised!) Sure, surrender can be scary, but how much more painful is it if we've got to figure it all out ourselves? It's stressful to think that we've got to write the script, act in it, direct it, build the stage, sew costumes, and cook for the crew in a one-woman show.

It feels good to release control and believe that God/dess has your back. Surrender is feeling safe. Spiritual surrender is not about giving up or being complacent. Surrender, handing the keys over to the Divine, includes complete acceptance and faith in where we are at this moment.

If you're trying to manifest and call in something greater than you've ever experienced, and you're leaning only on your own experiences, you cannot go further than that. Your brain can only show you what it has experienced if you're leaning only on your own understanding. We all have years of stories steeped in fear that we've been telling ourselves. "This is not going to work out because these kinds of people don't like me," "All men are this; all women are that." No wonder we resist surrendering!

A couple of years ago, I declared to the goddess circle that I wanted to share our message on TV as a vehicle for empowerment. Less than one month later, an opportunity to shoot a pilot showed up. I didn't have the concept of shooting a pilot for a talk show with a live audience and a DJ in a Midtown Manhattan studio, yet it happened! I surrendered and Spirit filled in the space with the show. If I were coming from a place of control, it would not have happened.

Before that I was chosen to shoot a Gap commercial in my underwear to promote body love as a self-love ambassador. Again, that was not something that I had conceived, especially not at my age, with my body type and non-mainstream type of beauty. It was beyond my puny vision. Spirit is dreaming a bigger dream for you. Surrender and leave room for it.

Here's how to surrender:

- Start with intention, which I call prayer. Ask the Divine for what you want to call into your life. Affirm: *"This or something greater for the good of all involved."*

- Stay in a state of gratitude and appreciation for your current blessings and blissings.

- Practice nonattachment and let go of your attachment to outcome.

- Release the reins of control with meditation. Set your alarm on your phone for 15 minutes a day to start, close your eyes, focus on your breathing, and observe your thoughts.

- Go high vibe. Raise your frequency with anything that makes you feel good. Have fun. The energy of joy is the energy of love. The energy of love is spiritual surrender.

- Lean into surrender. Spiritual teacher Dr. Deepak Chopra says when you think that you have surrendered all you can, there's still more. Relax into knowing that you are safe.

- Trust.

- Give yourself grace. Realize that you've never been fully in control anyway.

When you receive guidance, take inspired action. Inspired action comes from a place of sacred belief. Inspired action evolves your consciousness, opens possibilities, and moves your life forward.

Write in your Goddess Soulbook: *I am on the exact right path.*

HOW TO HONOR GODDESS ISET

When you honor Goddess Iset, you honor your faith in the secrets and mysteries of the Universe. You may choose to honor this energy inside yourself or invoke her energy according to your own tradition.

To honor the goddess in you: Put your hands on the crown of your head and feel the power of your own mysteries. Feel the energy that connects you to the Universe. Surrender.

Symbols: The "knot of Isis" or "girdle of Isis" is also called the tyet. The tyet resembles an ankh, but the "arms" point down instead. The tyet's original design may have been based on an early maxi pad.

Iset's stone, red jasper, is a potent healing stone that can represent menstrual blood in ceremonies. It has all of the energies of blood: life nurturing, courage giving, and support. Crystals used in Nubia include clear quartz and chalcedony. Iset is also associated with red jade, carnelian, lapis, and moonstone.

Iset's other symbols include red coral, ankhs, the flower of life, lotus flowers, scarabs, thrones, scorpions, cows, knots, Kyphi perfume, feathers, cobras, and sistrum rattles.

Colors: Her colors are blue, white, gold, and red.

Auspicious times: You can also honor her in alignment with your own menstrual cycle. Iset was celebrated across the region in spring. Her March 5 festival was known as Navigium Isidis all the way in Rome.

Music: "Goddess Isis Egyptian Mystery" by Egyptian Meditation Temple and "Nubian Queen" by Nelson Freitas

Suggested offerings: Iset's flower, lotus, represents rebirth. Ankhs, red coral, red crystals, and burning myrrh incense are great offerings to her, as is anything representing menstrual blood.

Alternate names: Isis, Auset, Aset, Wuset, The Great Magic, Queen of the Throne, Mother of the Gods, Great Virgin

Traditional Spiritual Surrender Ritual: Anointing

Anointing is the act of pouring sacred oil over someone's head or body to honor and bless or heal and comfort, surrendering them to the power of the Divine. Anointing is also used for spiritual protection, to block negative energy and bad spirits, and for medicinal purposes. In different historical periods and places, perfumes, milks, holy waters, and butters have all been used to anoint. There is plenty of anointing throughout the Bible and other holy books.

Historically, anointing was the domain of priests and royalty. But in Guyana, we "'noint babies," meaning massaging and blessing infants with oil, keeping their joints limber and happy.

The Queen of Sheba birthed a line of Ethiopian kings through King Solomon, so you may want the anointing oil that Solomon's father, King David, was anointed with. The holy anointing oil recipe from the Book of Exodus in the Bible is pure myrrh, sweet cinnamon, cassia, sweet calamus, kaneh bosem (most likely cannabis), and olive oil.

At the Temple of Hathor in Abu Simbel, Egypt, there is a wall painting of the deification of Queen Nefertari. In the relief, Goddesses Iset and Hathor bless Nefertari by anointing her forehead with oil. In another image, Nefertari holds two offering jars as she stands before Goddesses Iset, Ma'at, and Nephthys. They crown and anoint her.

Anointing is an ancient practice of blessing what is holy to protect and honor it. People are usually anointed, but you can also anoint sacred objects and locations. The seven sacred pools of Egypt were used to anoint deceased ancestors to help them participate fully in the afterlife. Essential essences, oils, resins, and botanicals were used for the practice.

The recipe for Kyphi perfume is on the walls of the Edfu Temple of Horus, a temple dedicated to Iset's son Heru, and on her own temple. Kyphi was used as a beacon for deities in their temples, to open dream travel or to sharpen intuition. There was a sun Kyphi and a moon Kyphi.[18] Wine, honey, frankincense, juniper berries, cinnamon, myrrh, mint, raisins, pine, and camel grass were added to the lesser-known sweet, flat cyperus, aspalathos, peker, and mastic.

In 2012, scientists were able to recreate ancient Egyptian scents using excavated residue, claiming that these may have been Cleopatra's recipes. Ingredients used for fragrance, skincare, and haircare include myrrh, cinnamon, cardamom, and green olive oil. Frankincense was also used as a fragrance.[19]

Your Spiritual Surrender Ritual: Anoint Thyself

Ritual intention: To anoint and bless your beautiful, divine self, surrendering to your God/dess power.

Grand rising! You have learned so much in this process. You also came in with much. Every strand of your hair, every fingernail, each DNA strand is coded with ancient secrets. You are a sacred vessel for divine knowledge. We honor that.

Anointing is pouring libations on the body altar and releasing control to the Divine. At my Miracles and Manifesting Retreat, I included a perfume-making manifesting workshop. Speaking your self-love and desires into a custom fragrance made just for you and anointing your body with it is ancient magic.

You will need:

- Red or pink roses (pesticide free)
- Distilled water
- A bowl and a glass
- Cooking pot and stove

What to do:

Part 1: Create Your Anointing Potion

Prepare your ritual space. Clean the roses. Remove the petals and put them into a pot. As you touch the petals, speak words of love and affirmation over your life using *"I am"* statements.

Add just enough distilled water to the pot to cover the rose petals. Continue to speak your intentions into the rose water. Simmer the roses and water on low heat for 28 minutes. Do not let it boil. Turn off the heat and let the liquid cool. Strain the liquid when it is at room temperature or let the petals marinate in the water overnight and then strain it. The water should be pink when it is ready, and the roses should be light pink or white. Dispose of the rose petals with gratitude and love.

Set aside one bowl of rose water for your anointing. Pour one glass of rose water for you to drink.

Part 2: Anoint Yourself

Prepare your ritual space. You may choose to do this in front of a mirror and/or your goddess altar. Pour libations. Set a new glass of clear water on your altar. Light a white candle. Where the instructions say, "Anoint," dip your fingers on your right hand into your bowl of rose water and touch the corresponding body part.

Pray according to your tradition. Speak this anointing blessing out loud: *Mother/Father God/dess, thank you for blessing me.*

Ancestors, I am so grateful for your guidance on this path.

I have been initiated into the sacred goddess circle of the divine feminine. I had it all along, and I am exactly where I should be.

I am [say your goddess name].

Anoint your feet:
Blessed is the Threshold;

I stand in the blessing of Goddesses Nana Buluku and Mawu-Lisa.

Anoint the bottom of your spine:
Blessed is my Temple of Ancestors;

I stand in the soil of Great Ancestresses Sawtche, Tituba, Mbuya Nehanda, Sara la Kali, and Marie Laveau.

Anoint your pelvic area:
Blessed is my Temple of Conjurers;

I stand in the magic of Goddesses Ngame, Modjadji, Ma'at, Tanit, and the Seven Sisters.

Anoint your belly button:
Blessed is my Temple of Warriors;

I stand in the power of Goddesses Oya, Atete, Sekhmet, Asase Yaa, and Sitira.

Anoint your breastbone:
Blessed is my Temple of Shadows;

I stand in the illumination of Shadows Long Bubby Suzi, Aunt Nancy, Soucouyant, Gang Gang Sara, and Medusa.

Anoint your heart:
Blessed is my Temple of Lovers;

I stand in the love of Goddesses Oshun, Qetesh, Erzulie Dantor, Mbokomu, and Ala.

Anoint your throat:
Blessed is my Temple of Griots;

I stand in the voice of Goddesses Mami Wata, Yasigi, Mama Djombo, Mame Coumba Bang, and Nunde.

Anoint your third eye (forehead):
Blessed is my Temple of Queens;

I stand in the insight of Great Ancestresses Queen Nandi, Queen of Sheba, Queen Mother Nanny, Queen Nefertiti, and Queen Yaa Asantewaa.

Anoint the top of your head:
Blessed is my Temple of High Priestesses;

I stand in the ecstasy of Goddesses Yemaya, iNkosazana, Ayizan, a-Bol-Nimba, and Iset.

May I be blessed in the name of the Most High God/dess;

May I be blessed in the name of my ancestors.

[You may name your ancestors.]

Àse, Àse, Àse!

Part 3: Celebration and Reflection

Drink your blessed rose water.
Additional initiation celebration ideas:

- Read your praise poem from Mama Djombo's sanctuary (Chapter 7).

- Read your ancestral lineage from Mbuya Nehanda's sanctuary (Chapter 2).

- Read your goddess mission statement from Mame Coumba Bang's sanctuary (Chapter 7).

YAY! Celebrate! Congratulations—you did it! Spend time at your goddess altar, going through your Goddess Soulbook and reflecting on your journey.

Congrats! You have completed the Temple of High Priestesses.

Temple of High Priestesses Ecstasy Mantras

- *I am receiving and radiating love.*
- *I am always being guided in the right direction.*
- *My life is full of miracles.*
- *We are always prospering.*
- *Everything I need to know finds me at the perfect time.*

Temple of High Priestesses Journal Questions

- What can you do (or not do) to surrender to Spirit?
- Are you moving in the direction of your dreams?
- What were the last three miracles you experienced?
- What matters to you most?
- What are you secretly manifesting right now?

Temple of High Priestesses Embodiment

- Add something to your altar that represents your ecstasy goddess power.

Temple of High Priestesses Integration

- Add the Temple of High Priestesses goddesses and your experience with these rituals to your Goddess Soulbook.

CONCLUSION

The Ascent: Moving Forward

It is written in our law. The Divine has spoken. You are God/dess.

You have your own God/dess magic. This sacred secret knowledge, wrapped in your soul, is a part of your purpose. These are the mysteries that you came to reclaim.

Mũmbi/Moombi, meaning Creator, is the first woman, primordial goddess for the Kikuyu people of Kenya. She and her husband had nine or ten daughters. It is forbidden to say which. Her husband, Gĩkũyũ, the first man, was distraught that they bore no sons. He was directed to sacrifice a goat under a fig tree, light a fire, and pray in the moonlight. One partner walked from the flames for each of their daughters, and each young woman became the head of her own nation. Each nation today still calls itself "Nyũmba ya Mũmbi," Mũmbi's people.[1] Thus the Kikuyu people are connected forever in the Divine's goddess web, and so are we.

Take the hand energetically of the goddess to the left of you in our Goddess Temple Circle that stretches around this beautiful globe. Take the hand energetically of the goddess to the right of you. Tune in to the highest vibration in the Universe, the holy energy of love.

"Mother-Father-God, thank you for helping us to awaken the Divine within. You called us forward and woke us up with a purpose. When everything feels like it is falling apart, may we remember that it is falling together. We know who we are and whose we are. For this, we are so grateful. And in your name we say, Amen! Àṣẹ! And so it is!"

A-women!

Trust your magic.

You are God/dess.

"I AM A GODDESS" MANIFESTA

I am magic.

Rooted.

Standing in power, light, heart, voice, insight, and ecstasy.

I am the Divine and She is Me.

At the Threshold, I am limitless.

My power shines forth from within.

I am the Soil.

Firmly planted and deeply rooted, I am my sister, and my sister is me.

I am a Conjurer.

What I desire desires me.

Divine blessings flow as I give and receive easily and freely.

I am a Warrior.

I make shift happen.

I am Illumination.

I am willing to know the truth.

I am a Lover.

I am supported by my loved ones, those who are seen and those who are unseen.

I am a Griot.

I am willing to be seen and heard.

I am a Queen.

Everything I touch turns to gold.

I am a High Priestess.

My life is full of miracles.

GODDESS EMPOWERMENT RESOURCE GUIDE

READ:

Daring Greatly by Brené Brown

for colored girls who have considered suicide when the rainbow is enuf by ntozake shange

Guyanese Komfa: The Ritual Art of Trance by Dr. Michelle Yaa Asantewa

Jambalaya: The Natural Woman's Book of Personal Charms and Practical Rituals by Luisah Teish

Mama Day by Gloria Naylor

Metegee: The History and Culture of Guyana by Ovid Abrams, Sr.

SHEROES of the Haitian Revolution by Bayyinah Bello and Kervin Andre

The Artist's Way by Julia Cameron

The Book of Forgiving by Desmond Tutu and Mpho Tutu

The Essential Law of Attraction Collection by Esther Hicks and Jerry Hicks

The Sacred Bombshell Handbook of Self-Love by Abiola Abrams

Their Eyes Were Watching God by Zora Neale Hurston

The War of Art by Steven Pressfield

WATCH:

Africa's Greatest Civilizations, documentary series by Henry Louis Gates, Jr.

Ancestral Voices: Esoteric African Knowledge, documentary by Dalian Adofo and Verona Spence-Adofo

Ancestral Voices: Spirit is Eternal, documentary by Dalian Adofo and Verona Spence-Adofo

Black in Latin America, documentary by Henry Louis Gates, Jr.

Cubamor, independent film by Joshua Bee Alafia

In Search of Voodoo: Roots to Heaven, documentary by Djimon Hounsou

Journey of an African Colony, The Making of Nigeria, documentary series by Olasupo Shasore

Juju: The Web Series, by Moon Ferguson

Lost Kingdoms of Africa, BBC documentary by Dr. Gus Casely-Hayford

YouTube Channel: Abiola Adams

YouTube Channel: TheMedicineShell

LISTEN:

Official Song: "Yeah I'm a Goddess" by afua danso

See Music Playlist on the next page

VISIT: (websites)

- HeartMath Institute®, heartmath.org
- Kathleen Booker, Breathwork Coach, kathleenbooker.net
- East Coast Reiki, Damali Abrams, damaliabramsart.com
- West Coast Reiki, Tomiko Fraser Hines, TheGoddessLifeWithTomiko.com
- The Food Alchemist, Chef Ameera, chefameera.com
- Online Yoga, Vivian Williams-Kurutz's Harlem Wellness Center, harlemwellness.org

Come play with me!

Meet a group of like-minded goddess sisters and find out how to join the Goddess Temple Circle.

Also, download free goodies on my site, including resources for this book, at Womanifesting.com/GoddessInitiation.

AFRICAN GODDESS INITIATION MUSIC PLAYLIST

Musical selections in order of appearance in the book

"Nanaê, Nanã Naiana" by Sidney da Conceição

"Cordeiro de Nana" by Thalma de Freitas

"Eshou/Mawu-Lisa" by Oxaï Roura

"Mawuse" by Petit-Pays Oméga

"For Sarah Baartman" by Nitty Scott

"Welcome Home—Sarah Baartman" by Robbie Jansen and Alou April

"Bruja" by La Perla

"Diamonds" by Rihanna

"Mbuya Nehanda" by the Harare Mambos

"Still I Rise (Caged Bird Songs)" by Maya Angelou, RoccStar, and Shawn Rivera

"Sara la Kali" by Dani Caracola & La Banda de Ida y Vuelta

"Mary Magdalene" by FKA Twigs

"Marie La Veau" by Papa Celestin's New Orleans Band

"My Power" by Beyoncé

"Yeah I'm A Goddess" by afua danso

"Orange Moon" by Erykah Badu

"Modjadji" by Sello Chicco Twala

"Rain Child" by Neith Sankofa and Ascended Breath

"Maat" by Sona Jobarteh

"Ma'at (Each Man)" by Jah9

"Goddess Code" by Lizzy Jeff

"PYNK" by Janelle Monáe

"Seven Sisters Blues" by John T. Smith

"Dreams" by Solange

"Oya" by Ibeyii

"Oya" by Lazaro Ros

"Sanyii Koo" by Seenaa Solomoon featuring Keeyeron Darajjee

"Breaths" by Sweet Honey in the Rock

"Sekhmet" by Lavva

"Empress" by Ray BLK

"Asaase Yaa (Great Mother)" by Sa-Roc

"Blessed" by Jill Scott

"Sitira Gal" by British Guiana Police Force Band

"Watch Me Work" by Melanie Fiona

"Song of the Jumbies" by Josephine Premice

"Zombie" by Fela Kuti

"Kwaku Ananse" by Apagya Show Band

"Anansewaa" by Kojo Antwi

"Suck Me Soucouyant" by Geoffrey Cordle

"Ma Soucouyant" by Slow Train Soul

"Ju Ju Warrior" by Calypso Rose

"Witch Doctor" by Mighty Sparrow

"She's a Bitch" by Missy Elliott

"De Jumbie" by Scrunter

"Me" by Oshun

"Oxum" by Serena Assumpção

"Qetesh" by Belle and the Beats

"Battle of Qadesh" by Sona Jobarteh

"Erzulie O" by RAM

"Black Girl Magic" by Chrisette Michele

"Coming Home" by Shingai Shoniwa

"Strong as Glass" by Goapele

"Eternal Bliss" by The Igbo Goddess

"African Queen" by 2Baba

"Free Your Mind" by En Vogue

"Ladies First" by Queen Latifah

"Expression" by Salt-N-Pepa

"My Life" by TLC

"If" by Janet Jackson

"Be Happy" by Mary J. Blige

"I Am Mami Wata" by Casey Malone

"Watra Mama" by Black Harmony

"Iyo Djeli" by Oumou Sangaré

"This Is for My Girls" by Michelle Obama and other artists

"Faibe Guiné" by Super Mama Djombo

"Casabe África" by Dulce Neves

"Coumba" by Orchestra Baobab

"Don't Play with Your Own Life" by Coumba Gawlo

"Koni Koni Love" by Klever Jay

"Nan Dòmi" by Riva Nyri Prècil

"KwaZulu (In the Land of the Zulus)" by Miriam Makeba

"Nandi's Suite" by Ndabo Zulu and Umgidi Ensemble

"Rainha Makeda" by Batuk

"Makeda" by Les Nubians

"Queen of the Mountain" by Burning Spear

"Grandy Nanny" by Group of Maroons of Scott's Hall

"Nefertiti" by Miss Amutha Nature

"I Am Light" by India.Arie

"Koo Koo Hin Koo" (Ghanaian folk song)

"Yaa Asantewaa" by Star Gal

"Nana Yaa Asantewaa" by Melz Owusu

"Yemaya" by Celia Cruz

"Iemanjá" by Serena Assumpção

"Nomkhubulwane" by Nduduzo Makhathini

"Mermaid" by Sade

"Ayizan" by Mizik Mizik

"When You Believe" by Whitney Houston and Mariah Carey

"Yingi yo su" by Baga Guiné

"Harvest Moon" by Cassandra Wilson

"Goddess Isis Egyptian Mystery" by Egyptian Meditation Temple

"Nubian Queen" by Nelson Freitas

GODDESS DIRECTORY:
Alphabetical Listing of Deities and Magical Beings You Met on This Journey

a-Bol-Nimba
a-Mantsho-ño-Pön
Abuk
Aha Njoku
Akongo
Ala
Almaqah
Amadioha
Amma
Ammit
Amun
Anansi
Anubis
Anyanwu
Arsa
Asar (Osiris)
Asase Yaa
Astarte
Atabey
Aten
Atete
Athena
Aunt Nancy
Ayida-Weddo
Ayizan (Velekete)
Baal Hammon
Babalú-Aye
Bastet
Bennu
Chukwu
Damballah Weddo
Dan
Dangbé (Da)
Dankoli
Ebenga
Erzulie Dantor
Erzulie Freda
Esu-Elegbara
Fa
Fairmaid
Gang Gang Sara
Geb
Golden stool

Hathor
Heru (Horus)
iNkosazana
Inna
iNyangu
Iset (Isis)
Ishtar
Ix Chel
Iya Nla
Iyami Aje
Iyami Osoronga
Jengi
Komba
KoniKoni
Kwaku Ananse
La Sirène
Legba
Loko
Long Bubby Suzi
Ma'at
Mama Djombo
Mama Nature
Mame Cantaye
Mame Coumba Bang
Mami Wata
Marie Laveau
Mawu-Lisa
(Mawu—moon goddess;
Lisa—sun god)
Mbaba Mwana Waresa
Mbokomu
Medusa
Menhit
Min
Modjadji
Moko
Mũmbi/Moombi
Mwari
Nana Buluku
Nehanda
(also Mbuya Nehanda)
Neith
Ngame

Niniganne
Nomkhubulwane
Nommo
Nunde
Nut
Nyame
Obatala
Ogou Feray/Ogun
Oladumare
Ole Higue
Omo/Ogo
Ora
Oshun
Oya
Poseidon
Qandisa
Qetesh
Queen Mother Nanny
Queen Nandi
Queen Nefertari
Queen Nefertiti
Queen of Sheba
Queen Yaa Asantewaa
Ra
Re
River Mumma
Sara la Kali
Sawtche
Sekhmet
Set
Sete
Seven Sisters
Shango
Sitira
Soucouyant (Boo Hag)
Tanit
Ti Jean Petro
Tituba
Twe
Waaqa
Wadjet
Yasigi
Yemaya

ENDNOTES

Chapter 1

1. Lydia Cabrera, *El Monte* (Havana: Editorial Letras Cubanas, 1993), https://salsainrussian.ru/wp-content/uploads/2016/02/cabrera-lydia-el-monte.pdf.

2. Raimundo Nina Rodrigues, *"Os Africanos no Brasil"* (São Paulo: SciELO—Centro Edelstein, 2010), https://www.facebook.com/IleOxossi/photos/a.407618175976419/924659990938899/?type=3&theater.

3. "Egyptian Magical Scrolls," Ethiopic Manuscript Production, http://larkvi.com/mss/eth/production/scrolls.php.

4. Joshua Hammer,*The Bad-Ass Librarians of Timbuktu and Their Race to Save the World's Most Precious Manuscripts* (New York: Simon & Schuster, 2016), 27.

5. South African Rock Art, Trust for African Rock Art, https://africanrockart.org/rock-art-gallery/south-africa/nggallery/page/2.

6. Credo Mutwa, "Awaken the Mother Mind (the Divine Feminine)," YouTube video, https://youtu.be/FAJ5-AXyRgg.

Chapter 2

1. "Rootedness: The Ancestor as Foundation" by Toni Morrison; referenced by Edwidge Danticat in "The Ancestral Blessings of Toni Morrison and Paule Marshall," *New Yorker*, August 17, 2019, https://www.newyorker.com/books/page-turner/the-ancestral-blessings-of-toni-morrison-and-paule-marshall.

2. Zola Maseko, *The Life and Times of Sara Baartman: The Hottentot Venus* (Brooklyn: Icarus Films, 1998), documentary, 53 min.

3. Suzanne Daley, "Exploited in Life and Death, South African to Go Home," *New York Times*, January 30, 2002, https://www.nytimes.com/2002/01/30/world/exploited-in-life-and-death-south-african-to-go-home.html.

4. Rachel Holmes, "African Queen: The Real Life of the Hottentot Venus," *New York Times*, January 14, 2007, https://www.nytimes.com/2007/01/14/books/chapters/0114-1st-holm.html.

5. "Symbols in Ndembu Ritual, Victor Turner," Anth Theory Fall 09, http://anththeoryfall09.wikifoundry.com/page/Symbols+in+Ndembu+Ritual%2C+Victor+Turner.

6. Victor Turner, "Symbols in Ndembu Ritual" in *The Forest of Symbols: Aspects of Ndembu Ritual* (Ithaca, New York: Cornell University Press, 1967), http://hayderalmohammad.weebly.com/uploads/2/2/9/6/22967004/victor-turner-symbols-in-ndembu-ritual.pdf.

7. A.E. Larsen, "Salem: Let's Look at What Actually Happened," *An Historian Goes to the Movies* (blog), March 30, 2015, https://aelarsen.wordpress.com/2015/03/30/salem-lets-look-at-what-actually-happened/.

8. "An Indian Slave Woman Confesses to Witchcraft," Digital History, from William E. Woodward, ed., *Records of Salem Witchcraft* (Roxbury, Massachusetts, 1864), 11–48, https://www.digitalhistory.uh.edu/disp_textbook.cfm?smtID=3&psid=67.

9. "Fake spirit mediums should," *Sunday Mail*, October 26, 2014, https://www.sundaymail.co.zw/fake-spirit-mediums-should.

10. "Mbuya Nehanda a.k.a Charwe Nyakasikana: 'My bones shall rise again,'" Rain Queens of Africa, March 10, 2011, http://rainqueensofafrica.com/2011/03/mbuya-nehanda-a-k-a-charwe-nyakasikana-my-bones-shall-rise-again/.

11. "Nehanda Hanging True Account," *Herald*, May 5, 2014, https://www.herald.co.zw/nehanda-hanging-true-account/.

12. Idah Mhetu, "Zimbabwe: Nehanda, Kaguvi Heads Found in London, Public Funeral Planned for Chimurenga Icons," All Africa, March 6, 2020, https://allafrica.com/stories/202003060161.html.

13. Sheunesu Mpepereki, "Nehanda: Tracing the Roots of the Great Shona Spirit Medium: Part Two," *The Patriot*, June 26, 2014, https://www.thepatriot.co.zw/old_posts/nehanda-tracing-the-roots-of-the-great-shona-spirit-medium-part-two/.

14. Kean Gibson, *Comfa Religion and Creole Language in a Caribbean Community* (New York: SUNY Press, 2001).

15. Ovid Abrams, *Metegee: The History and Culture of Guyana* (Queens, New York: Eldorado Publications, 1998).

16. Jarmila Balazova, "Religion among the Roma," Roma in the Czech Republic, February 26, 2000, http://romove.radio.cz/en/clanek/18906.

17. Vincent Philippon, *The Legend of the Saintes-Maries* (1521).

18. Balazova, "Religion among the Roma."

19. Quote from Franze de Ville's book, *Traditions of the Roma in Belgium,* in Andy T., "Myths of Black Sarah, Sarah-la-Kali, an 'Icon of Love and Welcome,'" *Daily Kos*, May 24, 2016, https://www.dailykos.com/stories/2016/5/24/1530286/-Myths-of-Black-Sarah-Sarah-la-Kali-an-Icon-of-Love-and-Welcome.

20. African Wisdomkeepers: Knowledge Preservation Initiative, http://africanwisdomkeepers.com/.

21. Carolyn Morrow Long, *A New Orleans Voudou Priestess: The Legend and Reality of Marie Laveau* (University Press of Florida, 2006), 21.

22. Denise M. Alvarado, "Dr. John Montanee: Father of New Orleans Voudou," ConjureDoctors.com, https://www.conjuredoctors.com/dr-john-montanee.html.

23. Beatriz Varela, "The Lexicon of Marie Laveau's Voodoo," http://amigospais-guaracabuya.org/oagbv004.php.

24. Wendy Mae Chambers, "Marie Laveau's Obituary," http://www.voodooonthebayou.net/marie_laveau.html.

25. Zora Neale Hurston, "Hoodoo in America," *The Journal of American Folklore* 44, no. 174 (1931): 317-417. www.jstor.org/stable/535394.

Chapter 3

1. G. Barra, *1000 Kikuyu Proverbs*, East African Literature Bureau (London: Macmillan, 1960).

2. Linda Iles, "Ngame, Mother Goddess of the Akan," Isis, Lotus of Alexandria Lyceum, https://sites.google.com/site/isislotusofalexandrialyceum/ngame-mother-goddess-of-the-akan.

3. Richard A. Parker, *The Calendars of Ancient Egypt* (Chicago: University of Chicago Press, 1950), https://oi.uchicago.edu/sites/oi.uchicago.edu/files/uploads/shared /docs/saoc26.pdf.

4. Robert Moss, "The White Goddess and the Habit of Coincidence," *The Robert Moss Blog*, November 29, 2013, http://mossdreams.blogspot.com/search/label/Ngame.

5. Harrie Leyten, "From idol to art: African 'objects with power': a challenge for missionaries, anthropologists and museum curators," African Studies Collection, Leiden University (2015), https://openaccess.leidenuniv.nl/bitstream /handle/1887/32748/ASC-075287668-3666-01.pdf?sequence=1.

6. Melissa Meyer, *Thicker Than Water: The Origins of Blood as Symbol and Ritual* (Oxfordshire, UK: Routledge, 2005).

7. "South Africa's Preteen Queen with 'Rainmaking' Powers," *Daily Sabah*, June 13, 2017, https://www.dailysabah.com/life/2017/06/13/south-africas-preteen-queen-with-rainmaking-powers.

8. Bjorn Rudner, "Omang? People of the Rain Queen," February 2020, YouTube video, https://www.youtube.com/watch?v=jq7FFUuHdHc.

9. "Modjadji, the Rain Queen," Rain Queens of Africa, March 10, 2011, http://rainqueensofafrica.com/2011/03/modjadji-the-rain-queen/.

10. Joshua J. Mark, "Ma'at," World History Encyclopedia, September 15, 2016, https://www.ancient.eu/Ma'at/.

11. Mai Sirry, "The Weighing of the Heart Ceremony," Experience Ancient Egypt, https://www.experience-ancient-egypt.com/egyptian-religion-mythology /egyptian-afterlife/weighing-of-the-heart-ceremony.

12. Gil Renberg, "Magic in Roman North Africa," https://faculty.georgetown.edu/jod /apuleius/renberg/MAINTEXT.HTML.

13. Rohase Piercy, "In Praise of Tanit," *Goddess Pages*, https://goddess-pages.co.uk /in-praise-of-tanit-2/.

14. "Sex Spell to Force a Man to Bed with His Female Admirer Discovered on Egyptian Papyrus," *Al Bawaba*, April 9, 2020, https://www.albawaba.com/editors-choice/ sex-spell-force-man-bed-his-female-admirer-discovered-egyptian-papyrus-1349898.

15. Owen Jarus, "Woman Seeks Man in Ancient Egyptian 'Erotic Binding Spell,'" Live Science, April 3, 2020, https://www.livescience.com/egyptian-erotic-binding-spell. html.

16. Owen Jarus, "Ancient 'Mad Libs' Papyri Contain Evil Spells of Sex and Subjugation," Live Science, May 20, 2016, https://www.livescience.com /54819-ancient-egyptian-magic-spells-deciphered.html.

17. Noah St. John , "Why Your Mind Is Like an Iceberg," updated December 6, 2017, *HuffPost*, https://www.huffpost.com/entry/why-your-mind-is-like-an-_b_6285584.

18. Jeffrey E. Anderson, *Conjure in African American Society* (Baton Rouge: LSU Press, 2008), 99.

19. John T. Smith, "Seven Sisters Blues," https://www.elyrics.net/read/f/funny-paper-smith-lyrics/seven-sisters-blues-lyrics.html.

20. "Fertility Figure: Female (Akua Ba)," The Met, https://www.metmuseum.org/art
/collection/search/312279#:~:text=The%20name%20akua%20ba%20comes,as%20
if%20it%20were%20real.

Chapter 4

1. David Warner Mathisen, "Shango and Oya of the Yoruba," Star Myths of the World, December 4, 2016, https://www.starmythworld.com/mathisencorollary/2016/12/4/shango-and-oya-of-the-yoruba.

2. Max Dashu, "Atete, Goddess of the Oromo People in Southern Ethiopia," *Veleda Blog*, Source Memory, https://www.sourcememory.net/veleda/?p=772.

3. Leila Qashu, "Toward an Understanding of Justice, Belief, and Women's Rights: Ateetee, an Arsi Oromo Women's Sung Dispute Resolution Process in Ethiopia" (PhD diss., Memorial University of Newfoundland, June 2016), https://core.ac.uk/download/pdf/77997929.pdf.

4. Ashenafi Belay Adugna and Eba Teresa Garoma, "The Poetics of Oromo Blessing Expressions: A Stylistic Analysis of a Verbal Art Genre," *International Journal of Sciences: Basic and Applied Research* 32, no. 1 (February 2017): 92–120, https://core.ac.uk/download/pdf/249335668.pdf.

5. Max Dashu, "Atete, Goddess of the Oromo People in Southern Ethiopia," Academia, 2010, https://www.academia.edu/9745568/Atete_Goddess_of_the_Oromo_People_in_southern_Ethiopia.

6. Cultural Coffee Ceremony, https://www.habeshawitcoffee.com/copy-of-home.

7. Lindsey Goodwin, "How to Perform an Ethiopian Coffee Ceremony," The Spruce Eats, April 11, 2019, https://www.thespruceeats.com/ethiopian-coffee-ceremony-765830.

8. "Capoeira Angola," Ancestral Movement, https://ancestralmovement.com/capoeira-angola/.

9. Spirits of Africa, "SAN (Bushman) Healing Dance Botswana Africa," February 2012, YouTube video, https://www.youtube.com/watch?v=IyLF3y1YJKA.

10. Alistair Boddy-Evans, "Trance Dance of the San," ThoughtCo, *updated February 12, 2019,* https://www.thoughtco.com/what-is-the-trance-dance-44077.

Chapter 5

1. Gemma Pitcher, "The Shetani Of Zanzibar," Zanzibar Travel Guide, http://www.zanzibar-travel-guide.com/bradt_guide.asp?bradt=1847.

2. Bongo, *Backra & Coolie: Jamaican Roots*, vol. 1, Folkways Records, https://folkways-media.si.edu/liner_notes/folkways/FW04231.pdf, liner notes.

3. Nathaniel Samuel Murrell, *Afro-Caribbean Religions: An Introduction to Their Historical, Cultural, and Sacred Traditions* (Philadelphia: Temple University Press, 2010), https://www.google.com/books/edition/Afro_Caribbean_Religions/9h5KDRfZ-JgC?hl=en&gbpv=1&dq=kumina+healing&pg=PA264&printsec=frontcover.

4. James Early, "The 'Re-communalization' of a Jamaican Kumina Drum," Folklife, August 15, 2014, https://folklife.si.edu/talkstory/2014/re-communalization-of-a-jamaican-kumina-drum.

5. Anne Hutchings, "Ritual Cleansing, Incense and the Tree of Life–Observations on Some Indigenous Plant Usage in Traditional Zulu and Xhosa Purification and Burial Rites," *Alternation* 14, no. 2 (2007): 189-218. http://alternation.ukzn.ac.za/Files/docs/14.2/11%20Hutchings.pdf.

6. Andy Newman, "Frankincense and Mirth," *New York Times*, July 17, 2008, https://www.nytimes.com/2008/07/17/fashion/17INCENSE.html?_r=1&ref=fashion&oref=slogin.

7. Charlie Kulander, "Limin' Time," *National Geographic Traveler*, https:

8. //www.nationalgeographic.com/traveler/articles/1068tobago.html.

9. Jonathan Skinner, "Interning the Serpent: Witchcraft, Religion and the Law on Montserrat in the 20th Century," *History and Anthropology* 16, no. 2 (2005): 143-165, https://doi.org/10.1080/02757200500116139.

10. Arley Gill, "Tracing the Origin of Trinidad's Carnival to Grenada," *Now Grenada*, April 19, 2014, https://www.nowgrenada.com/2014/04/tracing-origin-trinidads-carnival-grenada/.

Chapter 6

1. "Traditional Scent: Wusulan," The Silent Note, https://the-silent-note.tumblr.com/post/97019302120/traditional-scent-wusulan.

2. "Around-the-World Scented Trip: Perfume of Africa," Carrement Belle, March 18, 2020, https://www.carrementbelle.com/blog/en/2020/03/18/perfume-africa/.

3. Zora Neale Hurston, *Mules and Men* (1935), http://xroads.virginia.edu/~MA01/Grand-Jean/Hurston/Chapters/hoodoo4.html#2.

4. Café Da Silva, Café Percussion, https://www.cafepercussion.com/home.

5. "Qadesh," Beyond the Nile, http://beyondthenile.angelfire.com/Qadesh.html.

6. Nik Douglas, "The Temple of Africa," Tantra Works, http://www.tantraworks.com/tafrica.html.

7. Alissa Lyon, "Ancient Egyptian Sexuality," Archaeology of Ancient Egypt, October 23, 2014, http://anthropology.msu.edu/anp455-fs14/2014/10/23/ancient-egyptian-sexuality/.

8. Jenny Hill, "Kyphi," Ancient Egypt Online, https://ancientegyptonline.co.uk/kyphi/.

9. HeartMath Institute® Exercises, https://www.heartmath.org/resources/heartmath-tools/heartmath-appreciation-tool-and-exercises/.

10. "Bantu Proverbs," Proverbicals.com, https://proverbicals.com/bantu.

11. "Step on the Egg: The Path to Reconciliation,"*The Voice of Peace*, no. 13, January–April 2015, https://rc-services-assets.s3.eu-west-1.amazonaws.com/s3fs-public/VOP%2013,%20EN%20final.pdf.

12. Jill Carattini, "When Forgiveness Is Impossible," RZIM, https://www.rzim.org/read/a-slice-of-infinity/when-forgiveness-is-impossible.

13. Melanie Lidman, "African Tradition Blends with Religion to Illuminate Path to Forgiveness," Global Sisters Report, November 19, 2014, https://www.globalsistersreport.org/african-tradition-blends-religion-illuminate-path-forgiveness-15136.

14. "Significance of the New Yam Festival in Igbo Society of Nigeria," Igbo Union Finland, http://www.igbounionfinland.com/significance-of-new-yam-festival-in-igbo-society-of-nigeria.

15. Chinua Achebe, quoted in Herbert M. Cole, *Mbari: Art and Life among the Owerri Igbo* (Bloomington: Indiana University Press, 1982).

Chapter 7

1. Randy M. Browne, "The 'Bad Business' of Obeah: Power, Authority, and the Politics of Slave Culture in the British Caribbean," *The William and Mary Quarterly* 68, no. 3 (July 2011): 451-80, https://doi:10.5309/willmaryquar.68.3.0451.

2. Gordon Collier and Ulrich Fleischmann, eds., *A Pepper-Pot of Cultures: Aspects of Creolization in the Caribbean* (Matatu 27-28) (Leiden, Netherlands: Brill Academic Publishers, 2004).

3. Alex van Stipriaan, "Creolization and the Lessons of a Water Goddess in the Black Atlantic," in *Multiculturalismo, Poderes e Etnicidades na Africa Subsariana* [*Multiculturalism, Power, and Ethnicities in Sub-Saharan Africa*] (Porto, Portugal: Centro de Studios Africanos), 83–103. https://ler.letras.up.pt/uploads/ficheiros/6945.pdf.

4. Anne-Marie O'Connor, "The Many Faces of Mother Water," *Los Angeles Times*, April 20, 2008, https://www.latimes.com/archives/la-xpm-2008-apr-20-ca-mami20-story.html.

5. Vusamazulu Credo Mutwa, *Zulu Shaman: Dreams, Prophecies, and Mysteries* (Rochester, New York: Destiny Books, 2003).

6. Germaine Dieterlen, "Masks and Mythology among the Dogon," *African Arts* 22, no. 3 (May 1989): 34-43, 87-88, https://doi:10.2307/3336777.

7. Marcel Griaule, *Conversations with Ogotemmêli: An Introduction to Dogon Religious Ideas* (Oxford, UK: Oxford University Press, 1970).

8. "Hornbill Mask," early 20th century, Minneapolis Institute of Art, https://collections.artsmia.org/art/4776/hornbill-mask-dogon.

9. Polly Richards, "The Dynamism of Dogon Masks and Mask Performances," The Menil, https://www.menil.org/read/online-features/recollecting-dogon/dogon-now/dynamism-of-dogon-masks-polly-richards.

10. Mildred Europa Taylor, "The Bijagos of Guinea-Bissau Where Women Rule and Choose Their Own Husbands," *Face2Face Africa*, May 16, 2020, https://face2faceafrica.com/article/the-bijagos-of-guinea-bissau-where-women-rule-and-choose-their-own-husbands.

11. Alex Cobbinah, "Why Mumbo Jumbo?" GlobalMumboJumbo, https://globalmumbojumbo.wordpress.com/about/.

12. Lakshmi Gandhi, "Unmasking the Meaning and Marital Disputes behind Mumbo Jumbo," Code Switch, *NPR*, May 31, 2014, https://www.npr.org/sections/codeswitch/2014/05/31/317442320/unmasking-the-meaning-and-marital-disputes-behind-mumbo-jumbo.

13. "Super Mama Djombo," Light in the Attic Records website, https://lightintheattic.net/releases/873-festival-deluxe-edition.

14. "Oríkì," Poets.org, https://poets.org/glossary/oriki.

15. Judith Gleason, *Leaf and Bone: African Praise-Poems* (New York: Penguin, 1994).

16. Rebecca Cusworth, "The Residue of an Unspecified Ritual and Journeying to No End," *a-n* (blog), August 21, 2010, https://www.a-n.co.uk/blogs/the-residue-of-an-unspecified-ritual-and-journeying-to-no-end/.

17. Michelle Margoles, "Mame Coumba Bang: A Living Myth and Evolving Legend," Independent Study Project (ISP) Collection, 2007: 105, https://digitalcollections.sit.edu/isp_collection/105.

18. Yves Leonard, "The Baka: A People between Two Worlds" (master's thesis, Providence Theological Seminary, 1997), https://www.collectionscanada.gc.ca/obj/s4/f2/dsk2/ftp03/MQ26821.pdf.

19. Andrea Pink, "Fact or Myth: Does Music Affect Plant Growth?" Bloomscape, https://bloomscape.com/does-music-affect-plant-growth/.

20. Richard Alleyne, "Women's Voices 'Make Plants Grow Faster' Finds Royal Horticultural Society," *The Telegraph*, June 22, 2009, https://www.telegraph.co.uk/news/earth/earthnews/5602419/Womens-voices-make-plants-grow-faster-finds-Royal-Horticultural-Society.html.

21. Erik Davis, *Nomad Codes: Adventures in Modern Esoterica* (Portland, Oregon: Verse Chorus Press, 2011).

22. Ani Kalayjian and Dominique Eugene, *Mass Trauma and Emotional Healing Around the World: Rituals and Practices for Resilience and Meaning-Making* (Santa Barbara, California: Praeger, 2009).

23. Myron Eshowsky, "Shamanism and Peacemaking," dwij.org, https://dwij.org/pathfinders/steve_olweean/eshhowsky.html.

24. Sobonfu Somé, *The Spirit of Intimacy: Ancient African Teachings in the Ways of Relationships* (New York: HarperCollins, 2002).

Chapter 8

1. Maxwell Zakhele Shamase, "Shaka Zulu: Founding Father of the Zulu Nation," interview by Thuso Khumalo, *Deutsche Welle*, April 20, 2020, https://www.dw.com/en/shaka-zulu-founding-father-of-the-zulu-nation/a-52448409.

2. Soka Mthembu, "Queen Nandi: A Remarkable Woman," *News24*, August 29, 2014, https://www.news24.com/news24/mynews24/Queen-Nandi-A-remarkable-woman-20140829.

3. Alicia Keys, *More Myself: A Journey* (New York: Flatiron Books, 2020).

4. Stefano Boni, "Female Cleansing of the Community. The Momome Ritual of the Akan World," *Cahiers d'Etudes Africaines* 192 (2008): 765-90, https://journals.openedition.org/etudesafricaines/15502#tocto1n1.

5. Zora Neale Hurston, *Mules and Men* (1935), http://xroads.virginia.edu/~Hyper2/CDFinal/Hurston/hoodoo5.html.

6. Michael Wood, "Four Myths: The Queen of Sheba," *Myths and Heroes*, PBS, https://www.pbs.org/mythsandheroes/myths_four_sheba.html.

7. "Searching for the Queen of Sheba," *BBC News*, May 31, 1999, http://news.bbc.co.uk/2/hi/africa/353462.stm.

8. Bev Carey, *The Maroon Story: The Authentic and Original History of the Maroons in the History of Jamaica, 1490–1880* (Kingston, Jamaica: Agouti Press, 1997), 117–257.

9. Jenny Hill, "The Aten," Ancient Egypt Online, https://ancientegyptonline.co.uk /amarnareligion/.

10. Valerie Vande Panne, "Nefertiti as Sensual Goddess," *Harvard Gazette*, November 18, 2013, https://news.harvard.edu/gazette/story/2013/11/nefertiti-as-sensual-goddess /. Sobonfu Somé, "The Seen and the Unseen: Spirituality among the Dagara People," *Cultural Survival Quarterly*, March 2009, https://www.culturalsurvival.org/ publications/cultural-survival-quarterly/seen-and-unseen-spirituality-among -dagara-people.

11. "Sacred Xhosa Birth Rituals: South Africa," Spiritual Birth, March 8, 2011, http://www.spiritualbirth.net/sacred-xhosa-birth-rituals-south-africa.

12. Adelaide Arthur, "Africa's Naming Traditions: Nine Ways to Name Your Child," *BBC News*, December 30, 2016, https://www.bbc.com/news/world-africa-37912748.

13. Carrie S., "Kickass Women in History: Yaa Asantewaa," Smart Bitches Trashy Books, April 13, 2019, https://smartbitchestrashybooks.com/2019/04/kickass-women-in-history-yaa-asantewaa/.

14. Chantal Korsah, "Yaa Asantewaa: Queen Mother of the Ashanti Confederacy," Dangerous Women, July 22, 2016, http://dangerouswomenproject.org/2016/07/22/ yaa-asantewaa/.

Chapter 9

1. Judy Cantor-Navas, "Discover the Sacred Afro-Cuban Chants That Are Celia Cruz's First-Known Recordings," *Billboard*, July 16, 2020, https://www.billboard.com/ articles/columns/latin/9419552/celia-cruz-first-known-recordings/.

2. Penny S. Bernard, "The Fertility Goddess of the Zulu: Reflections on a Calling to Inkosazana's Pool," in *Deep Blue: Critical Reflections on Nature, Religion and Water*, eds. Sylvie Shaw and Andrew Francis (Durham, UK: Acumen Publishing, 2008), 49–66.

3. Penny S. Bernard, "Ecological Implications of Water Spirit Beliefs in Southern Africa," USDA Forest Service Proceedings RMRS-P-27, 2003, https://www.fs.fed.us/ rm/pubs/rmrs_p027/rmrs_p027_148_154.pdf.

4. James Wiener, "Gold and the Gods: Jewels of Ancient Nubia," History Et Cetera, November 10, 2014, https://etc.ancient.eu/interviews/gold-gods-jewels-ancient-nubia/.

5. Petra Habiger, "Menstruation, Menstrual Hygiene and Woman's Health in Ancient Egypt," A Note from Germany, http://www.mum.org/germnt5.htm.

6. "A1: An Important Egyptian Faience Amulet Gold Necklace," LiveAuctioneers, https://www.liveauctioneers.com/item/11447347_a1-an-important-egyptian-faience-amulet-gold-necklace.

7. Pawel Wolf and Ulrike Nowotnick, "The Almaqah Temple of Meqaber Gaʿewa near Wuqro," *Proceedings of the Seminar for Arabian Studies* 40 (2010): 367–80, https:// www.jstor.org/stable/41224035?seq=1.

8. Vusamazulu Credo Mutwa, *Zulu Shaman: Dreams, Prophecies, and Mysteries* (Rochester, New York: Destiny Books, 2003), 13.

9. "Vodou Spirits: Ayizan," Hougansydney.com, October 5, 2014, http://hougansydney.com/voodoo-spirits/ayizan.

10. "Ballets Africains," Mandebala.net, https://www.mandebala.net/references /kakilambe.php.

11. Mike McGovern, *Unmasking the State: Making Guinea Modern* (Chicago: University of Chicago Press, 2012), https://press.uchicago.edu/ucp/books/book/chicago/U /bo14365566.html.

12. Frederick John Lamp, "Mask with Superstructure Representing a Beautiful Mother (D'mba)," Object Narrative, in *Conversations: An Online Journal of the Center for the Study of Material and Visual Cultures of Religion* (2014), doi:10.223322/con. obj.2015.1.

13. John Middleton and Greet Kershaw, *The Kikuyu and Kamba of Kenya: East Central Africa, Part V* (London, UK: Routledge, 2017).

14. Patrick E. Iroegbu, "Significance of New Yam Festival in Igbo Society of Nigeria and in Diaspora," *Nigeria Village Square*, August 11, 2010, https://www. nigeriavillagesquare.com/articles/significance-of-new-yam-festival-in-igbo-society- of-nigeria-and-in-diaspora.html.

15. P.D.A. Garnsey and C. R. Whittaker, eds., *Imperialism in the Ancient World: The Cambridge University Research Seminar in Ancient History* (Cambridge, UK: Cambridge University Press, 1979), 37.

16. "Isis, Aset, Iset, Ast, Eset, Auset—Which Is It Anyway?," Isis Magic Articles, Hermetic Fellowship, http://www.hermeticfellowship.org/Iseum/Articles /IsetAsetName.html.

17. "The Hymn of Isis," from *The Thunder, Perfect Mind*, https://92d8dda75447112de0c1-0e939f13a06bd1dbeb5309286eaa14e5.ssl.cf5. rackcdn.com/ws_01_hymn_isis.pdf.

18. Lise Manniche, "Perfume," in *UCLA Encyclopedia of Egyptology*, Willeke Wendrich, ed., 2009, https://escholarship.org/content/qt0pb1r0w3/qt0pb1r0w3.pdf.

19. Sabrina Imbler, "Researchers Concocted an Ancient Egyptian Perfume Perhaps Worn by Cleopatra," *Atlas Obscura*, August 6, 2019, https://www.atlasobscura.com /articles/cleopatras-ancient-perfume-recreated.

Conclusion

1. Jomo Kenyatta, *Facing Mount Kenya: The Tribal Life of The Gikuyu* (London, UK: Mercury Books, 1961), 4, https://www.sahistory.org.za/sites/default/files/file%20 uploads%20/jomo_kenyatta_facing_mount_kenya_the_tribal_lifbook4me.org_.pdf.

INDEX

A

a-Bol-Nimba, 351–359
abosom, 11, 143, 294–295
Abraham-Hicks, 78, 141
Abrams, Damali, 22, 30, 58, 151–152, 308
Abrams, Ovid, Sr., 56
abundance
    about, 69–71
    ala-Bol-Nimba and, 352
    altar of, 350
    giving and receiving, 100
    herbs and spices, 41, 42
    Mawu-Lisa and, 21, 23
    scarcity comparison, 180
    symbol of, 181, 347, 350
    traditional rituals, 72–73, 355
    your rituals, 73–75, 347–350
Achebe, Chinua, 240
addiction, 128, 158–159
Adinkra symbols, 112–113, 143, 144, 243, 245
affirmations. See mantras
African dream root, 305, 307–308
African Goddess Creed, 10–11
Afro-Caribbean masquerade, 190. See also masks
Ahima, Ekua, 137
Aje, 149–150
Akan
    about, 10, 89, 150
    author's roots, 244
    calendar of, 85–86
    folklore, 171
    goddesses of, 48, 105 (See also Asase Yaa; Aunt
    Nancy; Ngame)
    life-force energy of, 33
    proverbs, 238, 245
    traditional rituals of, 55, 113–114, 224
akoben, 245. See also Temple of Griots
Akom, 10, 89
akomfo (okomfo), 55
Ala, 235–241
alchemy, 77, 108–109, 301–303, 312–315
alignment, 99, 100, 108, 282, 287, 337–342
altars
    abundance altar, 350
    ancestral altar, 57–58, 61
    ganda circle, 56
    goddess altar, 24–26, 72, 74, 94, 115, 282,
    367–369

god/dess womb bowl creation at, 27
    grief altar, 241
    traditional ritual, 23–24
álúsí, 11, 15, 235–236, 281
amadlozi, 30. See also Temple of Ancestors
Amenhotep IV (pharaoh), 311
amulets (talismans), 72, 85, 101–102, 339–340
Anaïs, 222
ancestors
    African Goddess Creed on, 11
    altars and shrines for, 57–58, 61
    blessing of, 29–30
    Mo'juba ancestral prayer, 63–64
    protection ceremony, 49–50
    soil energy channel and, 30, 32–35 (See also
    Temple of Ancestors)
    tribute prayer, 64
ancient Egypt. See Egypt
Angelou, Maya, 51, 54, 55, 283
ankh, 99, 105, 361
anointing, 365–369
anxiety, 38, 122, 223, 318, 326–327
aphrodisiac bath, 218–220
Arawak/Taino, 46, 48, 164
art
    brazen international visual and performance
    artist, healer, and professor, 151
    incense as, 175, 211
    Mbari temples as, 239–240
    oracle cards as, 301–303
    for paper vision doll, 115
    rock art, 17, 249
    for self-expression rituals, 259–260
    for wounded healer rituals, 140–141
    yoni art, 25, 89–90, 109
Arzu Mountain Spirit, 166, 285
Asantewa, Michelle Yaa, 56, 210
Asase Yaa, 48, 142–147
ascent, 371
Ashanti/Asante, 3, 30, 95, 171. See also Asase Yaa;
    Ngame; Queen Mother Nanny; Yaa Asantewaa
ash circle, 277–278
Atete, 130–135
Aunt Nancy, 170–176
awakening
    about, 323, 325–326, 331–332
    traditional rituals, 40, 49, 332–333
    of voice energy channel, 245
    of womb, 356–359

your rituals, 333–334, 356–359

awkward conversation challenge, 278–279

Ayizan, 145, 275, 343–350

B

Baba Credo Mutwa (Vusamazulu), 21, 62, 246, 253, 254, 282, 339, 340

baby naming, 313–314

Baga (a-Bol-Nimba), 351–359

Baker, Josephine, 31, 154, 286

Balobedu, 92, 94–95. See also Modjadji

Bantu, 229, 230. See also Mbokomu

Barbados, 45, 81, 171. See also Tituba

baths
    aphrodisiac bath, 218–220
    clearing baths, 95–97, 225–227
    for initiation to womanhood, 86
    spiritual cleansings, 107–108, 239, 332–334

Belize, 166, 320

Benin, 15, 197–198, 275, 277. See also Mawu-Lisa; Nana Buluku; Nunde

Bes Chamber, 218

betrayal, 126, 172–176, 237–238, 241

Bible, 52, 215, 253, 298, 365–366

birth, of a baby, 2, 78, 83, 106, 113–114, 313–314

Bishop Desmond Tutu, 204

Black Madonna, 59–60, 222

Blessing of the Threshold Guardians, 12

BMGV (Big Magical Goddess Vision), 87–88, 93–94, 109, 141, 287

BMGV vision doll, 114–115

body map, 168–169

bone-throwing ritual, 175, 300–301

Book of Fa (Ifá), 21

Book of Shadows, 18

Book of the Dead, 17, 361

Boukman Dutty, 270

brazenness, 150–155

breakups/divorce, 173, 223–224, 237–238, 262, 318. See also betrayal

breathwork, 5, 39, 78, 248, 296, 341–342

Brown, Brené, 166

burn-and-release visualization, 320–321

C

cacao, 190

calling in rapid lightning change ritual, 128–129

candles, 26, 213, 254, 295–296, 315

Candomblé chants, 15, 140

Capoeira, 140

Caribbean
    author's roots in, 3–4, 22, 55, 81–82, 151, 244, 306

diaspora and, 10, 81, 190

elemental system of, 26

goddesses of (See Ayizan; Erzulie Dantor; Mami Wata; Queen Mother Nanny; Sitira; Tituba)

Haitian Vodou, 67–68, 222, 236, 274, 332–333

masquerades of, 190

traditional rituals of the Caribbean, 23–24, 72, 182, 225–227

traditional rituals of Guyana, 55–57, 72, 182, 236, 355, 366

traditional rituals of Haiti, 145–146, 182, 189, 332–333, 355

traditional rituals of Jamaica, 72, 167–168, 182, 189, 236

traditional rituals of Trinidad, 72, 182, 236
    See also jumbies

carry the stone ritual, 233–234

Carter, Ida, 111, 113

chakras, 8

channeling/channel. See creation energy channel; ecstasy energy channel; insight energy channel; love energy channel; power energy channel; soil energy channel; voice energy channel

Charwe Nyakasikana, 51–52. See also Mbuya Nehanda

chi, 281–282, 283–284, 286, 291, 333. See also Temple of Queens

choosing your goddess name, 314–315

Chopra, Deepak, 364

Christianity, 2, 3, 10, 52–53, 101, 107, 131, 298

cinnamon, 41, 73–74, 102–103, 211, 348–350, 366

circles
    altars and, 26, 56
    ganda circle, 56
    goddess circle, 1–2, 4–5, 7, 8, 11
    for grief release, 240–241
    ritual circles, 140–141, 154, 238, 240–241, 277–278

cleansing, 294–295, 332–334

clearings, 95–97, 174–176, 225–227

Cleopatra's aphrodisiac bath, 218–220

clutter clearing, 175–176

coconuts, 9, 174, 175–176, 333–334

coffee rituals, 133–135

Collins, Adana, 22, 314

Comfa (Komfa), 55–57, 167, 189

conjure, 77–78. See also creation energy channel; Temple of Conjurers

conversation challenge, 278–279

cord cutting, 223–224, 225–227

cosmic power, 22–27

Coumba, 268–273

creation energy channel
    about, 77, 78–82

blockage of, 82–83
conjurers and, 76–116 (*See also* Temple of Conjurers)
power of guidance from, 106
creative visualization, 114–115
creativity, 82–83, 111–115, 187, 257–258
Credo Mutwa (Baba Credo, Vusamazulu), xv, 21, 62, 246, 253, 254, 282, 339, 340
Cruz, Celia, 4, 330, 332
crystals, 25, 39, 60, 74, 338–340, 365

D

dabtaras (debteras), 17, 72, 101–102
Dagara, 26, 240, 253, 277, 282, 313, 338
Damali Abrams, 22, 30, 58, 151–152, 308
dances and dancing
liberation dance, 154–155
of Mami Wata, 250
manifestation and, 93, 95
mask ceremonies and, 259, 353
raindancing rituals, 94–95, 295
resistance and, 189–190
of Sitira, 149, 154
traditional rituals, 40, 55–56, 140, 145, 167, 190, 347
death, 2, 143, 235–236. *See also* grief; rebirth
debteras (dabtaras), 17, 72, 101–102
depression, 165. *See also* shame
desire
about, 86–88
alchemy and, 312
alignment and, 335–336, 337
manifestation and, 93, 96–97
mantras, 116
pleasure and, 106, 108–109
shadow self and, 161
traditional rituals, 88–89, 105, 113–114
your rituals, 68–69, 89–90, 96–97, 108–109, 367
Desmond Tutu (bishop), 204
Diamond, Keisha, 305
diaspora
about, 6, 9, 10, 81, 236–237
film on, 208–209
goddesses of (*See* Aunt Nancy; Mami Wata; Soucouyant)
inner monsters of, 158–159 (*See also* Temple of Shadows)
masquerades and, 190
okra's symbolism, 224–225
queens of, 281 (*See also* Temple of Queens)
rituals of, 353–354
sacred sensuality and, 215–216
divination
about, 11, 299

defined, 302
tools for, 60, 131, 253, 301–303
traditional rituals, 17, 101–102, 253, 300–301
your rituals, 65, 102–103, 301–303
divine lineage, 61–65
divorce/breakups, 173, 223–224, 237–238, 262, 318. *See also* betrayal
Doe, Antranette, 106, 299
Dogon, 33, 190, 256–259, 299. *See also* Yasigi
dolls, 25, 72, 105, 113–115
dreams
about, 282, 305–307
cord cutting and, 223–224
fish dreams, 329
harvests and, 353–354
intuition and, 290, 292
oracle cards and, 286
resistance and, 185–186, 187–188
snake dreams, 325, 336
spiritual surrender and, 363–364
traditional ritual, 307–308
your ritual, 308–309
See also awakening
dream traveling, 308–309
drums/drumming
a-Bol-Nimba and, 351–353
Coumba and, 269
as illegal, 3
jumbie dances and, 189
traditional rituals with, 55–57, 95, 145, 153, 167, 294, 301, 355
Dunbar, Paul Lawrence, 209
Dutty Boukman, 270

E

ecstasy energy channel
about, 324–326
blockage of, 326–327
high priestesses and, 323–370 (*See also* Temple of High Priestess)
egg-stepping ritual, 232
Egun, 30, 190, 237
Egypt
altars, 24
carnivals of, 190
crystals, 339–340
goddesses of, 194, 281–282 (*See also* Iset; Ma'at; Nefertiti; Qetesh; Sara la Kali; Sekhmet)
heka (alchemy), 77, 107, 312
khaibit, 158
lunar calendar of, 86
numerology, 219
rebirth and, 53
sexuality and, 215, 217–218
traditional rituals of, 17, 102, 175, 253, 366
umbilini energy, 326

elements, 25–26, 57–58, 211, 338

emotional nakedness, 251–254

energetic womb. *See* womb and womb energy

energy-clearing incense, 174–175

energy cords, 223–227

erotic binding spells, 107–108

Erzulie Dantor, 221–227

Erzulie Freda, 222, 295

Ethiopia, 130–131, 133, 297–298, 340, 366.
    See also Atete; Queen of Sheba

Ethiopian healing scrolls, 17, 72, 101–102

F

family
    author's, 3–4, 22, 24, 47, 55, 81–82, 151, 180, 244, 284–285, 299, 306
    betrayal and, 172–173
    connections to, 32, 64, 70–71 (*See also* Temple of Ancestors)
    dreams and, 306
    forgiveness and, 230–231
    grief and, 237–238
    names and, 314
    rebirth and, 53, 236
    spirit family, 284–285, 286
    voice energy channel and, 244, 246, 247, 264, 271
feeling safe, 30, 32–33, 46–50, 363–364
fertility, 78–79, 111–115, 154, 339
fertility dolls, 113–114
Fit, Anna Jae, 70–71
floor baptism, 42–43
floor wash, 41–42
Florida Water, 9, 41, 49, 176, 226
Fon, 10, 15, 21, 67
forgiveness, 209–210, 230–234
foundation. *See* Temple of Ancestors
fourfold path, 233–234
frankincense, 39, 50, 72–74, 134, 175, 211, 218–219, 366

G

Gang Gang Sara, 185–192
Garifuna, 10, 164, 190, 236, 285. *See also* Long Bubby Suzi
Ghana
    author's roots in, 81
    folklore, 85
    goddesses of, 85, 250 (*See also* Asase Yaa; Yaa Asantewaa)
    proverbs, 245
    slave trade, 48
    traditional rituals of, 174, 224–225, 294, 355
    See also Akan

Giovanni, Nikki, 337
giving and receiving, 100–103
goddess altar, 24–26, 72, 74, 94, 115, 282, 367–369
Goddess City (hip-hop theater), 5
goddess coffee ceremony, 133–135
goddess directory, 377–378
Goddess Intention Incense, 102–103
goddess mission statement, 273
Goddess Soulbook
    abundance statements, 71
    alchemy statements and rituals, 312, 315
    alignment ritual, 342
    ancestral prayer, 64
    awakening ritual, 334
    betrayal healing ritual, 176
    brazen ritual, 155
    creation energy statements, 78–80
    creativity ritual, 115
    creativity statements, 111
    desire questions, 88, 90
    divination ritual, 303
    dream ritual, 309
    ecstasy energy statements, 325–326
    emotional nakedness statements, 252, 254
    energy cords ritual, 227
    feeling safe ritual, 50
    giving and receiving statements, 100
    grief release, 238, 241
    harvest ritual, 357, 359
    insight energy statements, 283–284, 286–287
    intuition statements and rituals, 292, 295
    love energy statements, 204–205
    miracle statements, 346
    power energy statements, 118–119, 121, 122
    preparation of, 18–19
    quantum leap ritual, 322
    rage healing ritual, 200
    resistance healing ritual, 192
    revolutionary love, 213
    sacred sensuality ritual, 220
    scarcity healing ritual, 184
    self-expression ritual, 260
    shadow statements, 161–162
    shame healing ritual, 169
    shine ritual, 267
    soil energy statements, 31, 33
    soul forgiveness ritual, 234
    speaking up statements, 270, 273
    spiritual surrender statements and rituals, 364, 369
    truth statements, 276–277, 279
    voice energy statements, 244, 245–246
    worthiness ritual, 135
    wounded-healer ritual, 141
Goddess Superhero You, 182–184
Goddess Temple Circle
    on abundance, 70

on ancestors, 31
ascent and, 371
on brazenness, 151–152
on creation energy channel, 79–80
on divination, 299
on dreams, 305
on grief, 236–237, 238
on insight, 285–286
on joy, 144
on pleasure, 106
on quantum leaps, 318
on resistance, 188
on shame, 165
on shine, 263–264
on spiritual surrender, 363–364
on Vodou, 344–345
on wounded healers, 137–138
god/dess womb bowl, 27
Grant, Antoy, 5
grief, 237–241
griots. See Temple of Griots
gris-gris bag, 72–74
grounding, 38–43
Guinea, 295, 351–352, 354. See also a-Bol-Nimba
Guinea Bissau, 262, 264. See also Mama Djombo
Gullah Jack, 270
Guyana
    author's roots in, 3–4, 22, 45, 81–82, 171, 244, 306
    diaspora and, 10
    goddesses of (See Tituba, Sitira)
    jumbies of, 158, 171, 178
    masquerades of, 190
    traditional rituals of, 55–57, 72, 182, 189, 236, 355, 366

H

hair, 67, 329–330, 333–334
Haiti (Saint Domingue)
    diaspora and, 10
    goddesses of, 355 (See also Ayizan; Erzulie Dantor)
    masquerades of, 190
    proverbs, 6
    sacred trees of, 23
    traditional rituals of, 145–146, 182, 189, 332–333, 355
    Vodou, 67–68, 236, 274, 326, 332
hamsa, 105, 106
Hannibal, 104, 314
happy list, 146–147
harvest, 353–359, 365–366
head washing, 332–334
healers, 22, 40, 69–70, 136–141, 166–168, 300, 330

HeartMath Institute, 224, 274
Heartsong, Claire, xvi
Heka, 137
heka, 77, 107–108, 218, 312. See also Temple of Conjurers
Hicks, Esther, 78
hidden lake ritual, 253–254
High John the Conqueror, 72–73
Hill, Lauryn, xvii
hip hop, 5, 63–64, 244, 265–266
honey, 135, 208–209, 211–213, 218–220, 234, 270
Hoodoo
    about, 10, 67, 70, 110–111
    traditional rituals of, 41, 72, 73–74, 128, 212–213, 295, 347–350
Hounsou, Djimon, 252
Hurston, Zora Neale, 31, 68, 72, 138, 212, 222, 295
hydromancy, 253

I

'I Am a Goddess' manifesta, 372
iboga, 159, 319–320
Ifá/ÒrìⅨà, 10, 17, 21, 332, 344, 353–354
Igbo, 30, 53, 85, 86, 150, 281–282, 355. See also Ala
ilu uwa, 53
imphepho, 50, 174–175, 300
incense, 50, 102–103, 134, 174–175, 211, 219, 300
Initiation Contract, 19
Initiation journal, 18
Inkosazana, 335–342
Inkulisela voice power, 272
inner monsters. See Temple of Shadows
insight energy channel
    about, 282–287
    blockage of, 287–288
    queens and, 280–322 (See also Temple of Queens)
integration. See Goddess Soulbook
intuition, 77, 85, 282, 287–288, 291–296, 326, 366
Irreechaa, 131
Iset, 360–369
isiZulu, 5
Islam, 10

J

Jamaica
    diaspora and, 10
    goddesses of (See Queen Mother Nanny)
    jumbies of, 158, 164
    Maroons of, 305
    masquerades of, 190
    traditional rituals of, 72, 167–168, 182, 189, 236

jebena buna coffee ceremony, 133, 134
journaling. See Goddess Soulbook; Initiation journal
joy, 70, 106, 131–132, 143–147, 179
Judaism, 10
juju, 10, 66, 69–71, 72, 94, 95, 149, 174–175
jumbie dance, 189
jumbies, 158–159, 187–188. See also Temple of Shadows
jumbie tree, 186

K

Kaguvi, Sekuru, 53
Kananga Water, 9, 41, 49, 56, 176, 226
Keene, Tynesha, 144
"Keeping Kumina" ceremony, 167–168
Kennedy, Imogene "Queenie", 167
Khoekhoen/Khoikhoi/Khoi-San. See Sawtche
King Asantehene Prempeh I, 317
King Kpassè, 198
King Lobengula, 52
King Menelik I, 298
King Tut, 340
Kopacz, Anita, xv-xvii
Komfa (Comfa), 55–57, 167, 189
Kongo, 72, 141, 158, 167–168
Koni Koni, 275, 277
kra, 85, 224, 317
Kumina, 10, 167–168, 189
kunkuma menstrual broom ritual, 88–89
Kwe Kwe celebration, 153–154

L

Lady Shepsa Jones, 236–237
La Madama, 301
La Regla Lucumi, 10, 209
Laveau, Marie
    how to honor, 71–75
    message from, 66
    story of, 66–69
Lave Tet head washing, 332–333
libations, 32, 49–50, 63, 64–65, 142, 237–238, 347
liberation dance, 154–155
Libya, 194, 197, 339–340. See also Medusa
life clutter clearing, 175–176
life force, 11, 31, 33, 49, 63, 118, 259–260, 301–303. See also Temple of Warriors
Lisa energy. See Mawu-Lisa
Long Bubby Suzi, 163–169
Lorde, Audre, 245
Love, Dr. Velma, xvi

love energy channel
    about, 205–206
    blockage of, 206
    lovers and, 202–242 (See also Temple of Lovers)
lucid dreaming, 308–309
lwa(s), 145, 221–222, 274, 332, 344

M

Ma'at, 98–103
Macumba, 10
Mali, 17, 211, 255, 257. See also Yasigi
Mama Djombo, 261–267
Mame Coumba Bang, 268–273
Mami Wata, 249–254
Mandela, Nelson, 38, 92, 204
manifestation
    about, 5, 77–78, 92, 93–94
    alchemy and, 212
    being brazen and, 154–155
    creation energy channel and, 78–80, 82–83
    creativity and, 112, 113–114
    desire and, 86–89
    gratitude for, 352
    of miracles, 347–350
    perfume for, 366–369
    of pleasure, 108–109
    sacred sensuality and, 216, 217
    spiritual surrender and, 363–364, 366–369
    traditional rituals, 88–89, 94–95, 113–114, 217–218
    wound healer and, 141
    your rituals, 95–97, 108–109, 141, 154–155, 347–350, 366–369
mantras (affirmations)
    for alignment, 340–342
    creation mantras, 116
    ecstasy mantras, 369–370
    emotion mantras, 242
    illumination mantras, 201
    insight mantras, 322
    power mantras, 156
    soil mantras, 75
    Threshold mantras, 28
    voice mantras, 279
Marie-Claire Heureuse Félicité (empress), 281
Marie Laveau. See Laveau, Marie
Maroons, 26, 149, 189, 304–305, 308. See also Queen Mother Nanny
Marshall, Nickeola, 22
Mary Jacobe, 61
Mary Magdalene, 60–61
Mary of Clopas, 60
Mary Salome, 60–61

masks
    masquerades, 190, 352–353
    resistance and, 187
    resistance healing rituals with, 190–192
    self-expression ritual with, 258–260
    that grins and lies, 191–192
    vision masks, 259–260
Mawu energy. *See* Mawu-Lisa
Mawu-Lisa, 20–27
"Mawuse" (Oméga), 23
"May I Be Cleansed" bath, 97
Mbari temples, 239–240
Mbokomu, 228–234
Mbuya Nehanda, 51–58
meditations, 5, 39, 292, 295–296, 318, 340–342,
    364
Medusa, 193–200
menstruation, 25, 86, 88–89
milk floor wash, 41–43
milk tree initiation, 40
The Mino, 118, 217
miracles, 11, 41–43, 291, 345–350, 352
mirrors, 160–161, 173, 206, 207–209, 295–296
Modjadji, 91–97
mojo bag, 53, 72–74, 350
Mo'juba ancestral prayer, 63–65
Momone community cleansing, 294–295
money spraying, 347
monsters. *See* Temple of Shadows
Montanee, John, 67
moon, 86, 356–359
moon water, 9
mother's milk miracle floor wash, 41–43
music playlist, 375–376
Muthi, 10
myrrh, 50, 72, 134, 175, 218–219, 365, 366

N

nakedness (emotional), 251–254
naming ceremonies, 313–315
Nana Buluku, 14–19
Nefertiti, 310–315
Nehanda, 51–58
new cycles, 14, 16–19
New Orleans, 66–67, 111, 112–113, 154, 190. *See
    also* Marie Laveau; Seven Sisters
Ngame, 84–86, 88–90
Nigeria
    author's roots in, 81
    divination and, 299
    festivals of, 332

gemstones of, 340
goddesses of, 281 (*See also* Ala; Oshun; Oya;
    Yemaya)
incense of, 174
poetry of, 266
shrines, 23
symbols of, 126
traditional rituals of, 181, 225, 333–334, 347
nkisi, 72, 102, 152
nomkhubulwane, 336
Nubia, 137, 338–339, 361, 365. *See also* Iset
Nunde, 274–279
Nyono Tong Gweno (Step on the Egg) ceremony,
    232

O

Obeah, 10, 45, 72, 186, 250
Odinani (Odinala), 10, 53, 235
okomfo (akomfo), 55
Okomfo Anokye, 317
okra slip, 224–225
okro, 225
Oméga, Petit-Pays, 23
oracle cards, 60, 301–303
Oríkì praise poetry, 265–266
Oromo, 130–133. *See also* Atete
Oshun, 207–213, 295
Oya, 124–129

P

Palo, 10, 209
Panti, Rosario, 119
parfum, 211
perfume, 49–50, 365–366, 367
personal storms, 126–129
Pharaoh Amenhotep IV, 311
pleasure
    about, 106–107
    creation energy channel and, 82
    creativity and, 112
    mantras, 242
    power energy channel and, 122
    traditional ritual, 107–108
    your ritual, 108–109
    See also sacred sensuality
poetry, 111, 265–267, 305
power energy channel
    about, 120–122
    blockage of, 122–123
    warriors and, 117–156 (*See also* Temple of
    Warriors)
praise poetry, 265–266

prayer, 5, 17, 63–64, 113, 284–285, 364
Pressfield, Steven, 187
protection, binding, and blocking ritual, 127–128
puberty, 37, 40

Q

Qetesh, 214–220
qi, 33, 282
quantum jumping, 307
quantum leaps, 317–321
Queen Aminatu, 281
Queen Makeda, 298, 300
Queen Mother Nanny, 304–309
Queen Nandi, 289–296
Queen Nefertari, 313, 366
Queen Nefertiti, 310–315
Queen of Sheba, 297–303, 366
Queen Yaa Asantewaa. *See* Yaa Asantewaa

R

rage, 195–200
rain dance/raindancing, 94–95, 295
rapid lightning change ritual, 128–129
Rastafarianism, 10
Rebienot, Bernadette, 159
rebirth
    about, 33, 34, 53–55
    in afterlife, 218
    alchemy ritual, 314–315
    goddess initiation as, 3
    Queen Nefertiti and, 311
    symbol of, 211, 365
    traditional ritual, 55–57
    your rituals, 57–58, 314–315
recording the sacred, 17
relationships, 173, 223–224, 237–238, 262, 318
releases, 240–241, 320–321
resistance, 108, 187–192, 325–326
retreats, 119–120, 128, 134, 166, 284, 320, 367
revolutionary love, 209–213. *See also* sacred
    sensuality
rewrite yourself, 198–200
rice, 178, 181, 347–350
rootwork, 17, 18, 111
Rozzel, Allison, 285–286
Rumi, 238

S

sacred erotic magic, 108–109
sacred sensuality, 215–220
sacred sexuality ritual, 107–108

sacrifice, 13, 49, 95, 143
safety (feeling safe), 30, 32–33, 46–50, 363–364
Saint Domingue. *See* Haiti
sangoma, 21, 175, 249, 253, 300–301, 340
Sankofa, 13. *See also* Threshold
Santeria, 10, 72, 330
Sara la Kali (Black Sara, Sainte Sara), 59–65
Sawtche (Sarah Baartman/Saartjie), 36–43
scarcity, 179–184
Sekhmet, 136–141
self-care, 106, 112, 139, 165, 200, 237
self-expression, 245–248, 257–260
self-love, 106, 112, 139, 165, 200, 211–213, 237
self-praise poetry, 266–267
Senegal, 62, 211, 262, 269. *See also* Coumba
sensuality. *See* sacred sensuality
Seven Sisters, 110–116
sex/sexuality/sensuality, 106–109, 215–220. *See
    also* pleasure
shadow self, 6, 159, 161, 162. *See also* Temple of
    Shadows
Shaka Zulu, 92, 217, 289–290
shame
    about, 7, 164–167
    brazenness comparison, 152
    grief and, 238
    soul forgiveness and, 230, 232
    traditional healing rituals, 167–168, 232
    wild feminine as shameful, 122
    your healing ritual, 168–169
shetani, 158
shine, 144, 247–248, 262–266
Shona, 52, 72. *See also* Mbuya Nehanda
shrines
    about, 23
    ancestral shrine creation, 58, 61
    grief shrine creation, 241
    gris-gris bags ritual, 74
    Mbari temples, 239–240
    of Nana Buluku, 16
    of Sara la Kali, 61
sisters of the mask, 258–289
Sitira, 148–156
slavery
    author's roots, 3–4, 10, 81, 151
    folklore, 152
    Gang Gang Sara's story, 186–187
    inner monsters and, 195–196, 198
    Native Americans and, 46
    okra and, 225
    Queen Mother Nanny's story, 304–305
    rituals arising from, 15, 72–73, 145, 167,
    224–225

Sitira's story, 149–150
Vodun and, 67–68
voice energy channel and, 250–251
Yemaya's story, 329, 330
snakes, 197–198, 325, 336
social masks, 191–192
soil energy channel
about, 30, 32–34
ancestors and, 29–75 (*See also* Temple of Ancestors)
blockage of, 34–35
Somé, Malidoma Patrice, 253
Somé, Sobonfu, 240
Soucouyant, 177–178, 181–184
soul, 11. *See also* Goddess Soulbook
soul forgiveness, 209–210, 230–234
sous sous, 181–182
South Africa
goddesses of, 249–250 (*See also* Inkosazana; Modjadji; Queen Nandi; Sawtche)
native plants of, 305
rock art of, 17
Stonehenge of, 62
traditional rituals of, 114, 154, 174–175, 314, 319
Ubuntu and, 204
umbilini energy, 319
speaking up, 246, 270–273, 278–279
spell/spellwork, 5, 17, 100, 105, 107–108, 334
Spiritpreneurs, 69
Spiritual Baptist, 3, 10, 41, 318
spiritual surrender, 363–369
spraying money, 347
Step on the Egg ceremony, 232
stone-carrying ritual, 233–234
stones, 338–340
stuckness, 54, 128–129
sun energy. *See* Mawu-Lisa
sun rises disc, 141
sun water, 9, 23, 26, 41, 176, 226
Superhero You, 182–184
Super Mama Djombo, 262, 264, 376
Suriname, 10, 26, 178, 250–251
sweetening the jar, 211–213
Swint, Tracey Bryant, 79

T

Taino/Arawak, 46, 48, 164
talismans (amulets), 72, 85, 101–102, 339–340
Tanit, 104–109
Teish, Luisah, 208, 295
tem, 29–75

Temple of Ancestors (amadlozi)
about, 30–32
blessing, 29–30
Marie Laveau, 66–74
Mbuya Nehanda, 51–58
Sara la Kali, 59–65
Sawtche, 36–43
soil energy channel, 30, 32–35
Tituba, 44–50
wrap-up, 74–75
Temple of Conjurers (heka), 76–116
about, 77–78
blessing, 76–77
creation energy channel, 77, 78–83, 106
Ma'at, 98–103
Modjadji, 91–97
Ngame, 84–90
Seven Sisters, 110–116
Tanit, 104–109
wrap-up, 116
Temple of Griots (akoben), 243–279
about, 244–245
blessing, 243–244
Mama Djombo, 261–267
Mame Coumba Bang, 268–273
Mami Wata, 249–254
Nunde, 274–279
voice energy channel, 245–248
wrap-up, 279
Yasigi, 255–260
Temple of High Priestess (umbilini), 323–370
about, 324
Ayizan, 343–350
blessing, 323
a-Bol-Nimba, 351–359
ecstasy energy channel, 324–327
Inkosazana, 335–342
Iset, 360–369
wrap-up, 369–370
Yemaya, 328–334
Temple of Lovers (ubuntu), 202–242
about, 203–205
Ala, 235–241
blessing, 202–203
Erzulie Dantor, 221–227
love energy channel, 205–206
Mbokomu, 228–234
Oshun, 207–213
Qetesh, 214–220
wrap-up, 242
Temple of Pythons, 197–198
Temple of Queens (chi), 280–322
about, 281–282
blessing, 280–281
insight energy channel, 282–288
Queen Mother Nanny, 304–309

Queen Nandi, 289–296
Queen Nefertiti, 310–315
Queen of Sheba, 297–303
Queen Yaa Asantewaa, 316–321
wrap-up, 322
Temple of Shadows (jumbies), 157–201
about, 158–162
Aunt Nancy, 170–176
blessing of the shadows, 157–158
Gang Gang Sara, 185–192
Long Bubby Suzi, 163–169
Medusa, 193–200
Soucouyant, 177–184
witnessing your shadow self, 162
wrap-up, 201
Temple of Warriors, 117–156
about, 118–120
Asase Yaa, 142–147
Atete, 130–135
blessing, 117–118
Oya, 124–129
power energy channel and, 120–123
Sekhmet, 136–141
Sitira, 148–156
wrap-up, 156
third eye, 281–282, 368–369
Threshold (Sankofa), 12–28
about, 12–13
blessing of, 12
Mawu-Lisa, 20–27
Nana Buluku, 14–19
wrap-up, 28
throwing bones, 175, 300–301
Tisdale, Jovhannah, 165
Tituba, 44–50
Tobago, 10, 186–187, 189, 190. See also Gang Gang
Sara
tolerations list, 146–147
trance/possession, 50, 55–56, 145, 167, 189, 207, 320, 324
Trinidad, 10, 72, 158, 190, 236. See also
Soucouyant
truth
about, 276–277
inner truth (See Temple of Shadows)
traditional ritual, 277–278
voice energy channel and, 245–248
your ritual, 278–279
See also alignment; emotional nakedness; grounding; shine; speaking up
Tubman, Harriet "Moses," 31, 329
Tunisia. See Tanit
Tutu, Bishop, 204, 233
Tutu, Mpho, 233

U

ubuntu, 204, 229, 232–233. See also Temple of
Lovers
Umbanda, 10
umbilini, 325–326. See also Temple of High
Priestess
Umbilini mantra meditation, 340–342
unfuckwithable, 118–119, 149, 151–152. See also
brazenness

V

vévé, 89, 222, 345, 346
Victor, Guerda, 344–345
vision board, 87, 93, 115, 160–161, 312
visualizations, 320–321
Vodou, 45, 67–68, 145, 222, 236, 274, 332–333, 344–345
Vodun, 10, 67, 343–344
voice energy channel
about, 245–247
blockage of, 247–248
griots and, 243–279 (See also Temple of Griots)
Voodoo, 66–68, 70–71, 72, 326
Vusamazulu Credo Mutwa (Baba Credo), 21, 62, 246, 253, 254, 282, 339, 340

W

warriors. See Temple of Warriors
water gazing in the hidden lake ritual, 253–254
water representations, 26–27
water whisperer ritual, 95–97
Watson, Joe "Frizzly Rooster," 212
Winti, 10, 26, 251
witches and witchcraft, 44–46, 186, 270
womanifesting womb awakening, 356–359
womb and womb energy, 7, 78–83, 111–112, 237, 356–359
womb bowl, 27
worthiness, 131–135
wounded healers, 121, 138–141

Y

Yaa Asantewaa (queen), 316–321
yam festival, 355
Yasigi, 255–260
Yemaya, 328–334
yoni, 7, 90, 106, 293
yoni art, 25, 89–90, 109
Yoruba
author's roots, 3
calendar of, 85–86, 332

goddesses of, 298 (*See also* Oshun; Oya; Yemaya)
Ifá, 17, 21, 332, 353–354
life-force energy of, 33, 282
soil energy channel and, 30, 33
traditional rituals of, 41, 49, 63, 72, 225, 265–266, 333

Z

Zimbabwe, 52, 72, 92. *See also* Mbuya Nehanda

Zulu
    ancestral spirits, 30
    on insight, 282
    on Mawu energy, 21
    meditations, 340–341
    praise poetry of, 265
    snake dreams and, 325, 336
    throwing bones, 175, 300–301
    traditional rituals of, 272, 353–354
    See also Inkosazana; Queen Nandi

ACKNOWLEDGMENTS

Thank you to my Creator.

Thank you to my ancestors.

African Goddess Initiation was written with, by, and for my ancestors. Birthing this book is a love letter to my sisters.

I am so grateful for you, my Goddess Temple Circle. You are my soul mate peeps! Thank you for joining me on adventures from your living room to Paris. You always tell me exactly what you need from me. I am so proud to be able to share some of your stories in this book. Thank you for sharing your dreams with me.

The village for this book started long before I was born. I am grateful to all those who helped me to seed, plant, and grow this beautiful garden.

Thank you to my mommy for having my back no matter what. Without your stories about Ma, Auntie, Granny, and Grandfather, this book would not exist. You said that when Ma would tell you about us being from the Ashanti and Fula people, she would speak a language that is lost to us today. Hopefully somewhere in these pages, the meaning of her words is recovered. You may not be able to sit in her guava tree to read this book like you used to, but hopefully you will enjoy it.

Thank you to my daddy, the first writer I ever met! I love you and appreciate your support. Thank you for letting me interview you for this book and teaching me to drum with my words. I am possible because of you.

Unlimited love and gratitude to my sister Damali Abrams, the Glitter Priestess, for always taking the time to give love, support, and feedback on anything I send your way. I also appreciate your unsolicited editing! You are a powerful healer, writer, and artist. So exciting to share this transformative journey with you. Walla Baby Tribe forever.

Much love and gratitude to my loving family, my brilliant brother Ovid Jr., my beautiful niece Ava, my cousins Michelle G. and Michelle H., Nickeola, Shondelle, Jonnelle, Julie, Yasmine, Shauntel, and Jeanine, just to name a few. Thank you to my "big cousins": Cousin Lorraine, Cousin Bernie, Cousin Dennis, Cousin Jean, Cousin Michael, Cousin Keith, and everyone in our family circle.

Special love and blessings to my smart, funny, and caring niece Tesha, nephew Quamel, and niece Akiela. I love you. Love to my NYC contingent of Diana, Dion, Kwesi, Dara, and your families. Love you! Thank you to all of my siblings, nieces, and nephews with special gratitude for my big brother, Deon, for lighting the way. Deon, you are a force to be reckoned with, and I am proud to be your sister. Love you!

Thank you to my beloved Hay House family for the most loving and supportive creative cocoon that I have ever experienced. Patty the Gift and Reid Tracy, I felt you channeling the supportive energy of Great Ancestors Louise Hay and Dr. Wayne Dyer. I am honored and grateful.

Blessings to my sister and editor Melody Guy for holding space for me. You make me feel safe to spread my dreams under your feet, even with my unlimited deadline extension requests. Somehow you miraculously respond all hours of the night or weekends. (By the way, stop it, Black woman. Even goddesses need sleep!)

Blessings and magic to my amazing artist Destiney Powell. The ancestors definitely sent you my way. You are Divine, my sister. Thank you for channeling your magical art with me.

Goddess Adaobi Obi Tulton, my good sis! When I read your bio to my sister we both agreed that we were somehow born to work together. You are an incredible editor, and I appreciate you making me better.

Big fat juicy love and gratitude to my beautiful, kind, supportive friend Jessica Ortner, without whom this project would not be possible. You are an incredible human, and I love our conversations. Looking forward to playdates! Thank you to Jess's brother (inside joke), the wise and generous Nick Ortner, who is not only my very astute "lawyer" but also my tapping guru.

Colette Barron-Reid, The Oracle herself, thank you for swooping in and making me feel at home. You are Venus meets Athena. Kyle Gray, thank you for asking questions that shift the winds of tides.

My back is had! Thank you to my talented and brilliant goddess sisters Kristal Mosely and Patranila Jefferson. Thank you for allowing me to go off the grid to manifest, channel, and create. I love you and I am proud of you.

Thank you to my shining healer sister-friends Kathleen Booker, Lainie Love Dalby, Leora Edut, and Jameelah Auset. All love, blessings, and blissings to my ancestor-ass friends (inside joke) Vivian Williams-Kurutz of Harlem Wellness, Aseantè Renee, and Patria Diaz.

Thank you to my supportive and inspirational teachers Chikwenye Okonjo Ogunyemi of Sarah Lawrence, who fittingly made history as the original creator of the word *womanist*, Frances Taliaferro, of Brearley and the late great Annette Feder.

Thank you to my friend Ken E. Ritz (name cemented, your granny is proud!) of Morningside Writers Group for the morning pages coaching and encouragement.

Thank you to Charli Penn, my friend and longtime *Essence* editor, and my other sisters who have given me a voice on your platforms—Nikki Woods, Jeanine Staples, Ari Squires, Rosetta Thurman, Kara Stevens, Sadia Sisay, Dr. Venus Opal Reese,

Lucinda Cross, and Brooke Emery. Thank you for believing in me, Elizabeth Lesser and Carol Donahoe of the Omega Institute, Yvette Hayward of the African American Literary Awards Show, and Gill Matini at the College of Psychic Studies, and Bob Proctor, PJ Gaz, and Koby Benvenisti of the Proctor Gallagher Institute.

All love and gratitude to my sister Antoy Grant, the Goddess of Fever and Tre's sweet mommy, who started this goddess journey with me in the last century. The Goddess of Nerve adores and appreciates you. And much love to our honorary Goddess of Rage, Daniel Banks.

I stand on the shoulders of giants. Àse to my empowerment lineage: Susan Taylor, Iyanla Vanzant, Sark, Louise Hay, Queen Afua, Lisa Nichols, Luisah Teish, and Sobonfu Somé . Àse to my literary foremothers Great Ancestresses Zora, Toni, Maya, Gloria, Ntozake, and Nikki. Because you did, I can.

Thank you, Michaela Paula Lopez, for being an awesome assistant. I am so excited about your next chapter.

A-women to Goddesses Shu Oceani, Blanche Haley, Samantha Sinclair, SenShe, Jamie Nicole, Janice Brantle, and Alisia Young for adding your intergalactic spark to the Goddess Temple Circle.

Thank you, Oshun, for following us across the waters. Ori Ye Ye O!

ABOUT THE AUTHOR

ABIOLA ABRAMS is an award-winning author, intuitive self-love coach, goddess oracle-card creator, transformational speaker, and international retreat leader.

As a spiritual teacher, Abiola harnesses the ancient divine feminine wisdom of goddesses and ancestors combined with embodiment rituals, shadow work, and channeled meditation.

Abiola's calling is to help you transmute your fears to manifest your personal power and embody the goddess within. She empowers women through online courses, virtual and global spiritual retreats from Belize to Bali, and with her popular Spiritpreneur® and Goddess Frequency podcasts and web video series.

As the founder of the Womanifesting.com empowerment platform and Goddess Temple Circle, Abiola's mission is to empower you to become who you were born to be.

Abiola has given uplifting advice on networks from the CW to the Discovery Channel, and in publications such as *Essence* magazine. Abiola studied sociology at Sarah Lawrence College and has a master's degree in women's storytelling from the Vermont College of Fine Arts.

A New York City native and daughter of Guyanese parents, Abiola is the first person in her family born in the United States.

Learn more at:

Womanifesting.com

YouTube @PlanetAbiola

Facebook and Instagram @abiolaTV

Hay House Titles of Related Interest

YOU CAN HEAL YOUR LIFE, *the movie*, starring Louise Hay & Friends
(available as a 1-DVD program, an expanded 2-DVD set,
and an online streaming video)
Learn more at www.hayhouse.com/louise-movie

THE SHIFT, the movie,
starring Dr. Wayne W. Dyer
(available as a 1-DVD program, an expanded 2-DVD set,
and an online streaming video)
Learn more at www.hayhouse.com/the-shift-movie

✦ ✦ ✦

*A FIERCE HEART: Finding Strength, Courage,
and Wisdom in Any Moment*, by Spring Washam

*GODDESS WISDOM MADE EASY: Connect to the
Power of the Sacred Feminine through Ancient Teachings
and Practices*, by Tanishka

*LETTERS TO A STARSEED: Messages and Activations
for Remembering Who You Are and Why You Came Here*,
by Rebecca Campbell

*PEACE FROM BROKEN PIECES: How to Get Through
What You're Going Through*, by Iyanla Vanzant

*YOU ARE A GODDESS: Working with the Sacred
Feminine to Awaken, Heal and Transform*,
by Sophie Bashford

All of the above are available at your local bookstore,
or may be ordered by contacting Hay House (see next page).

✦ ✦ ✦

We hope you enjoyed this Hay House book. If you'd like to receive our online catalog featuring additional information on Hay House books and products, or if you'd like to find out more about the Hay Foundation, please contact:

Hay House, Inc., P.O. Box 5100, Carlsbad, CA 92018-5100
(760) 431-7695 or (800) 654-5126
(760) 431-6948 (fax) or (800) 650-5115 (fax)
www.hayhouse.com® • www.hayfoundation.org

———

Published in Australia by: Hay House Australia Pty. Ltd.,
18/36 Ralph St., Alexandria NSW 2015
Phone: 612-9669-4299 • *Fax:* 612-9669-4144
www.hayhouse.com.au

Published in the United Kingdom by: Hay House UK, Ltd.,
The Sixth Floor, Watson House, 54 Baker Street, London W1U 7BU
Phone: +44 (0)20 3927 7290 • *Fax:* +44 (0)20 3927 7291
www.hayhouse.co.uk

Published in India by: Hay House Publishers India,
Muskaan Complex, Plot No. 3, B-2, Vasant Kunj, New Delhi 110 070
Phone: 91-11-4176-1620 • *Fax:* 91-11-4176-1630
www.hayhouse.co.in

———

Access New Knowledge.
Anytime. Anywhere.

Learn and evolve at your own pace
with the world's leading experts.

www.hayhouseU.com

Listen. Learn. Transform.

Listen to the audio version of this book for FREE!

Connect with your soul, step into your purpose, and find joy with world-renowned authors and teachers—all in the palm of your hand. With the *Hay House Unlimited* Audio app, you can learn and grow in a way that fits your lifestyle . . . and your daily schedule.

With your membership, you can:

- Expand your consciousness, reclaim your purpose, deepen your connection with the Divine, and learn to love and trust yourself fully.

- Explore thousands of audiobooks, meditations, immersive learning programs, podcasts, and more.

- Access exclusive audios you won't find anywhere else.

- Experience completely unlimited listening. No credits. No limits. No kidding.

Try for FREE!